VICTORIA CROSS HEROES

VOLUME II

MICHAEL ASHCROFT

D0100799

This edition published in Great Britain in 2017 by
Biteback Publishing Ltd
Westminster Tower
3 Albert Embankment
London SE1 7SP
Copyright © Michael Ashcroft 2016, 2017

Michael Ashcroft has asserted his right under the Copyright, Designs
and Patents Act 1988 to be identified as the author of this work.

All rights reserved. No part of this publication may be reproduced,
stored in a retrieval system or transmitted, in any form or by any means,
without the publisher's prior permission in writing.

This book is sold subject to the condition that it shall not, by way of trade
or otherwise, be lent, resold, hired out or otherwise circulated without the
publisher's prior consent in any form of binding or cover other than
that in which it is published and without a similar condition,
including this condition, being imposed on the subsequent purchaser.

Material has been reproduced with kind permission from the British Medical
Journal (p. 253), the South African Military History Society (p. 117–19), the Royal
Green Jackets (Rifles) Museum Trust (pp. 59–60) and the National Archives (p. 100).
Every reasonable effort has been made to trace copyright holders of material
reproduced in this book, but if any have been inadvertently overlooked the
publishers would be glad to hear from them.

ISBN 978-1-78590-248-2

10 9 8 7 6 5 4 3 2 1

A CIP catalogue record for this book is available from the British Library.

Set in Garamond Three by Adrian McLaughlin

Printed and bound in Great Britain by
CPI Group (UK) Ltd, Croydon CR0 4YY

MIX
Paper from
responsible sources
FSC
www.fsc.org
FSC® C020471

In 2011, Alex Jerome, along with his wife Susie, gifted the medal group awarded to Captain (later Major-General) Henry Jerome VC to the Ashcroft VC Collection. Captain Jerome, who was honoured for his bravery during the Indian Mutiny, was Alex Jerome's great-grandfather. In view of this extraordinarily generous action, I am dedicating this book to Alex and Susie Jerome to thank them for the faith that they have shown in the integrity and the future of my VC collection. Sadly, Alex died in March 2017, aged 80.

CONTENTS

ACKNOWLEDGEMENTS

I am grateful to the fifty-eight brave men whose stories feature in this book: without their acts of remarkable heroism there would have been no book to write. Sadly, all the men who feature in this book are now dead, but I am grateful, in some cases, to their families, friends and former comrades for providing me, directly or indirectly, with details of the VC recipients' lives.

I would particularly like to thank Michael Naxton, the curator of the Ashcroft Medal Collection, for his immense contribution over the past thirty years. Michael's formidable expertise and good judgement have enabled me to build the world's largest collection of VCs. Michael shares my enthusiasm for the decoration and everything that it stands for. He also takes enormous pride in my VC collection and he has provided great assistance in writing this book.

My gratitude goes to Angela Entwistle, my corporate communications director, who has worked for me for even longer than Michael Naxton. Angela and her team at my private office enabled me to get this project off the ground and to promote the book.

I am grateful to Iain Dale and his team at Biteback Publishing for publishing a book of mine on gallantry for the first time: my other five books on bravery were the work of another publisher. Iain and his team usually specialise in political books but I am glad that they were willing and able to broaden their horizons in order to publish a book on bravery, a subject so close to my heart.

I am grateful to David Erskine-Hill, of DNW (Dix Noonan Webb) auctioneers, for – along with Michael Naxton – reading and correcting the original draft of this book. However, any errors (and in a project of this size there will inevitably be some) are entirely down to me.

My thanks go to Jane Sherwood for her diligent picture research, Christopher Cox for photographing some of my medal collection and its accompanying memorabilia, and to all those who have allowed me to reproduce the photographs contained in this book.

Many authors have penned authoritative books on the VC and its recipients that have been invaluable for this project. These men and women are listed in my Select Bibliography at the end of the book. However, some deserve particular thanks. I was delighted to have access to the *VCs of the First World War* series for information on the recipients of Great War decorations: authors Gerald Gliddon and Stephen Snelling, in particular, deserve special praise for the exceptional professionalism of their research. For the Welsh VCs in my collection, I was fortunate enough to be able to use splendid material gleaned by the thorough research work of W. Alister Williams, the author of the two-volume *Heart of a Dragon: The VCs of Wales and the Welsh Regiments*.

However, *Victoria Cross Heroes: Volume II* is crammed full of exclusive material too: many of the medal groups I have purchased were accompanied by rare, even unique, letters, diaries, photographs and items of memorabilia kept by the medal recipients and/or their families.

I would like to thank the Victoria Cross and George Cross Association and, in particular, its secretary, Rebecca Maciejewska, for their help with some historical information on the VC. Three years ago, too, the association was responsible for publishing what is already widely regarded as the 'bible' of the VC: the three-volume *Victoria Cross and the George Cross: The Complete History*. I have relied heavily on some of the information in these superbly researched publications for personal and career details of many of the VC recipients who feature in this book.

Once again, I must also thank a group of largely unsung heroes. They are the cataloguers who have researched the lives of the VC recipients before their medals were sold at auction or sold to me privately. I do not know the identities of all who carried out this research but the auction houses include DNW (Dix Noonan Webb), Spink & Son and Morton & Eden. The individual cataloguers who deserve my gratitude include Pierce Noonan, David Erskine-Hill, Nimrod Dix, John Hayward, Mark Quayle, Oliver Pepys and Richard Black (albeit in his capacity as a dealer).

I am grateful to the Imperial War Museum, London, for allowing me special access to its VC papers and to a private research room, and I would like to thank The Salvation Army for allowing me to study its papers and books on Henry 'Harry' Andrews VC.

My thanks also go to Anthony Staunton, the military historian, for permitting me access to his paper entitled 'Forfeited Victoria Cross Myths' – and for allowing me to quote freely from it.

I am grateful to the Danish Embassy in London and, in particular, Thomas Bech Hansen, the embassy's communications and press officer, for their assistance in relation to Private (later Lieutenant) Thomas Dinesen VC.

Last but certainly not least, I am enormously grateful to Lance-Sergeant Johnson Beharry VC for writing the Foreword to *Victoria Cross Heroes: Volume II*. Johnson is a thoroughly deserving recipient of Britain and the Commonwealth's most prestigious award for bravery in the face of the enemy. I have got to know him fairly well in recent years and I feel privileged that such a brave man should have been willing to pen such generous words to begin this book.

www.lordashcroft.com
www.lordashcroftmedals.com
www.victoriacrossheroes2.com
@LordAshcroft

FOREWORD

BY LANCE-SERGEANT JOHNSON BEHARRY VC

The Victoria Cross is 160 years old this year and it is entirely appropriate that Lord Ashcroft, one of the decoration's greatest supporters, should be marking the anniversary with a new book. Few, if any, men have done more over the years than Lord Ashcroft to champion bravery and to support the Armed Forces. By writing and publishing *Victoria Cross Heroes: Volume II*, he is once again bringing the courage of British and Commonwealth soldiers, sailors and airmen to a wide audience.

In 2005, I became the first living recipient of the VC for nearly forty years, so it will come as no surprise that I am an enthusiastic supporter of the decoration that was created by Queen Victoria in 1856. As one of eight children and someone who was born and raised in a poor family in Grenada, I share Lord Ashcroft's fondness for an egalitarian gallantry medal that can be awarded to anyone, regardless of their birthplace, wealth, colour, rank, religion or creed. At the time of my two VC actions, I was a private serving in the 1st Battalion, The Princess of Wales's Royal Regiment, and just trying to do my job – no more, no less. When I was growing up in my home country, I had not even heard of the VC, let alone knew that it was Britain and the Commonwealth's most prestigious award for bravery in the face of the enemy. Now, of course, I know quite a bit about the VC's rich and wonderful history.

More than a decade after the event, I can still remember exactly how I learned that I was going to be awarded the VC. Along with three comrades, I was summoned to see the commanding officer (CO).

It was 16 March 2005, just two days before decorations for the Iraq War and its aftermath were to be published in the *London Gazette*. The CO told two of my three comrades that they were to be awarded the Military Cross (MC) and the third that he was to be awarded the Conspicuous Gallantry Cross (CGC) – second only to the VC for bravery in the face of the enemy. After a long pause, the CO turned to me and said: 'Beharry, this one's rather special. They haven't handed out one of these for quite a while. It gives me the very deepest pleasure to tell you that you are going to receive the Victoria Cross.' I heard what he said but for a time it did not really register with me.

The next day, after I had attended a press briefing the day before the awards were made public, my CO told me: 'You know, like it or not, Beharry, this medal is going to have a profound impact on your life. All the awards that are going to be announced tomorrow are precious, but the VC is something else again. It will change things – now and for the rest of your life.' He was right, of course, starting with a visit to Buckingham Palace on 27 April 2005, when I received my decoration from Her Majesty The Queen. It took nearly fifteen minutes for my citation to be read out, describing how, as the driver of a Warrior armoured personnel carrier, I had twice been able to save the lives of my comrades under fire in Iraq in 2004, receiving serious head injuries during the second action. And then, of course, I was presented with the VC by The Queen, who told me: 'You're a very special person.' As she pinned my medal to my chest, she added with typical understatement: 'It's been rather a long time since I've awarded one of these.' Overawed by the occasion and stuck for words, I replied simply: 'Thank you, Your Majesty.'

I recount these events because I want to give an indication of quite how proud and humbled I felt to be awarded the VC. I have no doubt that it is a feeling shared by every single recipient. Behind every award there is a wonderful story, and *Victoria Cross Heroes: Volume II* recounts those of nearly sixty recipients of the VC. Even though I now have more than fifteen years of service in the Army, it never ceases to astonish me just what servicemen and women are capable of doing for their country and for their comrades when duty calls and their blood is up.

The VC collection that Lord Ashcroft has built up, now 200-strong, is by far the largest in the world and it will never be matched. However, Lord Ashcroft has done more than simply establish the collection over a period of thirty years: he has also donated £5 million so that it could go on public display, free of charge, in a gallery bearing his name at the Imperial War Museum, London. Yet, perhaps Lord Ashcroft's greatest achievement in highlighting bravery has been to write six books on gallantry that have been read and appreciated all over the world. *Victoria Cross Heroes, Volume II* has been meticulously researched by someone with a real passion for bravery in general and for the VC in particular: I have no doubt that it will be read and enjoyed for many decades to come.

AUTHOR'S ROYALTIES

Lord Ashcroft is donating all his author's royalties from *Victoria Cross Heroes: Volume II* to military charities.

LORD ASHCROFT
AND BRAVERY

All the individual write-ups in this book are based on VCs that form part of Lord Ashcroft's collection, the largest such collection in the world.

Lord Ashcroft also owns substantial collections of Special Forces gallantry decorations, gallantry medals for bravery in the air and some George Crosses (GCs). His collection of VCs and GCs is on display in the Lord Ashcroft Gallery at the Imperial War Museum, London, along with VCs and GCs owned by, or in the care of, the museum.

For more information visit: www.iwm.org.uk/heroes

For more information on Lord Ashcroft's books on bravery visit:

www.victoriacrossheroes.com
www.specialforcesheroes.com
www.georgecrossheroes.com
www.heroesoftheskies.com
www.specialopsheroes.com
www.victoriacrossheroes2.com

For more information on Lord Ashcroft's VC collection (including when and where the VCs in this book were acquired) visit: www. lordashcroftmedals.com

For more information on Lord Ashcroft and his work visit: www. lordashcroft.com

Follow him on Twitter: @LordAshcroft

PREFACE

Ten years ago, to mark the 150th anniversary of the Victoria Cross, I wrote my first book on gallantry based largely on my VC collection. At the time that *Victoria Cross Heroes* went on sale in November 2006, I was the proud owner of 142 VCs that had been amassed, sensitively and discreetly, over the previous twenty years. The book told the remarkable stories of the brave actions behind those awards, along with a small number of additional VCs – not in my collection – that had been carefully chosen for a television series of the same name.

Since then, my VC collection, the largest of its kind in the world, has been boosted by the purchase of nearly sixty further VCs. *Victoria Cross Heroes: Volume II* tells the stories of these VC recipients and the courageous deeds behind the medal groups that I have purchased over the past decade. If anything, *Victoria Cross Heroes: Volume II* tells even more astonishing stories than my first book on the subject. This is because, as I explain in the first chapter of this book, over the past ten years I have become more selective with those that I have purchased. The criteria that I used for buying a new VC became stricter, so that almost every one of the fifty-eight VCs featured in this book is, for one reason or another, quite exceptional.

Victoria Cross Heroes: Volume II is published to mark the 160th anniversary of the creation of the VC, Britain and the Commonwealth's most prestigious medal for gallantry in the face of the enemy. At the same time, my new book marks the thirtieth anniversary of the purchase of my first VC, the decoration awarded to Leading Seaman James Magennis at the end of the Second World War.

At the time I bought the Magennis VC in the summer of 1986, I intended that the purchase should be a one-off, and yet, three decades on, I am the proud custodian of 200 VCs – more than one in seven of the total number of VCs that have been awarded since the medal was instituted by Queen Victoria in 1856 to reward acts of outstanding bravery during the Crimean War.

In September 2016, I reached a notable landmark when I purchased the 200th VC for my medal collection. The 200 VCs that I now own span every force – Army, Royal Navy and RAF – and nearly 128 years, from deeds of great bravery in 1854 to an astonishing act of courage during the Falklands War of 1982. The VC has been awarded 1,358 times to 1,355 men, including the American 'Unknown Warrior', and three recipients have received 'Bars' – the equivalent of a second VC (these totals do *not* include the separate Commonwealth VCs that can now be awarded by Australia, New Zealand and Canada).

This book takes a brief look at the history of the VC along with how and why I amassed my collection. The bulk of the book, however, details the lives and deeds of those men who deserve to be regarded as 'the bravest of the brave'. Every VC that has been awarded has the story of one man's courage behind it: how a soldier, sailor or airman decided to risk his life to such a degree that he was decorated with what is widely regarded as the world's premier gallantry award.

The aim of *Victoria Cross Heroes: Volume II* is primarily two-fold: to champion acts of great bravery and to raise money for good causes. I have decided to donate every penny of my author's royalties from the book to military charities.

I hope you will enjoy reading about the courageous actions of those brave men who have shown such dedication to duty in the service of their monarch and their country. If you consider their actions to be inspirational, I hope that you will pay a visit to the Lord Ashcroft Gallery at the Imperial War Museum, London, so that you can see these brave men's medal groups and the fascinating memorabilia that so often accompanies them. The aim of the gallery, which houses the 'Extraordinary Heroes' exhibition, is to intrigue, inspire and amaze in equal measures.

1

A PASSION FOR THE VC

A short history of the
Victoria Cross

The Victoria Cross was instituted by a Royal Warrant announced on 29 January 1856. It thereby became the first British decoration that could be awarded to any serviceman irrespective of rank. The notion of awarding a gallantry medal to low-ranking soldiers and sailors had first come under serious consideration in Britain in the autumn of 1854. Until then, the government and military leaders had felt there was no real need to reward 'ordinary' men for their courage.

It was the outbreak of the Crimean War in 1854 – after nearly forty years of peace – that resulted in the need to reassess whether simply serving monarch and country, in return for a modest wage, was sufficient reward for some of the acts of outstanding bravery that soon emerged in the war against Russia. Stories of outstanding gallantry started circulating about remarkable soldiers even though they were often operating in the most appalling conditions, coupled with a lack of adequate clothing and provisions to protect them from the harsh Russian winter. There was a general feeling that thousands of men were being asked to fight in conditions far worse than any army had ever encountered before. Furthermore, if they were seriously injured, the hospitals tending the wounded were hopelessly inefficient and seriously under-equipped.

Significantly, too, the Crimean War came under greater public scrutiny than any war previously: it was the first conflict to be covered by a corps of war correspondents and reports from *The Times*'s William Howard Russell and others meant that the war captured the public's imagination as never before. A series of perceptive and critical articles highlighted both the lack of adequate equipment and the ravages of cholera and typhoid: in all, the two diseases claimed some 20,000 lives, compared with the 3,400 killed and mortally wounded in battle.

Both Russia, Britain's enemy, and France, Britain's ally, had gallantry award systems in place that were not contingent on high rank, thereby leaving some British troops with a feeling of being undervalued, even though campaign medals were already in existence. Until the Crimean War, officers – usually majors and above – were given the junior grade of the Order of the Bath for acts of bravery, but there was no such equivalent award for junior officers, Non-Commissioned Officers (NCOs) or ordinary soldiers or sailors. As the Crimean War intensified, there was a growing feeling that a new award was needed to recognise examples of gallantry irrespective of a man's station in life, or his lengthy or meritorious service.

Both Queen Victoria and her husband, Prince Albert, were enthusiastic about addressing the problem. Indeed, shortly after the start of the war, the Conspicuous Gallantry Medal (CGM) for the Royal Navy and Distinguished Conduct Medal (DCM) for the Army were instituted in order to recognise the gallantry and leadership of NCOs. However, these awards continued to provide no medal that recognised the bravery of junior officers.

Pressure mounted for an egalitarian decoration that was open to all and would reflect the courage of men on the frontline. The idea for such an award was advocated in the House of Commons for the first time on 19 December 1854 by Captain G. T. Scobell, an MP and former naval officer who had served during the Napoleonic Wars.

It was the Duke of Newcastle, the Secretary of State for War, however, who seized the initiative on 20 January 1855, writing to Prince Albert:

> It does not seem to me right or politic that such deeds of heroism
> as the war has produced should go unrewarded by any distinctive
> outward mark of honour because they are done by privates or by
> officers below the rank of major ... The value attached by soldiers
> to a little bit of ribbon is such as to render any danger insignificant
> and any privation light, if it can be attained.

It was the Duke who broke the news of the radical new bravery award
to the public when he told the House of Lords nine days later that
the government had advised The Queen 'to institute a Cross of Merit
which would be open to all ranks of the Army in future'. However,
the Duke conceded that more thought was needed as to the precise
nature of the award, and matters were not helped when he lost his
job a few days after making the speech. Initially, the civil service,
under the guidance of Lord Panmure, the new Secretary of State for
War, came up with a plan for the award that was both clumsy and
long-winded.

It needed the intervention of Prince Albert to veto the 'Military
Order of Victoria' and suggest instead the 'Victoria Cross'. He felt
the word 'order' had unwanted aristocratic overtones and noted:
'Treat it as a cross granted for distinguished service, which will make
it simple and intelligible.' Victoria herself chose the design and
the inscription: 'For Valour'. At first, the government suggested the
cross be inscribed 'For the Brave', but The Queen was rightly concerned that this would imply that non-recipients were not brave.

The Royal Warrant signed on 29 January 1856 announced the
creation of the VC, a single decoration available to the British Army
and the Royal Navy. It was intended to reward 'individual instances
of merit and valour' and which 'we are desirous should be highly
prized and eagerly sought after'. The warrant laid down fifteen 'rules
and ordinances' that had to be 'inviolably observed and kept'.

'Firstly. It is ordained that the distinction shall be styled and designated the "Victoria Cross", and shall consist of a Maltese Cross of

bronze with Our Royal Crest in the centre, and underneath which an escroll bearing this inscription, "For Valour".' The second rule stated that the cross should be suspended from the left breast, by a blue ribbon for the Navy and a red ribbon for the Army. The third decreed that the names of those receiving the decoration should be published in the *London Gazette* and registered in the War Office. The fourth regulation was forward-thinking enough to give instructions about what should happen if an individual who had already received a VC were to perform an act of bravery that would entitle him to a second medal. It instructed that any second or further acts of bravery entitled the VC holder to an additional Bar, attached to the ribbon suspending the cross. The fifth rule made it clear that the VC was intended only for wartime courage, to be awarded to officers or men who had served Britain 'in the presence of the enemy, and shall have then performed some signal act of valour, or devotion to their country'.

The sixth instruction showed a welcome support for meritocracy in the British Armed Forces:

> It is ordained, with a view to place all persons on a perfectly equal footing in relation to eligibility for the Decoration, that neither rank, nor long service, nor wounds, nor any other circumstance or condition whatsoever, save the merit of conspicuous bravery shall be held to establish a sufficient claim to the honour.

This clause made the VC, at a stroke, the most democratic decoration in naval and military history.

The seventh regulation enabled a senior commanding officer in the Army or Navy to confer the decoration 'on the spot' if he had witnessed it, 'subject to confirmation by Us [the government]'. The next rule made provision for someone to be awarded the VC even if his (or her) bravery had not been witnessed by his commanding officer. In such a case, the 'claimant' had to prove his act of courage to the satisfaction of his commanding officer, 'who shall call for such description and attestation of the act as he may think requisite'. Under the ninth instruction, it was ruled that anyone receiving an 'on-the-spot' award should be decorated in front of his Army or Royal Navy colleagues. The man's name should appear in a 'General Order, together with the cause of his especial distinction'. Regulation ten, which applied to those receiving an award not witnessed by their commanding officer, indicated that the recipient should simply receive his decoration 'as soon as possible'. Similarly, the man's name should appear in a General Order issued by his commanding officer. Rule eleven made provision for the General Orders relating to the awarding of VCs to be transmitted 'from time to time' to 'our Secretary of State for War, to be laid before Us, and shall be by him registered'.

Instruction twelve tried to be all-encompassing, providing for the VC to be awarded in cases 'not falling within the rules above'. It allowed for the Secretary of State for War and the head of the Royal Navy or Army to make a joint award, 'but never without conclusive proof of the performance of the act of bravery for which the claim is made'. Regulation thirteen was longer and more complex and was intended to apply to a situation in which a large number of men – in some cases scores of them – were considered to have been 'equally brave and distinguished'. In this case, for every group of seamen or troop of soldiers, one junior officer and two servicemen should be chosen to receive the medal on behalf of their comrades.

The fourteenth rule made a generous financial provision for the recipient of a VC. Any junior officer, seaman or soldier receiving the medal would also be entitled to a special pension of £10 a year. For any additional Bar awarded under the fourth rule, he received a further £5 a year.

The final instruction was intended to ensure that the VC was held only by men of good character. It declared that if any VC holder was later convicted of 'treason, cowardice, felony, or of any infamous crime, or he be accused of any such offence and doth not after a reasonable time surrender himself to be tried for the same', he should have his name erased from the register and lose his special pension. There was, though, a glimmer of hope for anyone forced to forfeit his VC: 'We [the government] shall at all times have power to restore such persons as may at any time have been expelled both to the enjoyment of the Decoration and Pension.'

With this Royal Warrant, the VC came into being in the nine-teenth year of The Queen's 64-year reign, and with the blessing of the monarch and her consort. Over the previous two years there had been some discussions as to whether the VC should be made from a precious metal – such as gold or silver – to make it even more valu-able to the recipient, but it was finally decided that it should be of little intrinsic value. It was intended that the bronze for the med-als would be taken from two cannon supposedly captured from the Russians at Sebastopol during the Crimean War.

Indeed, until 2005, it was still widely believed that every cross was made in this way – the bronze coming from the cascabels (the ball found at the rear of a cannon's barrel) of the cannon, which are now kept at the Royal Arsenal at Woolwich. However, John Glanfield claimed in his book *Bravest of the Brave* that this was a myth. He scoured historical documents and used scientific analy-sis to show that the cascabels from the pair of Woolwich cannon were not used for this purpose until 1924, sixty-eight years after the first VCs were produced. Furthermore, he says that the precious cascabels disappeared for a time during the Second World War, so a different metal was used for five crosses awarded between 1942 and 1945. 'The truth has been fogged by time, myth and misinforma-tion,' wrote Glanfield, who also claimed there was no evidence that the Chinese-made cannon at Woolwich had even been captured at Sebastopol, the last major battle of the Crimean War. He had good news for anyone hoping to be awarded the VC in the near future, though: there remains enough of the historic cascabels – currently stored by the Royal Logistic Corps at Donnington – for a further eighty-five crosses.

It was more than a year after the Royal Warrant was announced that the first awards of the VC were published in the *London Gazette*, on 24 February 1857. The Queen had told Lord Panmure that she wished to bestow as many of the awards as possible herself and so on 26 June she invested sixty-two of the 111 Crimean recipients in a ceremony in Hyde Park in front of 4,000 troops and 12,000 spectators. Dressed in a scarlet jacket, black skirt and plumed hat, Victoria remained on horseback throughout the ceremony. One by one, she pinned a cross onto each man's jacket, while Prince Albert stood a short distance away, saluting each recipient. The ceremony and the new award were both greeted with great enthusiasm by the public.

Over the years, there have been several significant amendments to the fifteen rules, but the basic principle – that the award is for conspicuous bravery – has remained to this day. The first changes to the regulations came little more than a year after the announcement that the VC had been awarded for the first time. A Royal Warrant of 10 August 1858 extended the medal to 'non-military persons'. Under this new clause, four people received the cross for their voluntary service in the Indian Mutiny. The same instructions also allowed the VC to be awarded, subject to the existing rules, for 'acts of conspicuous courage and bravery under circumstances of extreme danger, such as the occurrence of a fire on board ship, or the foundering of a vessel at sea, or under any other circumstances in which, through the courage and devotion displayed, life or public property might be saved'. Just six crosses have been awarded over the years under this provision.

Most of the regulations have been tested at some time or other, and this has occasionally led to the rules being altered. Between 1863 and 1908, eight men had their VCs cancelled for various misdemeanours in accordance with the final rule of the original regulations. This rule never specifically stated that the cross itself should be forfeited, but for the best part of half a century it seems that the regulation was interpreted to mean that the medal had to be surrendered, along with the special pension. In 1908, the Treasury Solicitor reversed this practice, saying that holders of the medal should be able to keep it, even if their record of having won it was erased. Several years later, however, George V was evidently still concerned by the prospect of future confusion because, in a letter of 26 July 1920, it was declared: 'The King feels so strongly that, no matter the crime committed by anyone on whom the VC has been conferred, the decoration should not be forfeited. Even were a VC to be sentenced to be hanged for murder, he should be allowed to wear his VC on the scaffold.'

A Royal Warrant of 1 January 1867 stated that eligibility for a VC was extended to include members of local forces serving with imperial troops under the command of a 'general or other officer'. The warrant was retrospective and had been drawn up to reward the bravery of those who were dealing with the 'Insurgent native tribes of Our Colony of New Zealand'. This meant that Major Charles Heaphy became the first non-regular serviceman to be awarded the VC. His actions were 'gazetted' – announced in the *London Gazette* – on 8 February 1867 for an act of bravery three years earlier. On 11 February 1864, Heaphy, while serving in the Auckland Militia – part of the New Zealand military forces – went to the aid of a wounded soldier on the banks of the Mangapiko River. While tending to his comrade, Heaphy was fired upon by Maoris, with five musket balls piercing his clothes and cap. Despite being injured in three places, the major stayed with the soldier all day and saved his life.

From 1880 to 1881, there was a rethink over the 1858 Royal Warrant that had extended the decoration to non-operational duties. A further Royal Warrant of 23 April 1881 essentially revoked this order by declaring unequivocally that the VC should be for 'conspicuous bravery or devotion to the country in the presence of the enemy'. Another potentially unfair area was cleared up by a Royal Warrant of 6 August the same year. This extended eligibility to members of the Indian ecclesiastical establishments on the grounds that if they were attached to an army in the field they would be required to perform the same roles as military chaplains, who were eligible for the medal. This Royal Warrant was issued as a direct result of the bravery of the Revd James Adams, who had shown formidable courage in an incident during the Second Afghan War. At Killa Kazi, on 11 December 1879, some men of the 9th Lancers had fallen into a deep ditch along with their horses and the enemy was closing in on them. Adams, under heavy enemy fire, jumped off his mount and rushed into the waist-deep water. He dragged the horses off the men so they were free to escape at a moment when the enemy was only a matter of yards away. Under the initial rules, Adams, who managed to escape on foot, would not have been entitled to the VC, but the new Royal Warrant meant that he was 'gazetted' on 26 August 1881, nearly two years after his act of courage.

In July 1898, the government took action to look after recipients of the VC who were struggling financially, even with their annual £10 special pension (in 1859, this would be the equivalent of more than £600 in today's money). New regulations were enacted that enabled recipients below non-commissioned rank to receive, if need dictated, up to £50 a year (equivalent of nearly £4,000 in 1898). Since then, there have been several increases to the size of the pension received by VC recipients: most recently, in 2015, George Osborne, as Chancellor, increased it to £10,000 per annum, linked to the Consumer Price Index (CPI).

The original Royal Warrant of 1856 made no mention of whether the award could be won posthumously. However, the government and the military authorities decided from the beginning that a cross would not be given to a potential recipient if he had been killed in action or had died shortly afterwards. Instead, in cases of outstanding bravery, an announcement would be made in the *London Gazette* that indicated that, had the man survived, he would have been recommended for the VC.

During the Second Anglo-Boer War, fought in Africa between 1899 and 1902, an exception was made to this practice that caused great controversy and later prompted the rules to be rewritten. The Hon. Frederick Roberts was the son of Field Marshal Earl Roberts, who had himself been awarded the VC for an act of bravery in 1858 during the Indian Mutiny. Frederick was twenty-seven when he was seriously wounded on 15 December 1899, at the Battle of Colenso, when heroically trying to rescue the guns of the 14th and 66th Batteries of the Royal Field Artillery. He died from his wounds the next day. It was therefore a surprise to everybody when he was gazetted on 2 February 1900, and awarded a posthumous VC. Although nobody doubted his courage, there was some anger that he had been treated as a special case apparently because of the seniority and influence of his father. The families of other potential recipients of posthumous VCs began to ask why their relatives had not been similarly rewarded. As a result of this, there was much discussion and considerable research into the backgrounds of potential recipients. Nearly two years later, in the *London Gazette* of 8 August 1902, Edward VII approved the award of six posthumous VCs, all relating to incidents during the Boer War. Although the families of these recipients were satisfied with this outcome, those of six other men who had been gazetted between 1859 and 1897 were still unhappy that their relatives had not been awarded the medal. The King twice resisted attempts by the War Office to award the VC to the six soldiers, but eventually a war widow succeeded where the government had failed. Sarah Melvill, whose husband, Lieutenant Teignmouth Melvill, was killed in Zululand in 1879, made a direct appeal to The King and, in 1906, he reversed his earlier decision. Since Melvill's case could hardly be considered apart from the other five, the following year all six crosses were gazetted and were thought to have been delivered to the families of the dead men. The controversy surrounding Frederick Roberts's decoration, therefore, ultimately meant that the precedent for awarding the VC posthumously was established once and for all.

In the run-up to the First World War, new regulations relating to the VC were introduced. A Royal Warrant of 21 October 1911 extended eligibility to native officers and men of the Indian Army and additional guidelines were set out relating to their special pensions. Specifically, in the event of the recipient's death, these pensions were to be continued until his widow either died or remarried.

After the First World War, further changes were made to the rules. It was decided in 1918 that the crimson ribbon used by the Army should be adopted by all services, including the newly formed Royal Air Force (RAF). A committee was also formed in 1918 to consider the whole question of the VC. The following year its recommendations formed the basis of a new Royal Warrant that was eventually signed on 20 May 1920. This was the first wholesale shake-up of the initial 1856 regulations. The Royal Warrant used simpler language and – according to P. E. Abbott and J. M. A. Tamplin, the authors of *British Gallantry Awards* – it 'consolidated, varied and extended the previous provisions'. There were some significant alterations, and the 1856 rules were renumbered to incorporate amendments made in previous Royal Warrants. The list of those eligible for the VC – both men and women – was widened and the regulations regarding the award of a VC to groups for bravery were amended. Perhaps the most significant change came in the enlarged conditions under which an award could be made: for 'most conspicuous bravery or some daring or pre-eminent act of valour or self-sacrifice or extreme devotion to duty in the presence of the enemy'. Specific provision was made for posthumous awards, while erasures and restorations of the VC would be published in the *London Gazette*.

Since 1920, only relatively minor changes to the regulations have been made. A Royal Warrant of 5 February 1931 gave permission for a half-sized replica of the decoration to be worn 'on certain occasions'. It also provided that forfeiture of a VC and any future restoration of it should be entirely discretionary. This rule followed a recommendation from the inter-departmental Rewards Committee that gallantry awards should be considered irrevocable, except in cases of extreme infamy. There has been no erasure of a VC since 1908 – and hopefully there never will be another. Whatever crime a man commits in life, one cannot and should not erase a past act of bravery.

As the make-up of the British Armed Forces, international borders and the Commonwealth changed in the twentieth century, a few further changes to the regulations were deemed necessary. A Royal Warrant of 9 May 1938 enabled members of the Burmese military to be entitled to a VC. This was needed because Burma had stopped being part of India the previous year. A Royal Warrant of 24 January 1941 made all ranks of the newly formed Indian Air Force eligible, while another, issued on 31 December 1942, extended eligibility to the Home Guard, the Women's Auxiliary Services and the paramilitary forces of India and Burma. To allow for inflation, the size of the special pensions gradually rose in the UK and other countries in the Commonwealth.

Constitutional changes in the Commonwealth led to a Royal Warrant of 30 September 1961 that made servicemen and women eligible, provided the government of each country was prepared to agree to take on the terms of the warrant. A further Royal Warrant was needed on 24 March 1964 to transfer responsibilities relating to the VC from the Secretary of State for War to the newly named Secretary of State for Defence.

In recent decades, several Commonwealth countries have taken it upon themselves to introduce both their own honours systems and their own decorations for gallantry. Three countries have introduced a system by which they award their own VCs: Australia (1991), Canada (1993) and New Zealand (1999).

The method of recommending anyone for the VC has changed little over the years, though the system is today more stringent and the number of awards far fewer than in the past. Today, an incident of extreme bravery is initially reported by eyewitnesses to the commanding officer of the unit concerned. The commanding officer then writes up his, or her, account of the action and passes it up the chain of command for endorsement by the local commander-in-chief. Next, it is sent to London to the Ministry of Defence Armed Forces Operational Awards Committee, which is composed of officers from the three services, all with operational experience. If a recommendation passes through all these levels of scrutiny, a special Victoria Cross Committee is convened, which includes the Chiefs of Staff and the Permanent Under-Secretary. Eventually, a recommendation is passed from the Defence Secretary to The Queen for her final approval.

Each VC, along with its citation, is published in the *London Gazette*, the government's official public record. Sometimes such an announcement is in conjunction with other gallantry awards, but occasionally they are published separately. There are no rules on when or how quickly an announcement has to be made: sometimes it has been made within days, but usually it is weeks, months or even years after the act of bravery has taken place. By tradition, all VC recipients are now presented with their decoration by the reigning monarch at an investiture at Buckingham Palace. In the past, however, often a deputy, such as another member of the royal family or a senior figure in the military, has invested individuals with their VC.

Since its institution, the VC has been made and supplied by Messrs Hancocks (now Hancocks & Co.), the London jewellers, who were originally based in Bruton Street in Mayfair but are now situated a couple of hundred yards away in Burlington Arcade. There have been many attempts to produce fakes and copies, but most forgers have been unable to get everything exactly right: the size, the thickness, the weight, the colour and the engraving. Hancocks pride themselves on being able to tell a genuine VC from a fake under close examination, including testing the metal. In addition, since 1906, the company has made a minuscule, secret mark of authenticity on each cross to deter forgers further. On rare occasions, replacement VCs have been issued, provided the recipient has been able to prove, beyond reasonable doubt, that the original cross had been destroyed or stolen. Most gallantry medals in the world are unidentified and unmarked, so each VC, with its clear inscription of the name and rank of the recipient, is a unique record of the man and his achievement.

The shape of the cross is described as a 'cross pattée' and the medal is 1.375 inches wide and weighs 0.87 troy ounces, together with the suspender bar and V-shaped link. The face of the suspension bar is embossed with laurel leaves, while the recipient's details are engraved on the reverse. The date of the act of bravery is engraved in the centre of the circle on the reverse of the cross. The details given on the suspender bar may vary but the norm is to provide the rank, name and unit of the recipient. In most cases only the recipient's initials are given, but there have been occasions when his first name has appeared on the cross. The medal is worn on the left breast, suspended from a crimson ribbon which is 1½ inches wide.

As stated earlier, the VC has been awarded 1,358 times to 1,355 men, including the American 'Unknown Warrior'. Among this 1,358 total is the award of three Bars (a second VC to an individual). At the time of writing, there are six living VC holders (not including the separate awards from Commonwealth countries).

Finally, it is a little-known, but intriguing, fact that a small number of gallantry awards have remained secret. This was because the action that merited such an award was so highly sensitive that it led to a delayed announcement in the *London Gazette* or an extremely guarded one (i.e. an announcement that was brief or couched in general terms). However, all awards of the VC and GC are eventually announced: they cannot remain secret for ever.

Championing bravery:
the fulfilment of a dream

It was one of the proudest moments of my life. On an autumn evening in 2010, HRH The Princess Royal officially opened the Lord

Ashcroft Gallery at the Imperial War Museum in London. By doing so, the world's largest collection of VCs was made accessible to the public, free of charge – and, after a journey of more than half a century, my dream had become a reality.

As I explained in a speech to my guests that evening – Armistice Day, 11 November 2010 – my journey had begun with a passion for bravery that I had developed as a boy. This grew partly from my general interest in events from the Second World War but, more specifically, because I had been inspired by my father, Eric Ashcroft. My late father was a modest man but eventually, after much prompting from his persistent son, he told me of his own terrifying experiences on 6 June 1944 during the D-Day landings. He movingly recalled how he and other officers had been told to expect 75 per cent casualties – dead or wounded – as they landed. My father's CO, a colonel, was, in fact, shot dead at his side shortly after arriving on 'Sword Beach'. My father himself was wounded by shrapnel but he fought on until he was eventually ordered from the battlefield.

As a small boy, I sat wide-eyed as he painted a vivid picture of his small landing craft crashing through the waves towards the Normandy coast. He conjured up the sense of fear as he and his men approached the inevitable hail of machine-gun fire that would 'welcome' them as they raced towards French soil. I felt a surge of pride that my father – Lieutenant Eric Ashcroft – had played such a courageous part in the war effort.

Gradually, my interest in bravery grew and grew. Courage is a truly wonderful quality, yet it is so difficult to understand. You can't accurately measure it, you can't bottle it and you can't buy it, yet those who display it are, quite rightly, looked up to by others and are admired by society. Wiser – and braver – men than me have struggled to comprehend gallantry and what makes some individuals risk the greatest gift of all – life itself – for a comrade, for monarch and country, or sometimes even for a complete stranger.

Over the years, my general passion for bravery transformed itself into one for gallantry medals in particular. Such medals are the tangible record of an individual's service and courage. When I was in my early twenties, I hoped one day to own a VC, the ultimate decoration in Britain and the Commonwealth for bravery in the face of the enemy. Yet, I was a man of few means and the cost of such decorations was then prohibitive.

But what was the dream that it turned into? I will fast-forward nearly two decades until shortly after my fortieth birthday. By then I was fortunate enough to have made a little money as an entrepreneur and so – in July 1986 – I bought at auction my first VC. It was the decoration that had been awarded to Leading Seaman James Magennis for valour during the closing months of the Second World War. Although I had initially intended the purchase to be a one-off, I soon decided to try to build a collection. One VC became two, soon the collection hit double figures and so on. On the night of the gallery opening, the total number of VCs in my collection stood at 164.

As my collection became the largest in the world, I wanted to bring the decorations to a wider audience. I knew I wanted them to be enjoyed by thousands of people but the difficulty was how to achieve it. In short, the dream was to somehow get the collection on show in a suitable location – but I was a businessman, not a museum curator.

Once again, in my speech that evening, I fast-forwarded two decades, this time to the summer of 2008. As a result of a great deal of behind-the-scenes discussion, I was able to announce that I had given a sizeable donation so that the largest collection of VCs in the world would go on display in a new gallery. The location was what I considered to be not just a *suitable* location, but quite literally the *best* possible location for the VCs – the world-renowned IWM.

Today my collection of VCs stands at 200 decorations. This is because in September 2016, just as I was putting the finishing touches to this book, Michael Naxton, the Curator of the Ashcroft

Medal Collection, concluded a private deal for me to buy the gallantry and service medals of Flight Lieutenant Andrew Beauchamp Proctor VC, DSO, MC and Bar, DFC. Beauchamp Proctor, who was an acting captain at the time he was awarded his VC, was the Allies' sixth-highest-scoring ace of the Great War and South Africa's leading ace: unusually, his fifty-four 'victories' all came in the final year of the conflict. I was thrilled when I learned that, after lengthy negotiations, my offer had been accepted – not only is it a simply superb medal group but the '200 mark' was not one I had ever imagined was possible when I started my collection fully thirty years earlier. Cared for and protected by a trust, it covers most of the campaigns in which the VC has been awarded over the past 160 years, and there are a number of hugely impressive individual stories. It includes the very first VC bestowed upon a recipient – Lieutenant (later Rear-Admiral) Henry Raby, who was presented with his decoration by Queen Victoria in 1857; the twentieth century's first VC – to Private John Barry for bravery in South Africa in 1901; and the last VC of the twentieth century – to Sergeant Ian McKay for gallantry in the Falklands in 1982. It has a truly international flavour too: home to the first VC to be awarded to a Sikh – to Sepoy Ishar Singh for courage on the North-West Frontier in 1921 – and the first VC awarded to a Muslim – to Sepoy Khudadad Khan for bravery in battle in 1914, early in the First World War. The collection also includes the first aviation VC – a posthumous award to Second Lieutenant William Rhodes-Moorhouse in 1915; a string of submarine awards; two of the five civilian VCs and one of the only three double VCs in the world. For, in 2009, the collection took possession of the decorations of Captain Noel Chavasse, a medical officer, who earned a VC both on the Somme and at Ypres, thereby becoming the only man to receive a 'VC and Bar' during the First World War.

With the publication of *Victoria Cross Heroes* ten years ago, I made a conscious decision to do all I could to champion bravery and, in particular, the courage of VC recipients. I became convinced that we all have a duty to highlight the gallantry of our servicemen and others who have risked, and often given, their lives for their country, their monarch and wider freedoms.

By the time *Victoria Cross Heroes* was published in 2006 – the 150th anniversary of the creation of the VC – I had recently turned sixty and, despite my ongoing commitments and interests in business, politics, philanthropy and other areas, I decided to devote more time and resources to championing bravery.

Victoria Cross Heroes: Volume II is my sixth book on bravery and, by donating my author's royalties from these publications to various military charities, I have been able to help some good causes along the way. As stated earlier in this chapter, I found a way – through the Lord Ashcroft Gallery at the IWM – of putting my collection of VCs and GCs on public display. Since the gallery was opened in 2010, hundreds of thousands of people have visited the 'Extraordinary Heroes' exhibition that seeks to intrigue, inspire and amaze by re-telling forgotten stories of bravery that show how, when faced with extreme situations, some people can do extraordinary things. The IWM has long had a deserved reputation for helping the public to understand the experience of modern conflict and I wanted the gallery to concentrate on helping visitors to try to understand the concept of courage and how grateful we should be to those who display it.

I have found other ways, too, of championing bravery. In 2011/12, I donated more than £1 million to a £7 million appeal for a new Bomber Command Memorial. A successful appeal meant that in June 2012 Her Majesty The Queen was able to unveil a new monument in Green Park dedicated to the memory of more than 55,000 airmen. I made my donation because I wanted the memorial to be built while some Bomber Command veterans, then in their late eighties and early nineties, were still alive. Rarely, if ever, can any group of servicemen have been more deserving of a memorial to their courage than Bomber Command. The new monument is and will remain a fitting tribute to the men who helped to shape the free world in which we live.

In recent years, I have established two major medal collections on top of the one featuring VCs. These are my Special Forces medal collection and my collection of medals for gallantry in the air. Furthermore, I now own nineteen GCs, having started this collection as recently as 2010. I have regularly lectured on bravery, including at the Cheltenham Literary Festival, and my medal collections often provide the starting point for my talks.

Today I also write regularly for newspapers and magazines about bravery. I have a regular 'hero of the month' slot in *Britain at War*, the country's bestselling history monthly, and I have penned numerous articles in national and local newspapers. For example, in the early summer of 2014, to mark the 70th anniversary of the D-Day landings, I wrote in the *Sunday Telegraph* of my visit to 'Sword Beach', where my father had landed on 6 June 1944. As part of my research for the project, I discovered – to my joy – that my father had given a recorded interview to the IWM on his military exploits that remains in their archives.

In the aftermath of the opening of the Lord Ashcroft Gallery, I sat down with Michael Naxton, the curator of the Ashcroft VC Collection, to decide upon the direction we would take in future. Michael, who formerly worked as the head of the Sotheby's medals and coins department, has helped me to build my entire VC collection. Michael and I concluded that in future we would concentrate on buying only VCs with quite remarkable stories behind them or ones that filled a gap in the existing collection. In essence, our aim was only to purchase medals with a 'wow' factor or ones that made the collection more rounded and more historically complete. The result of this decision was that, in recent years, I have turned down the opportunity of buying VCs that I might previously have added to my collection. However, it has meant that the rarity, by circumstance or campaign, of the stories behind the VCs that I have purchased has been higher than ever before.

I should stress that it is rare, if not unheard of, for any VC recipient to have only the quality of bravery. So often, in my experience, these men have many more strengths, including a sense of duty, loyalty, sacrifice and comradeship. Every VC tells a story of one man's bravery in the face of the enemy: a tale of how a soldier, sailor or airman showed courage so far beyond any sense of expectation, or duty, that his country decided to bestow upon him its foremost honour for valour. This book tells the stories of fifty-eight men whose gallantry must be cherished and never forgotten.

2

THE
CRIMEAN WAR

The Crimean War lasted from 1854 to 1856 and was a conflict between Imperial Russia, on one side, and the Ottoman Empire, Britain, France and Sardinia, on the other. The majority of the fighting took place on the Crimean peninsula in the Black Sea. The war was won by the Ottoman Empire (later Turkey) and its Western allies. Britain and its allies lost well over 200,000 personnel to both the battlefield and disease, and the Russian losses were far greater.

In the 1840s, Lord Palmerston and other British leaders had become concerned that Russia would encroach into India and Afghanistan. Tensions grew in the 1850s and, when Tsar Nicholas I sent troops into Moldavia and Wallachia, Britain despatched a fleet to the Dardanelles, the entrance to the Black Sea. By 1853, Russia and the Ottoman Empire were at war, and when the former ignored an Anglo-French ultimatum to withdraw from Moldavia and Wallachia, Britain and France too declared war on 28 March 1854.

The Crimean War saw some fierce battles and several grim sieges. It also marked the introduction into warfare of railways and the telegraph, as well as trenches and blind artillery fire (whereby gunners rely on 'spotters' rather than being on the field of battle themselves). For this reason it was thereafter labelled the first 'modern war'. The poor treatment of wounded soldiers in the harsh conditions prompted the work of Florence Nightingale and the development of modern nursing methods. Basic ambulances were also used for the first time during the conflict.

The first major confrontation between the two sides came at the Battle of the Alma on 20 September 1854. On 25 October, the Russians were driven back at the Battle of Balaclava, noteworthy for the foolhardy Charge of the Light Brigade. Eleven days later, the two sides fought the Battle of Ink-erman, again with heavy casualties. On 11 September 1855, the British and French forced the fall of Sebastopol. Peace was eventually concluded in Paris the next year.

The Crimean War led directly to the creation of the VC. In 1856, 111 men were awarded the medal for their contribution to the war. The trust has fifteen of these medals in its collection, including seven that were purchased in the past decade and which make up this chapter.

LIEUTENANT (LATER REAR-ADMIRAL) JOHN BYTHESEA

Royal Navy

DATE OF BRAVERY: 12 AUGUST 1854

GAZETTED: 24 FEBRUARY 1857

Special feature of the VC: the second award ever 'won', the first awarded for a Special Forces-type action, and the earliest surviving award (the very first one having been 'lost' in the 1890s).

John Bythesea was born in Freshford, Somerset, on 15 June 1827. He was the youngest of five sons of the Revd George Bythesea, the rector and patron of Freshford, Somerset, and his wife Mary (*née* Glossop). Bythesea was educated at Grosvenor College, Bath, before he left school aged fourteen to embark on a military career. Bythesea's four older brothers all served in the Army but he broke with family tradition and opted instead for a life at sea, joining the Royal Navy on Christmas Eve 1841 as a volunteer 1st class. For the next four years, he served in HMS *Alfred*. Bythesea's eldest brother, Lieutenant G. C. G. Bythesea, of the 81st Foot, was killed in action at Feroze-shuhur (also spelled Ferozeshah), a hard-fought battle in the Punjab in 1845, when the British defeated the Sikhs.

After passing the necessary examination, Bythesea was promoted to mate in February 1848 and, between that month and June 1848, he served in HMS *Victory*. For the next year, he served in HMS *Pilot* in the East Indies, and was promoted to lieutenant on 12 June 1849. He was appointed to HMS *Arrogant* in September 1852 and served with the Fleet under Admiral Sir Charles Napier's command in the Baltic during the Crimean War.

On 18 May 1854, the *Arrogant*, together with HMS *Hecla*, came under fire from a force of Russian troops situated behind a protective sandbank. The Russian troops were, however, soon dispersed, and the next morning the two ships proceeded up a narrow channel to the town of Ekness. Here they faced determined opposition from two artillery batteries and the *Arrogant* suffered two killed and four wounded before the enemy's guns were silenced.

On 7 August 1854, with the British Fleet patrolling off the Russian-held island of Wardo, Captain Hastings Yelverton, the *Arrogant*'s commander, paid an official visit to Admiral Sir Charles Napier, the Commander of the Fleet. In fact, the first Special Forces-style raid of the Crimean War was a result of a mild rebuke delivered by Napier to Yelverton. The former gently ticked off the latter for the fact that despatches from the Russian Tsar were being constantly landed on Wardo and forwarded from there to the commanding officer of the fortress at Bomarsund. Napier's gripe was that the British forces had taken no action to prevent this.

Upon returning to his ship, Yelverton mentioned this state of affairs to his men and one of them, Lieutenant Bythesea, by then twenty-seven, determined to do something to disrupt the flow of mail that British intelligence sources had identified. Bythesea came up with an ambitious plan to slip on to Wardo and try to intercept the Russian mail as it was being moved across the island. He suggested that a foreign national, Stoker William Johnstone, whom he had discovered spoke Swedish, should accompany him on the mission. Yelverton's initial reaction was that a much larger force should accompany Bythesea but — in true Special Forces tradition

– it was eventually decided that a larger party was more likely to draw unwanted attention.

On 9 August 1854, just two days after Napier's and Yelverton's conversation, and clearly with minimal planning, Bythesea and Johnstone rowed ashore on their own. They made their way to a local farmhouse, where the owner had been forced to hand over all his horses to the Russians and was therefore only too willing to help them. He not only gave them food and shelter but informed them about how the Russians had improved a nine-mile stretch of local road to make it easier and quicker for messengers carrying the despatches to Bomarsund. However, the two men had not managed to arrive on the island unnoticed. Informants had told the Russians that a small shore party from the British Fleet was on the island and search parties had been sent out to capture them. Bythesea and Johnstone were able to avoid capture only because the farmer's daughters had given them old clothes to disguise themselves as Finnish peasants.

On 12 August, having been on the island for three days, Bythesea was told by the well-informed farmer that the Russian mail boat had landed and that the despatches were to be sent down to the fortress at Bomarsund at nightfall, with a military escort to accompany them part of the way. That night, Bythesea and Johnstone hid in bushes along the route. They watched from a safe distance as the military escort, reassured that the route was clear, turned back, leaving five unarmed messengers on their own. Bythesea and Johnstone knew the moment had come to strike. Armed with just a single flintlock pistol, they ambushed the five men. Two fled into the night, while the other three were captured along with the despatches. Bythesea and Johnstone returned to the hidden boat on which they had arrived and forced the three men to row to the *Arrogant*. Johnstone steered the craft as Bythesea held the pistol and instructed their prisoners to row. On their arrival at the ship, the prisoners were taken on board while the despatches were taken straight to Admiral Sir

Charles Napier and General Baraguay d'Hilliers, the French commander. Napier was thrilled by their actions, while d'Hilliers's admiration for the men was said to be 'unbounded'.

Bythesea's reward for the daring and successful mission was to be given command of the three-gun steam vessel HMS *Locust*, which was present at the fall of Bomarsund, as well as at the bombardment of Sveaborg in August 1855. He was promoted to commander in May 1856. Neither Bythesea nor Johnstone expected their bravery to be officially recognised as both, somewhat modestly, considered they had just been doing their duty. However, at Queen Victoria's behest, the VC was instituted on 29 January 1856 for extreme bravery in the face of the enemy and the awards were able to be backdated to the beginning of the Crimean War. The first action that had led to an awarding of the VC was the bravery of Lieutenant Charles Lucas, who served in HMS *Hecla*. Lucas had thrown a live shell overboard on 24 June 1854 after it landed on the ship's deck. However, the second and third VC actions – although, in fact, the twenty-second and twenty-third to be announced officially in the *London Gazette* – were those of Bythesea and Johnstone. Bythesea's VC, which was the result of recommendations from both Napier and d'Hilliers, was gazetted on 24 February 1857.

The first investiture, intended for the first ninety-three recipients of the medal, took place amid great pomp in Hyde Park, London, on 26 June 1857. At the occasion, sixty-two servicemen received their medal from The Queen. The remaining thirty-one were serving overseas and received their medals at a later date. Bythesea was the second man – after Commander Henry Raby – to have his VC pinned on him by The Queen, who remained mounted on her horse, Sunset, while conferring each award. Johnstone was one of those serving overseas and his medal was sent out for presentation aboard his ship.

Bythesea went on to serve at sea around the world, including in the operations against China from 1859 to 1860. For his final sea-going command, in 1870, he was appointed to the battleship HMS

Lord Clyde. This, however, was to end in disgrace for the courageous commander. In March 1872, *Lord Clyde* went to the aid of a paddle steamer that had run aground off Malta. However, in doing so, *Lord Clyde* also ran aground and had to be towed off by her sister ship, HMS *Lord Warden.* As a result of this episode, Bythesea and his navigating officer were court-martialled and severely reprimanded, with instructions that neither were to be employed at sea again. It was a sad end to Bythesea's previously distinguished and unblemished naval career.

However, typical of the man, Bythesea bounced back from his humiliation. On 26 March 1874, and by then forty-six, Bythesea married at Bathwick Parish Church, Somerset, to Frances 'Fanny' Prior, the daughter of an Army colonel. Later that year, Bythesea took up the post of Consulting Naval Officer to the Indian government. This enabled him, over the next six years, to restructure – from the old Indian Navy – the Royal Indian Marine. Further honours followed – a Companionship of the Military Division of the Most Honourable Order of the Bath (CB) in 1877 and a Companionship of the Most Eminent Order of the Indian Empire (CIE) the following year.

Bythesea retired from the active list on 5 August 1877, only to be promoted to rear-admiral seventeen days later. He died at his home in South Kensington, London, on 18 May 1906, aged seventy-eight. A guard of honour, made up of petty officers from HMS *Victory*, was mounted at the funeral. Bythesea is buried in Bath Abbey cemetery in his home city, while a memorial was erected to him and his brothers in his father's old church at Freshford. There is also a street – 'Bythesea Road' – named after him in Trowbridge, Wiltshire, and his name is on the Bomarsund memorial in Finland, which was unveiled in 2004, on the 150th anniversary of his action.

Incidentally, there was always some debate and confusion relating to Stoker William (also known as John) Johnstone, Bythesea's fellow VC recipient. The three-volume *Victoria Cross and the George*

Cross: The Complete History, first published in 2013, sought to clear up any ambiguity. It stated that the man who received the VC was Stoker William (or 'John') Johnstone, from HMS *Arrogant*, who had been born in Hanover, Germany. Sadly, for someone with such a distinguished military career, Johnstone's life came to an abrupt and unhappy end. On 20 August 1857, and by then aged thirty-four, he committed suicide on board HMS *Brunswick* in the West Indies having, in a 'fit of insanity', attacked one of his fellow crew before slitting his own throat. It is not known whether he was even presented with his VC prior to his death. Johnstone was buried at sea and his name is also on the recently unveiled Bomarsund memorial.

In April 2007, there was a great sense of anticipation when Bythesea's VC came up for auction at Spink in London. Not only was it the second VC ever 'won' but, for me, with a dual passion for the VC and Special Forces medals, it was in many ways the ultimate military decoration from this period. As detailed above, Bythesea's VC had been awarded for an early Special Forces-style operation, using a small, undercover force against a larger one for a specific target. I was therefore absolutely thrilled when I became the successful bidder for Bythesea's VC, albeit saddened that his other medals and awards had been stolen some thirty years earlier and were never recovered.

SERGEANT (LATER BREVET MAJOR) JOHN SIMPSON KNOX

Army: Scots Fusilier Guards

DATES OF BRAVERY: 20 SEPTEMBER 1854
AND 18 JUNE 1855

GAZETTED: 24 FEBRUARY 1857

Special feature of the VC: one of the first batch of six VCs ever awarded to soldiers. The medal group was accompanied by the cannon ball that blew off Knox's arm.

John Simpson Knox was born in Calton, Glasgow, on 30 September 1828. He was the son of John Knox of Inverkeithing and his wife Rebekah (*née* Living). John Knox Sr served with both the 90th Regiment and the 28th Regiment (Militia), before working as a grocer and labourer. Little is known of John Knox Jr's early life, including his education. However, he enlisted into the Scots Fusilier Guards in Glasgow on 15 May 1843, aged fourteen and having run away from home. It appears that Knox, who was unusually tall for his years, may have bought himself out of the Army but then re-enlisted a short time later (although it is also possible his real age was discovered by the authorities and he had to leave the Army for a short time).

In July 1845, Knox was promoted to acting corporal, although he was still only sixteen years old. Over the next nine years, he received a series of promotions so that four days after arriving in the Crimea, on 18 September 1854, he was promoted to colour-sergeant. On 19 September, the very day after his promotion, he was involved in the Scots Fusilier Guards' first action of the war en route to Sebastopol: this involved dispersing with fixed bayonets Russian troops who had earlier fired on a village.

On 20 September 1854, during the Battle of the Alma, Knox fought courageously, playing a key role at a time of great chaos and misunderstanding during the fighting. The Scots Fusilier Guards were part of the 1st Division that was at the extreme left of the Allied line and furthest inland. It was initially in reserve to the Light Division as the two divisions halted a short distance before the Alma River. At this point, the Russians had taken up defensive positions on the other side of river. This meant that, in order to attack, British troops faced fording the river itself and then climbing the bank on its far side – all this before they confronted a Russian earthworks bristling with artillery. The British force was ordered forward at 2.45 p.m., the French having managed to force a crossing further downstream. The Light Division crossed first, but came under fire from the Russian artillery and began to withdraw. The Guards'

Brigade was ordered forward and crossed the river, with the battalions beginning to re-establish their ranks on the other side, having scrambled up the banks on that side of the river. As the confusion mounted, the brigadier ordered them forward without delay, and the Scots, in the middle of the Guards' line, obeyed. However, as they started their advance, the retreating troops of the Light Division broke their line, and some of the Scots Guards joined the retreat. Further chaos followed an attempt by the Russians to seize the regiment's colours. It was left to their officers and Non-Commissioned Officers (NCOs), notably Knox, to regain control of the situation, which they were eventually able to do.

In a letter home, Knox described the horrors of battle:

> The scene that met my gaze was the most awful description: it made me shudder. The bodies of our opponents were so thick on the ground that for some distance I had to go on tiptoe to pass without touching ... the enemy cheered, and endeavoured to drive us back; however, we stuck to them until we were masters.

Knox took part in major battles at Balaclava, Inkerman and Sebastopol, where he was Mentioned in Despatches. Knox's talents as a fine soldier and a leader of men were further rewarded by his appointment to ensign in the 2nd Battalion, the Rifle Brigade, in March 1885. This had come about because the performance of the Scots Fusilier Guards at Inkerman had so impressed the Prince Consort that he offered several of them commissions in his own regiment. The men were individually selected by General Lord Rokeby, who put forward the names of Knox and others.

On 18 June 1855, during an action at the Redan fort, Sebastopol, Knox, who was now a lieutenant and aged twenty-six, once again excelled himself in battle. He volunteered for the ladder party (men carrying ladders with which to scale the enemy barricades) in the attack, knowing the dangers that he would face at the forefront of the battle. He fought valiantly, even though he was wounded twice: in fact, a cannon ball severed his left arm.

It was for his bravery at the Alma and the Redan that he was awarded the VC soon after it was instituted by Queen Victoria. His action at the Alma was the earliest for which VCs were awarded to members of the British Army – earlier actions leading to the award of the decoration were carried out by members of the Royal Navy. His VC was announced on 24 February 1857, when his citation read:

> When serving as a Serjeant in the Scots Fusilier Guards, Lieutenant Knox was conspicuous for his exertions in reforming the ranks of the Guards at the Battle of the Alma.
>
> Subsequently, when in the Rifle Brigade, he volunteered for the ladder-party in the attack on the Redan, on the 18th of June, and (in the words of Captain Blackett, under whose command he was) behaved admirably, remaining on the field until twice wounded.

Knox was among the sixty-two men at the first presentation of the VC by Queen Victoria in Hyde Park on 26 June 1857. Despite the loss of his arm, he continued to serve, and in January 1856 he was appointed as acting paymaster at the Regimental Depot, Winchester, Hampshire. In April of the same year, he was appointed as adjutant of the Rifle Brigade at Aldershot, Hampshire. Knox was appointed as Instructor of Musketry in January 1858, and was promoted to captain in April of that year. Other positions as an Instructor of Musketry followed and he briefly returned to regimental duties in January 1872. On his retirement from the Army in June 1872, he was given the honorary rank of brevet major.

Knox left the Army to take up the position of governor of Cardiff Prison. In September 1886, he was given the same role at Kirkdale Prison, Liverpool. In October 1891, he was appointed governor of Hull Prison, but poor health prevented him from taking up this role. In fact, he retired from the prison service in January 1892, aged sixty-three.

Knox had married Harriet Gale in Winchester, Hampshire, in July 1862, and the couple went on to have a son and six daughters. In his retirement, Knox lived in Cheltenham, Gloucestershire. He died at his home in the spa town on 8 January 1897, aged sixty-eight, and was buried four days later at Cheltenham Cemetery. Knox's name is on the Rifle Brigade Memorial at Winchester Cathedral, Hampshire.

The sale of Knox's medal group at a Spink auction in April 2010 created a great deal of media interest – this was because it was one of the first VCs to a serving soldier and because the sale included the Russian cannon ball that had severed Knox's arm. Oliver Pepys, of Spink auctioneers, said at the time:

> Major Knox showed incredible bravery, losing his arm to cannon fire in the process. The medal is being sold with a Russian cannonball, the very one that smashed into Knox's arm. In all my years of working with rare medals and war artefacts, I have never seen a more unusual keepsake.

PRIVATE SAMUEL PARKES

Army: 4th (The Queen's Own) Regiment of Light Dragoons
DATE OF BRAVERY: 25 OCTOBER 1854
GAZETTED: 24 FEBRUARY 1857
Special feature of the VC: an outstanding Charge of the Light Brigade award to the oldest man to be awarded the VC for action in the Crimean War.

Samuel Parkes was born in Wigginton, Tamworth, Staffordshire, in September 1813. He was the son of Thomas Parkes, a labourer, and his wife Lydia, and he was baptised on Christmas Eve 1815 at St Editha's Church, Tamworth. Little is known of his early life (including where he went to school) but he had two sisters, one older and one younger than him. He had been working as a labourer when he enlisted at Tamworth as a private in the 4th Light Dragoons on 30 July 1831, aged seventeen (although it appears he gave his age as eighteen). A formidable man of 6ft 2in., with fair hair and grey eyes, he joined his regiment during a time of active recruitment because at least one third of the lower ranks serving in India were dying from cholera each year.

For most of the next decade, Parkes was based in India with his regiment. However, in 1839, he served during the Afghanistan campaign and in July of that year played his part in the British capture of Ghuznee, the supposedly impregnable fort situated between Kabul and Kandahar. Indeed, for his part in that campaign, he received the Ghuznee Medal.

After his regiment's return to Britain in March 1842, Parkes served during the 'Rebecca Riots' in south Wales and, later, in Ireland. In November 1848, he was sentenced at a Regimental Court Martial to fifty-six days' imprisonment for being drunk on duty: one of a few run-ins that he had with military authority.

After the declaration of war by Britain and France on Russia on 28 March 1854 – the start of the Crimean War – Parkes was chosen by Colonel Lord (George) Paget, the regiment's commanding officer, as his personal orderly (effectively his bodyguard). In mid-September, the Allied forces made unopposed landings in the Crimea, with the 4th Light Dragoons arriving on 15 September. On 20 September, the British troops inflicted a heavy defeat on the Russians but the Allies did not follow up on this by pursuing the enemy to Sebastopol, as a result of which the Russians were given vital time to regroup.

The ill-fated Charge of the Light Brigade took place on 25 October 1854. Lord Raglan, who was in overall command of the British forces, had intended to send the Light Brigade in pursuit of a retreating artillery battery, a task well suited to such a force. However, due to a breakdown in communications, the Light Brigade was instead sent into a full-frontal assault on a different and well-prepared artillery battery. Of some 670 men who rode into battle, 110 were killed, 134 were wounded and fifty-seven were taken prisoner. The charge on horseback was led by a force that included the 4th and 13th Light Dragoons.

It was during the thick of the fighting that Parkes, aged forty-one, showed such bravery that he was later awarded the VC. His citation, eventually published on 24 February 1857, stated:

> In the charge of the Light Cavalry Brigade at Balaklava, Trumpet-Major Crawford's horse fell, and dismounted him, and he lost his sword; he was attacked by two Cossacks, when Private Samuel Parkes (whose horse had been shot) saved his life, by placing himself between them and the Trumpet-Major, and drove them away by his sword. In attempting to follow the Light Cavalry Brigade in the retreat, they were attacked by six Russians, whom Parkes kept at bay, and retired slowly, fighting, and defending the Trumpet-Major for some time, until deprived of his sword by a shot.

In more detailed accounts provided by eyewitnesses, it seems that at one point Private John Edden, also from the 4th Light Dragoons and also, coincidentally, from Tamworth, had had his horse shot from under him during the fighting. Edden and Crawford, who had been wounded, assisted Parkes in trying to rescue the seriously wounded Major Halkett. Parkes refused an offer to surrender and fought on until, as stated in the VC citation, he was wounded in his right hand by a shot. Halkett did not survive the battle, while Edden managed to escape the scene. Parkes and Crawford were thought to have been killed during the battle but, in fact, both men had been taken as Prisoners of War. The two prisoners were handed over by the Cossacks to the regular troops, who treated them well. General Liprandi, a Russian, is said to have looked at Parkes's huge frame and joked: 'If you are a Light Dragoon, what sort of men are your Heavy Dragoons?'

Parkes and Crawford were held for a year and a day before being exchanged for Russian prisoners on 26 October 1855. Both men were then charged under the Mutiny Act. However, they were cleared of any wrongdoing and, when the circumstances of their disappearance became known, they were awarded full arrears of pay. Furthermore, a number of survivors from the Charge of the Light Brigade provided statements relating to Parkes's bravery at Balaclava and he was awarded the VC soon after the award was created by Queen Victoria. Parkes was the oldest man to be awarded the VC for bravery in the Crimean War.

Parkes did, in fact, provide his own account of the Battle of Balaclava, but this did not come until he filed an affidavit on 2 June 1863 as part of a lawsuit taken out by Lord Cardigan following criticism of him by Colonel Calthorpe (Cardigan won the legal battle). Parkes stated:

I was twenty-six years and four months in the service and I have got the Victoria Cross. I remember the Charge of the Light Cavalry Brigade on the 25th of October 1854 at Balaklava. I acted as orderly to Lord George Paget on that day, and took part in the Charge. I saw Lord Cardigan leave the Heavy Cavalry Brigade, ride through the right of our squadrons and heard him give orders to Lord George Paget that the Light Brigade should advance, and he ordered them to 'Trot Gallop.' At the time the first line of our cavalry was about 250 yards in front of our line. We then all charged, and as we passed the redoubts on our right and left they fired on us. When our line arrived past the redoubts and the smoke and dust had cleared away we saw no sign of the first line and could not imagine what had become of them. We continued our charge and reached the guns in front of us and got through them, cutting down the drivers and gunners and silencing the guns. Whilst we were so engaged we observed the 11th Hussars were being cut up by the enemy and a number of the 4th Light Dragoons, together with Lord Paget and myself, charged down to their support. We then saw that the Russians had drawn back; but at the same time we saw a regiment of Lancers in our rear. Lord George Paget first thought they were the 17th Lancers, but on discovering they were the enemy's troops he called out to some officers near him 'Where is Lord Cardigan?' and then I heard someone (whom I have always thought to be Captain Lowe) say, 'Lord Cardigan has gone back some time.' Lord George Paget then ordered us to get through the Russians in the best way we could and so we retreated right through the Russian cavalry, who opened up right and left and let us pass, showing no resistance to us. When we were retreating and just after I had passed the first redoubt, my horse was shot and we were attacked by the Cossacks. I defended myself for a long time, but at length, whilst so engaged with a Cossack, a shot struck the hilt of my sword and wounded my hand, two Russians officers galloped up, took me prisoner, and took me to General Liprandi. Later that evening he sent for me again, with others, and asked us many questions relevant to our positions and strength and also asked me if we had been made drunk before the charge. He further asked me if it was Lord Cardigan who went to the rear on a chestnut horse with white legs; we said, 'Yes' and he then said: 'If he had not had a good horse, he would never have got back.' The water kegs, haversacks, etc., were taken from all the other prisoners, but the General then gave orders that mine should not be taken, and nothing was taken from me except my scabbard and belt. From the time we commenced to charge I did not see Lord Cardigan again until my return to England. He gave no order to our line except the order to 'Charge' as before stated.

Unfortunately, Parkes did not give a detailed account of his own VC action as it was not relevant to the legal case.

Parkes was discharged from the Army at his own request on 1 December 1857, while in possession of three good conduct badges and having served for more than twenty-six years. On 13 February 1858, he married Ann Jeffrey, a Yorkshire farmer's daughter, at St George's Church, Hanover Square, central London. The couple lived in London and Parkes worked for the Royal Parks, stationed at Hampton Court Palace. In the same year that he got married, he was appointed an inspector in the Hyde Park Constabulary.

Parkes died in Hyde Park, central London, on 15 November 1864, apparently aged fifty-one, and was buried at Brompton Cemetery, Fulham, west London. However, both his death certificate and the burial register give Parkes's age as forty-nine. There are no known photographs of Parkes in existence. There was, however, a Victorian postcard published depicting his VC action and also a painting of him by artist Louis William Desanges.

The man who deserves credit for uncovering new information about Parkes's military career is Peter Elkin, the VC recipient's great-great-great-nephew and the author of the book *Tamworth's Forgotten Hero*. Elkin also discovered his illustrious ancestor's unmarked grave in 1999 and arranged for a memorial stone to be erected. Furthermore, Elkin arranged that on 24 October 2004, for the 150th anniversary of the Charge of the Light Brigade, a plaque dedicated to Parkes's memory was positioned inside St Editha's Parish Church in Tamworth, where Parkes was baptised in 1815. Elkin owns a sword that used to belong to Parkes, although it is uncertain whether this was the weapon that he had during the Charge of the Light Brigade.

LIEUTENANT (LATER LIEUTENANT-COLONEL) FREDERICK MILLER

Army: Royal Regiment of Artillery
DATE OF BRAVERY: 5 NOVEMBER 1854
GAZETTED: 6 MAY 1859
Special feature of the VC: an award for exceptional bravery at the Battle of Inkerman but its announcement was severely delayed due to mislaid papers.

Frederick Miller was born in Radway under Edge, Warwickshire, on 10 November 1831. He was the son of Lieutenant-Colonel Fiennes Miller, of the 6th (Inniskilling) Dragoons, and his wife Georgiana (*née* Story). Details of his early education are not known but he attended the Royal Military Academy (RMA), Woolwich, London, as a cadet from January 1847, when he was fifteen.

From December 1848, Miller served as a lieutenant in the Royal Regiment of Artillery. He saw action during the Crimean War and was present at the Battles of the Alma, Sebastopol and Balaclava. However, it was for his courage at the Battle of Inkerman in Russia (now Ukraine) that he was awarded the VC. During the height of the fighting on 5 November 1854, Miller, aged twenty-two, managed to prevent Russian soldiers from seizing valuable British guns. His citation stated:

> For having, at the battle of Inkermann personally attacked three Russians, and with the gunners of his Division of the Battery, prevented the Russians from doing mischief to the guns which they had surrounded.
>
> Part of a Regiment of English infantry had previously retired through the Battery in front of this body of Russians.

In April 1855, Miller was promoted to second captain and in November of the same year he was elevated to brevet major. He later worked as a tutor in military tactics at RMA, Woolwich, where he taught both The Prince of Wales (the future King Edward VII) and Prince Alfred, Duke of Edinburgh.

After the creation of the VC in 1856, Miller was recommended for the decoration in January 1857. However, the recommendation was mislaid by the War Office and so nothing happened to progress it. In January 1859, Miller wrote to the authorities putting himself up for the award, although at this point a decision had been taken not to award any further VCs for the Crimea. However, after the mislaid statements were located, his claim was accepted and his VC was sanctioned on 6 May 1859, nearly five years after his action. He received his award from Queen Victoria at an investiture at Buckingham Palace on 8 June 1859.

Miller was promoted to captain in December 1861 and was given the brevet rank of lieutenant-colonel in February 1867. He served in India from 1868 to 1869, on St Helena from 1871 to 1872 and in Cape Colony, South Africa, from 1872 to 1874. In August 1873, he was promoted to lieutenant-colonel. As well as being an accomplished landscape artist, Miller wrote a number of military histories.

Miller died in service while in Cape Town, South Africa, on 17 February 1874, aged forty-two. He was buried in St Peter's Cemetery, Cape Town, although his remains were later interred at the Ossuary Garden of Remembrance, Observatory, Cape Town. Additionally, his name is commemorated on a family obelisk in the graveyard of Radway Parish Church, Warwickshire, and his name is also inscribed on the Royal Artillery Memorial, Woolwich.

CAPTAIN (LATER HONORARY MAJOR-GENERAL) MATTHEW CHARLES DIXON

Army: Royal Regiment of Artillery
DATE OF BRAVERY: 17 APRIL 1855
GAZETTED: 24 FEBRUARY 1857
Special feature of the VC: one of the first awards to be announced.

Matthew Charles Dixon was born in Avranches, Brittany, France, on 5 February 1821. He was the eldest son of Major-General Sir

Matthew Dixon, of the Royal Engineers, and his second wife Emma (*née* Dalton). Indeed, the Dixons were a formidable military family: Dixon Jr's grandfather was Sir Manley Dixon, an admiral of the fleet. Dixon Jr attended the Royal Military Academy (RMA), Woolwich, and was commissioned as a second lieutenant in the Royal Regiment of Artillery in March 1839, aged eighteen.

From March 1840 to June 1848, Dixon served in Ceylon (now Sri Lanka) and during this time he was promoted first to lieutenant (March 1841) and then to second captain (June 1848). From December 1848 to January 1854, he served in Jamaica, before being promoted to captain in February 1854.

Captain Dixon arrived in the Crimea early in 1855 and he was soon involved in the thick of the fighting. His VC action took place on 17 April 1855, when, aged thirty-four, he was manning No. 9 Battery of the Siege Train on the Second Parallel of the British Right Attack on the Woronzov Ridge, east of the Woronzov Road leading to Sebastopol, Russia (now Ukraine). The citation for his VC stated:

> On the 17th April, 1855, about 2 p.m., when the battery he commanded was blown up by a shell from the enemy, which burst in the Magazine, destroyed the parapets, killed and wounded ten men, disabled five guns, and covered a sixth with earth; for most gallantly re-opening fire with the remaining gun before the enemy had ceased cheering from their parapets (on which they had mounted) and fighting it until sunset, despite the heavy concentrated fire of the enemy's batteries, and the ruined state of his own.

Dixon's VC was one of the initial batch of awards announced on 24 February 1857. Furthermore, he had been promoted to brevet major on the same day as his VC action and he was later Mentioned in Despatches. His other bravery and service awards included the Légion d'Honneur (5th Class) from France. In November 1855,

Dixon was promoted to brevet lieutenant-colonel and the following year he served on the Channel Islands.

Dixon did not attend the initial VC award ceremony, when, on 26 June 1857, Queen Victoria invested sixty-two of the 111 Crimean War recipients in a ceremony in Hyde Park in front of more than 4,000 troops and 12,000 spectators. Instead, he received his VC from The Queen at an investiture on Southsea Common, Portsmouth, Hampshire, on 2 August 1858. In April 1862, he was promoted to lieutenant-colonel and the following month he was married at St Andrew's Church, Enfield, Middlesex, to Henrietta Bosanquet, the daughter of Admiral Charles Bosanquet (the couple never had children).

In June 1862, Dixon was promoted to brevet colonel and from that year until July 1866 he served in Jamaica. From January 1867, he served for exactly a year in Gibraltar. In August 1868, he was promoted to colonel and he retired in March 1869 with the honorary rank of major-general.

After his retirement, Dixon moved to a house in the village of Pembury, near Tunbridge Wells, Kent. He died at his home on 7 January 1905, aged eighty-three, and he is buried at Kensal Green Cemetery, north-west London. Additonally, there is a plaque in his honour at Pembury Church and his name is listed on the Royal Artillery Memorial in Woolwich, south-east London.

LIEUTENANT (LATER REAR-ADMIRAL) HENRY JAMES RABY

Royal Navy (Naval Brigade)
DATE OF BRAVERY: 18 JUNE 1855
GAZETTED: 24 FEBRUARY 1857
Special feature of the VC: Raby was the first VC recipient ever to receive the award from Queen Victoria and the only one to be 'wounded' during an investiture, when Her Majesty pinned the medal's brooch pin straight into his chest.

Despite coming from a traditional British family, Henry James Raby was born in Boulogne, France, on 26 September 1827. He was born into a family of wealthy industrialists: his grandfather, Alexander, had built a family fortune in the iron industry in south Wales. However, after the depression that followed the Napoleonic Wars, the Raby family had hit hard times. Following another disaster – the family's home in Llanelli, Cae Mawr Cottage, was destroyed in a fire in 1824 – Henry, his father Arthur and mother Henrietta (*née* Smith) were travelling around Europe. Henry was born where they were staying in France, while on their way to Germany.

Raby Jr was educated at Sherborne School in Dorset before joining the Royal Navy on 8 March 1842, aged fourteen. A volunteer first class, he was assigned to HMS *Monarch*. For the next six years, he served in a number of ships, gaining promotion and, while serving in HMS *Trafalgar*, completing his first foreign tour in the Mediterranean in 1848.

On 2 October 1850, he joined HMS *Wasp* as a newly promoted lieutenant, first being involved in anti-slavery duties off West Africa before operating along the Circassian coast between the Black and Caspian Seas until September 1854. On 23 October 1854, with the Crimean War raging, Lord Raglan called for naval assistance to reinforce land troops whose numbers had been ravaged by disease. A Naval Brigade was formed with sailors from four ships, including HMS *Wasp*.

Raby, by then twenty-seven, arrived with the Naval Brigade in the Crimea in October 1854 and served on land, rather than at sea, for the remainder of the war. He fought with the Naval Brigade at the Battle of Inkerman on 5 November 1854.

In June 1855, the Naval Brigade was instructed to provide some manpower to form some of the ladder parties for the assault on Sebastopol. This involved a two-pronged Anglo-French attack on two features, the Malakoff, a two-storey stone tower, and the Redan, a triangular, purpose-built fort. The ladder parties faced a daunting challenge because they were at the front of the assault and would face the full might of the defensive fire. Indeed, ladder parties from years earlier had been known as the 'Forlorn Hope' because, for many, membership meant almost certain death in battle.

In the event, Raby was assigned to duties in the trenches besieging Sebastopol. On 17 June 1855, some 800 Allied guns began firing in a massive bombardment of the Russian forces. Although the Russian resistance was formidable, their soldiers soon started to run short of ammunition and the Allies began to gain the upper hand. The next day, the Anglo-French force began a major offensive targeting both the Malakoff and the Redan. Both attacks went badly, with the men of the Naval Brigade, along with the 57th Regiment and the Rifle Brigade, taking heavy casualties.

It was on 18 June that Raby took part in an action for which he would be awarded the VC. During the attack on the Redan, a soldier serving with the 57th Regiment became stranded in no-man's land having been seriously wounded. He had been shot through both legs but, despite clearly being in great pain, was sitting up and calling for assistance. Raby, along with another officer who had seen what had happened, seized the initiative and they decided to rescue the wounded man, accompanied by two other seamen.

Climbing over the breastwork of the advanced trench, Raby and the other men faced a daunting challenge: the wounded man was fully 70 yards away and the enemy had opened up a heavy fire from a position looking down on where he lay. However, the rescue party succeeded in reaching the man, before lifting him up and, after supporting his injured legs, scurrying back to their own lines. The heavy enemy fire continued but they eventually managed to get the wounded soldier back to a place of safety.

Sir Stephen Lushington later prepared a report of the incident that noted the bravery of Raby and others. However, Raby became aware of Lushington's report and tried to correct what he felt had been an injustice in the nomination because Lieutenant Edward D'Eath, the first man to see that a soldier needed rescuing, had not been given sufficient credit for his bravery, and nor had the other two soldiers.

Having returned home after the war, Raby wrote directly to Lushington, telling him:

> I have only on my return to England become aware of your having already forwarded to Admiral Sir Edward Lyons, Commander in Chief of the Mediterranean Fleet, the names of such officers and men amongst those who had the honour of serving under your command in the Royal Navy Brigade who you consider to have deserved the distinction of the 'Victoria Cross' by any special act of 'valour or devotion to their country' in the presence of the enemy during the late war.
>
> Under these circumstances, I have the honour to request that you will allow me, in justice to the memory of my lamented comrade and brother officer the late Lieutenant Edward Hughes D'Eath, R. N. of Her Majesty's ship 'Sidon' to bring the following action to your notice.
>
> On the 18th June 1855 Lieut D'Eath commanded the 4th party of seamen detailed to carry the scaling ladders to which party I had also the honour of being attached; in the morning soon after the repulse of the troops from the Redan, I was standing in the advanced sap in front of the Quarries when Lt D'Eath came to me and said that there was a soldier laying out in front of the sap badly wounded who he thought we might get in, and asked me if I would assist him to do so, to which I agreed readily. Lieut D'Eath on again looking at the man considered that from his being wounded in the legs it would require more than ourselves to bring him in, he therefore asked John Taylor ... and Henry Curtis ... if they would volunteer to go with us, they immediately assented...
>
> As Lieut D'Eath unfortunately fell victim to cholera soon after this event, I as the survivor take the liberty of laying this simple statement of the facts before you trusting that you consider it worthy of

being classed with those 'deeds of valour' which are already known to
you [and] will be pleased to use your influence to procure the Honour of 'The Victoria Cross' for him and those others concerned, and
I feel that by the family of my friend the late Lieut D'Eath nothing
would be more highly prized than such a testimony to his bravery.

I have the honour to be, Sir, your obedient and humble servant
HENRY J. RABY

At the actual time of Raby's bravery, the VC did not exist, although,
in fact, a new decoration, for everyone from the lowest ranks to the
most senior officers, was under active consideration. As stated in
Chapter 1, the VC was instituted by a Royal Warrant of 29 January
1856, which, with fifteen 'rules and ordinances', created a new decoration to reward 'individual instances of merit and valour'.

It is likely that Lushington knew that the VC could not be
awarded posthumously, and so had not mentioned D'Eath when
he drew up his report. D'Eath had died on 7 August 1855, thereby
making him ineligible for the award. In the event, however, Raby,
Taylor and Curtis were all awarded the VC.

Eventually, the first awards of the VC, including Raby's, were
announced in the *London Gazette* on 24 February 1857. Four months
later, on 26 June 1857, there was a wonderful gathering in Hyde
Park for the first presentation of the medals. Queen Victoria herself was on horseback and dressed in scarlet jacket, black skirt and
plumed hat as she prepared for one of the most remarkable investi-
tures in the history of the royal family.

Just seventeen months after instituting the VC, The Queen was
about to bestow the award on sixty-two of the initial 111 medal
recipients in a ceremony attended by an estimated 4,000 troops and
12,000 spectators. Just one of the medal recipients would go in the
history books as the first ever man to receive the VC, and that honour was given to Commander Henry Raby, then just three months

short of his thirtieth birthday. By virtue of being the most senior officer in the most senior service (the Royal Navy), he was chosen as the first person to whom The Queen bent down towards from her horse in order to pin the VC firmly on his chest.

In fact, she was a little too firm as she thrust the medal forward and the brooch pin of Raby's VC penetrated the thick jacket of his uniform and pierced his skin. As J. D. Davies notes in his book *Britannia's Dragon: A Naval History of Wales*: 'The investiture proved to be rather more painful than the action for which he was being rewarded, as The Queen pinned the medal straight into his chest.' Raby is said not to have flinched as the pin went deep into his skin but, in his latter years, he joked that he had survived the VC action unscathed only to be wounded by The Queen. Raby received several other decorations from foreign countries, including the Légion d'Honneur (3rd Class) from France.

Raby went on to enjoy a distinguished career in the Royal Navy. In October 1859, he was appointed to the command of HMS *Weser* and, the following year, he was given command of HMS *Alecto*. During this time, based on the West Africa Station, Raby carried out a great deal of work against the slave trade. In April 1861, he commanded the gunboats that seized and destroyed Porto Novo, the large slaving fort. During this fighting, he was involved in spiking one of the guns when it exploded, leaving him with facial injuries.

Raby was promoted to captain in November 1862, the year before he married Judith Foster in Holt Parish Church, Wiltshire. The couple went on to have three sons, two of whom served in the Armed Forces.

In October 1875, after more than twenty-seven years' service, Raby was appointed a Companion of the Order of the Bath (CB). He was placed on the retired list in 1877 but early in the following year was promoted to rear-admiral.

Raby never forgot his Llanelli links: at the time of his investiture, he is believed to have owned thirty-six cottages in the town. In 1878, a year after retiring, he returned to Llanelli and was welcomed as a hero by an affectionate crowd. He also visited the dock and furnace that his grandfather had created two generations earlier.

In retirement, Raby spent most of his remaining years living in Southsea, Hampshire, where he was involved in several charities. He died on 13 February 1907, aged seventy-nine, and was buried in Highland Road Cemetery, Portsmouth, with full military honours. The memorials to Raby include a brass tablet in Llanelli Town Hall, while there is also a painting depicting his VC action at Sherborne School in Dorset.

LIEUTENANT (LATER MAJOR-GENERAL SIR) CHRISTOPHER CHARLES TEESDALE

Army: Royal Regiment of Artillery
DATE OF BRAVERY: 29 SEPTEMBER 1855
GAZETTED: 25 SEPTEMBER 1857
Special feature of the VC: the unique award of the decoration for the Siege of Kars and the first VC awarded to a recipient born in South Africa.

Christopher Charles Teesdale was born in Grahamstown, the Cape of Good Hope, South Africa, on 1 June 1833. He was the third son of Lieutenant-General Henry Teesdale, of the Royal Horse Artillery, who was posted to South Africa, with his wife Rose (*née* Dobrée), prior to their baby's birth. Christopher was just two years old when he returned to England with his family. For the rest of his childhood, he was brought up in England and Guernsey, where his mother's family lived. In 1848, Teesdale was accepted as a gentleman cadet in the Royal Artillery and he was commissioned into the regiment as a second lieutenant on Waterloo Day, 18 June 1851, shortly after his eighteenth birthday.

On 22 April 1853, he was promoted to lieutenant and served with the British Forces in the Crimean War, where he was given an important role fairly early on in the conflict. The British and French forces had made their way to the Crimea with the intention of destroying the Russian Black Sea Fleet and the port of Sebastopol. Their other objective was to prevent a Russian naval assault on Constantinople, while the land route through the Caucasus and Asia Minor was protected by the large Turkish Army, guarding against a Russian invasion from Tiflis (now Tbilisi). The Russians had moved 35,000 troops into the area in early 1854, hoping to open up a second front against a weak and disorganised Turkish Army.

On 3 and 6 August, the Russians twice routed the Turks on the battlefield. Smarting from two heavy defeats, the Turkish Army fell back on the town of Kars, south-west of Tiflis. Realising the seriousness of the situation, the British decided in September 1854 to send a British Commissioner, accompanied by a small staff, to join the Turkish force. The man tasked with this key role was Colonel Sir Fenwick Williams, of the Royal Artillery, who was accompanied by his aide-de-camp, Lieutenant Christopher Teesdale, and Dr Humphry Sandwith, who had been appointed Inspector General of Hospitals in Asia Minor. The intention was that Williams would liaise between the Ottoman Porte in Constantinople and Lord Raglan's headquarters in the Crimea.

The three-strong party, headed by Williams, arrived in Kars in late 1854. Although a barren, harsh location, the town was strategically important. If the Russians could capture it, they could march on into the Ottoman Empire, which would, in turn, significantly boost their chances of winning the Crimean War. While Williams and Sandwith spent the winter travelling through Asia Minor, Teesdale was left as the sole British representative in Kars. He lamented his misfortune in a letter home:

> I am not so enamoured of the 'Sunny East' as to wish to stay six months in a mud hovel on my own, unable to get out more than six times during that period. As to the fair ones, I have had a fine opportunity of seeing them during our inspection of these winter

quarters. They are about as fair as an old boot and if you can imagine anything between a chimney-sweep and a dancing bear you will form a better idea of their costume and grace than it is possible for me to give you.

In April 1855, Williams and Sandwith returned to Kars, where they were joined by three more Englishmen, including two Army officers. Williams, who had been given the temporary rank of brigadier-general, and Teesdale, in the rank of major, and the rest of the British party attempted to strengthen the town's defences in preparation for the inevitable Russian siege, which began in June 1855. At the end of this month, the Russians moved between 35,000 and 40,000 men into the area. They were under the command of General Nikolay Mouravieff, who, as a young subaltern, had taken part in the capture of the town in 1828. During July, and with Mouravieff absent, there were skirmishes after the Russians had probed the town's defences. However, on 8 August, the Russian assaults became more aggressive, leading Teesdale to write home:

> To this moment I do not know what the demonstration against our position was meant for. The only explanation I can imagine is that, in the absence of Mouravieff, General Brumer wished to do something – what, no one probably knows except himself. The Russians were quite deceived by our silence on the day of the demonstration in that quarter as to the range of our guns, and therefore came within easy reach of them before they were made painfully aware of the fact. The number of enemy killed included a General, a Lieutenant-Colonel, and eight or nine officers of superior rank.

Teesdale himself could not resist a swipe at the retreating Russian Army. He galloped up to a position overlooking the battle scene and ordered a large cannon to be elevated and fired, causing chaos amid the fleeing Russians. The enemy's reverse led to a change of tactics:

they patiently decided to starve the town into submission. News of the fall of Sebastopol reached Kars on 17 September, by which point the town was suffering: cavalry horses were dying and the population was on half rations. When Mouravieff learned of Allied plans to send a relief force to Kars, he decided on an all-out attack.

Following the spirited defence of Kars on 29 September 1855 in response to a major assault, Williams wrote a despatch dated that day:

> I have the honour to inform your Lordship that General Mouravieff, with the bulk of his army, at day-dawn this morning, attacked our entrenched position on the heights above Kars, and on the opposite side of the river. The battle lasted, without a moment's intermission, for nearly seven hours, when the enemy was driven off in the greatest disorder, with the loss of 2,500 dead, and nearly double that number of wounded, who were, for the most part, carried off by the retreating enemy. Upwards of 4,000 muskets were left on the field. Your Lordship can, without a description on my part, imagine the determination of the assailants, and the undaunted courage of the troops who defended the position for so many hours. I have great gratification in acquainting your Lordship with the gallant conduct of Lieutenant-Colonel Lake, Major Teesdale, and Captain Thompson, who rendered the most important service in defending the redoubts. I beg to recommend these officers to your Lordship's protection. I also beg to name my Secretary, Mr. Churchill, an Attaché of Her Majesty's Mission in Persia. He directed the fire of a battery throughout the action, and caused the enemy great loss. Dr. Sandwith has been most active and efficient in the management of the ambulances and in the hospital arrangements. Our loss was about 700 killed and wounded.

The ferociousness of the battle was relayed in a letter home from Teesdale written the next day. It began: 'I dare say when this reaches you that you will have heard of the desperate action we had here yesterday; I wish you to know as soon as possible that, by God's mercy, I came out of it unhurt.'

After a lengthy description of the bloody battle, Teesdale ended his letter:

> Tired of acting so long on the defensive I mounted my horse which had remained unhurt and led a charge against the enemy's chasseurs and stragglers who, favoured by the ground, still kept shooting our men at leisure. This was no easy task, and on reaching the exterior of Tachmach tabia we found ourselves confronted by a regiment of the enemy – fresh men firing heavily along their front. It was the last remnant of the Russian infantry. The Turks still left alive in Tachmach tabia could no longer be restrained; seeing our plight they burst forth like a pent-up torrent from the redoubt and rushed with the blind fury of wild animals to our assistance – and the Russian regiment seemed to melt before them. In a moment the ground was thick with corpses and the survivors flying as best each one might. Our men could not be stopped until they had passed the road at the bottom of the hill – but the affair was over. A few more shots were fired at the fugitives when a band struck up and the soldiers were dancing amidst all the horrors of a battle ground.

The battle had raged uninterrupted for seven hours: the Turkish losses were 362 dead and 631 wounded. The townspeople of Kars suffered an additional 101 dead and 202 wounded. Of the Russian dead, General Williams wrote in a later despatch:

> Their loss was immense – they left on the field more than 5,000 dead, which literally covered the country, and it took the Turkish infantry four days to bury. Their wounded and prisoners in our possession amount to 160, whilst those who were carried off are said to be upwards of 7,000.

A Russian officer later painted an even grimmer picture:

> At the muster call in camp more than a third, and nearly a half, were
> missing from the night before. The whole of the following day was
> spent in collecting the dead and wounded. The Tsar's personal regi-
> ment of Carabiniers had suffered most – all of its thirty-two officers
> had either been killed or wounded, and we had up to 15,000 hors-
> de-combat as a result of the battle.

That night, having spent the afternoon burying their own dead and
treating their wounded, the defenders of Kars slept out in their positions, but no further attack was made.

In the weeks following the battle, it became apparent to both
sides that there was little likelihood of an Allied relief force being
sent to Kars. However, having suffered such heavy losses in one battle, Mouravieff was in no hurry to do so again, and instead refocused
his efforts on maintaining the siege, and starving the defenders into
submission. Teesdale described the situation vividly in another letter home:

> The horrors of the concluding part of the siege are almost too terri-
> ble to recall – men too proud to beg locked their doors and lay down
> to die in their houses. The misery within the town increased by the
> day, and the vigilance of the Russians doubled. A stock of wood
> eked out to the last had vanished, and the cold at night became so
> bitter that numbers of men were found every morning to be frozen
> to death in their tents. Horses and mules had long ceased to be of
> any service except for food. Towards the middle of November snow
> began to fall, and so intense did the cold now become that to sleep
> under canvas became nearly impossible. General Williams was now
> increasingly employed in nursing the remaining strength of the
> men. For some time past the health of Captain Thompson had been
> failing but he kept gallantly at his post until the cold and exposure

had entirely unfitted him for further exertion. At last so few days {*sic*} provisions remained that it became evident that the place was untenable for any further length of time, and unless some very unexpected piece of good news reached us we should have to abandon the city we had so long defended. By November 20th the state of weakness and complete prostration to which the garrison was now reduced had increased so terribly that the prospect of cutting our way out through the Russian lines – which at one time had seemed feasible – now appeared utter recklessness.

Dr Sandwith described scenes of desperately hungry men tearing up grass to eat the roots and of vultures competing with dogs to eat the corpses left in shallow graves. He wrote: 'The soldiers are dying at a rate of one hundred a day of famine. They were skeletons and were incapable of fighting. The city was strewn with dead and dying.'

Following a Council of War on 24 November, and with no prospect of Kars being relieved, the decision to surrender was taken. Teesdale wrote:

I was sent from the Council with the flag of truce to the Russian Camp. Having arrived at the outposts the Cossacks approached me. Having explained the object of my mission I was blindfolded and led towards their camp. Arriving at the headquarters of General Mouravieff I was admitted at once and presented the note from General Williams which I carried. An interview was arranged for the following day at noon and having been treated with great civility I took my leave. The following day General Williams, accompanied by his secretary Mr. Churchill and myself, presented ourselves at the Russian headquarters at the appointed time and, after the ordinary civilities, the two Generals were left alone to proceed to the settlement.

The formal surrender took place at an old Genoese church about 3 miles from Kars. The officers and regular troops of the garrison, around 8,000 in all, were all made Prisoners of War and the irregulars, numbering 6,000 in total, were allowed to go free. Under a clause in the surrender, personally inserted by General Mouravieff, 'Officers of all grades will be allowed to retain their swords, in consequence of the brave defence made by the garrison of Kars.' Sandwith, as a non-combatant, was allowed free to find his own way home. Armed with a Russian passport, he finally arrived back in England some three months later. The four British officers, including Teesdale, together with Churchill, as a volunteer prisoner, were all taken into custody at the Russian town of Tiflis.

On the conclusion of hostilities in the Crimea, and the signing of the treaty of peace on 30 March 1856, the four British officers were released. Teesdale arrived back in England on 11 June 1856, reverting to his substantive rank of lieutenant, Royal Artillery, having been created a Companion of the Order of the Bath (CB) the previous month in recognition of his distinguished services before the enemy in Kars (there were awards for all the British officers present at Kars).

Teesdale was also created an Officer of the French Légion d'Honneur and ultimately received the VC, the only one awarded for Kars. His award was announced on 25 September 1857, when his citation stated:

> For gallant conduct, in having, while acting as Aide-de-Camp to Major-General Sir William Fenwick Williams, Bart., K. C. B., at Kars, volunteered to take command of the force engaged in the defence of the most advanced part of the works, – the key of the position – against the attack of the Russian Army when, by throwing himself into the midst of the enemy, who had penetrated into the above redoubt, he encouraged the garrison to make an attack, so vigorous, as to drive out the Russians therefrom, and prevent its capture; also for having, during the hottest part of the action, when the enemy's fire had driven the Turkish Artillerymen from their guns, rallied the latter, and by his intrepid example induced them

to return to their post; and further, after having led the final charge which completed the victory of the day, for having, at the greatest personal risk, saved from the fury of the Turks, a considerable number of the disabled among the enemy, who were lying wounded outside the works, – an action witnessed, and acknowledged gratefully before the Russian Staff, by General Mouravieff.

Teesdale was presented with his VC by Queen Victoria on 21 November 1857 at Windsor Castle, thereby becoming the first South African-born recipient of the award. He also received the Turkish campaign medal for the defence of Kars – a unique occurrence of the VC being paired with a 'non-mainstream' foreign campaign medal.

Teesdale was promoted to captain and, later, brevet major in January 1858, and in November of that year was appointed equerry to The Prince of Wales. The two men shared a good relationship, as evidenced by a letter written by the Prince in June 1861: 'My dear Teesdale, I enclose two Post Office orders for £1 the sum you won here by successfully drawing the winner of the Oaks ... I remain, yours very sincerely, Albert Edward.' Teesdale was also an enthusiastic amateur artist and later developed a close friendship with the French painter Gustave Doré.

A decade after his release from captivity in Russia, Teesdale returned to St Petersburg to take part in the Garter Mission for the Investiture of His Imperial Majesty the Emperor of Russia with the Order of the Garter. Teesdale was promoted brevet lieutenant-colonel in December 1868, major in July 1872 and lieutenant-colonel in September 1876. He was appointed a brevet colonel and an aide-de-camp to Queen Victoria in October 1877, before being promoted to colonel in October 1882 and to his ultimate rank of major-general in April 1887. In July of that year, he was also created a Knight Commander of the Order of St Michael and St George (KCMG) in celebration of Her Majesty's Golden Jubilee. His final appointment was that of Her Majesty's Master of Ceremonies, a job he held from

May 1890. Teesdale retired from the Army in the spring of 1892 in order to become a Justice of the Peace. He died at home in South Bersted, near Bognor, Sussex, on 1 November 1893, aged sixty, the day after suffering a second stroke. Teesdale was buried in the village churchyard and his name was later added to the memorial at the Royal Artillery Chapel in Woolwich, south-east London.

3

THE INDIAN MUTINY
AND BEYOND

The Indian Mutiny

The Indian Mutiny broke out in 1857 and comprised a prolonged period of armed uprisings in northern and central India. The sepoys – native Indian soldiers from the Bengal Army serving under British officers – were protesting against British occupation of that part of the subcontinent. Small pockets of simmering discontent had begun in January 1857, but in May a large-scale rebellion broke out that turned into a fully fledged war in the affected regions. The mutiny lasted for thirteen months: from the rising at Meerut on 10 May 1857 to the fall of Gwalior on 20 June 1858 (although there were still 'mopping up' operations in 1859). The mutineers were eventually suppressed by the British – with the help of soldiers from other Indian armies – but not before a considerable loss of life on both sides.

Even the phrase 'Indian Mutiny' is controversial. Many Indians, along with some historians, prefer to refer to it as the 'First Indian War of Independence' or the 'War of Independence of 1857'. The British East India Company had expanded substantially in India over the previous hundred years. This had inevitably caused tensions among local inhabitants and an army was needed to secure the company's commercial interests.

The trigger for the rebellion was the introduction of a new gun that, unlike the old musket, required soldiers to bite open a cartridge and pour the gunpowder it contained into the muzzle. According to local rumour, the cartridge had been greased – to make it waterproof – with lard (pork fat) or tallow (beef fat). This was offensive to Muslim and Hindu soldiers alike, who were forbidden by their religions to eat pork or beef, respectively.

There were large uprisings in Cawnpore, Lucknow (where the British resi-
dency was besieged for ninety days) and Jhansi, which became the heart of
the rebellion. The principal outcome of the conflict was the end of the East
India Company's hegemony in the subcontinent and the onset of almost a
century of direct rule of India by Britain.

Of 182 VCs awarded for acts of bravery in the Mutiny, I own twenty,
including five purchased in the past decade.

COLOUR-SERGEANT STEPHEN GARVIN

Army: 60th Rifles (later The King's Royal Rifle Corps)

DATE OF BRAVERY: 23 JUNE 1857

GAZETTED: 20 JANUARY 1860

Special feature of the VC: the unique VC and DCM combination awarded
for action in the Indian Mutiny, making the recipient the most decorated
Non-Commissioned Officer of the whole conflict.

Stephen Garvin was born in Cashel, Co. Tipperary, on 19 August
1825. He was the son of James Garvin, a fur skinner, and his wife
Frances (*née* Ryan). Stephen Garvin enlisted into the Army, initially
into the 74th Regiment, on 6 July 1842, but within two years he
had transferred to the 60th Rifles. He embarked for India with the
regiment's 1st Battalion on 24 November 1845.

In just over two years, he had two quick promotions: from private to corporal in October 1845 and from corporal to sergeant
in December 1847. Garvin saw action in the Punjab Campaign of
1848–49, when he was present at the siege and capture of Mooltan (also spelled Multan) and in the Battle of Goojerat (also spelled
Gujrat) in which the Sikh Army was defeated. Garvin was also present in operations on the North-West Frontier in December 1849,
when the 60th Rifles, under Lieutenant-Colonel J. Bradshaw, took
part in two difficult attacks: the uphill assaults against the villages
of Sanghoo and Pali.

Garvin was still serving with his regiment's 1st Battalion in May 1857, by then as a colour-sergeant and thirty-one years old, when he witnessed the outbreak of the Indian Mutiny at Meerut on the 10th. He is mentioned in Wolmer Whyte's *Histories of the Regiments of the British Army*, in which the author writes that 'the Riflemen picked up some of the bodies of the murdered victims, then returned, and having formed a ring of picquets round English women and children who had taken refuge in the lines, they bivouacked on the Mall'.

Whyte added:

> When, next morning, the Riflemen made a reconnaissance they came across the bodies of two Riflemen of A Company, mutilated almost beyond recognition. They also found the body of Mrs. Chalmers, who had only lately arrived from England. Both officers and men knew and loved her for her devotion to the women and children of the regiment, and when her dismembered remains were seen in a ditch by the roadside, the Riflemen raised their weapons in the air and swore that her death would be avenged ... so well did the Riflemen keep their oath that in a few weeks they were known by the natives as 'the Regiment from Hell.' The scenes of massacre and outrage which were now so commonly met with strengthened the determination of all ranks to overcome the enemy, who, it was discovered, were retreating from Meerut and marching on Delhi, 40 miles away.

In their book *Focus on Courage*, Lieutenant-General Sir Christopher Wallace and Major Ron Cassidy take up the story of the events in Delhi:

> On 23 June 1857 it was anticipated that the rebels would mount a major attack to seize Delhi Ridge and avenge the decisive British victory at the Battle of Plassey exactly 100 years previously.

When the attack was launched at 5 a.m., the defenders were prepared and for the next twelve hours the battle raged until eventually
the rebels withdrew at sunset behind the city walls of Delhi. Quot-
ing from the Regimental History:

'During the course of the day Captain Fagan – a hero among
heroes – commanding the right [artillery] battery in front of Hin-
doo Rao's house, asked Lieutenant Hare to drive the enemy from
a temple – the Swansi (or idol), but corrupted by the British soldier into the "Sammy House" [at the south-eastern extremity of
Delhi Ridge closest to the city] – which the mutineers had occupied as a post of vantage, and whence a well-directed fire upon our
embrasures was being maintained. This fire could not be returned;
for, although the distance was only about 250 yards, the temple
stood on ground so much below Fagan that he could not sufficiently depress his guns. The men of Hare's company were by this
time lying on the ground utterly exhausted: the task appeared desperate; but at Hare's call for volunteers the whole Company at once
rose and rushed down upon the Sammy House, which was soon in
its possession. Sergeant Stephen Garvin set an example of distinguished valour, for which, in due course, he received the Victoria
Cross. The Sammy House thus taken was never again occupied by
the enemy.'

The citation that accompanied Garvin's award of the VC shed a little
more light on his actions:

For daring and gallant conduct before Delhi on 23 June 1857, in
volunteering to lead a small party of men, under a heavy fire, to the
'Sammy House' for the purpose of dislodging a number of the enemy
in position there, who kept up a destructive fire on the advanced
battery of heavy guns, in which, after a sharp contest, he succeeded.
Also recommended for gallant conduct throughout the operations
before Delhi.

However, on 3 September 1857, Garvin received a gunshot wound in the left side of his groin, most probably in the action that later led to the award of his Distinguished Conduct Medal (DCM). The award of the DCM was very rare during the Indian Mutiny, with the decoration going to no more than a dozen or so men.

Garvin returned to Britain with the 1/60th in early 1860 and his VC was formally announced in the *London Gazette* on 20 January of that year, alongside that of Rifleman Samuel Turner, who had shown great bravery the day before Garvin's VC action, also at Delhi. The same edition of the *London Gazette* also included the names of five other members of the 1/60th who received VCs based on the ballot arrangements listed under Clause 13 of the Royal Warrant dated 29 January 1856.

Garvin received his decoration from Queen Victoria at an investiture held in Home Park, Windsor, on 9 November 1860. He thereby entered the record books as the most decorated non-commissioned soldier from the Indian Mutiny. At the end of 1861, Garvin transferred to the 64th (2nd Staffordshire) Regiment and was discharged as a sergeant-major in April 1865, having completed twenty-two years' 'exemplary' service. During this time, Garvin served for more than fourteen years in India. Five years later, after further service in the Militia, he was appointed a Yeoman of the Guard.

During and after his time in the Army, Garvin married three times: on 7 May 1851 in Kasauli, India, he married Harriet Reardon and the couple went on to have two daughters; on 18 September 1862 in Farnborough, Hampshire, he married Emma Samways and the couple went on to have one son and a daughter; and on 6 June 1871 at St Mary the Great, Cambridge, he married Mary Smith, a bricklayer's daughter.

Garvin died at Chesterton, Cambridgeshire, on 23 November 1874, aged forty-nine. He is buried in the cemetery at St Andrew's Church, Chesterton.

LIEUTENANT (LATER MAJOR-GENERAL)
GEORGE ALEXANDER RENNY

Indian Army: Bengal Horse Artillery

DATE OF BRAVERY: 16 SEPTEMBER 1857

GAZETTED: 12 APRIL 1859

Special feature of the VC: a splendid Indian Mutiny award to an officer from the only native artillery troop to stay loyal during the uprising. A stolen VC, too, that was returned to his family five years later.

George Alexander Renny was born in Riga, Russia (now Latvia), on 12 May 1825. He was the son of Alexander Renny, a Scottish merchant living in Riga. However, when Renny was very young, his father died and his mother returned to Scotland with her family. Renny was educated at Montrose Academy, Scotland, and Addiscombe College, Surrey: the purpose of the college was to train young officers to serve in the East India Company's Army in India. Renny was commissioned into the Bengal Horse Artillery as a second lieutenant in June 1844. He served during the Sutlej Campaign of 1845–46, and was present at the Battle of Sobraon on 10 February 1846.

In October 1846, Renny was promoted to lieutenant and spent the next eleven years in India. Renny married in Naini Tal, India, in October 1849, to Flora McWhirter, the daughter of Dr John McWhirter, who had been president of the Royal College of Physicians of Edinburgh. The couple went on to have three sons and three daughters. By 1857, Renny held the command of the 5th Troop, 1st Brigade (Native), Bengal Horse Artillery. On 10 May 1857, the Great Sepoy Mutiny began at Meerut and it soon spread throughout the subcontinent. Renny at this time was stationed in Jalandhar, and four weeks later, on the night of 7 June, he was first called into action, ordering his native gunners to fire upon the mutinous cavalry and infantry.

There were soon mutinous outbreaks in twenty-six regiments of infantry, seven regiments of cavalry and eight companies of artillery.

Yet, Renny's troop remained faithful, the only battery of native artillery to do so. Next, Renny marched with his men to Delhi, arriving in late June to find that the city had fallen to the rebels.

On 9 July, after an attack by the rebel cavalry on the right of the British camp on Delhi Ridge, it was thought advisable, as a precaution in case they mutinied, to take away the guns and horses of Renny's troop. The native officers and men were desperate to be allowed to prove their loyalty, but to no avail, and they were placed in charge of the mortar battery on the ridge. Their loyalty was again put to the test that evening when a group of rebels approached and urged them to join them, and to return to inside the city's walls. The native Indians were adamant and replied that they obeyed orders only from their own officers. Instead, they returned to their mortar battery, which they worked and manned without relief until the end of the siege.

Brigadier Nicholson's movable column arrived outside Delhi in August, and, on 4 September, a siege train of thirty-two howitzers and heavy mortars also arrived, along with more than 100 bullock carts of ammunition. This meant that an attack on the rebels, inside their formidably walled city, was, at last, possible. With the forward batteries complete, the bombardment of Delhi got under way on 12 September. The rebels responded with a storm of mortar, artillery and musket fire that resulted in more than 300 British casualties. The battering of Delhi's defences continued, and on 14 September, the all-out attack finally started.

Renny, then thirty-two years old, who had been given command of No. 4 Siege Battery, provided covering fire for the initial assault on the city, but casualties were high: on the first day alone the Delhi Field Force lost sixty-six officers and more than 1,000 other ranks were killed or wounded. However, the primary objectives had been achieved, providing the potential for a further offensive.

On the afternoon of 14 September, conveying by hand a couple of twelve-pounder mortars, Renny and some of his troop entered Delhi.

Once inside the city proper, they successfully shelled several houses that were being used to shelter rebel snipers. On 15 September, the British consolidated their earlier gains, and further artillery fire was directed onto the centre of the city by Renny's troop. Overnight and into the morning, the rebels withdrew from the suburb of Kishanganj, leaving behind five heavy guns that were soon used to fire on them, resulting in a breach of the main magazine. By noon, the magazine had been stormed and seized, along with it 171 guns and howitzers, plus a vast stock of ammunition.

However, during the afternoon of 16 September, the enemy, realising the enormity of their arms loss, made a frantic attempt to recapture the magazine, as well as the workshops adjoining it. Advancing under covering fire, they succeeded in seizing the workshops, and seemed set to recapture the magazine too. However, with the outcome of the battle finely balanced, Renny sprang into action. He leapt onto the magazine's burning roof and pelted the enemy with shells handed to him, their fuses already burning. As the enemy withdrew, Renny and his troop turned the mortars captured in the magazine onto Fort Selimghur and the Red Palace and started a major bombardment, which they continued for the next four days. Finally, on 20 September, after five days of fierce fighting, Delhi fell at last.

Lieutenant Renny, who was mentioned in General Wilson's despatch, was promoted to captain in April 1858 and then brevet major in July the same year. With the city back under British control, he and his troop served in the subsequent operations in Muzaffarnagar District and in Rohilkhand, their final engagement of the campaign being the action at Sisseah in January 1859. Renny's men, whose loyalty had been total and owed a great deal to their commander's leadership, were singled out for rich praise. Every native officer received the Order of British India and every Non-Commissioned Officer received the Indian Order of Merit for their services. Furthermore, following Delhi's capture, the native soldiers had their guns and horses restored to them.

Renny's VC was eventually announced on 12 April 1859, when his citation ended:

> The roof [of the magazine] having been again set on fire, Captain Renny [although he was a lieutenant at the time of the battle] with great gallantry mounted to the top of the wall of the magazine, and flung several shells with lighted fuses over into the midst of the enemy, which had an almost immediate effect, as the attack at once became feeble at that point, and soon after ceased there.

Renny was presented with his decoration by Queen Victoria at an investiture at Home Park, Windsor, on 9 November 1860.

Second Lieutenant (later Colonel) Edward Thackeray, of the Bengal Engineers, who had braved heavy enemy musketry fire to put out the fire on the thatched roof of the magazine at the time of Renny's VC action, was also awarded the VC. However, his decoration was not announced until 29 April 1862, nearly five years after his action.

In June 1867, Renny was promoted to brevet lieutenant-colonel and the following year he served during the Hazara Campaign on the North-West Frontier, as part of the expedition against the Bazoti Black Mountain tribes. This three-week campaign was the last of the sixteen punitive expeditions carried out in the region over a twenty-year period that qualified for the India General Service Medal's North-West Frontier clasp. On 30 July 1868, a tribal force of some 500 tribesmen had attacked the police station in the Agror Valley, and for the next fortnight the rebels carried out raids in the area. A punitive force was assembled, and Renny travelled the 65 miles from Rawalpindi to the base camp near the village of Koongullee. In the early hours of 3 October 1868, the force set out from its camp, with Renny in command of D Battery, F Brigade, Royal Horse Artillery. The force had its four nine-pounder guns and two 24-pounder howitzers mounted on elephants. The following morning, Renny's battery went into action against the enemy, which was located on a knoll about 1,000 yards in front of the British position. The enemy was driven off and, later in the campaign, Renny and his men attacked a redoubt called 'Muchaie Peak' which, at 10,200 feet, became one of the highest points at which a British force had ever operated. The assault was successful, with few casualties, and for this role Renny was Mentioned in Despatches.

Renny eventually retired from the military in December 1878, with the honorary rank of major-general. He died at his home in Bath, Somerset (now Avon), on 5 January 1887, aged sixty-one. Renny was buried in the city's Locksbrook Cemetery. There is a memorial in his honour in Freshford Church, Somerset, and his name is listed in the Royal Artillery Chapel, Woolwich, south-east London.

In 1978, Renny's medal group, including his VC, was stolen during a burglary from the Renny family home in Waldringfield, Suffolk. However, in March 1983, a person using a metal detector on Sheen Common, London, located an unusual object, and this turned out to be the stolen Renny medal group. The discovery was subsequently publicised on 22 March 1983 and a day later the grand-daughter-in-law of Renny became aware of the find and claimed the VC back into the safety of the family. For several years, the medal group was on display – and on loan – at the Royal Artillery Museum in Woolwich. However, I purchased the medal group at a Spink auction in 2010.

LIEUTENANT (LATER ADMIRAL SIR) NOWELL SALMON

Royal Navy (Naval Brigade)
DATE OF BRAVERY: 16 NOVEMBER 1857
GAZETTED: 24 DECEMBER 1858
Special feature of the VC: a splendid and very rare fighting sailor's Indian Mutiny VC.

Nowell Salmon was born in The Vicarage at Swarraton, Hampshire, on 20 February 1835. He was the son of the Revd Henry Salmon, the rector of Swarraton, and his wife Emily (*née* Nowell), the daughter of a vice-admiral. Salmon, who was also the maternal grandson of Admiral Nowell, was educated at Marlborough College, Wiltshire, and entered the Royal Navy in May 1847 as a cadet, aged only twelve. Just days later, he was appointed to serve in HMS *Dragon*. In May 1849, Salmon was promoted to midshipman and from June 1850 to February 1854 served in HMS *Thetis* on the South America station. In March 1854, he transferred as mate to HMS *James Watt*, serving in the Baltic Campaign. In January 1856, Nowell was promoted to lieutenant, serving from March of that year on HMS *Ant*. In September 1856, he was appointed to HMS *Shannon*, which was then under orders to sail to Singapore. However, after the outbreak of the Indian Mutiny, *Shannon*, commanded by Captain William Peel, was ordered to Calcutta.

Within days of the ship's arrival, Peel had formed the celebrated *Shannon* Naval Brigade of 408 seamen and marines from his crew. The brigade, together with six 68-pounders, two eight-inch howitzers and eight 24-pounders, began its march to Allahabad on 13 August 1857. On 23 October, Peel sent a party of 120 seamen, consisting of Lieutenant Salmon's company and some gunners, to proceed with four of the 24-pounders to Cawnpore.

However, by mid-November, Salmon's party had rejoined the brigade, which was advancing towards Lucknow. Reaching the Alumbagh on 15 November, the brigade came under the command of Sir Colin Campbell's Second Relief Force, who ordered it to start bombarding the enemy's defences. Salmon was awarded the VC for the courage that he displayed on 16 November 1857, when aged twenty-two. On this day, the men of the *Shannon*, during an attack on the Residency, attempted to gain a position nearby in the Shah Nujjiff Mosque. Their intention was to use the building as a temporary fort and refuge for their weary comrades. However, the wall to the mosque was 20 feet high and, with no scaling ladder available, they had to breach it. The 24-pounder guns could not blast their way through the wall and an enemy sniper shot those who came too near it. A few of the sailors climbed a neighbouring tree, but they were also targeted by the sniper, who killed and wounded several men.

Salmon, however, succeeded in climbing the tree and shooting the sniper. Leading Seaman Harrison then joined him, passing up loaded rifles as Salmon shot yet more rebels until he was himself shot and severely wounded in the thigh by a musket ball. Harrison then took over and continued to pick off more of the enemy. Finally, a breach in the wall was made, through which some of the men managed to drag a gun. From that vantage point, they used the gun to cover the retreat of their comrades. This gun now occupied such a commanding position that the mutineers directed a heavy fire on it and the men who were manning it.

Eventually, the order was given to abandon the gun. However, Seaman William Hall, who had been manning one of the other guns, saw that this would be a disastrous move and so left his position to assist Lieutenant Thomas Young in manning it. Despite facing a heavy fire of musket balls, the two men succeeded in retaining possession of the gun until nightfall, when the mutineers withdrew with heavy losses. Eventually Shah Nujjiff was taken and the next morning the assault on Lucknow was completed.

Salmon was mentioned in Sir William Peel's final despatch of 31 March 1858: 'Lieutenant Nowell Salmon – An excellent officer, distinguished himself in the Shannon's Brigade at the relief of Lucknow, was severely wounded, and named for the Victoria Cross. Recommended for promotion.' VCs for both Salmon and Harrison were announced on Christmas Eve 1858, although it was not until an investiture at Buckingham Palace on 8 June 1859 that the two men received their decorations from Queen Victoria. Hall, who had done so much to save the gun, was also awarded the VC, thereby becoming the first black man to receive the award. In total, twenty-three VCs were earned for bravery on that single day – 16 November 1857.

In 1859, Salmon, having been promoted to commander the previous year, was given command of HMS *Icarus*, serving in the West Indies and the Mediterranean. Salmon captured William Walker, the notorious American 'Filibuster', in 1860 in the port of Trujillo, Honduras. Walker was an American lawyer and adventurer who had organised several private military expeditions into Latin America, with the intention of establishing English-speaking colonies under his personal control. This was known as 'filibustering' (the word was derived from the Spanish *filibustero*, meaning pirate or buccaneer).

The British government, which controlled some neighbouring regions, had considerable strategic and economic interest in the construction of an interoceanic canal through Central America, and regarded Walker as a persistent and unwelcome menace in the region. Salmon handed Walker over to the Honduran authorities (rather than hand him back to the United States), which executed him by firing squad on 12 September 1860, aged thirty-six. For his part in defeating Walker, Salmon received the thanks of the Central American States (Honduras and Nicaragua), which presented him with a unique gold medal. Congratulations were also received from Government House, Honduras (now Belize).

In December 1863, Salmon was promoted to captain and he later commanded HMS *Defence* in the West Indies and the Mediterranean, *Valiant* as the guard-ship in the River Shannon, and *Swiftsure* in the Mediterranean. In January 1866, he married Emily Saunders, with whom he had a son, Geoffrey (later Colonel G. N. Salmon, CMG, DSO, the Rifle Brigade), and a daughter, Eleanor.

In 1874, he was appointed Aide-de-Camp to Queen Victoria, in which role he was created a Companion of the Order of the Bath (CB). He was promoted to rear-admiral in August 1879, and from 1882 to 1885 he served as Commander-in-Chief, Cape of Good Hope. Salmon was promoted to vice-admiral in July 1885 and was created a Knight Commander of the Order of the Bath (KCB) in celebration of Her Majesty's Golden Jubilee in 1887. In the same year, he took up the appointment of Commander-in-Chief, China Station, serving for the next four years until he was promoted to admiral in September 1891.

Salmon was appointed Commander-in-Chief at Portsmouth in June 1894. Having been created a Knight Grand Cross of the Order of the Bath (GCB) in celebration of The Queen's Diamond Jubilee in 1897, his three-year term was extended for two months so that he could command the Fleet at the Diamond Jubilee Fleet Review at Spithead, Hampshire, on 26 June 1897.

In August 1897, Salmon was appointed First and Principal Naval Aide-de-Camp to The Queen. He was promoted to his ultimate rank of admiral of the fleet in January 1899, finally retiring from the active list in February 1905 after almost fifty-eight years' Navy service: an astonishing career length for anyone. Salmon died in his home at Southsea, Hampshire, on 14 February 1912, aged seventy-six. He was buried in the cemetery at St Peter's Church, Curdridge, Hampshire. There is a memorial in Salmon's honour in St Ann's Church, Portsmouth Dockyard, and a memorial window in his honour at St Peter's Church.

LIEUTENANT (LATER MAJOR-GENERAL) HENRY EDWARD JEROME

Army: 86th Regiment of Foot
DATES OF BRAVERY: 17 MARCH, 3 APRIL AND 28 MAY 1858
GAZETTED: 11 NOVEMBER 1859
Special feature of the VC: the unique triple-dated Indian Mutiny award and the only VC ever gifted to the Ashcroft VC Collection.

Henry Edward Jerome was born in Antigua, West Indies, on 2 February 1830. His father was Captain Joseph Jerome, who served with the 86th Regiment of Foot, and his mother was Jane (*née* Walker).

His uncle, Major John Jerome, also served with the 86th Regiment (later the Royal Irish Rifles).

Little is known about Henry Jerome's early life, but he attended the Royal Military College, Sandhurst, and, on 21 January 1848, commenced his military service as an ensign without purchase in his father's and uncle's regiment. On 30 April 1852, he was promoted to lieutenant. Jerome served in India at the time of the Indian Mutiny and was Mentioned in Despatches three times. For some ten weeks between mid-March and the end of May 1858, Jerome was in the thick of the fighting and served with great distinction.

Jhansi is the historic city on the banks of the Pahuj River and now part of the Indian state of Uttar Pradesh. It had been the capital of the princely state of Jhansi until it was annexed by the British Governor-General in 1854. Jhansi was ruled by Rani Lakshmibai from June 1857 but at dawn on 3 April 1858, Sir Hugh Rose stormed the walled city with a strong force. At first, the attack on the right was frustrated by the failure to get sufficient scaling ladders in place, but then some men made their way through a breach in the walls and cleared the ramparts. The 86th Regiment, including Jerome, was responsible for the left attack that was more successful after soldiers scaled the wall and captured the palace. By 4 April, most of the city was in British hands, although the Rani of Jhansi (Rani Lakshmibai) had managed to escape.

During the fighting on 3 April, Lieutenant Sewell had been badly wounded and was exposed to enemy fire. Jerome, aided by Private Byrne, raced to his assistance and carried him to safety despite being under a heavy fire.

At this point in his service, Jerome, aged twenty-eight, had already shown great bravery during the capture of the fort of Chanderi on 17 March 1858. He then went on to display exceptional gallantry when confronting a larger enemy force on the Jumna (also spelled Jamuna) River on 28 May 1858. During this battle, Jerome was seriously wounded.

Despite this, he survived his injuries and was promoted to captain on 23 July 1858. His VC was announced on 11 November 1859, when his three separate acts of bravery were all mentioned in his citation. Jerome received his VC from Queen Victoria at an investiture at Windsor Castle on 4 January 1860. He remained in the Army after the end of the Indian conflict and, on 18 April 1863, married Inez Cowper, the daughter of The Queen's Consul to Havana (Cuba), at St Thomas's Church, Portman Square, London. The couple went on to have a son, Lucien.

On 1 July 1859, Henry Jerome was transferred as a brevet major to the 19th Regiment and, after further promotion to major, took part in the Hazara Expedition of 1868. From 1876 to 1884, Jerome served in Britain until he retired in 1885 with the rank of major-general.

Jerome died at his home in Bath, Somerset (now Avon), on 25 February 1901, aged seventy-one, and he was buried in the city's Lansdown Cemetery. In March 2006, it was reported that Jerome's headstone, made of a rare Indian rose granite, had been badly damaged by vandalism. However, it was later discovered that the damage was probably caused by over-enthusiastic cemetery workers. Whatever the cause, the headstone was replaced.

Jerome's valuable medal group has a special place in my VC collection for one reason: it was gifted by his family in 2011. Alex Jerome, supported by his wife Susie, donated the VC awarded to his great-grandfather, thereby waiving his right to the estimated £100,000–£150,000 that such a decoration might have fetched at auction or in a private sale. It was the first and, so far, only time that I have been gifted a medal for my VC collection.

Alex Jerome later spoke publicly about why he had gifted the VC. He revealed that it was because he was so impressed with the way the collection had been built up and then, in 2010, made available to the public through the Lord Ashcroft Gallery at the Imperial War Museum. Speaking from his home in America, Alex Jerome said:

> I got to hear about the collection of VCs built up by Lord Ashcroft
> and, the more I looked into it, the more impressed I became by what
> he had achieved. I was particularly impressed that Lord Ashcroft
> had gone to such lengths to put the collection on public display.
> I eventually decided that I wanted my great-grandfather's VC to be
> returned to Britain and put on display alongside the finest collec-
> tion of such medals in the world.

Alex Jerome said he was aware that VCs fetch considerable sums
when sold but he added: 'I never contemplated selling our medal.
I felt that would have dishonoured my great-grandfather's memory
and achievements.'

In fact, Alex Jerome, a father of two, gifted his ancestor's VC and
two campaign medals to my VC collection, along with his service
sword, carried in all his VC actions, and an engraved silver-plated
cup given to Henry Jerome by his fellow officers and on which there
are details of his Indian Mutiny service.

Michael Naxton, the curator of my VC collection, carried out
the behind-the-scenes negotiations with the Jeromes for the medal
group to be gifted to my collection and so he personally went to
America to collect the VC. To this day, he remains in touch with
the Jerome family.

The generosity of Alex Jerome and his family was made public
on Armistice Day 2013, when details of my VC collection became
public knowledge on a new website (www.lordashcroftmedals.
com). The *Daily Express* carried a story about the whole episode
headlined 'Indian Mutiny hero's £150,000 VC given to museum
for free'.

Alex Jerome also revealed that his great-grandfather's descendants had given great public service too: his son, Lucien, served as a
senior British diplomat all around the world, while his grandson,
'Toby', served as a Royal Navy captain during the Second World
War and was awarded the Distinguished Service Order (DSO) for his

significant part in 'Operation Pedestal', the famously ill-fated convoy carrying vital supplies to the beleaguered island of Malta in 1942.

At the time, I said of the decision to gift the VC to my collection:

> I am enormously grateful to Mr and Mrs Jerome for their wonderfully generous act. I am also immensely flattered that they have made the gift because they were so impressed by my VC collection and my decision to make it accessible to everyone. Major-General Henry Jerome was an incredibly brave and distinguished soldier, and I am honoured to have his VC in my collection and on public display in the gallery.

It is because of their generous act that I have dedicated this book to the Jeromes in recognition of the faith that the couple had in the integrity and the future of my collection. Sadly, Alex died in 2017.

MR GEORGE BELL CHICKEN

Indian Naval Brigade: Civilian volunteer
DATE OF BRAVERY: 27 SEPTEMBER 1858
GAZETTED: 27 APRIL 1860
Special feature of the VC: the only naval award for gallantry on horseback.
Chicken was also one of only five civilians to be awarded the VC.

George Bell Chicken was born on 2 March 1833 in Howden Pans, Northumberland. He was the son of George Chicken and his wife Elizabeth (*née* Bell). George Chicken Sr was a master mariner, hence his son's interest in the sea from an early age. In 1847, aged just fourteen, he joined the Merchant Marine (or Merchant Navy). In 1852, he was promoted twice, first to mate and then to second mate. As second mate, Chicken served in the *Anna*, which sailed to the United States. In July 1852, he sailed to Valpariso, Chile, as first mate in the *Darlington*, and the following year he travelled to Copenhagen,

Denmark, and some of the Baltic ports. In 1855, and by then being a master mariner like his father before him, he served in *Hastings*, which sailed to Madras, India, and in August of the same year he travelled on to Calcutta. Chicken left the Merchant Marine later in 1855 for the 'Country Merchant Service', operating in Batavia, Singapore, Penang and Malacca. However, after extensive travel, he left this service after losing money on a speculative financial venture.

In 1857, the year that the mutiny broke out, Chicken took up a position in India with the Government River Surveying Service. However, Chicken wanted to take on the mutineers and on 31 July 1858 was appointed to the Indian Naval Brigade and made acting master at Fort William. A few months later, he joined 3 Detachment Indian Naval Brigade as a volunteer, serving under Brigadier Douglas at the Battle of Jagdishpur.

On 27 September 1858, Chicken, aged twenty-five, attached himself to a mixed party of fifty-four troopers of the 3rd Sikh Irregular Cavalry and sixty-eight men of Captain Thomas Rattray's mounted police. They were all under the command of Lieutenant Charles Baker, of the Bengal Police, and, when action loomed, Chicken apparently told his comrades of his determination to be awarded the VC for his bravery that day.

Baker's men attacked a force of 700 mutineers who were encamped at a village called Suhejnee, near Peroo, in Bengal. The mutineers were routed and quickly fled, pursued on horseback by Chicken and others. In his book *The Victoria Cross at Sea*, John Winton writes: 'Chicken quickly forged ahead, driving his horse recklessly across river nullahs and through sugar cane and thick jungle. When he caught up with a party of about twenty armed mutineers he was quite alone.'

The citation for his VC, announced on 27 April 1860, detailed the full extent of his bravery, which resulted in him being wounded:

> For great gallantry on the 27th September, 1858, at Suhejnee, near Peroo, in having charged into the middle of a considerable number

of the rebels, who were preparing to rally and open fire upon the scattered pursuers. They were surrounded on all sides, but, fighting desperately, Mr. Chicken succeeded in killing five before he was cut down himself. He would have been cut to pieces, had not some of the men of the 1st Bengal Police and 3rd Sikh Irregular Cavalry, dashed into the crowd to his rescue, and routed it, after killing several of the Enemy.

On receiving the despatches of Colonel Turner, commanding the Cavalry Column, Sir Colin Campbell (later Lord Clyde) had recommended Chicken and Lieutenant Charles Baker for the VC. Despite concerns over Chicken's eligibility as a volunteer, his award, along with Baker's, was approved. In fact, Chicken was only eligible for the decoration because Queen Victoria had signed a Royal Warrant on 13 December 1858 that made volunteers who had borne arms against the mutineers at Lucknow and elsewhere entitled to the VC.

However, it is highly unlikely that Chicken ever knew that he had been awarded the VC. He had been given command of a schooner, *Emily*, which was lost with all hands during a violent storm in the Bay of Bengal in May 1860. Chicken died, aged twenty-seven. It is believed that the original VC prepared for Chicken was sent to India, intended for presentation. However, it subsequently vanished – lost or stored somewhere in India rather than returned to the War Office as it should have been when Chicken died. The War Office later posted a replacement VC – similarly engraved because Chicken had no rank – to his father's home in Shadwell, east London, on 4 March 1862.

Intriguingly, the VC that I purchased at a Morton & Eden auction in London in 2006 is almost certainly *not* the medal sent to Chicken Sr. It was therefore offered for sale at auction as the 'original but unawarded' VC, and it was acknowledged that a 'duplicate but official cross' had also been presented to Chicken's next of kin.

The Second China War, 1857–60

Tensions grew between Britain and China in the mid-nineteenth century as the Western powers sought to expand their influence but the Emperor of China lacked any desire to have diplomatic relations with them. The First China War (also known as the First Opium War) took place between 1840 and 1842. In 1856, an already tense situation was exacerbated by the execution of a French missionary and the seizure of the Chinese crew members on the Arrow, *a British-registered ship. These two incidents were, in fact, major causes of the Second China War the following year.*

As part of the British offensive in the north of China, they seized the strategically important Taku Forts at the mouth of the Peiho River. Instead of trying to advance to Peking, the British negotiated a treaty with the Chinese commissioners at Tientsin. The treaty, allowing for greater trade with the West, was due to be ratified at Peking in 1859. However, relations deteriorated again and the British, along with the French, launched a fresh attack on the Taku Forts, which was repulsed. A third attack on the Taku Forts was mounted in August 1860. Only eight VCs were awarded for the two distinctly separate campaigns. Tensions continued, however, and eventually led to the Third China War – or Boxer Rebellion – in 1900.

LIEUTENANT (LATER MAJOR-GENERAL) ROBERT MONTRESOR ROGERS

Army: 44th Regiment of Foot

DATE OF BRAVERY: 21 AUGUST 1860

GAZETTED: 13 AUGUST 1861

Special feature of the VC: an award for exceptional bravery during the attack on the North Taku Fort, China.

Robert Montresor Rogers was born in Dublin on 4 September 1834. He was the son of James Rogers QC and was educated in the Irish capital city. In February 1855, he was commissioned into the 44th Regiment of Foot as a second lieutenant, subsequently promoted to lieutenant in August of the same year. Rogers, then aged twenty, served in the Crimean War from 27 August 1855 and was present at the siege and fall of Sebastopol.

Lieutenant Rogers embarked with his regiment for China in 1860, when he was one of the 17,700-strong Anglo-French force accompanying the British and French ambassadors, Lord Elgin and Baron Gros, to Peking. The party set sail in a combined fleet of 206 ships and transports, under the command of Lieutenant-General Sir James Hope Grant. On 3 August 1860, the Anglo-French force arrived at the mouth of the Peiho River, the main waterway to Peking, at a time when tensions were already high.

The Chinese were determined not to let the Anglo-French force advance up the Peiho River and the formidable Taku Forts were guarding its mouth. Indeed, on each side of the river stood both a principal fort and a detached fort. The Anglo-French force assessed that the detached northern fort was the key to the entire fortification: it overlooked both the principal northern fort and the detached southern fort, and would therefore render both untenable in the event of its capture.

Grant devised a plan to attack from behind the targeted northern fort but he knew that it, like the other forts, was surrounded by a thick brick wall and, furthermore, in front of the wall was a succession of three water-filled ditches, each separated by open ground covered with sharpened bamboo stakes. This meant that there were several obstacles to be surmounted before the wall could even be reached, let alone scaled.

After nearly three weeks of preparation, the Anglo-French force began its assault at dawn on 21 August, when the Allied batteries opened fire on the two northern forts and the Chinese guns retaliated. By 6 a.m., several Chinese guns had been disabled and at this point an 8-inch mortar shell scored a direct hit on the detached fort's magazine, causing black smoke to spiral into the air. Shortly afterwards, a shell from a British gunboat blew up the magazine in the principal northern fort.

At around 7 a.m., with the guns in the detached northern fort largely silenced, Sir Hope Grant ordered the assault. This was led by two companies of the 44th Foot, one commanded by Captain Gregory, the other, E Company, by Lieutenant Rogers, and two companies of the 67th Foot. The enemy's fire was heavy and there was no cover as the soldiers advanced with bullets, spears and arrows descending from all directions. There were chaotic scenes as the ditches in front of the fort were strewn with casualties.

With the situation finely balanced, Rogers, then aged twenty-five, pushed through a water-filled ditch, pulling out some of the defending stakes as he advanced. Soon he reached the parapet wall and his brave deeds inspired the storming parties of the 67th, whose blood was also up. Some swam across the ditches, while others waded across, but eventually several men reached the wall despite being under a constant withering fire from the 500-strong Chinese force that was defending the fort.

When the storming party's ladders were placed against the fort's defending wall, they were either pulled into the fort by the enemy or pushed away. It was at this point that Rogers attempted to force his way through one 'embrasure' (an opening in a wall or parapet) but he was driven back. When he raced towards another embrasure, it was too high for him to climb. However, Lieutenant Edmund Lenon, of the 67th Foot, then came to his aid, forcing the point of his sword into the wall so that it acted as a step. By positioning one foot on the sword, Rogers was able to get through the embrasure, closely followed by a private of the 44th Foot. Lenon later said: 'Lieutenant Rogers acted with conspicuous gallantry. He was the first Englishman in the place, and was afterwards, despite being severely wounded in the side by a matchlock ball, of the greatest service in assisting others through the embrasure.'

At about the same time, the French soldiers succeeded in entering through another embrasure and soon British and French troops were pouring into the fort. By 8.30 a.m., the crucially positioned, detached northern fort was in Allied hands. However, the British had lost seventeen men, with a further nineteen officers and 165 men wounded. The brunt of the casualties had been borne by the 44th Foot.

The fort's guns were then turned on the other three forts, while fresh infantry were brought up for a second assault – but they were never needed. After a short bombardment from the seized fort, white flags appeared in the remaining three. The battle had been won and the route to Peking was open.

Rogers was awarded the VC for his courage in being the first attacking soldier into the fort. Two other men who fought at his side were also awarded the VC: Lieutenant Lenon and Private John McDougall of the 44th Foot. The awards for the three men were formally announced on 13 August 1861, when they received a joint citation:

> For distinguished gallantry in swimming the Ditches, and entering the North Taku Fort by an embrasure during the assault. They were the first of the English established on the walls of the Fort, which they entered in the order in which their names are here recorded [Rogers being listed first], each one being assisted by the others to mount the embrasure.

In the meantime, Rogers had been promoted to captain in November 1860, which was his rank when he was presented with his VC by General Sir Hugh Rose, Commander-in-Chief, India, in Calcutta on 22 November 1862. Rogers was appointed as captain in the 90th Regiment in February 1861, in place of Captain (later Field Marshal Sir) Garnet Wolseley. Furthermore, Rogers was promoted to major in April 1873. In January 1878, the 90th Light Infantry stood first on the regimental roster for foreign service and, as a result, they were ordered to South Africa to assist in suppressing a local insurrection.

He subsequently led the Perthshire Volunteers throughout the Zulu War of 1879, and was present at the engagement at Zunyin Nek, Kambula, where the regiment suffered four killed and sixteen wounded, and Ulundi. Rogers, who was twice Mentioned in Despatches during the conflict, was popular with his men. This meant that when he was awarded the brevet of lieutenant-colonel in November 1879, his officers and men were so angry and disappointed at the lack of recognition that they collectively wrote to the *Daily News*. The letter, published on 3 February 1880, stated:

> The brevet lieutenant-colonelcy bestowed upon him after the Zulu business was finished amounted to no reward at all, as it merely anticipated his promotion to the same grade regimentally. It is therefore perfectly true to say that the officer who commanded throughout the Zulu War the very regiment which gained the greatest distinction in that campaign has received no recognition of his valuable services, while other regimental commanding officers with less conspicuous records have C.B. attached to their names.

The letter appears to have achieved its aim and Lord Chelmsford and Sir Evelyn Wood (as he had become) strongly recommended Rogers to Horse Guards. Within ten days, Rogers was given the brevet of colonel. Rogers received his South Africa Medal in April 1881, along with the rest of the regiment, at a grand medal ceremony and Trooping the Colour at Fort William in India. This was, in fact, the last time the colours of the Perthshire Light Infantry were trooped, because, on 1 July 1881, the Perthshire Regiment was reorganised, as part of the Childers Reforms, and redesignated the 2nd Battalion, Scottish Rifles, consequently not requiring, as a rifle corps, any colours.

Colonel Rogers brought the old colours with him on his return from India, and in March 1885 presented them to hang in St Mary's Church, Hamilton, Perthshire, by the memorial window, dedicated to the men of the regiment who had fallen in South Africa.

In July 1885, Rogers retired from the Army and within a year he was appointed a Companion of the Order of the Bath (CB): it was the award the officers under his command had wanted for him in the aftermath of the Zulu War. Furthermore, in December 1889, Rogers was granted the honorary rank of major-general 'in recognition of his services in the Army'.

Rogers died at home in Maidenhead, Berkshire, on 5 February 1895, aged sixty, and he was buried in the town's All Saint's Churchyard. He is also the subject of a painting by artist Louis William Desanges, which is held by the National Army Museum in London.

Malay Peninsula, 1875–76

The Malay Peninsula in the mid-nineteenth century was divided into a number of small states. Despite the rivalries and jealousies between them, they were jointly anxious over Siam to the north and the British presence in Singapore to the south. In theory, Britain was reluctant to get involved in the internal affairs of the various states but, in practice, it could not resist intervening.

The death of the Sultan of Perak in 1871 led to a lengthy dispute over the succession to the throne. In 1874, one of the claimants backed the appointment of a British Resident in Perak in return for British support for his claims to the throne. However, when James Birch took up the post of British Resident in 1874, he upset the locals by trying to assume too much power. Rival claimants to the Sultanate therefore colluded in his murder on 1 November 1875, which, in turn, led to full-scale military and political intervention from Britain. Brigadier-General Ross, commanding an Indian force, reached Penang on 27 November 1875, while Major-General Colbourne, with troops from Singapore and Hong Kong, advanced to Kuta, which fell on 17 December 1875. Pockets of resistance continued but these were put down by half a battery of artillery and some 250 Gurkhas.

CAPTAIN (LATER GENERAL) GEORGE NICHOLAS CHANNER

Indian Army: 1st Gurkha Regiment

DATE OF BRAVERY: 20 DECEMBER 1875

GAZETTED: 14 APRIL 1876

Special feature of the VC: the only VC ever awarded for an action in Malaya and the unique VC for the campaign in Perak.

George Nicholas Channer was born at Allahabad, India, on 7 January 1843. He was the eldest surviving son of eight children of Colonel George Girdwood Channer, of the Bengal Artillery, and his wife Susan (*née* Kendall). In fact, young Channer's mother was the eldest daughter of Nicholas Kendall, a Justice of the Peace and the vicar of Talland and Lanlivery, Cornwall. Channer was educated at Truro Grammar School, Cornwall, and Cheltenham College, Gloucestershire. After leaving school in 1859 and aged only seventeen, he passed in September of that year directly into the Indian Army as an ensign. However, Channer served with the 89th and 95th Regiments until August 1866, when he entered the Bengal Staff Corps. By this point, he was a lieutenant, having been promoted in August 1861.

Channer was first employed on active service in the North-West Frontier campaign from 1863 to 1864. He served in the Umbeyla (also spelled Ambela) expedition, and was present at the actions of 16 and 17 December 1863 against the Sitana fanatics. Afterwards, in 1864, he was with General Wilde's column in Jadur country and from 1871 to 1872 he also participated in the Lushai operations. Channer married Annie Watson, the daughter of a wine merchant, at Christ Church, Greenwich, Kent, in June 1872, and the couple went on to have ten children: six sons and four daughters.

Channer was awarded his VC for outstanding bravery while serving as a captain with the 1st Gurkhas in the Malay Peninsula in 1875–76. *The 1st King George's Own Gurkha Rifles, the Malaun Regiment 1815–1921,* edited by Petre F. Loraine, takes up the story of how the 1st Gurkhas, with a force of more than 250 men, moved into action at Sungei Ujong in late December 1875:

The insurrection had spread to Sunghie Ujong [*sic*] in the neighbourhood of Malacca, where Colonel Clay with this force sailed from Penang in the S.S. Malda on the 6th December, reaching Malacca two days later. There one hundred men under Captain Rankin were left to protect the place whilst the rest, with some of the Buffs and half a battery of artillery, proceeded to the mouth of the Lookut River, where they disembarked on the 9th December and moved forward to Rassa. The enemy were in the Terrachee Valley and on a very strong position at the Bukit Putoos (pass). It was arranged to divide the little force into two columns: the first, under Lieut.-Colonel Sale-Hill with about one hundred of the 1st Gurkhas and some naval and artillery details, was to march by a circuitous route for the villages of Pantay and Terrachee; the other column, in which were the rest of the 1st Gurkhas, a detachment of the 10th Foot, etc., was to give Colonel Sale-Hill a day's start to get on his way to the rear of the pass, which would then be attacked in front by Colonel Clay's column.

Colonel Clay, on arriving at the foot of the pass about 10 a.m. on the 20th December, had sent forward Captain Channer with a detachment of the 1st Gurkhas to reconnoitre it. So thick was the jungle that, at first, Captain Channer said it was impossible to discover the exact location of the stockade. Being directed to push up as close as possible, and try to find a suitable place for the use of guns and rockets, he and Lieutenant North, R.E., went on along the bed of a torrent till brought up by trees felled across it. Leaving a rearguard to cut through these obstructions, Captain Channer sent out his men on either side, himself going with the left party. Moving cautiously forward through the jungle, he and the twenty-five men with him presently saw smoke from the enemy's fires, and one of the stockades, which was of logs surrounded by a palisade with numerous obstructions of pointed bamboo. The Malays, lulled into a false security, were cooking and talking, and were quite unaware of Channer's proximity. Having satisfied himself as to the easiest point of entry, he and two of the Gurkhas leapt the palisade and without hesitation went for the twenty or thirty Malays forming the garrison of the fort. Each of the gallant trio shot a Malay. Two more were killed, and then the rest of the twenty-five Gurkhas came in to the sound of the shots. The Malays, believing they were surrounded and lost, made for the two other stockades, one about eighty yards distant, and the other, which completely blocked the pass, about twice that distance.

Then Channer and his men opened fire from cover on the nearer stockade. Half an hour's firing sufficed to drive the garrison from this stockade into the farther one across the pass, which also, under the steady fire, they evacuated. In the first fort a four pounder iron gun was found.

The loss on the British side was two killed (Naick Bhagat Sing Rai and Sepoy Daljit Thapa) and two wounded. The Malay loss was certainly severe, though, as the dead and wounded had been removed, its amount was not known.

For his gallant action Captain Channer received the Victoria Cross and a brevet-majority, whilst the sepoys Balbir Gharti and Jitman Thapa, who were with him in the first assault, received the Order of Merit.

The bravery of Channer, who was thirty-two at the time of his VC action, and his colleagues virtually brought the brief campaign to a close, although men remained in the area until well into the New Year. Channer's VC was announced on 14 April 1876, by which point he had been promoted to brevet major. His citation read:

For having, with the greatest gallantry, been the first to jump into the Enemy's Stockade, to which he had been dispatched with a small party of the 1st Ghoorkha Light Infantry, on the afternoon of the 20th December, 1875, by the Officer commanding the Malacca Column, to procure intelligence as to its strength, position &c.

Major Channer got completely in rear of the Enemy's position, and finding himself so close that he could hear the voices of the men inside, who were cooking at the time, and keeping no look out, he beckoned to his men, and the whole party stole quietly forward to within a few paces of the Stockade. On jumping in, he shot the first man dead with his revolver, and his party then came up, and entered the Stockade, which was of a most formidable nature, surrounded by a bamboo palisade; about seven yards within was a log-house, loop-holed, with two narrow entrances, and trees laid latitudinally, to the thickness of two feet.

The Officer commanding reports that if Major Channer, by his foresight, coolness, and intrepidity, had not taken this Stockade, a great loss of life must have occurred, as from the fact of his being unable to bring guns to bear on it, from the steepness of the hill, and the density of the jungle, it must have been taken at the point of the bayonet.

Channer was also Mentioned in Despatches for further bravery during the campaign. He next served with the expedition against the Jowaki Afridis in 1877–78 and then with the 29th Punjab Infantry in the Second Afghan War of 1878–80, when he was again Mentioned in Despatches. Over the next few years, he received a steady succession of postings and promotions, including being made colonel in November 1883 at the age of just forty.

In 1888, Channer commanded the 1st brigade of the Hazara Field Force, under General Sir John McQueen, in an expedition to the

Black Mountain (also known as the Hazara Expedition), undertaken to punish the tribes for an attack on British troops. During this period, he excelled, displaying great energy and determination, and in the following year he was rewarded with a Companionship of the Order of the Bath (CB). Further senior postings and promotions followed until he received his final rank, that of general, in January 1899. In November 1901, he was placed on the unemployed supernumerary list.

Channer died in Westward Ho!, Devon, on 13 December 1905, aged sixty-two, and was buried at East-the-Water Cemetery in nearby Bideford. There is a plaque in his honour at Norham Parish Church in Devon and his name is both on the roll of honour and given to a classroom at Cheltenham College.

The Second Afghan War, 1878–80

During the 1860s and 1870s, Russia expanded in Central Asia and Britain and other countries became concerned by this increase of power. The 'Eastern Crisis' of 1877–78 was the result of Britain's fears that Russia also wanted to expand its influence in the Balkans and the Turkish Empire. When the Russians then sent a mission to Kabul, Britain responded by insisting that Sher Ali, the Amir of Afghanistan, should also receive a British mission. The Amir took offence at the British tone and declined to accept a mission, even though he too was concerned by Russian expansion.

This led to the Second Afghan War, and British troops crossed into Afghanistan on 21 November 1878. The British soon launched attacks on three fronts and over the next two years there were several memorable battles between the two sides. Sixteen VCs were awarded for the Second Afghan War and five of these are in my collection, including one purchased over the past decade.

GUNNER JAMES COLLIS

Army: Royal Horse Artillery

DATE OF BRAVERY: 28 JULY 1880

GAZETTED: 17 MAY 1881

Special feature of the VC: a fine award for gallantry during the Second Afghan War to a soldier who was at the centre of controversy over his forfeited VC.

James Collis was born in Cambridge, Cambridgeshire, on 19 April 1856. He was the son of William Collis, a coal porter, and his wife Mary (*née* Peacock). James Collis had three brothers: one was a conductor in the Indian Ordinance Corps; another was a quartermaster sergeant with the Lancashire Regiment; and the final one served with the Suffolk Regiment.

It is not known where Collis was educated, but, for a time after leaving school, he worked as a groom in Newmarket, the heart of horse-racing country. In 1872, and when still aged only sixteen, he enlisted into the 46th Regiment. In November 1877, he transferred to the Royal Horse Artillery and served with his regiment in the Second Afghan War.

The extraordinary tale of this VC begins on 28 July 1880, when Collis and his comrades were making their way back to Kandahar after the disastrous British defeat at Maiwand, Afghanistan, then, as now, a desperately difficult country in which to fight a war against local forces. During the battle, an estimated half of the 2,000-strong British force was lost against a vastly larger army that was estimated to have outnumbered Brigadier G. S. R. Burrows's force by four to one and also had superior firepower. Collis, who was then twenty-four, was part of the British force that was attacked by the Afghans as it retreated. The officer commanding the battery was attempting to bring in a limber (a two-wheeled cart designed to support the trail of an artillery piece) carrying wounded men who were under a crossfire. Seeing the dangers and difficulties faced by his comrades, Collis raced forwards and, in doing so, drew the enemy's fire, thereby taking the snipers' attention away from the limber at great danger to himself.

Collis survived his daring act of bravery and his VC was announced on 17 May 1881 (although his surname was misspelled as 'Colliss' in his official citation). After being discharged from the Army, Collis joined the Bombay Police in India in 1881, rising to the rank of inspector. Soon afterwards, on 14 March 1882, Collis married Adela Skuse, a widow, at the Mission Church, Girgaum, Bombay, and the couple went on to have three sons and a daughter.

In 1884, Collis returned to the UK and in September 1887 he re-enlisted into the Army, this time joining the Suffolk Regiment, before transferring to the Royal Artillery a year later. Collis returned to India in 1888 as part of his service, but in 1891 was invalided home suffering from rheumatic fever, returning without his wife. At some point, he met Mary Goddard, who was apparently unaware that he had a wife in India. The couple were married at St Paul's Chapel of Ease, Battersea, south London, on 26 February 1893.

In 1895, his deception was discovered and Collis was convicted of bigamy and sentenced to eighteen months' hard labour. Later that year, his VC was declared forfeit for his crime under the original statutes of the Royal Warrant of 1856. By this point, however, Collis had already pawned his VC for a mere eight shillings (40p), having apparently hit hard times. The decoration was retrieved by police for the same sum from a pawnbroker's shop for the Crown on the instructions of the Home Office.

After leaving prison and settling in Bury St Edmunds, Suffolk, Collis pursued a number of jobs but in 1914, after the outbreak of the First World War, he re-enlisted into the Suffolk Regiment, aged fifty-eight, as a drill instructor. However, he was dogged by poor health and was invalided out of the Army on medical grounds in August 1917, moving into lodgings in Battersea, south London. Collis was admitted to Battersea General Hospital with heart problems, and he died there on 28 June 1918, aged sixty-two.

Two years later, Collis's sister Hannah Haylock petitioned the War Office on behalf of the family for the forfeiture to be cancelled. George V was sympathetic to the family's wishes but Winston Churchill, then Secretary of State for War, opposed the reinstatement. Churchill believed that because Collis had pawned his medals he placed little value on them. Furthermore, Churchill noted that the family had not kept in contact with Collis and it was only twenty-five years after the forfeiture that they had decided to raise their grievance with the authorities.

However, The King would not let this matter rest. Lord Stamfordham, George V's private secretary, stated on 26 July 1920:

> The King feels so strongly that, no matter the crime committed by anyone on whom the VC has been conferred, the decoration should not be forfeited. Even were a VC [recipient] to be sentenced to be hanged for murder, he should be allowed to wear the VC on the scaffold.

The King also insisted that Collis's name should be inscribed, along with all the corps' other VC recipients, on the Royal Artillery Memorial in Woolwich, south-east London.

In a paper entitled 'Forfeited Victoria Cross Myths', Anthony Staunton writes:

> No Victoria Cross (VC) has been cancelled following the views expressed by King George V, to his Private Secretary, Lord Stamfordham, in 1920. Prior to this, eight VC recipients, one a Royal Naval officer and seven British Army soldiers, had their awards cancelled between 1861 and 1908 in accordance with clause fifteen of the original VC warrant signed by Queen Victoria on 29 January 1856 and published on 5 February 1856 in the *London Gazette*.

The original VC warrant of 1856 contained provision for both the cancellation and restoration of awards. The warrant that was redrafted in 1920 included the same cancellation and restoration provisions (except for minor grammatical corrections) but also added the requirement that cancelled and restored VC awards be published in the *London Gazette*.

Staunton continues:

> Despite the cancellation provisions of the VC warrant, the King's views prevailed during the 1920s and no action was taken thereafter to deprive any VC recipient of their medal following misconduct or conviction of an offence. An interdepartmental committee met in the late 1920s to review the matter; their recommendation was that all gallantry awards should now be regarded as irrevocable.

In 1931, the words of the 1856 and 1920 warrants' cancellation clause referring to 'treason, cowardice, felony, or of any infamous crime' were modified to the less emotive 'to cancel and annul'. These provisions continue to this day. Staunton pointed out that, contrary to some inaccurate reports, none of the eight forfeited VCs was ever restored to the original recipient.

In his book *The Evolution of the Victoria Cross*, M. J. Crook writes of the forfeitures:

> So far as the eight men in question are concerned time has practically annulled their expulsion, since virtually all lists of VC recipients (even including one prepared by the WO [War Office] itself in 1953) do include the names of these eight, even though the subsequent forfeiture may also be indicated.

The precise whereabouts of the Collis VC between late 1896 and 1938 are not known, although it would seem that it went initially, as was required at the time, into the possession of the Solicitor General, and a later holder of the office had a personal interest in gallantry medals. When that Solicitor General died unexpectedly and the VC was found in his medal collection, it was decided to sell it as no one involved knew its background.

The Collis VC was sold at auction by Glendining's on 10 June 1938 to Colonel H. J. P. Oakley, who was himself a recipient of the Military Cross (MC). After his death, the VC passed to Oakley's daughter, who resold it by auction in 1980. The buyer at that auction, after keeping it for thirty-four years, decided to sell it, and this enabled me, privately, to purchase this fine award with such an intriguing and unique history.

I am delighted that VCs are no longer forfeited for minor crimes. A man (or woman) who displays great gallantry should not have his (or her) medal taken away just because of some relatively low-level misdemeanour. Soldiers from past eras – and indeed soldiers today – are not always angels, but if they have shown great bravery then that act cannot be denied simply because of a crime committed months or years later. Whatever his personal failings, James Collis was an extremely brave individual and I will always do all I can to champion his gallantry.

As previously stated, Collis died in June 1918. He was buried in Earlsfield Cemetery, Wandsworth, south-west London, and for eighty years he lay in an unmarked grave. However, on 22 May 1998, a ceremony was held at Wandsworth's Council Cemetery in Magdalen Road to mark the erection of a headstone in Collis's honour, resplendent with the carving of a VC. As well as his new headstone, Collis's name is on the war memorial at the cemetery.

The First Anglo-Boer War, 1881

As Britain sought to extend its influence in southern Africa, it annexed the South African Republic, the Boer state in the Transvaal, in 1877. At the time, the Transvaal was bankrupt and leaderless and so the British attempted to portray the annexation as being popular with the Boers.

However, this was not the case, and, after three tense and difficult years, the Boers declared their independence in 1880.

This, in turn, led to the First Anglo-Boer War of 1881 (although, in fact, it began in late 1880). The conflict started badly for the British, largely due to the fact that at the outbreak of hostilities it had just 1,800 soldiers garrisoned around the Transvaal. In contrast, the Boers had access to a force of 7,000, plus volunteers from the Orange Free State. A British force en route to Pretoria was routed, and several garrisons were surrounded and besieged.

Despite still waiting for reinforcements from Britain, Sir George Pomeroy Colley decided to take the initiative in late January 1881. On the 24th, he advanced from Newcastle towards the Transvaal with a force of 1,200 men, but he found his way blocked by an army of several thousand Boers. Colley tried to advance at Laing's Nek on 28 January but the Boers repulsed his force and left it with heavy casualties. Two men were awarded the VC for their bravery at Laing's Nek that day. Six VCs were awarded for the First Anglo-Boer War and one of these is now in my medal collection.

SUB-LIEUTENANT (LATER MAJOR)
ALAN RICHARD HILL (LATER HILL-WALKER)

Army: 58th Regiment of Foot

DATE OF BRAVERY: 28 JANUARY 1881

GAZETTED: 14 MARCH 1882

Special feature of the VC: an outstandingly rare award for the calamitous First Anglo-Boer War of 1881, the only major conflict for which no campaign medal was ever sanctioned.

Alan Hill was born in Northallerton, Yorkshire, on 12 July 1859. He was the son of Captain Thomas Hill, the Chief Constable of North Riding, Yorkshire, and Frances Hill (*née* Walker). Hill was educated at Richmond Grammar School, Yorkshire, and he enlisted into the North Yorkshire Rifles in 1877.

In 1879, Hill transferred to the 58th Regiment and served in the Anglo-Zulu War, where he was present at the Battle of Ulundi, the last major battle of the conflict. In 1881, he served in the First Anglo-Boer War, and it was here that he showed such bravery that he was awarded the VC for rescuing two wounded comrades – and trying to rescue a third – in the heat of battle. His decoration was announced on 14 March 1882, when his citation stated:

> For gallant conduct at the action of Laing's Nek on the 28th January, 1881, in having, after the retreat was ordered, remained behind and endeavoured to carry out of action Lieutenant Baillie, of the same Corps, who was lying on the ground severely wounded. Being unable to lift that officer into the saddle, he carried him in his arms until Lieutenant Baillie was shot dead. Lieutenant Hill then brought a wounded man out of action on his horse, after which he returned and rescued another. All these acts being performed under a heavy fire.

Hill was promoted, aged twenty-one, to lieutenant on the very day after his VC action and he was also Mentioned in Despatches for further bravery. In February 1881, he was present at the Battle of Ingogo River (also known as the Battle of Schuinshoogte) on the 8th and the Battle of Majuba Hill on the 27th, when he was seriously wounded in the fighting that saw the Boers win the day. Once again, however, he was Mentioned in Despatches for his courage in action. Having recovered from his injuries, Hill received his VC from Queen Victoria at an investiture at Windsor Castle on 13 May 1882.

Hill served in Natal and Cape Town, Cape Colony, from 1883 to 1885. In September 1886, he was promoted to captain and from 1887 to 1892 served as adjutant to the 3rd and 4th Battalions of the Northampton Militia. From 1892 to 1895, he served as Station Staff Officer in Bangalore, India. He was promoted to major in 1896 and during the same year served with the 1st Battalion, Northamptons, in India. In 1897, he was appointed Assistant Adjutant-General in Mandalay, Burma, and during that year took part in the Tirah Campaign, including being present in operations in the Bara Valley.

Hill retired from the Army on 12 October 1901, aged forty-two, in order to pursue a life as a country gentleman. In April 1902, he married his first cousin, Muriel Walker, at St Saviour's Church, Chelsea, central London. After his wife's two brothers died without heirs, Hill changed his surname to Hill-Walker so that the Walker family could continue to live at their family home, Maunby Hall, in Thirsk, Yorkshire.

Hill-Walker died at his home in Thirsk on 21 April 1944, aged eighty-four. He was buried in Maunby Churchyard.

Chitral, North-West Frontier, India, 1895

In the late nineteenth century, Chitral was a small state on the North-West Frontier, India. Despite being only a little larger than Wales, it had great strategic importance, and as a result Britain showed great interest in its internal affairs. During the rule of the Mehtar, Aman-ul-Mulk, from 1857 to 1892, Chitral was stable. However, for the next three years there was bloody infighting over which member of his family should rule. After successfully plotting the murder of one of his brothers, Amir-ul-Mulk seized power, supported by his uncle, Sher Afzul. To make matters worse, parts of Chitral were then invaded by Umra Khan, the ruler of the neighbouring state of Jandola.

Britain took the initiative on 31 January 1895, when Surgeon-Major George Robertson, the British Political Agent at Gilgit, occupied Chitral Fort with a force of some 400 men. Further British intervention took place on 2 March 1895, when Robertson deposed Amir-ul-Mulk at Mehtar, replacing him with his younger brother, Shuja ul-Mulk. As Robertson became concerned that Sher Afzul would attack and overrun Chitral Fort, he sent

Captain Colin Campbell out with 200 men to reconnoitre the area. Camp-
bell's men were attacked by Sher Afzul's forces, suffering heavy casualties.
The remains of Campbell's force retreated back to Chitral Fort, some carry-
ing their wounded, where they would be besieged for the next six weeks until
the arrival of the Chitral Relief Force.

SURGEON-CAPTAIN (LATER SURGEON-MAJOR) HARRY FREDERICK WHITCHURCH

Indian Army: Bengal Medical Service

DATE OF BRAVERY: 3 MARCH 1895

GAZETTED: 16 JULY 1895

Special feature of the VC: the unique award for the defence/relief of Chitral
Fort, North-West Frontier.

Henry Frederick Whitchurch was born in Kensington High Street, west London, on 22 September 1866. He was the son of Frederick Whitchurch, a grocer, and his wife Sarah (*née* Chapman). Whitchurch Jr was educated at various private schools in England, France and Germany before studying at St Bartholomew's Hospital in London.

In March 1888, aged twenty-one, he joined the Indian Army as a surgeon-captain at a time of general unrest on the North-West Frontier. From 1889 to 1890, he served during the Chin Lushai Expedition, including the Relief of Aijal and at Changsil, India. In October 1891, Whitchurch was appointed officiating surgeon for the 24th (Punjab) Regiment of the Bengal Infantry. In 1895, he served during the defence and relief of Chitral Fort in India (now Pakistan) and it was during this time that he showed such exceptional gallantry, aged twenty-eight, that he was awarded the VC. The citation for his VC, announced on 16 July 1895, does full justice to his courage when a comrade officer was badly wounded a mile and a half from the fort:

During the sortie from Chitral Fort of the 3rd March last, at the commencement of the siege, Surgeon-Captain Whitchurch went to the assistance of Captain Baird, 24th Bengal Infantry, who was mortally wounded, and brought him back to the fort under a heavy fire from the enemy. Captain Baird was on the right of the fighting line, and had only a small party of Gurkhas and men of the 4th Kashmir Rifles. He was wounded on the heights at a distance of a mile and a half from the fort. When Surgeon-Captain Whitchurch proceeded to his rescue, the enemy, in great strength, had broken through the fighting line; darkness had set in and Captain Baird, Surgeon-Captain Whitchurch, and the sepoys were completely isolated from assistance. Captain Baird was placed in a dooly [similar to a stretcher] by Surgeon-Captain Whitchurch, and the party then attempted to return to the fort. The Gurkhas bravely clung to the dooly until three were killed and a fourth was severely wounded. Surgeon-Captain Whitchurch then put Captain Baird upon his back and carried him some distance with heroic courage and resolution. The little party kept diminishing in numbers, being fired at the whole way. On one or two occasions Surgeon-Captain Whitchurch was obliged to charge walls, from behind which the enemy kept up an incessant fire. At one place particularly the whole party was in imminent danger of being cut up, having been surrounded by the enemy. Surgeon-Captain Whitchurch gallantly rushed the position, and eventually succeeded in getting Captain Baird and the sepoys into the fort.

Nearly all the party were wounded, Captain Baird receiving two additional wounds before reaching the fort.

Just as they reached the fort, Baird had suffered what proved to be a fatal wound when he was shot in the face. He died the next day – 4 March 1895 – but not before he had secured a promise from Surgeon-Major George Robertson, the British Political Agent at Gilgit, that Whitchurch's gallantry would be recognised. The announcement of Whitchurch's VC came well after the siege of the fort was raised. The reference to the Gurkhas is confusing because there was no Gurkha Regiment involved. However, three companies of the 4th Kashmir Rifles were of Gurkha composition and the citation refers to these men. Whitchurch was presented with his VC by Queen Victoria at an investiture at Osborne House, Isle of Wight, on 27 July 1895, just eleven days after his award was officially announced.

From 1897 to 1898, Whitchurch served in the defence of the Malakand, the relief of Chakdara and action at Landakai on the North-West Frontier, in which he was twice Mentioned in Despatches. He was promoted to surgeon-major in March 1900, and the following year served in China, where he was again Mentioned in Despatches, and was present at the relief of the British Legation, Peking, and at actions at Yangstan and Pertsand (for which he was yet again Mentioned in Despatches for a fourth time). In October 1901, he was appointed Surgeon of the 1st Gurkha Rifle Regiment, based in Dharamsala, the Punjab, India.

While still serving as a surgeon-major, Whitchurch, who never married, died from enteric fever at Dharamsala on 16 August 1907, aged forty. He was buried in Dharamsala, where there is a headstone in his memory. There is also a brass plaque in his honour at the Cathedral of the Resurrection, Lahore, Pakistan.

Mamund Valley, North-West Frontier, India, 1897

Tensions continued on the North-West Frontier of India for many decades after the Indian Mutiny. The Mohmands, who lived near the Kabul River to the north-west of Peshawar, attacked the border post of Shabkadr on 6 August 1897. A British Mohmand Field Force was sent to deal with the uprising. However, the Mohmands proved to be worthy opponents and so the Malakand Field Force was ordered to support the original British contingent.

On the night of 16/17 September, the Malakand Field Force's 2nd

Brigade had been carrying out punitive actions when Brigadier-General P. D. Jeffreys and his small force found themselves under heavy attack as they tried to gain control of the village of Bilot in the Mamund Valley. Three VCs were awarded for bravery during the battle.

LIEUTENANT (LATER LIEUTENANT-COLONEL) THOMAS COLCLOUGH WATSON

Army: Royal Engineers, attached Corps of Bengal Sappers and Miners
DATE OF BRAVERY: 16/17 SEPTEMBER 1897
GAZETTED: 20 MAY 1898
Special feature of the VC: an outstanding North-West Frontier VC for a very rare night action, and believed unique award to a recipient born in the Netherlands.

Thomas Colclough Watson was born in Velsen, the Netherlands, on 11 April 1867. The son of Thomas Colclough Watson and his wife Eliza (*née* Reed), he was educated at Lough Grammar School, Lincolnshire. In February 1888, when aged twenty, he was commissioned as a lieutenant into the Royal Engineers. In January 1892, Watson married Edythe Welchman, the younger daughter of the late Major-General John Whateley Welchman, of the Indian Army, and who had been awarded the Royal Red Cross (RRC) for her work during the Black Mountain Expedition of late 1888.

In 1897–98, while attached to the Bengal Sappers and Miners, Watson served during the Mohmand Expedition. The Mohmands, a Pashtun tribe who inhabit the hilly country to the north-west of Peshawar, attacked the border post of Shabkadr on 6 August 1897. The British response was to form the Mohmand Field Force, under General E. R. Elles, to deal with them. However, the rebels were a formidable foe and – as previously stated – the Malakand Field Force, which had been active in Bajaur, was sent to support the Mohmand Field Force.

On the night of 16/17 September, during a mission being carried out by the Malakand Field Force's 2nd Brigade, Brigadier-General P. D. Jeffreys, who commanded the brigade, found himself with a small force, including half a company of the 4th Bengal Sappers and Miners and twelve men of the Buffs (East Kent Regiment), outside the village of Bilot. The village was full of heavily armed tribesmen who opened fire on the British. Lieutenant Watson and Lieutenant James Colvin were tasked with taking the village.

In his book *The Sapper VCs*, Gerald Napier summed up the seriousness of the situation facing Watson and his comrades during the early hours of 17 September:

> Worse still, part of the force had not made it back at all. The brigade commander, the gunners and their guns, a party of 12 of the Buffs and 45 sappers including Watson and Colvin had come together at the village of Bilot and decided to take shelter there. Unfortunately, the Mamunds had beaten them to it and a bitter struggle now ensued. The area round the houses was full of burning '*bhoosa*', a kind of chopped straw, so that attempts to break in were prevented and the beleaguered party were illuminated as targets for the enemy fire at 30 yards range, from loopholes on two sides of their position.

It was at this point that Watson courageously went forward with charges to destroy the main tower of Bilot village, an action carried out successfully despite a heavy enemy fire. Napier continued: 'Watson and Colvin led a party of sappers and the 12 Buffs in repeated attempts to break in and drive the enemy out [of the village] with the bayonet.'

When Watson returned from this attack, he had been hit in the thigh but he insisted on going out again. Relief eventually arrived in the area in the form of two companies of the Guides and 38th Dogras, and, at around dawn, a squadron of the 11th Bengal Lancers. Winston Churchill, then a young war correspondent at the scene with the Bengal Lancers, takes up the story in his book *The Malakand Field Force: An Episode in Frontier War*:

Half an hour before dawn on the 17th the cavalry were mounted, and as soon as the light was strong enough to find a way through the broken ground, the squadron started in search of the missing troops. We had heard no more of their guns since about two o'clock. We therefore concluded they had beaten off the enemy. There might, of course, be another reason for their silence. As we drew near Bilot, it was possible to distinguish the figures of men moving about the walls and houses. The advanced files rode cautiously forward. Suddenly they cantered up to the wall and we knew some at least were alive. Captain Cole, turning to his squadron, lifted his hand. The sowars, actuated by a common impulse, rose in their stirrups and began to cheer. But there was no response. Nor was this strange. The village was a shambles. In an angle of the outside wall, protected on the third side by a shallow trench, were the survivors of the fight. All round lay the corpses of men and mules. The bodies of five or six native soldiers were being buried in a hurriedly dug grave. It was thought that, as they were Mahommedans, their resting-place would be respected by the tribesmen. Eighteen wounded men lay side by side in a roofless hut. Their faces, drawn by pain and anxiety, looked ghastly in the pale light of the early morning. Two officers, one with his left hand smashed [Watson], the other shot through both legs, were patiently waiting for the moment when the improvised tourniquets could be removed and some relief afforded to their sufferings. The brigadier, his khaki coat stained with the blood from a wound on his head, was talking to his only staff-officer, whose helmet displayed a bullet-hole. The most ardent lover of realism would have been satisfied. Food, doolies [similar to stretchers], and doctors soon arrived. The wounded were brought to the field hospitals to be attended to. The unwounded hurried back to camp to get breakfast and a bath. In half an hour the ill-omened spot was occupied only by the few sowars engaged in shooting the wounded mules, and by the vultures who watched the proceedings with an expectant interest.

Additionally, Churchill wrote more in specific praise of Watson's bravery during the night-time battle:

> The general now ordered the battery and sappers to go into the village, but it was so full of burning *bhoosa* that this was found to be impossible, and they set to work to entrench themselves outside. The village was soon full of the enemy. From the walls and houses, which on two sides commanded the space occupied by the battery, they began to fire at about 30 yards' range. The troops were as much exposed as if they had been in a racket court of which the enemy held the walls. They could not move because they would have had to desert either the guns or the wounded. Fortunately not many of the tribesmen at this point were armed with rifles. The others threw stones and burning *bhoosa* into the midst of the little garrison. By its light they took good aim. Everybody got under such cover as was available. There was not much. Gunner Nihala, a gallant native soldier, repeatedly extinguished the burning *bhoosa* with his cloak at the imminent peril of his life. Lieutenants Watson and Colvin, with their sappers and the twelve men of the Buffs, forced their way into the village and tried to expel the enemy with the bayonet. The village was too large for so small a party to clear. The tribesmen moved from one part to another, repeatedly firing. They killed and wounded several of the soldiers, and a bullet smashed Lieutenant Watson's hand. He however continued his efforts and did not cease until again shot, this time so severely as to be unable to stand. His men carried him from the village, and it was felt that it would be useless to try again. The attention of the reader is directed to the bravery of this officer. After a long day of marching, and fighting, in the dark, without food and with small numbers, the man who will go on, unshaken and unflinching, after he has received a severe and painful wound, has in respect of personal courage few equals and no superior in the world. It is perhaps as high a form of valour to endure as to dare. The combination of both is sublime.

In a hastily written letter to his wife four days after the fighting, which included a sketch of the scene of battle, Watson provided a detailed account of the events at Bilot, but with great modesty. He also reassured his wife that his wounds were not serious, when, in fact, the last of his wounds was sufficiently bad to put him out of action for several months:

My own darling, I had got as far as this – or rather I have just written the above final sketch of our movements when I think I would rather write to you an account of our doing(s) on the 16th.

I went out with the Guides under Major Campbell to burn some villages. I had 2 sections of Sappers with me. About 11 a.m. a chit to say the 35th Sikhs & the guns were hard pressed further up the valley & we were to go to their assistance. Off we went & got up about 1.30 p.m. I personally saw very little of what was going on except in my immediate front where the enemy kept most tantalisingly just out of range. Finally we were told to retire & I had part of the retirement to cover. I was holding my bit of ground very nicely when the Genl. [General] sent to say he wanted a certain tower blown up – so I took 4 men & went to do it.

'I found one of the enemy installed about 250 yards off with a Martini [rifle] and very pretty shooting he made – getting the extreme edge of the tower 3 times – he could just see my shoulder round the corner. I had just blown the tower and got back to my place when I got the order to join the Genl. with my sappers I went there & found he wanted me to act as escort to the Guns together with Colvin's sections which in all gave me about 70 men with an average of 20 rounds a piece. Our mules with tools had gone on as I did not consider them necessary for escort work. About this time about 5.30 p.m. we got the order for the Guns and Sappers to go back, that one company of the 35th Sikhs were cut off & we must remain out the night. I rode off to try and get the tools back but failed & when I got back I found that we were to take up a position alongside a ruined village. It is too late to discuss the advisability of the position & we were paid for our stupidity. Before we had finished scratching a trench with our own hands along the dotted line a man fired a shot from A. [relating to his sketch]

Along the double dotted line were 12 men of the Buffs who had been off as escort to a dooley but could not find it. I got these men together and we ran round the corner, clearing some 30 to 40 Pathans from that side. Then I went to the next corner & finding more collected these I came back for the Buffs and we cleared that side with a couple of volleys. Just then I got touched on the right leg, only a graze, but one of the Buffs was badly hit, so I went back to get some Sappers up & to tell Colvin the state of affairs. I hurried back & was pointing out where the devils were sneaking up when I got a slight flesh wound in the inside of the right arm – nothing of consequence but unfortunately almost immediately afterwards I got hit badly on the left hand. I asked the Buffs to hang on till I could get another officer & went & shouted for Colvin but I fear my directions to him were not very clear. The General and Hamilton put on a tourniquet for me & I hung on thro' the night. The dooleys & doctors came out at 7 a.m., but a relief party of 2 company's [sic] of Guides & 2 Comps (35th) Dogras came out [at] 1.30 – but for them I do not think any of us would have got off.

I hear the wounded are to be sent down in a day or two – the usual arrangements is I believe to send them to Murree. But darling, of course I want to be with you, so make any arrangements you like & wire or write me to Malakand & Nowshera – I will try & work whatever you propose.

I can't write anymore today. Much love my own from your loving T.

Watson's VC, one of three awarded for bravery that night, was announced on 20 May 1898, when his citation ended: 'After being wounded and driven back, he made a second attempt to clear the village, and only desisted after a second repulse and being again hit and severely wounded.'

During the Mohmand Expediton, Watson had also twice been Mentioned in Despatches. Lieutenant Colvin, who fought at Watson's side during the night in question, was also awarded the VC for his gallantry. The third VC was awarded to Lance-Corporal James Smith, of the Buffs, whose award was on the basis of a report from Watson. Smith had gone out with a detachment of twelve men, two of whom were killed and four wounded, including Smith. Of the party, four privates received the Distinguished Conduct Medal (DCM).

As a result of his final battle wound – to his hand – Watson was incapacitated for several months. However, he was well enough to receive his VC from Queen Victoria at Windsor Castle, during a period of home leave, on 25 June 1898. On being awarded his VC, Watson and his wife became the only husband-and-wife 'VC – RRC' in the country, with the exception of Lord and Lady Roberts.

On 17 November 1898, Watson was promoted to captain and on 18 August 1906 promoted to major. Before the outbreak of the Great War, Watson undertook a number of senior roles in India. After the war began, he was promoted to lieutenant-colonel and appointed Commanding Engineer of the 12th Indian Division. He served with distinction in Mesopotamia (now Iraq), fighting against the Turkish forces, but, in June 1915, he was invalided back to the UK with a serious illness.

Watson never recovered from this unspecified illness and he died in Cavendish Square, central London, on 15 June 1917, shortly after his fiftieth birthday. He was cremated at Golders Green Crematorium in north London, where his ashes were interred. His name is on the crematorium's war memorial.

4

THE SECOND ANGLO-BOER WAR AND BEYOND

The Second Anglo-Boer War, 1899–1902

The Second Anglo-Boer War – generally known as the Boer War – was fought at the turn of the twentieth century between the British Empire and the two independent Boer republics: the Orange Free State and the South African Republic (the Transvaal). After a long and hard-fought campaign, the two republics were defeated and absorbed into the British Empire. The war cost around 75,000 lives, including 22,000 British soldiers.

After the discovery of gold in the Transvaal, thousands of British and other prospectors and settlers streamed over the border from the Cape Colony as well as further afield. Johannesburg sprang up and there were tensions between the newcomers and locals. There was gamesmanship, too, between Joseph Chamberlain, Britain's Colonial Secretary, and the leaders of the Orange Free State and the Transvaal. War was declared on 11 October 1899, the Boers striking first by invading Cape Colony and Natal Colony before the end of January 1900. In a period known as 'Black Week', 10–15 December 1899, the British forces led by General Redvers Buller suffered devastating losses at Magersfontein, Stormberg and Colenso. The Boers also besieged the towns of Ladysmith, Mafeking and Kimberley, where the townspeople all suffered terrible hardship. There were further defeats for the British in the first five weeks of 1900, but, when reinforcements arrived on 14 February, troops under the command of Field Marshal Lord Roberts launched a series of successful counter-offensives. Kimberley was relieved the very next day, and there were further victories before the relief of

Ladysmith. However, it was the relief of Mafeking in May that prompted the biggest celebrations in Britain. As 250,000 British troops, under the overall command of Lord Kitchener, gained control of both republics, the enemy resorted to guerrilla tactics, while the British built large-scale concentration camps to hold refugees, including women and children, created by their 'scorched earth' policy. The war rumbled on until the Boers finally conceded defeat in 1902.

Seventy-eight VCs were awarded during the Boer War, of which the trust owns eighteen, including three purchased in the last decade.

SERGEANT WILLIAM BERNARD TRAYNOR

Army: The Prince of Wales's Own (West Yorkshire Regiment)
DATE OF BRAVERY: 6 FEBRUARY 1901
GAZETTED: 17 SEPTEMBER 1901
Special feature of the VC: a superb Boer War award for a very rare night action and the only VC awarded to an NCO or private soldier from the West Yorkshire Regiment during the conflict.

William Bernard Traynor was born in Hull, Yorkshire (now Humberside), on 31 December 1870. He was the son of Francis Traynor, a flax dresser originally from Co. Monaghan, and his wife Rebecca (*née* Longfield). After being educated at Pryme Street Roman Catholic School in Hull, Traynor Jr worked as a labourer. On 14 November 1888, Traynor, just a month short of his eighteenth birthday, joined the 2nd Battalion, West Yorks Regiment (The Prince of Wales's Own Regiment) at Beverley, Yorkshire. From January 1891, he served with his regiment in India, including postings to the garrisons at Mooltan, Lahore and Lucknow. On 12 June 1897, he married Jane Martin and the couple went on to have two daughters and four sons, including twin boys.

On 20 October 1899, and having earlier extended his service to twelve years, Traynor went with his regiment to South Africa, where he took part in the Second Anglo-Boer War. He was present at several of the major engagements: Colenso, Spion Kop, Laing's Nek, Tugela Heights and the relief of Ladysmith in Natal, and was promoted to sergeant on 1 June 1900.

He received his VC for bravery at Bothwell Camp, Transvaal. As a result of the Boer attacks on the Delagoa Bay (now Maputo Bay) railway line, Lieutenant-General J. D. P. French was ordered to clear Boer commandos from the area south of the line as far as the Johannesburg to Natal railway. The aim was to encircle General Louis Botha and his troops near Ermelo. On 5 February 1901, French's column camped at Bothwell, at the northern end of Lake Chrissie and around halfway between Ermelo and Carolina. At 3 a.m., the Boers attacked the camp and for an hour they kept up a relentless assault. In his book *After Pretoria: The Guerilla War*, H. W. Wilson paints a vivid picture of the day's events:

> On 5 February, General Smith-Dorrien, on the British left, reached Bothwell Farm, in the neighbourhood of Lake Chrissie, which is famous as being one of the very few sheets of fresh water in South Africa. Here he halted for the night and, with the studious attention to all reasonable precautions, which had won him so good a reputation in this protracted war, entrenched his camp strongly. The night was intensely dark, and the obscurity was increased by a heavy mist which hung over these uplands, rendering it impossible for the sentries and outposts to see anyone at a few yards' distance. It was fortunate that so much care was shown on the British side, as Louis Botha during the day had reinforced Lukas Meyer, who was conducting the Boer retreat in this quarter, and had determined upon a night attack with 2,000 men, to cover the withdrawal northwards of the great bulk of his force, now menaced with the danger of being driven into Natal or penned in upon the Swazi frontier. At 3 a.m. on the 6th the assault was delivered.
>
> The Boers were able to crawl close in to the British outposts

before they were seen and challenged. Their forlorn hope then rushed between two trenches held by the West Yorkshires, driving in front of them a troop of loose horses, so as to confuse the British troops and lead them to think they were being charged by mounted men. They did cause momentary confusion, but the men of G and H Companies of the West Yorkshires were good soldiers, tired by months of war, and they held fast, while the supports coming up caught the Boer stormers and fought them hand-to-hand, speedily hurling them back in wild disorder. The enemy left on the ground Commandant Spruyt and some twenty burghers dead, close to or inside the British lines. Spruyt was a man of exceptional bravery. He had previously been taken prisoner, and had escaped, without any taint of treachery or unfairness, by leaping from a train in motion.

While the main attack was going forward, the Boers had opened a heavy rifle fire upon the camp and had also feinted its eastern corner. The crackle of the fusillade, the hail of bullets and the stampeding of the horses caused a great confusion. Many men were killed or wounded as they lay asleep. But order was swiftly restored; the tired troops as they awoke collected their wits, snatched up their rifles, and dashed forth to repel their assailants. They had no mark at which to fire except the fitful flashes of the Martinis and Mausers, yet there is evidence that many of the British bullets found billets in the enemy's ranks. Long before day broke, seeing that their onset had failed, the Boers withdrew, well knowing that the British were too ignorant of the ground to attempt pursuit until day came. They seem to have made off to the north, sending a detachment eastwards to make the British think that they were retiring in that direction. At daybreak Smith-Dorrien despatched his mounted infantry to follow them up, but they had already got so far that touch could not be recovered.

The British casualties in this affair were heavy, and the large proportion of killed in the figures points to desperate hand-to-hand fighting. Twenty-four officers and men were killed and fifty-three

wounded. The West Yorkshires were hardest hit. Their conduct in
the face of surprise attack, with the odds heavily against them, was
admirable. Among the Boer killed, besides Commandant Spruyt,
were two Field Cornets, and Commandant Raademeyer was severely
wounded.

The fiercest fighting had been on the perimeter of the camp defended
by the 2nd Battalion, The Prince of Wales's Own Regiment. Despite
fending off the enemy, the British received heavy casualties and
the Boers were able to escape from the encirclement that French
has been hoping to achieve. It was during the height of the battle
that Traynor showed such great courage that he was awarded the
VC. He was, however, badly wounded – so badly injured that his
wife initially received a telegram saying that he had been killed.
In fact, he had received splinter and bullet wounds to his chest
and thigh.

Traynor's VC was announced on 17 September 1901, when his
citation stated:

> During the night attack on Bothwell camp, on 6 February 1901, Ser-
> geant Traynor jumped out of a trench and ran out under an extremely
> heavy fire to the assistance of a wounded man. While running out
> he was severely wounded, and being unable to carry the man him-
> self, he called for assistance. Lance-Corporal Lintott at once came to
> him, and between them they carried the wounded soldier into shelter.
> After this, although severely wounded, Sergeant Traynor remained
> in command of his section, and was most cheerful in encouraging
> his men till the attack failed.

Traynor's injuries forced his discharge from the Army in September 1901, the same month that his VC was announced. He was not
well enough to travel to London for his investiture and so, instead,
a presentation was made to him at the West Yorks Barracks, York,

close to his home. His VC was presented to him by Colonel Edward Browne, who had been awarded his own VC for bravery during the Zulu War.

The *Daily Mail* reported on the event:

> A brief but interesting ceremony took place at a full-dress parade of the troops of the York garrison at the infantry barracks this morning, when Sergeant W. B. Traynor, 2nd Battalion, West Yorkshire Regiment, was presented with the Victoria Cross gained during the South African War ... The officer making the presentation of the trophy, Colonel E. S. Browne, Assistant Adjutant-General, North Eastern District, is himself a Victoria Cross man.
>
> Having referred to the circumstances under which Sergeant Traynor risked his life to help one under his command, Colonel Browne, V.C., said one could not conceive a brighter example of true devotion to duty in a commander.
>
> Colonel Browne then called Sergeant Traynor, who was in mufti, forward and pinned the Cross to his breast, and also the South Africa Medal with six clasps [thin strips of metal detailing the specific battles at which an individual had been present]. Colonel Browne addressed the troops, remarking that owing to the state of Sergeant Traynor's health, it had not been possible for him to journey to London to receive the Cross, in the way he otherwise would, but that circumstances had its compensating advantage for it enabled Sergeant Traynor to receive it in the very cradle and home of the distinguished regiment to which he had belonged and earned honour for (cheers) ... At the conclusion of the ceremony, Sergeant Traynor received numerous personal congratulations.

For a short time, Traynor worked as an orderly room clerk with the Royal Engineers but in September 1902 he was given the job of barrack warden at Dover: during the Great War he was praised for his valuable service in this role. Following a dinner for holders of the

VC in the Royal Gallery of the House of Lords in 1929, at which The Prince of Wales was present, Traynor joined the Dover branch of the Royal British Legion and became one of its most enthusiastic supporters, at one point serving as the branch's vice-chairman.

In 1935, he retired from his post as barrack warden, but he continued living in Dover until his death on 20 October 1956, aged eighty-five. In his twilight years, Traynor had been honoured with an invitation to Queen Elizabeth's Coronation lunch held at Dover Town Hall. Throughout his post-military career, Traynor had also remained a loyal friend of his old regiment, regularly travelling north to attend reunions. At the time of his death, he had a son serving in the Royal Engineers and a granddaughter serving in the Women's Royal Army Corps (WRAC). Traynor's funeral was attended by numerous representatives of the West Yorkshire Regiment, as well as the Mayor of Dover. He was buried in Charlton Cemetery in Dover.

LIEUTENANT (LATER LIEUTENANT-COLONEL) WILLIAM JOHN ENGLISH

Army: 2nd Scottish Horse
DATE OF BRAVERY: 3 JULY 1901
GAZETTED: 4 OCTOBER 1901
Special feature of the VC: a splendid Second Anglo-Boer War VC to a very young officer who ended up serving in three major conflicts.

William John English was born in Cork, Ireland, on 6 October 1882. He was the son of Major William English and his wife Marian. He is believed to have attended Folkestone Grammar School (or Harvey Grammar School, Folkestone), in Kent before attending Campbell College, Belfast.

Originally, English served in the Merchant Marine but on 25 November 1900 he enlisted as a private into the 2nd Scottish Horse, a locally raised South African regiment. He served in the Boer War and was present at operations in Orange River Colony, Cape Colony and the Transvaal. On 17 March 1901, he was commissioned as a second lieutenant.

By early July 1901, a number of British columns were operating north of the Delagoa Bay railway line in north-east Transvaal. Their objective was to try to pin down the Boer general Ben Viljoen, who had become an expert in guerilla fighting during the war. On 3 July, Lieutenant-Colonel G. E. Benson set out from Machadodorp for Dullstroom. At the time, it appeared the Boers were in retreat but they suddenly turned and attacked the Scottish Horse. It was the gallantry of English, then only eighteen, that prevented the column from being outflanked. His bravery earned him the VC that was announced on 4 October 1901, when his citation stated:

> This Officer with five men was holding the right of a position at Vlakfontein on the 3rd July, 1901, during an attack by the Boers. Two of his men were killed and two wounded, but the position was still held, largely owing to Lieutenant English's personal pluck. When the ammunition ran short he went over to the next party and obtained more; to do this he had to cross some 15 yards of open ground under a heavy fire at a range of from 20 to 30 yards.

English's bravery meant that the vulnerable flank was secured and the position was held. In the end the engagement cost the Scottish Horse three men and nine wounded. His VC was announced in the *London Gazette* just two days before his nineteenth birthday and he received his medal from The Prince of Wales (later George V) at an investiture at Horse Guards Parade, London, on 2 July 1902. The war had ended on 31 May 1902, when English was released from military service.

On 6 April 1905, English re-enlisted into the 2nd Dragoon Guards in South Africa and on 7 October of that year was made a lance-corporal. On 17 October 1906, he was promoted to second lieutenant in the Army Service Corps (ASC). He returned with his unit to the UK in 1906 and in the following year served in Ireland, where he was promoted to substantive lieutenant on 27 October 1907. In 1909, he joined the Freemasons and was responsible for initiating United Service Lodge No. 3285 in Pinelands, South Africa. English returned to the UK once again in 1912 and the following year he was based in Portsmouth, Hampshire.

On 5 August 1914, immediately after the outbreak of the First World War, English was promoted to captain and went to France. He was promoted to acting major on 30 November 1914 and throughout the First World War served with distinction before, in late 1918, serving with the Occupation Forces in Germany at the end of the conflict. In the same year, his first wife, May (*née* Dunne), had died.

English reverted to the rank of captain in 1920 and two years later married Mary Pyper, the daughter of William Pyper, a master at Campbell College, Belfast, where English himself had once studied. The couple went on to have two sons and a daughter. In March of the same year, English embarked for Sierra Leone, returning to the UK the following year. He served on the Rhine and in India before retiring from the military on 5 December 1930. Next, English became an organiser for the Northern Ireland National Association for Employment of Regular Soldiers, Sailors and Airmen.

On 29 August 1939, after the outbreak of the Second World War, English commanded the Northern Ireland group of National Defence Companies (later the 6th Battalion, the Royal Ulster Regiment) and on 1 November 1939 he was promoted to lieutenant-colonel. However, on 24 April 1941 he relinquished command of the 6th Battalion to take up a post in the Middle East. He was the senior officer on a troop ship when it was attacked by enemy aircraft based in West Africa. In the bombing, his cabin was wrecked and he suffered shell-shock.

On 4 July 1941, English died, aged fifty-eight, from a brain haemorrhage while on board the transport HMT *Orduna* in the Red Sea. English was buried in Ma'alla Cemetery, Aden (now Yemen). There is a memorial in his honour at Campbell College, Belfast, and a plaque in his memory at King's Road, Belfast.

DRIVER (LATER HONORARY MAJOR) FREDERICK HENRY BRADLEY

Army: Royal Field Artillery
DATE OF BRAVERY: 26 SEPTEMBER 1901
GAZETTED: 27 DECEMBER 1901
Special feature of the VC: a superb VC awarded for the heroic defence of Fort Itala, South Africa.

Frederick Henry Bradley was born in Shoreditch, east London, on 27 September 1876. He was the son of Edmund Thomas Bradley, who served with the Royal Engineers, and his wife Caroline (*née* Smith). After leaving school, Frederick Bradley got a job as a blacksmith's hammerman before, on 12 March 1894, enlisting in the 2nd Depot Division of the Royal Field Artillery (RFA) aged just seventeen.

On 1 May 1894, Bradley joined the 41st Battery of the regiment as a driver. He also served with the 44th Battery before transferring to the 69th Battery in April 1897. Soon afterwards, his unit embarked for South Africa as part of the 1st Brigade, RFA. After the start of the Second Anglo-Boer War in October 1899, Bradley was present at several of the early battles, including the Battle of Talana Hill (also known as the Battle of Glencoe) in October 1899, the first major clash of the conflict, and the Siege of Ladysmith in Natal, which lasted from early November 1899 until late February 1900.

In August 1900, Bradley was among a handful of gunners chosen to accompany the Fifth Division, Mounted Infantry Battalion, raised by Major A. J. Chapman. He was present on 26 September 1901 – the day before his twenty-fifth birthday – at the Defence of Fort Itala, a two-day battle that some historians have compared to the defence of Rorke's Drift. In both cases, Natal was saved from an invasion by a small detachment of British soldiers who made a gallant stand despite being vastly outnumbered.

The battle at Fort Itala took place as a result of Commandant General Louis Botha's second expedition to Natal, when he was keen to exploit his earlier success over the British at Blood River Poort. The Commandant General ordered Assistant Commandant Chris Botha to attack a British position situated on the lower spur of the 4,800ft summit of Itala. Known as Fort Itala, its defences were, in fact, limited to shallow trenches and low-lying stone walls. The two sides were far from evenly matched: Botha had 1,400 men while the British force, under Major Chapman of the Royal Dublin Fusiliers, stood at around 300. The British initially had two fifteen-pounders and a Maxim gun at their disposal, though the latter jammed and the two fifteen-pounders were soon withdrawn from service because the gun crews suffered such heavy casualties from Boer marksmen. The seventeen-hour engagement soon developed into a duel of rifles and bayonets, during which the British force eventually expended a staggering 70,000 rounds during an intense and bloody action.

An article on the battle, entitled 'Itala – Monument to Valour', was written by M. C. Carter in the *South African Military History Society Journal* (Volume 2, No. 1, June 1971) and this provides a wonderful insight into the ferocity of the action:

> A tornado of lead enveloped the post. Bullets screamed and howled, the ground rapidly became covered with a shower of broken branches and chopped leaves, the screams and groans of stricken men and of the pathetic unprotected horses filled the air; dust and earth flew in all directions and the constant ear-shattering crash of hundreds of rifles made a sound to match all the thunderbolts of hell, as the Boers

tried to batter the defences to pieces with rifle fire. No cover could withstand this inferno, and men fell thick and fast, yet each attack melted away under the galling return cross-fire of the defenders...

By late afternoon after 17 hours of heavy, unrelenting attack, both sides were exhausted.

Chapman's force had taken a fearful toll of the attacking Commando, but they had suffered 81 killed and wounded and lost a further 40 as prisoners. This was nearly half his total strength. The troops, bleary-eyed, with hands burned, shoulders raw and faces scorched, their ammunition nearly exhausted, could hardly be expected to withstand another concerted attack. They were ready but hardly able. Chapman himself, shot through the right leg, waited and listened as the Boer fire slackened and died away. After an hour he sent out scouts who returned with the heartening news that Botha's men were drawing off ... No less than 153 British horses had been killed, while the rest had been injured or had bolted. There were more men defending Fort Itala than had been defending Rorke's Drift in 1879, but the scale of the task facing the British force was still immense.

The diary of the 69th Battery also provides a vivid description of the battle: 'At about 12.15 a.m. a very heavy fire was opened on the camp from all sides. The guns opened fire at once, firing shrapnel at the flashes at a range of 1,100 yards. There was a full moon. At about 3 a.m. Gunner Miller was wounded. The guns ceased firing about this time as the moon had gone down. The Boers at this time rushed one of our advanced trenches but the Sergeant with his twenty men fixed bayonets and charged, driving the Boers back. He lost ten men.

At 4 a.m. fire ceased and it was thought that the Boers had cleared. Day broke about 4.45 a.m. and at 5 a.m. the Boers again opened fire hotter than ever. The guns opened fire again using magazine fire as the Boers were now very close, in fact could have been reached with case shot if there had not been one of our own trenches in front of us.

Lieutenant Herbert was hit almost at once then Corporal Flowers and Gunner Spence. Major Chapman then ordered them to leave the guns as it was evident the guns could not be kept in action and men could not bring up ammunition. The guns at this time were under fire from the rear as well as the front and one gun had been turned round to check the fire from the rear.

After taking cover those who could get rifles worked in the trenches and others dressed the wounded and carried ammunition to the trenches.

About 11 a.m. Major Chapman called for volunteers to carry ammunition to a trench on the hill a distance of about 300 yards under a heavy fire. Six men volunteered. Gunner Duddy and Driver Lancashire started with the first box and got half way when Driver Lancashire was hit. Gunner Rabb and Driver Bradley ran out to carry him in and brought him back. Major Chapman then ordered no more men were to be sent but Gunner Ball and Driver Bradley ran out before they could be stopped and succeeded in getting one box to the top of the hill. Gunner Rabb and Driver Bradley were recommended for the V.C....

Canon W. M. Lummis carried out research that provided further information on Bradley's bravery:

When Major Chapman called for volunteers to take ammunition up the hill to the infantry at Fort Itala on the Zululand border, Bradley was one of the volunteers. A tiny man, his services were declined; but Bradley insisted, and when others were wounded, he instantly rushed out to carry them out to shelter and then carried the ammunition uphill. Before doing so, however, he knelt down by a bush and prayed for God's help.

Bradley's VC was announced on 27 December 1901, when his citation stated:

During the action at Itala, Zululand, on 26 September 1901, Major Chapman called for volunteers to carry ammunition up hill; to do this a space of about 150 yards swept by a heavy cross fire had to be crossed. Driver Lancashire and Gunner Ball at once came forward and started, but half-way across Driver Lancashire fell wounded. Driver Bradley and Gunner Rabb without a moment's hesitation ran out and caught Driver Lancashire up, and Gunner Rabb carried him under cover, the ground being swept by bullets the whole time. Driver Bradley then, with the aid of Gunner Boddy, succeeded in getting ammunition up the hill.

Bradley's VC was presented to him by Lord Kitchener at an investiture at Pretoria on Peace Thanksgiving Day, 8 June 1902, after which he was promoted to bombardier. After initially being placed on the 1st Army Reserve in South Africa, Bradley was later discharged from the Army on 11 March 1906. In that year, too, for reasons best known to himself, Bradley changed his two first names from 'Frank George' to 'Frederick Henry'.

In late March 1906, Bradley enrolled as a corporal in the Central South African Railway Volunteers (CSARV). However, he was serving with the Transvaal Mounted Rifles during the so-called Natal Rebellion of 1906 (also known as the Bambatha Uprising), a revolt against British rule and taxation in Natal. In 1907, he married Florence Hillary, who was from South Africa, and the couple went on to have two sons. After being discharged in February 1908, he rejoined the CSARV as a sergeant in January 1910. The following year, he, at his own expense, accompanied the South African contingent to the coronation of George V in London.

Bradley transferred to the 10th Infantry, the Witwatersrand Rifles, in January 1913, in which regiment he was commissioned as a second lieutenant in July of that year, before being promoted to lieutenant in March 1914.

After the outbreak of the Great War, Bradley served in German

South-West Africa (now Namibia) from August 1914 until September 1915. He initially served as Commanding Officer of C Company before switching to work as a Railway Transport Officer. Bradley was involved in the same train crash that claimed the life of Sir George Farrar and later provided a detailed written account of what happened:

> Sir George had his own rail trolley which he used for getting about the country. I was offered a lift on the trolley by Sir George which I gratefully accepted, and we arranged to leave for Kuibis at dusk. The driver's name was Henwood. The line was single track and it was essential that the stationmaster at both ends should know in advance what traffic was on the way, so that we would not meet any traffic.
>
> Sir George, therefore, gave instructions to Captain Pigg, the military stationmaster at Kuibis, to allow no train to leave until the trolley arrived from Bukkels-Bron. Unfortunately, the telephone wires were continually overburdened with calls on important military matters, and Captain Pigg received only a portion of the message. The vital part, that no train was to leave Kuibis, did not reach him. Our trolley was lit by an acetylene lamp. It was a terrible night. A gale was blowing at 70 to 80 miles an hour, carrying with it lumps of grit that stung our faces. Only tightly fitting goggles prevented our being blinded. Henwood, the driver, sat on the left of the trolley, Sir George Farrar was on his right, and I sat immediately behind him with my arm over the seat. Sir George chatted to me in a friendly manner, and we were about two miles from our destination when the accident occurred.
>
> I do not remember very much but I have been able to piece the story together from my fleeting recollections and what I was later told by those who arrived first on the scene. By a tragic mischance as I have explained, a mixed goods train left Kuibis shortly before we were due to arrive, and the vision of the driver was obscured by a large cylindrical tank of water, commonly known

as a 'Torpedo'. Neither Henwood nor the driver of the goods train was able to avoid the impact. Henwood, poor fellow, was terribly injured and did not live long afterwards. Dr. Pratt, of the Natal Carbineers, told me later that Sir George saw a collision was imminent when a 'Torpedo' loomed up, and he jumped to the side. He was struck on the hip and critically injured. He had spells of consciousness before he died, bravely, like a real soldier, at 5 o'clock the following morning.

And now, what happened to me! Mercifully, I suppose, I do not seem to have been aware that we were about to be struck by a train. I was exchanging a few words with Sir George in the howling gale and then I woke up in the hospital at Kuibis. I was flung 70 yards by the impact, and was picked up by Major Pirie, of the Treasury. He told me that he found me 'out on my feet' with blood streaming from my face. As soon as he began to talk to me I collapsed. I was under medical care for two months with a variety of injuries, such as broken ribs, broken ankles, a broken nose and head wounds. Looking back on it I do not think Providence intended me to die in a railway accident.

Once Bradley had recovered from his injuries, he applied for a transfer to France at the end of 1915 and, on arrival in England, was appointed a lieutenant in the Royal Field Artillery, attached to the Royal Engineers. Major Geoffrey Tylden later recalled that Bradley was looked after at this stage of his career: 'His old C.O. offered him a cushy job with the St John's Wood Depot Battery.'

In early 1916, Bradley travelled to France as adjutant of 5th Trench Mortar Battery, 5th Brigade, 2nd Division. Later still, with the rank of acting captain, he commanded six batteries of mortars on the Somme and was seriously wounded at Delville Wood. All in all, the Great War had presented him with two close brushes with death and, in July 1917, he returned to South Africa to recuperate from his injuries. Here, from 1 July 1917, he served in the South

Lieutenant (later Rear-Admiral) John Bythesea, Royal Navy, was awarded the VC in February 1857 for the first Special Forces-type action of the Crimean War. His courage in August 1854 involved him and a comrade hiding on the Baltic island of Wardo in order to capture vital Russian despatches from their armed escort.

A portrait of Sergeant (later Brevet Major) John Knox, after he lost his left arm in battle, features in the Library of Nineteenth-Century Photography. Knox was awarded the VC in February 1857 for two acts of bravery during the Crimean War. When his medal group was sold at auction, it was accompanied by the cannon ball that severed his arm.

The VC action of Private Samuel Parkes during the Crimean War is depicted in a painting by the artist Louis William Desanges. Parkes's VC was announced on 24 February 1857 for bravery in rescuing a comrade during the legendary Charge of the Light Brigade at the Battle of Balaclava in October 1854. Aged forty-one, Parkes was the oldest VC recipient of the conflict.

The VC action of Lieutenant (later Rear-Admiral) Henry Raby during the Crimean War is depicted in a postcard illustration. His VC was announced in February 1857 for bravery in June 1855 when he rescued a wounded comrade. Raby was the very first VC recipient to receive his award from Queen Victoria but during the investiture she inadvertently pushed the medal's brooch pin deep into his chest.

Lieutenant (later Major-General Sir) Christopher Teesdale received the unique VC for the protracted Siege of Kars (in eastern Turkey) during the Crimean War. His was also the first VC awarded to a recipient born in South Africa.

Colour-Sergeant Stephen Garvin was awarded the unique VC and DCM combination for the Indian Mutiny, making him the most decorated Non-Commissioned Officer of the whole conflict. His VC was awarded in January 1860 for bravery in Delhi in June 1857, when he led a successful attack on a key enemy position.

Lieutenant (later Major-General) George Renny, Indian Army, was an officer in the only native artillery troop to stay loyal during the Indian Mutiny. His decoration was announced in April 1859 for bravery in September 1857, when he leapt onto the burning roof of a magazine to see off an enemy attempt to recapture it.

Lieutenant (later Admiral Sir) Nowell Salmon, Royal Navy, was awarded a rare sailor's VC for action on land with the Naval Brigade during the Indian Mutiny. His decoration was announced in December 1858 for bravery in November the previous year at Lucknow in a daring attack on an enemy position.

Lieutenant (later Major-General) Henry Jerome was awarded the unique triple-dated VC in November 1859 for his repeated bravery during the Indian Mutiny the previous year. His VC medal group is the only one to have been gifted to my collection, thanks to the generosity of his great-grandson, Alex Jerome.

Captain (later General) George Channer, Indian Army, was awarded the only VC for an action in Malaya. His decoration was announced in April 1876 for gallantry in December the previous year, when he led an attack on a vital enemy stockade in Perak.

Gunner James Collis was awarded the VC in May 1881 for bravery in the heat of battle during the Second Afghan War in July the previous year. However, his decoration was later forfeited for the crime of bigamy, leading eventually to the personal intervention of George V, who was opposed to the practice of forfeiture.

Sub-Lieutenant (later Major) Alan Hill (later Hill-Walker) was awarded a rare VC for the calamitous First Anglo-Boer War of 1881, the only major conflict for which no campaign medal was ever sanctioned. His decoration was announced in March 1882 for bravery in January the previous year, when he rescued three wounded comrades at the Battle of Laing's Nek, South Africa.

Surgeon-Captain (later Surgeon-Major) Harry Whitchurch, Indian Army, was awarded the unique VC for the defence/relief of Chitral Fort, North-West Frontier. His decoration was announced in July 1895 for bravery in March that year, when he carried a wounded officer to safety on his back.

Lieutenant (later Lieutenant-Colonel) Thomas Watson was awarded an outstanding North-West Frontier VC for a very rare night action. His decoration, believed unique to a recipient born in the Netherlands, was announced in May 1898 for bravery in September the previous year. He was twice wounded, the second time seriously, but survived. Winston Churchill, who later visited the scene of the action, described Watson's gallantry as 'sublime'.

Sergeant William Traynor meets Sir Winston Churchill on 14 October 1946, long after receiving his VC for outstanding bravery during the Second Anglo-Boer War. Traynor's decoration, announced in September 1901, was for courage when he ran out to save a wounded man during a night attack at Bothwell Camp, South Africa, in February that year. Traynor was severely wounded but survived.

Lieutenant (later Lieutenant-Colonel) William English was awarded the VC in October 1901 for bravery in July of that year during the Second Anglo-Boer War. His decoration came after he determinedly held a vital position despite a fierce enemy attack, in which two of his comrades were killed and two wounded. He went on to serve in both world wars.

Driver (later Honorary Major) Frederick Bradley was awarded the VC in December 1901 for gallantry in the Second Anglo-Boer War during the heroic defence of Fort Itala, a two-day battle in September 1901 that some historians have likened to the famous battle at Rorke's Drift in 1879.

Lieutenant (later Colonel) John Grant (right), Indian Army, is pictured with another highly decorated officer. Grant was awarded his unique VC in January 1905 for bravery during the Tibet campaign when, in July 1904, he led an attack, under heavy fire, up a steep, bare rock face during the storming of the Gyantse Jong.

LEFT A new statue to commemorate Driver (later Sergeant) Job Drain was unveiled in Dagenham, Essex on 10 November 2009 – the day before Armistice Day. Drain, who was born in Essex and died in Dagenham, was awarded the VC in November 1914 for bravery at Le Cateau, France during the opening phase of the Great War that August.

BELOW LEFT Second Lieutenant (later Captain) James Leach was awarded the VC in December 1914 for great gallantry in France in October that year. Along with a sergeant and ten volunteers, he retook a crucial trench, killing eight of the enemy, wounding two and taking sixteen as prisoners.

BELOW RIGHT Sepoy (later Subadar) Khudadad Khan was both the first Indian and the first Muslim recipient of the VC. His award was announced in December 1914 for bravery during a battle in Belgium in October that year, when he continued to man a machine-gun even though his five comrades were all killed. After being wounded and left for dead by the enemy, he crawled back to rejoin his unit.

Captain Arthur Kilby was awarded a posthumous VC in March 1916 for outstanding bravery during the Battle of Loos in September the previous year. Despite having his left foot blown off, he cheered on his men up to the enemy's wire, where he was shot and killed.

Temporary Captain Angus Buchanan, the so-called blind VC, is photographed being led from the dais by a comrade after receiving both the VC and MC from George V in Bristol in November 1917. His VC had been announced in September 1916 for bravery in April that year, when he rescued an officer in Mesopotamia. Buchanan later lost his sight after being hit in the head by a sniper's bullet.

Private William Boynton Butler (second left) is photographed on the day of his investiture in December 1917 with three other soldiers who had also been awarded the VC. Butler's decoration had been announced in October 1917 for an unselfish act of gallantry in August that year. While serving on the Western Front, he grabbed a live shell in his trench, held it to protect passing infantry from danger and, finally, threw it into a safe area.

Captain Noel Chavasse was awarded the VC and Bar (the equivalent of a second VC) – on top of an earlier MC. Serving with the Royal Army Medical Corps, he saved countless lives on the frontline. His second VC was posthumous, awarded after his death on 4 August 1917 from serious injuries received when rescuing wounded soldiers. Only three VCs and Bars have been awarded in the decoration's 160-year history and Chavasse's is the only VC and Bar of the Great War.

The iconic posthumous VC & Bar, MC group of Captain Noel Chavasse, Royal Army Medical Corps, one of only three 'double VCs' ever awarded and the unique 'double' for the Great War.

African Defence Force, once again with the Witwatersrand Rifles. By the time the First World War ended in November 1918, Bradley was forty-two years old, but still his military career was not over.

In December 1919, he transferred to the 2nd Mounted Rifles (the Natal Carbineers) from the Supernumerary List of the Active Citizen Force. While serving with this regiment, he received promotion to the substantive rank of captain in December 1923.

During the 1920s, Bradley was awarded the Colonial Auxiliary Forces Long Service Medal and the Colonial Auxiliary Forces Officers' Decoration. Bradley also attended the coronation of George VI in 1937 as a member of the South African contingent. He remained on the Reserve of Officers until September 1938 and was granted the honorary rank of major.

During the later years of his career, Bradley worked as a publican and manager of a general store. A keen shot and angler, he was also a prolific writer, penning books with such titles as *Dengue Fever: How Caused and How Avoided*, *The Deadly Fly*, *Winged Death*, *When the Mail Train Passes* and *Filtration of Slops*. Bradley was also a member of the Far East Rand Squadron of the Legion of Frontiersmen.

As a publican, Bradley was not the first, and will not be the last, to drink too much while doing his job. Major Geoffrey Tylden, who knew him well, said:

> He was a damn good chap and kept a pub in Zululand ... He used to say 'My nerve is gone, so I drink,' and he did, poor chap. He always spoke of himself as an ex-driver and he looked it! I liked him very much ... I admired his lack of swank. A fine soldier of the old type.

It seems that Bradley's bravery was matched by his generosity, too. In 1935, the *Cape Argus* reported: 'In the balance sheet of the Royal Chelsea Hospital there appears a brief entry reading: "From the Bradley V.C. Fund. £10."' In an act of great generosity – since £10 was a not inconsiderable sum at the time – Bradley had secretly started donating his VC pension paid by the British government to the local hospital.

Bradley finally settled in Gwelo, Southern Rhodesia (now Zimbabwe), where he worked as a telephone exchange operator. He died on 10 March 1943, following an operation in the local hospital the previous day. He was sixty-six.

A newspaper reported:

> The day that he [Bradley] went to hospital was the day when H.E. [His Excellency] the Governor, Sir Evelyn Baring and Lady Mary Baring paid their first official visit to Gwelo, and it is reported that the Governor had a long chat with Major Bradley, to whom he showed his medals (which he had taken to hospital with him) and it is stated that H.E. was very pleased indeed to converse with the old hero, and learn something of his campaigning.

Bradley is buried in Gwelo Cemetery and his name is listed on a memorial at the Royal Artillery Chapel in Woolwich, south-east London.

Tibet campaign, 1904

In the early 20th century, Tibet was, technically, a vassal – or subordinate – state of China, even though it chose to ignore agreements negotiated between British and Chinese officials at the end of the 19th century. In July 1903, the British government in India sent a commercial mission led by Colonel Francis Younghusband into Tibet, only to have it ignored by the local rulers. As British fears grew of Russian expansion in the area, Younghusband left Tibet and returned with a far larger force under the command of Brigadier-General J. R. L. Macdonald. In March 1904, Tibet was given an ultimatum: to open negotiations with the British by 25 June or the

British force would march on Lhasa. Still the Tibetans remained defiant and on 6 July 1904 the British attacked, starting with Gyantse and the fort overlooking it. On 3 August, they reached Lhasa and, after the Tibetans had taken heavy casualties, a peace treaty was signed on 7 September.

LIEUTENANT (LATER COLONEL) JOHN DUNCAN GRANT

Indian Army: 8th Gurkha Rifles
DATE OF BRAVERY: 6 JULY 1904
GAZETTED: 24 JANUARY 1905
Special feature of the VC: the unique VC for the Tibet campaign of 1903–04 and the highest altitude action for any VC.

John Duncan Grant was born in Rurki (also spelled Roorkee), United Provinces, India, on 29 December 1877. He was son of Colonel Suene Grant, Royal Engineers, and his wife Caroline (*née* Napper), the daughter of a colonel in the Bengal Staff Corps. John Grant, usually known as 'Jack', was educated in Britain, first at Manor House School, Hastings, Sussex, then Cheltenham College, Gloucestershire, and finally at the Royal Military College, Sandhurst. He was commissioned as second lieutenant (unattached) on 22 January 1898. After briefly joining the Indian Staff Corps, Grant was appointed to the 30th Punjab Regiment in 1899 before his promotion to lieutenant in April 1900 following service with the Malakand Force. In August 1900, he transferred to the 44th (Gurkha Rifle) Regiment, which was retitled the 8th Gurkha Rifles in 1902.

From 1903 to 1904, Grant served in Tibet at a time when tensions in the country were high. He was initially Mentioned in Despatches but on 6 July 1904 showed such outstanding bravery in the attack on Gyantse and its hilltop fort that he would eventually be awarded the VC.

Perceval Landon, *The Times*'s correspondent at the scene, takes up the story:

> About two o'clock Colonel Campbell, to whom had been commit-
> ted the command of the attacking force, sent across to Pala village,
> where the General was watching operations with his staff, urgently
> recommending that an attack should be made at once upon the
> extreme east part of the upper works of the jong [fort]. The rock of
> Gyantse is so steep that it seemed accessible nowhere except along
> the main approach which was well defended.
>
> But at the point which Colonel Campbell chose there was just a
> bare possibility of scaling the rock. It was a fearful climb, and the top
> of it was crowned by a well-made wall flanked by two projecting bas-
> tions. At first the General was unwilling to press forward any further
> that day, and was in some doubt whether to accede to this request. He
> determined, however, to be guided by the advice of Colonel Campbell
> on the spot. At a little past three, a concentrated fire from all points was
> ordered to be directed upon the wall at the head of this steep climb.
> The common shell used by the ten-pounders was now employed with
> terrific effect, and one could see, second by second, a large ragged hole
> being torn open at this point. Clouds of dust arose and slowly drifted
> away to the west in the slight breeze, and whenever a lull in the can-
> nonade allowed a clear sight, the breach was wider by a yard or two.
> A constant cataract of stone and brick fell down the face of the rock
> below, which here was almost sheer for 40 feet. It was not shell alone
> that did this work. Magazine fire was concentrated at the same point,
> and under this whistling canopy of ball and shell, the Gurkhas were
> soon seen moving upwards and onwards from the houses at the base
> of the rock. It was a moment tense with excitement, Lieutenant Grant
> was in charge of the storming party, and soon the first figures appeared
> over the belt of houses and trees which hem in the rock on this side.
> Instantly the fire redoubled, and from three points a converging fire
> hammered and bit upon the wall above the heads.

Absolutely confident in the skill of the gunners, the Gurkhas climbed on. Not a Tibetan was seen on the wall above, but through the loop-holes of the bastions a few shots were fired, at what was becoming point blank range, and caused one or two casualties among the little figures clambering up on their hands and knees.

To those who watched from a distance, it seemed as if more loss was being inflicted when again and again one of the escalading force was knocked backwards by the masses of stone and brick dislodged by our shells. The steepness was so great that a man who slipped almost necessarily carried away the man below him also. But little by little the advance was made, and conspicuous in front of the small company was Grant, with one Sepoy, who was clearly determined to rival his officer in one of the pluckiest pieces of work ever known on the Indian frontier. The men now reached a point fifteen or 20 feet below the level of the breach, and it was no longer safe to allow the cannonade to continue. The guns had been tested with a success which almost surpasses belief. The chief danger lay in striking too low and exploding the shells on the outside, but not a single missile had struck the rock at the base of the wall. The marksmanship displayed was astonishing; inferiority in the gun itself was the only real danger to be feared, but these new ten-pounders seem to have reached mechanical perfection for all practical purposes.

Just at this moment, when the General himself was issuing orders that the fire should cease, the thin high pipe of the Ghurka bugler cried again and again from the distant rocks in the four shrill consecutive notes which call for silence, and silence reigned. Then, uncovered by our guns, the last desperate climb was made, and up the higher ridges of an ascent so sheer that it was almost impossible for our men to protect themselves, one or two of these little figures scrambled. They reached at last the crumbling wreckage of the Tibetan wall. Lieutenant Grant and his faithful follower were the first two men over, and the great semi-circle of the watching British force held their breath for a second to see if they would be at once shot down.

For the moment it was two men against all the enemy that were in the jong – for the third man slipped and carried away in his fall his immediate successor – and it was patent enough to us all that if the Tibetans had but reserved their fire and waited in the bastions, they might well have picked off, one by one, each man as his head appeared above the breach...

When I purchased Grant's medal group at a Morton & Eden auction in London in 2014, it was accompanied by several family letters. One of them was written by Grant to his uncle, Arthur Grant, who served in the 4th Gurkha Rifles, and was dated 7 July 1904 – the very day after his VC action. He wrote:

You will have seen that we snaffled the jong yesterday ... we started going up a rocky slope when the Tibetans at once started heaving stones & also firing ... several men were hit by small bore bullets – including a flesh one behind my knee – just a scratch – the approach to the breach was beastly steep and all loose stones & mud which kept slipping from under one. However we finally made an extra effort & got in. My Q.M. [Quartermaster] havildar was A.1 and got in first ... The G.O.C. [General Officer Commanding] congratulated us and Iggulden told our C.O. this morning that the general had wired to the C in C [Commander-in-Chief] saying how well the 8 G.R. had done which is satisfactory ... we had 18 casualties in the regiment during the day and about 4 occurred as we were going up to the breach...

On the same day, 7 July 1904, Grant's mother's Caroline, who had clearly learned of her son's bravery, wrote to him to say: 'My dear Jack – You are a brave fellow.' On 8 July, Arthur Grant wrote to his brother (Jack's father) and told him:

My dear Suene, I do feel proud of old J & his Goorkhas & so thankful that he was not bowled over altogether storming the Jong on the 6th July. It must have been a real tough business and with any luck Jack ought to get something out of it...

Arthur Grant's prediction was spot-on: Jack Grant's VC was announced on 24 January 1905, when his citation stated:

On the occasion of the storming of the Gyantse Jong on 6th July, 1904, the storming Company, headed by Lieutenant Grant, on emerging from the cover of the village, had to advance up a bare, almost precipitous, rock-face, with little or no cover available, and under a heavy fire from the curtain, flanking towers on both sides of the curtain, and other buildings higher up the Jong. Showers of rocks and stones were at the time being hurled down the hillside by the enemy from above. One man could only go up at a time, crawling on hands and knees, to the breach in the curtain.

Lieutenant Grant, followed by Havildar Karbir Pun, 8th Gurkha Rifles, at once attempted to scale it, but on reaching near the top he was wounded, and hurled back, as was also the Havildar, who fell down the rock some 30 feet.

Regardless of their injuries they again attempted to scale the breach, and, covered by the fire of the men below, were successful in their object, the Havildar shooting one of the enemy on gaining the top. The successful issue of the assault was very greatly due to the splendid example shown by Lieutenant Grant and Havildar Karbir Pun.

The latter has been recommended for the Indian Order of Merit.

In an article for the *Journal of the Victoria Cross Society*, Gerry Birch writes:

One might think all awards of the VC are unique but in this case the VC awarded to Lt Grant of the 8th Gurkha Rifles has a special claim. It was the only VC awarded in the Tibet campaign and was

won in action on the Tibetan Plateau, so it is the highest altitude
action for which a VC has been won.

Brian Best, the respected author, has quite rightly pointed out that
Havildar Karbir Pun would also have been awarded the VC had the
statutes so allowed in 1904: his actions were the equal of Grant's
bravery. In fact, a Royal Warrant extending eligibility to 'Native
Officers and Men' was to be signed by The King in 1911. Grant's
VC was to be the last awarded before the Great War and he received
it from Edward VII at an investiture at Buckingham Palace on
24 July 1905. In January 1907, Grant married Kathleen Freyer at
All Saints Church in London's West End, and his captaincy in the
8th Gurkhas was announced just three days after his wedding.

During 1908, Grant attended the Staff College at Quetta (now
Pakistan) and, following various Indian postings, embarked for New
Zealand, where he served on the Imperial General Staff, Otago District, arriving in Dunedin on 14 November 1911 with the temporary
rank of major in the New Zealand Defence Force.

After the outbreak of the Great War in August 1914, Grant
returned to India before being appointed brigade major in the 35th
Indian Infantry Brigade, with orders to join the Tigris Corps. Grant
was tasked with the relief of Sir Charles Townshend's Anglo-Indian
Force besieged in Kut, Mesopotamia (now Iraq). Grant, who had
twice been wounded serving in Tibet, was more seriously injured
in the thigh at Orah on 13 January 1916 (for which he was Mentioned in Despatches too). After being repatriated to England, he
spent time convalescing at Lady Ridley's Hospital in London and
was promoted to substantive major just nine days after receiving
his injury. After 'light duty' in England until the spring of 1917,
Grant's sailing orders to return to India were revoked in favour of a
temporary secondment to II Anzac Corps. There is little doubt that
his pre-war experience in New Zealand helped him to get this position. He briefly served with the Anzacs in France and Belgium before

embarking again for India in the *Nagoya* out of Marseilles, France, on 16 August 1917.

In May 1918, Grant was once more on his way to Kut, disembarking at Basra, in the south of the country, as acting lieutenant-colonel in command of 3rd Battalion, 11th Gurkha Rifles. Later, he was yet again stationed in India, at Manmad in the Bombay Presidency.

After the Great War ended in November 1918, Grant took extended leave before going with the 3/11th to fight in the Third Afghan War. He was afterwards actively employed in the Waziristan operations and was awarded the Distinguished Service Order (DSO) on 19 December 1922, when his citation stated his decoration was: 'For distinguished service rendered in the Field with the Waziristan Force, 1920–1921.'

In 1921, Grant assumed command of a Training Battalion of the 13th Rajput Regiment before returning to the Gurkhas in command of 1st Battalion, 10th Gurkha Regiment. Between 1925 and 1928, he was Assistant Adjutant-General, Army HQ, India, and was promoted a full colonel in September 1926. Grant retired in June 1929 and this coincided with his final decoration: the Companionship of the Order of the Bath (CB), announced in The King's Birthday Honours List of 1929. In 1934, he was appointed honorary colonel of the 10th Gurkha Rifles.

Grant served with the Home Guard in London during the Second World War. He attended the 1960 Gurkha Association Dinner in the presence of the King of Nepal and was one of the oldest VC recipients present at the fourth Victoria Cross and George Cross recipients' reunion, in the presence of Queen Elizabeth The Queen Mother, on 16 July 1964.

Grant died at his nursing home in Tunbridge Wells, Kent, on 20 February 1967, aged eighty-nine. Four days later, he was cremated at Tunbridge Wells Crematorium and his ashes were scattered there in the Garden of Remembrance. Grant's name is on an Honours Board at Cheltenham College and there is a painting of him at the same location. There is also a plaque to his memory at Quetta Staff College, Pakistan.

5

THE FIRST WORLD WAR
AND BEYOND: ARMY VCS

The Great War was 'total war' and led to a scale of casualties that had never been seen before. By the end, more than ten million military personnel and civilians had been killed. The war was eventually won by the Allied Powers: principally Britain, France and, latterly, the United States of America. They defeated the Central Powers, led by Germany, Austria-Hungary and the Ottoman Empire. Before America entered the war in 1917, Britain, France and Russia were sometimes referred to as the Triple Entente, and the Central Powers as the Triple Alliance. These pre-war diplomatic alliances were intended to make war less likely because no country would relish taking on three major powers. However, once the conflict broke out, the alliances made it more widespread. The 'spark' for the war was the assassination of Archduke Franz Ferdinand, the heir to the Austrian throne, in Sarajevo on 28 June 1914, which set off a rapid chain of events: Austria-Hungary declared war on Serbia, Russia mobilised its forces in defence of the Serbs, Germany declared war on France and Russia and also invaded (officially neutral) Belgium en route to France, and Britain declared war on Germany.

The war took place in many theatres but much of it was fought on the Western Front: both sides 'dug in' along a meandering line of fortified trenches stretching from the Channel to the Swiss frontier with France. The conflict is perhaps best remembered for its trench warfare. Advances in military technology meant that defensive firepower outweighed offensive capability, yet military commanders persisted in using nineteenth-century tactics against twentieth-century technology: millions of men were sent 'over the top' to face barbed wire that slowed their advance, artillery that was far more lethal than ever before and machine-guns that were deadly against an advancing infantry. Furthermore, the Germans began using poison gas in 1915, and soon the Allies followed suit. Yet, still thousands of men were sent to their deaths as military leaders desperately tried to make minuscule advances. On 1 July 1916, the first day of the Battle of the Somme, the British Army saw the bloodiest day in its history, suffering 57,470 casualties, of whom 19,240 were killed. Battles such as Ypres, Vimy Ridge, the Marne, Cambrai, Verdun and fruitless operations like Gallipoli also saw horrific levels of casualties. By the end of 1917, however, both sides had modernised considerably; wireless communications, armoured cars, tanks and tactical aircraft were all in wide use.

America joined the war on the Allied side in 1917 – the same year as the Bolshevik Revolution occurred in Russia. The United States had been angered by the fact that German U-boats had attacked its merchant ships, sinking three of them, so Congress declared war on Germany on 6 April 1917. The Americans' participation eventually proved decisive, more than making up for the withdrawal of Russia from the Allied side. The Allies managed to withstand the German Spring Offensive of 1918, then countered with their own Hundred Days Offensive from 8 August, during which they gradually gained the upper hand. The Central Powers collapsed in the autumn, and on 11 November the opposing armies on the Western Front agreed a ceasefire. The fighting did not start again, although a formal state of war persisted between the two sides until 1919, when the Treaty of Versailles was the first in a series of peace treaties to be signed between the various combatants.

The horrors of the First World War led to the award of 626 VCs – at the time of writing, almost half of the total number ever awarded. The trust now has eighty-two of them in its collection, including twenty-five purchased in the past decade and which (along with the Henry 'Harry' Andrews VC for a post-Great War action) make up the next two chapters.

The Western Front

The Western Front is arguably the best-known battle line in history. During the Great War, it was a narrow battlefield some 460 miles in length and up to 20 miles in depth. Yet, during a period of fifty months, more than six million soldiers were killed and fourteen million wounded along the Western Front alone. Thousands of men lost their lives day after day in often deadlocked trench warfare that saw endless offensives and counter-offensives from both sides.

By the end of 1914, both sides had dug in along a meandering line of trenches – fortified by machine-gun nests, artillery and barbed wire – stretching from the North Sea to the Swiss frontier with France. This line remained largely unchanged for much of the war. Eventually, in 1918, the Allies, by this time supported by American troops, gained the upper hand in the Hundred Days Offensive beginning in August.

DRIVER (LATER SERGEANT)
JOB HENRY CHARLES DRAIN

Army: Royal Field Artillery
DATE OF BRAVERY: 26 AUGUST 1914
GAZETTED: 25 NOVEMBER 1914
Special feature of the VC: a fine award for one of the earliest battles of the Great War.

Job Henry Charles Drain was born in Barking, Essex, on 15 October 1895. One of four children, he was the son of Job Drain Sr, a labourer at a local chemical works, and his wife Susan (*née* Stokes). Drain Sr had served in the Army Service Corps during the Second Anglo-Boer War of 1899–1902 and he went on to serve in the Great War. Drain Jr was educated at Barking Church of England School before leaving to become a factory worker.

On 27 August 1912, when he was aged just sixteen, Drain enlisted at Stratford, east London, into the Royal Field Artillery. After the outbreak of the First World War in August 1914, Drain soon found himself on the Western Front, having disembarked in France after sailing from Dublin. He arrived in Le Havre on 19 August as part of the 37th (Howitzer) Battery, Royal Field Artillery. Within exactly a week of his arrival, Drain, by then still only eighteen, displayed such bravery that he was later awarded the VC.

After the retreat of the British Expeditionary Force (BEF) from Mons in the face of a far superior enemy force, General Sir Horace Smith-Dorrien decided that II Corps should stand and fight at the ridge south of Le Cateau-Cambrésis. In the event, the Battle of Le Cateau lasted for two days and saw the British troops, despite suffering from extreme exhaustion, inflict heavy casualties on the enemy.

The 37th (H) Battery was part of the 5th Division and it had arrived at Le Cateau on the evening of 25 August, having been part of the withdrawal from Mons. When the Battle of Le Cateau began the next day, the 37th (H) Battery was at first positioned in a covered and camouflaged location on a minor road that led to the main road to Reumont. The German force was largely situated on high ground to the west of Le Cateau but at 6 a.m. its forces began firing from a forest position to the north-east of the town. The 37th (H) Battery played a role in silencing some of the enemy's batteries but soon the British forces were taking heavy casualties, as Drain noted in the wartime diary that he kept.

Drain, a driver, wrote [slightly edited because of his limited writing skills]:

> There was little cover or hiding place and when the battle began there were 18-pounder batteries on either side, with a siege battery to the rear of them and hundreds of infantrymen were going up to meet up with the enemy. Terrible shells came over in sixes and were bursting all over the place and over the tops of our guns and wagon lines with plenty of bullets flying about. Man after man was becoming wounded and horses were being killed and batteries were being smashed to pieces. I just don't think there was a man on the field who did not say his prayers for a general retirement to be ordered.

For a teenage soldier having his first taste of war, the experience must have been terrifying. As the morning progressed, the fighting intensified and the enemy was getting the upper hand. It seemed only a matter of time before the British would be forced to withdraw their guns and men. Captain Douglas Reynolds, of the 37th (H) Battery, frantically searched for limber teams to move two of the Howitzers before they fell into enemy hands (a limber was a two-wheeled horse-drawn vehicle used to tow a field-gun). When he could not find the men he needed, he disabled the guns so they were of no use to the enemy.

After Reynolds had withdrawn his men down the road towards Reumont, he again looked for available limber teams to rescue further Howitzers that the British had been forced to leave behind. This time he was not short of volunteers and two teams were chosen for the role, with one driver for each pair of harnessed horses. As they galloped forwards, it looked as if they were all facing certain death and one team was quickly shot down by enemy fire no more than 100 yards away from the Howitzer.

The other four-man team, which included both Reynolds and Drain, arrived at the gun position, wheeled the gun round, limbered up and brought one of the Howitzers back to the Allied position. However, one of the drivers, Ben Cobey, was shot and killed in the process. Reynolds, Drain and Driver Frederick Luke, who had accompanied them, were all recommended for the VC and received it (although there was some consternation that Driver Cobey was not awarded a posthumous VC). Reynolds's VC was announced in the *London Gazette* on 16 November 1914, while Drain's and Luke's were announced more than a week later, on 25 November. Reynolds was later promoted to major but died in hospital on 23 February 1916 of septicemia from gas poisoning. Drain and Luke both survived the war, having been promoted to sergeant.

Drain's VC was presented to him by George V at Locon, northern France, on 1 December 1914. The young soldier had little time to prepare for such a momentous event: he was in the trenches near Béthune when he was informed that The King wanted to see him. Without even time to clean himself up, he was soon in the inspection line at Locon, where he was presented with his VC. Back in Barking, residents were immensely proud of their East End boy made good. On his return, he was given a hero's welcome, an 'illuminated address', a purse filled with sovereigns and a watch at Barking Town Hall. In this instance, the illuminated address was a fine-quality, hand-decorated parchment recording Barking's gratitude to Drain.

In 1919, Drain was demobbed (he was discharged from the Reserve five years later) and in the same year married Patricia Murray at Poplar, east London, and the couple went on to have a son and a daughter. After leaving the Army, Drain did a number of different jobs: he worked as a messenger in Whitehall from 1919 to 1920, as a fish porter in Billingsgate from 1920 to 1924, and as a London bus driver from 1924 until his retirement.

Drain's job as a bus driver led to him being charged with obstruction after he was accused of blocking a tramway in Plaistow with his bus. However, in court on 28 October 1929 and defended by Brett Cloutman VC, Drain claimed he could not drive off because his path was blocked by cyclists, and he was acquitted and awarded two guineas' costs. In 1931, he was appointed as a special constable in Barking and in the same year, on 5 October, and while wearing his bus driver's uniform, he was presented to Prince Albert, the future George VI, as part of Barking's Charter Day celebrations.

Drain and Luke remained firm friends for decades and both attended the VC Centenary Service at Westminster Abbey on 25 June 1956. While living in Barking, Drain died in nearby Dagenham on 26 July 1975, three months short of his eightieth birthday. He is buried at Ripplesdale Cemetery, Barking.

Long after Drain's death the people of Barking have continued to celebrate the life and achievements of one of their favourite sons. In 1986, his career featured in an exhibition by local library services in honour of VC recipients from Essex. There is a plaque outside his last home and a bronze statue of Drain was unveiled in the Broadway, Barking, on 10 November 2009. Drain's name is also on a memorial at the Royal Artillery Chapel, Woolwich, south-east London.

SECOND LIEUTENANT (LATER CAPTAIN) JAMES EDGAR LEACH

Army: The Manchester Regiment
DATE OF BRAVERY: 29 OCTOBER 1914
GAZETTED: 22 DECEMBER 1914
Special feature of the VC: a splendid award for the first year of the Great War.

James Edgar Leach was born at Bowerham Barracks, Lancaster, Lancashire, on 27 July 1894. He was the son of Colour-Sergeant James Leach, of The King's Own (Royal Lancaster) Regiment, and his wife Amelia (*née* Summerfield), a bookbinder. James Leach Sr served in the West Indies from 1880 to 1881 and saw action in the Second Anglo-Boer War from 1900 to 1901, before being discharged later in 1901 and becoming an agent for the Royal Liverpool Friendly Society Insurance Company. James Leach Jr, who had four brothers and a sister, was educated at Bowerham Council School in Lancaster and Moston Lane Municipal School, Manchester. His family had moved to Blackley, Manchester, in 1901 before moving again, this time to Leicester, in 1907. Leach worked as an apprentice chemist before enlisting into the 3rd (Special Reserve) Battalion, the Northamptonshire Regiment, in August 1910.

At the time that he enlisted, Leach stated that he was a fishmonger, added two years to his actual age and said his parents were dead (he gave no next of kin). In January 1911, Leach joined the 2nd Battalion, the Northamptonshire Regiment, and, on 15 March of that year, transferred to the 1st Battalion. He was promoted to lance-corporal in November and, in June 1914, was promoted to corporal. At the outbreak of the First World War in August 1914, Leach and his battalion were based at Aldershot, Hampshire, and on 13 August were part of the 2nd Brigade of the 1st Division that landed in Le Havre, France. The following month his battalion took part in the fighting at the Battle of the Aisne and, soon afterwards, Leach was promoted to sergeant and Mentioned in Despatches. On 1 October, as a result of his sterling work on the battlefield and his leadership skills, he was commissioned in the field and transferred to the 2nd Battalion, the Manchester Regiment. Just eight days later, he transferred to the regiment's 1st Battalion as a second lieutenant. On 23 October, he joined the battalion on the Western Front and, because it was short of officers, he was given command of A Company.

By late October 1914, the war was going reasonably well for the Allies in northern France and the British II Corps had crossed the Béthune-La Bassée Canal and was fighting its way northwards. The Corps' aim was to reach the Lille-La Bassée road supported by the French 10th Army. However, the Germans had ambitions of their own and to the south of Armentières they intended to break through the Allied line in what turned into the Battle of La Bassée. Although the Germans succeeded in pushing the line back, they failed in their ultimate aim of breaking through the line.

After two days of heavy fighting from 27 October, in which the Germans captured and then lost the village of Neuve Chapelle, there was further intense fighting on 29 October. That morning, the Germans shelled the Manchesters near Festubert, west of La Bassée, and during one prolonged assault, under cover of a smokescreen, the enemy managed to enter the British trenches. This was despite a heroic defence from the Manchesters, who lost two officers in the fighting. Two attempts were made to recapture the lost trench but both failed.

At 2 p.m., Leach, aged twenty, and Sergeant John Hogan, aged thirty, aided by ten volunteers, mounted a third attempt to recapture the trench. Initially, they surprised the enemy and then worked up the trench, skilfully going from one side to the other with fixed bayonets, until the trench was back in Allied hands. During close-quarter fighting, the twelve men killed eight of the enemy, wounded two and captured sixteen as Prisoners of War, according to their later citation.

Word soon spread of their bravery and VCs were announced for both Leach and Hogan on 22 December 1914; a surprise Christmas 'gift' as both had simply expected to be Mentioned in Despatches.

Leach later explained in more detail to the press what had happened on 29 October. That morning, he had been in an advanced trench capable of holding some thirty-five men. The advanced trench was about 150 yards ahead of the main trench and only 120 yards from the enemy. Leach estimated that his position had been attacked by some 250 enemy troops who made a 'wailing' noise as they advanced. Although he thought the Manchesters had cut down some 150 of the enemy, the remaining 100 German soldiers seized the advanced trench, killing a dozen British soldiers in the process. Afterwards, the enemy made their way down the communication trench and eventually took the main trench too.

Leach explained that, on learning that the 2nd Manchester's position was to be taken over the next day by the Gurkhas, he felt he should try to recapture the lost trench. When he asked for volunteers, Hogan and ten other men agreed to join him. The aim, as they advanced, with Leach clutching his officer's pistol, had been to try to push the enemy back and shoot them as they retreated. This worked and meant that they were also able to free some British PoWs who had been taken earlier that day. Leach estimated the raiding party had captured fourteen enemy soldiers and a German officer, along with twenty wounded.

Leach also told how, having driven the enemy through the last traverse, he was surprised to hear an English voice calling 'Don't shoot, sir!' The words had come from one of his own men who had been taken prisoner in the morning. The man had been sent forward by a German officer who had told him that the enemy wished to surrender. This was accepted and when Leach and Hogan finally emerged from their trench Leach's cap had been shot to pieces and the scarf he had worn around his neck had been shredded.

During his VC action Leach had become badly concussed and, on 25 November, he was evacuated to Britain for treatment at Lady Evelyn Mason's Hospital for Officers in central London. He underwent Medical Boards on 3 and 27 December that both found him unfit for service and so he went on leave. During his leave, he was promoted to lieutenant on 11 December, less than two weeks before his VC was announced. While in Manchester, Leach returned to Moston Lane, his former school, where he received a hero's welcome. Additionally, in early February 1915, Leach took part in a recruiting drive in Manchester. He was presented with his award by George V at an investiture at Buckingham Palace on 13 February 1915, while Hogan, his comrade, received his decoration from The King exactly a week later.

After being declared fit for general service on 1 March, he also took part in the training of troops at Cleethorpes, Lincolnshire. On 15 April, he returned to his battalion in France, only to be concussed again two days later and evacuated to Britain a second time, on this occasion on the *St Andrew* on 17 April. After being treated at Taplow Priory in Buckinghamshire, Leach was again found unfit for service and he was sent on leave until 20 June. On 21 June, a Medical Board found him fit for light duties and he was posted to 15th Royal Fusiliers, 7th Reserve Brigade, at Purfleet, Essex. On 20 August, he was posted to No. 1 Army School of Signalling, HQ First Army Central Force, Caius College, Cambridge. Here, he apparently met Gladys Digby: the couple married in Cambridge on 23 December 1915. Sadly, the marriage was short-lived because his bride died just months later. However, on 3 March 1917, Leach married a second time, on this occasion to Josephine Butt, the daughter of a Grimsby trawler owner, at Old Clee Parish Church, Cleethorpes. The couple went on to have two sons and a daughter.

On 1 January 1917, Leach was promoted to temporary captain and on 24 March he returned to France to resume active service. The next day he went to 30th Infantry Base Depot and on 17 April he rejoined the 2nd Manchesters. After completing a two-week Lewis gun course ending on 2 July, he was medically examined but was again found unfit for active service. Three Medical Boards in Britain on 13 September, 16 October and 20 November still found him unfit and he was in hospital for much of this time, including a spell at Craiglockhart Hospital in Edinburgh, a military institution that specialised in treating nervous illness. Fellow patients at Craiglockhart in 1917 included the war poets Wilfred Owen and Siegfried Sassoon. On 2 January 1918, a Medical Board found him permanently unfit for active service and he was placed on half pay from 9 February. The next month he took up the position of Adjutant, South-West London Cadet Battalion. Finally, after more than three years of poor health, and having apparently suffered from some kind of mental breakdown, a Medical Board on 24 July found him unfit for any further general service and he was discharged from the Army, after eight years' service, on 7 August 1918. Because he had lied about his age from the start of his military career, Leach was still only twenty-four years old.

After the war, Leach did a large number of wide-ranging jobs. On 6 January 1921 and at a time of great tensions in Ireland, he joined the Royal Irish Constabulary, Auxiliary Division (the so-called 'black and tans'), where he was stationed at Glengarrif, Co. Cork. The following year, he returned to England and was employed by his father-in-law as a clerk at Grimsby fish docks. At the same time, he studied to become a Fellow of the Chartered Institute of Secretaries (FICS). From 1927, he worked at the Bank of England in London, only to lose his job because of redundancies during the Great Depression of 1930–31. He worked for some three years as a chartered secretary with an exporting business, during which time he worked in the South Pacific while his family remained in Britain. From 1934, Leach worked with the stockbrokers Foster and Braithwaite, in the City of London. However, after the death of his wealthy father-in-law, Walter Butt, in 1936, he was able to give up work and study for the Bar. While training, he was cited as the co-respondent in a divorce case and, having had an affair with the wife of a company director, had costs of £500 awarded against him at Devon Assizes. Leach's own marriage also ended, and he was divorced at a time when such an event was rare and caused considerable embarrassment to the family. After the divorce, Leach worked as a chartered secretary and served as a councillor in Hammersmith, then part of Middlesex.

After the outbreak of the Second World War in 1939, Leach worked for the Ministry of Aircraft Production before switching in 1943 to a job at the Osram lighting factory in Hammersmith. From early December 1941, Leach served as a lieutenant in the 27th City of London (Roehampton) Battalion of the Home Guard, a role he performed for fifteen months. Meanwhile, Leach's elder son, a third generation to be called James, who had been commissioned into the Royal Fusiliers in September 1937, also served throughout the war and survived the conflict. Leach himself had married for a third time in 1944, this time to Mabel Folland. After the war, Leach worked for the Danish Bacon Company and was a Hammersmith councillor from 1949 to 1955.

Leach attended several VC reunions, which included the Centenary Review of 1956 and a dinner held in the same year by the Manchester Regiment to honour their surviving VC recipients (at this event he was a guest speaker). He made his last major public appearance on 23 April 1958 when he was introduced to Queen Elizabeth The Queen Mother at the bicentenary celebrations of the Manchester Regiment, held at Warley Barracks in Brentwood, Essex.

Leach died at his home in Shepherd's Bush, west London, on 15 August 1958, aged sixty-four, leaving a widow and, apparently, a total of six children from his second and third marriages. He was cremated at Mortlake Crematorium, west London, and his ashes were scattered in its Garden of Remembrance.

SEPOY (LATER SUBADAR)
KHUDADAD KHAN

Indian Army: 129th Duke of Connaught's Own Baluchis, attached to
the 3rd Cavalry Brigade, British Cavalry Corps

DATE OF BRAVERY: 31 OCTOBER 1914

GAZETTED: 7 DECEMBER 1914

Special feature of the VC: the iconic first VC awarded to an Indian
recipient and also the first to a Muslim.

Khudadad Khan was born on 26 October 1888 in Dab Tehsil, Chakwal District, Jhelum, Punjab, India (now Pakistan). He enlisted as a sepoy in the 129th Duke of Connaught's Own Baluchis, Indian Army, on 3 August 1914 at a time when the regiment was recruiting on the North-West Frontier.

Initially, Sepoy (the equivalent to a private) Khan was sent to the Suez Canal Zone but he was then diverted to France because of the urgent need for more Allied troops. On 18 October 1914, he moved with the Ferozepore Brigade from Orleans, France, to be attached to the British Cavalry Corps that was attempting to hold the line between Zandvoorde and Ploegsteert Wood, Belgium. On 22 October, his regiment joined the 3rd Cavalry Brigade.

By late October 1914, fighting was raging all along the frontline as both sides tried to gain the advantage during the First Battle of Ypres. On 30 October, the enemy repulsed the advancing British 2nd Cavalry Division and captured the Belgian town of Hollebeke. However, the Germans were determined to push forwards as they tried to break through the Gheluvelt sector of the Ypres Salient.

Early on 31 October, during further fighting, one of the Baluchi regiment's two Maxim machine-guns was destroyed by enemy fire in an attack that had wounded a British officer. Also wounded by the relentless enemy fire was Sepoy Khudadad Khan, then twenty-six, one of six men from his detachment who had been tasked with manning the second Maxim gun.

As the battle intensified, Khan shrugged off his serious injuries and continued to work his gun as German shells rained down on the six men. One by one, Havildar Ghulam Mahomed, Sepoy Lal Sher, Sepoy Said Ahmed, Sepoy Kassib and Sepoy Afsar Khan were killed by enemy fire. When his position was eventually overrun by the Germans, Khan initially feigned death, but not before putting the machine-gun out of action so that the much-prized weapon would not fall into enemy hands. Eventually, he crawled back to rejoin his company and to receive medical aid.

Khan was treated in hospital for his wounds and then transferred for further treatment to the UK, where he spent several weeks at the Indian Convalescent Home, New Milton, Hampshire. During the battle, 164 Baluchis were killed or wounded and sixty-four others were missing in action. A further three British officers were killed and three more wounded, while three Indian officers were killed and three wounded.

Khan's VC was announced in the *London Gazette* on 7 December 1914, when his brief citation stated:

> On 31st October, 1914, at Hollebeke, Belgium, the British Officer in charge of the detachment having been wounded, and the other gun put out of action by a shell, Sepoy Khudadad, though himself wounded, remained working his gun until all the other five men of the gun detachment had been killed.

Khan was both the first Indian and the first Muslim to be awarded the VC: he received it as an Indian under the terms of the Royal Warrant of 1911, which extended the reward to native troops. Previously, Indians who showed exceptional gallantry received the Indian Order of Merit. The five men who had died manning the second machine-gun on 31 October received other posthumous gallantry awards.

Initially, Khan was too weak to attend his planned investiture, but he eventually received his VC from George V at Buckingham

Palace on 26 January 1915. On the same day, the *Daily Mail* ran an article heralding Khan as a hero: 'This is Sepoy Khudadad ... He was the first Indian soldier to win the coveted honour of the VC through gallantry on the field of battle. He worked a gun single-handed although wounded. All his comrades were killed.'

In 1917, Khan was promoted to jemadar and the following year was made senior jemadar. He survived the war and, in 1919, was promoted to subadar. After retiring in 1921, he worked as a farmer and in 1956 he took part in the VC centenary celebrations in London.

Khan, who was married twice and had two sons and a daughter with his second wife, died at the Military Hospital, Rawalpindi, Pakistan on 8 March 1971, aged eighty-two. He is buried in a suitably impressive grave in a cemetery in the Punjab, Pakistan. His name is engraved on the Memorial Gates, Hyde Park Corner, London, and there is a statue in his honour at the Army Museum in Rawalpindi.

For a time, Khan's medal group was on display at the Army Museum in Rawalpindi, but it remained in the ownership of his descendants. When the relative decided to offer the medal group for sale, I was able to secure it in a private deal.

We should never forget that Muslims made an immense contribution to the Allied effort during the Great War, and beyond. Of the 1.3 million Indians who constituted the volunteer force during the 1914–18 global conflict, approximately 400,000 were Muslims. It has been estimated that some 50,000 Indians were injured and 8,500 killed on the Western Front alone. Around a third to a half of these war-dead were Muslims, who fought – and sometimes died – alongside their fellow Hindu and Sikh countrymen. Many of those who went missing in action, and are named on the Menin Gate war memorial in Belgium, were Muslim.

In a world when a tiny minority of Muslims – notably those fighting for Islamic State (IS) and those extremists responsible for terrorist acts around the world – tarnish their religion, my VC purchase provided a wonderful opportunity for people to recognise the many, many loyal and brave Muslims who have risked, and sometimes given, their lives for Britain, its Allies and for wider freedoms.

In 2014, two former heads of the Army called for greater recognition of Khan's bravery as the first Muslim soldier to be awarded the VC. Their call was intended as a 'riposte' to the 'sickening extremism' of IS militants. General Lord Dannatt and General Lord Richards led a group of peers, MPs, historians and religious leaders who argued that children should be told about the role played by Muslim troops in the Great War.

In November 2014, Lord Ahmad, then the communities minister, unveiled a commemorative stone at the National Memorial Arboretum in Sepoy Khan's memory. He said: 'In honouring the courage of Khudadad Khan we not only remember our shared history, we also cherish the long tradition of Muslims fighting bravely alongside British soldiers, for a just cause in the service of this country.' I echo every word of those sentiments.

CAPTAIN ARTHUR FORBES GORDON KILBY

Army: The South Staffordshire Regiment
DATE OF BRAVERY: 25 SEPTEMBER 1915
GAZETTED: 30 MARCH 1916
Special feature of the VC: an outstanding posthumous award for the Battle of Loos.

Arthur Forbes Gordon Kilby was born in Cheltenham, Gloucestershire, on 3 February 1885. He was the only son of Sandford Kilby, from the Customs and Salt Department of the Bengal Police in India, and his wife Alice (*née* Scott). Arthur Kilby was educated at Bilton Grange, near Rugby, and Winchester College, Hampshire, before preparing for a military career by spending some time in Frankfurt, Germany. Kilby then attended the Royal Military College, Sandhurst.

In August 1905, aged twenty, he was commissioned into the 1st Battalion, the South Staffordshire Regiment, as a second lieutenant. On 31 October 1907, Kilby was promoted to lieutenant and on 1 April 1910 he was promoted to captain. Kilby was a talented linguist, speaking French, Spanish, German and Hungarian – the only officer in the Army to be fluent in the latter language at the outbreak of the war. He was also an enthusiastic ornithologist and had a passion for traditional architecture, declaring York Cathedral one of the most beautiful in England.

In December 1910, Kilby transferred to the 2nd Battalion of his regiment, which had then just returned from South Africa. After the outbreak of the Great War in August 1914, his battalion was one of the first to embark for the Western Front. Kilby arrived in France on 13 August as part of the British Expeditionary Force and, within just twelve days, he saw his first action at Maroilles. On the following day – 26 August – his brigade was ordered to withdraw and Kilby was sent to the rearguard to supervise their retreat. After being subjected to intense fire from the German artillery, he was badly concussed by a shell. In the chaos, Kilby became separated from his unit and wandered alone for hours without food and water, before collapsing again.

After being found, he was treated for shell-shock, spending nearly a month in hospital before rejoining his battalion on 24 September. By this time, his battalion was involved in the Battle of the Aisne. Apparently feeling guilty at missing so much action in the previous four weeks, including the Battle of the Marne, he volunteered for several solitary sniping expeditions. This was highly dangerous work and yet, on at least two occasions, he penetrated deep behind enemy lines in order to bring back valuable information.

There was to be no let-up for his battalion: in October, it moved north to the Ypres sector before heading north-west of Becelaere. After leading a counter-attack, Kilby was praised by his Commanding Officer: 'The British line being reported to be broken,

Captain Kilby was sent with his Company to the point of danger.' Although this report proved to be premature, the troops to the right of Kilby's new position did subsequently fall back from their trenches, which the Germans thereupon occupied. Kilby at once took action as effective as it was gallant, executing 'a brilliant counter-attack, in which, by rapid fire, he bluffed the enemy, whose force was several times the strength of his own, and turned them out of the re-occupied trenches and a wood which they had just taken.' This action gained immediate recognition, the following message being passed down the lines to him: 'Bravo, Kilby! Your colonel is proud of you and your Company. Hearty congratulations on good work.'

On 12 November, there was severe fighting around the position held by 6th Brigade. At about 6.30 a.m., the enemy made a surprise attack on the French 17th and 18th Divisions, on the British left, and forced them back some 600 yards. This exposed the extreme left of the British line, where the 2nd South Staffordshires were the flank battalion. After the Germans penetrated behind the British line, both Kilby and Captain Johnson commanded a group of men who held their trenches all day in the most difficult of circumstances. At one point, the position had been critical, but eventually the South Staffordshires extended their line and fell slightly back to re-connect with the French 18th Division.

For his outstanding courage and leadership, Kilby was awarded the Military Cross (MC), as well as subsequently being Mentioned in Despatches by Field Marshal Sir John French on 14 January 1915:

> The gap that was caused by the retirement of the French formed a gap between the trenches held by the South Staffordshire Regiment and the new line taken up by the French. The gap was filled by a portion of the South Staffords, and this exposed line was held by a portion of the Regiment all day. This manoeuvre was supervised by Captains A. F. G. Kilby and S. G. Johnson,

both of the South Staffords. Both these officers were wounded on
this occasion.

In fact, Kilby had been wounded in the right arm and lung by a rifle
bullet and was forced to return to England for treatment. Although
he never fully recovered the strength in his right hand, he rejoined
his battalion in May 1915. Once again, he became involved in the
thick of the fighting and, in late September, he was recommended
for the Distinguished Service Order (DSO). The original recommendation stated:

> For consistent good work, making some very useful reconnaissances,
> imbuing all ranks with keenness by his example. On the night of
> the 5th to 6th September, he went out along the canal tow-path
> under cover of darkness, accompanied by Lieutenant Thompson,
> 1st King's, and closely reconnoitred the German position on the
> embankment redoubt and brought back most useful information.
> The reconnaissance was a very dangerous one, as the canal bank is a
> hot-bed of snipers, and it required the greatest skill and courage to
> get right up to the German position as Captain Kilby did. This is
> only one specific instance. This officer constantly made night recon-
> naissances of this nature.

However, Kilby never received his DSO because of the regulations –
then and now – which stipulate that this award cannot be awarded
posthumously. For before a decision on his recommendation could
be taken, the chaotic events of 25 September 1915 – the opening
day of the Battle of Loos – intervened.

After four days of artillery bombardment, the 2nd Battalion,
South Staffordshire Regiment, was in the frontline at Cuinchy,
immediately south of the La Bassée Canal. At 5.35 a.m., some fifteen minutes before a discharge of poisonous gas was due to begin,
the officer in charge of the gas on the 6th Brigade front considered

the wind so unfavourable that he declined to turn on the gas cylinders and reported the situation to the 2nd Division Headquarters. However, a reply came through that the gas attack must be carried out regardless. The cylinders were opened at 6 a.m., but in some areas the gas-cloud was so dense that, despite wearing smoke-helmets, the South Staffordshire's companies were badly affected. Many men became violently sick and 130 of them were unable to take any further part in the day's operations.

The South Staffordshires' attack began at 6.30 a.m.: men from both A and B companies crossed no-man's land but, on reaching the first German wire entanglement, found it unbroken. Furthermore, they faced a fierce machine-gun and rifle fire. On the left, C Company, under Captain Kilby, went forward along the narrow tow-path beside the canal despite most of the men being badly gassed. Kilby and his men were under intense enemy fire from both sides of the canal and, early on in the fighting, Kilby was wounded in the hand, but still he and his men pressed on towards the enemy wire. As they were exposed to an onslaught of stick grenades thrown at them from the enemy redoubt, one of Kilby's feet was blown off. Yet still he defied terrible pain to urge his men on, even firing at the enemy with his rifle.

The situation, however, eventually became utterly hopeless. The company's repeated attempts to breach the enemy positions were repelled and, at 8 a.m., orders were given to withdraw. Only twenty men succeeded in making it back to the British trenches and the battalion suffered eleven officers and 280 other men killed or wounded. Kilby was one of the many whose whereabouts were not known, despite his men carrying out a prolonged search for him. In fact, after nightfall on the day he fell, forty of the forty-nine fit men volunteered to take part in the search for the dead and missing, during which they came under intermittent enemy fire.

Colonel Moss, the battalion's Commanding Officer, wrote a letter to Sandford Kilby, the missing officer's father, in the aftermath of the battle. He stated:

The Regiment had to attack the very strongest section of the German line. We started under very unfavourable conditions, as everyone was suffering badly from gas before we charged. Your son led his company against the embankment redoubt with the most magnificent gallantry. He was wounded at the very start, but still insisted in cheering on his men right up to the German wire, which our guns had been unable to destroy. He was again wounded, but still continued to cheer on his men. This is the last we know of him.

When no trace of Kilby could be found, he was posted as missing, presumed killed. He had died aged thirty.

For his gallantry at Loos, Kilby was recommended for a posthumous VC by Brigadier Daly, of the 6th Brigade. Daly also wrote to Kilby's parents, telling them:

He had such a sound military instinct, serene courage, and unbounded confidence. It was a great hope that the search parties would find him. No men could have done more; they all loved him, and they all risked their lives in the search ... In all the losses of friends one has, there has hardly been a day since the 25th September that your son has not been in my thoughts. Amongst the many gallant officers in this brigade he always stood out ... Before the big fight your son's company was often in that part of the trenches just opposite the railway embankment immediately south of La Bassée Canal. He asked me himself if ever there was a serious attack to let him attack at that point. It was a very tough nut, but he was convinced it could be done. He knew the ground well, and had all his plans cut and dried. I used to go up there with him and examine the German position and talk it all out. If anyone could have done it your son was the man. When the orders came for the big attack I made him promise me that he would not go over until at least half the company had gone; it was so essential to have his brain and judgment to direct the men and not get knocked out at once. On the actual day, as you know, things went wrong with the gas, and my own idea is that your son realized that it was going to be a failure, and went in front to lead what he considered was a forlorn hope, for he was leading the men when last seen.

Kilby's VC was announced on 30 March 1916 when his citation read:

> For most conspicuous bravery. Captain Kilby was specially selected, at his own request, and on account of the gallantry which he had previously displayed on many occasions, to attack with his company a strong enemy redoubt. The company charged along the narrow towpath, headed by Captain Kilby, who, though wounded at the outset, continued to lead his men right up to the enemy wire under a devastating machine-gun fire and a shower of bombs. Here he was shot down, but, although his foot had been blown off, he continued to cheer on his men and to use a rifle.
>
> Captain Kilby has been missing since the date of the performance of this great act of valour, and his death has now to be presumed.

Kilby's VC was presented to his father by George V in a private ceremony in the ballroom of Buckingham Palace on 11 July 1916. His body was recovered by the Germans where he fell, and buried by the side of the tow-path. The enemy acknowledged his heroism by erecting a simple wooden cross which they inscribed: 'The Kilby Family May Think Of Their Son With Pride, As We Remember Him With Respect.' It was also reported, but never confirmed, that another British regiment had erected a cross at the scene of the battle in memory of Kilby, Lieutenant D. M. Williams and thirteen members of their company. It is believed to have been inscribed: 'For King and Country – died like heroes.'

Long after the war ended – on 19 February 1929 – Kilby's body was found and identified, and he was later reburied in the Arras Road Cemetery at Rodincourt, France. His name is also listed on the Loos Memorial at Dud Corner Cemetery, north-west of Loos. Additionally, a marble memorial, with his bust, was erected in his honour at St Nicholas's Chapel, York Minster, the cathedral that he had always admired so much.

TEMPORARY CAPTAIN ANGUS BUCHANAN

Army: The South Wales Borderers
DATE OF BRAVERY: 5 APRIL 1916
GAZETTED: 26 SEPTEMBER 1916
Special feature of the VC: Buchanan became well known as 'the blind VC', the only recipient of the decoration to have lost his sight in action during the Great War.

Angus Buchanan was born in Coleford, Gloucestershire, on 11 August 1894. His father, Peter, a doctor, had served as a major and company commander in the Glosters. His mother Hannah (*née* Williams) had been married before, to a tin works' manager, with whom she had four daughters and a son. After being widowed, she married Peter Buchanan and the couple had two sons together, Angus and Hugh. The Buchanans were a well-off, middle-class family: they lived in a large house, holidayed regularly, had enough money to send their children to private school and Peter Buchanan even owned a motor car. Educated locally, at St John's Boys School in Coleford and Monmouth Grammar School in Gwent, Angus Buchanan was a talented sportsman, captained his school rugby team and was a member of the cricket XI. He won a scholarship to read classics at Jesus College, Oxford, where he embarked upon university life with enthusiasm and played for the university's A team during the 1913–14 season.

After the outbreak of the First World War, he was commissioned as a temporary second lieutenant in the 4th Battalion, the South Wales Borderers, on 27 November 1914. Buchanan left for Gallipoli on 28 June 1915 and was promoted to temporary lieutenant the same day. However, he was wounded at Suvla Bay on 7 August, soon after B Company landed, and sent to a hospital in Cairo, Egypt.

In early December 1915, and having been made a temporary captain, he returned to the peninsula and was soon back in the thick of the action. After taking part in the eventual evacuation of the peninsula, he was twice Mentioned in Despatches and was awarded the Military Cross (MC) on 7 January 1916 for bravery at Helles, when in command of B Company in trenches east of Gully Ravine. Unfortunately, neither the battalion war diary nor the *London Gazette* indicates exactly what bravery Buchanan showed in order to be awarded his MC.

Buchanan arrived in Mesopotamia (now Iraq) on 4 March 1916 and it was there, on 5 April, that he took part in the action for which he received the VC. On that day, the British advanced on the Turkish positions north of the Tigris River at Hanna, but found they had been evacuated. The British then continued west to the next Turkish position at Fallahiyeh. During the fighting, one officer, Captain Stewart Hemingway, was seriously wounded. Two soldiers went out into no-man's land to try to rescue Hemingway but one was shot and fell to the ground wounded.

Buchanan, then aged twenty-one, broke cover and ran some 150 yards to reach Hemingway. With the aid of the uninjured soldier who had initially gone to assist Hemingway, he carried the wounded officer back to safety despite being under a heavy fire. Buchanan then raced out into no-man's land a second time to bring the wounded soldier back to cover, once again under a heavy fire.

Buchanan was wounded in the arm during the fighting against the Turks later on the day of his VC action and his Commanding Officer wrote a letter to his parents saying:

> I regret to say that your son Angus was wounded in the arm on the
> evening of 5 April, when we were attacking and driving back the

Turks, but I am very glad to tell you that the wound was only a slight one. The real reason for my letter is a far more pleasant one. During our advance in the morning we came under very heavy machine-gun fire, and suffered rather heavily. One of our officers, Lieut. Hemingway, was badly wounded, and lying in the open about 150 yds from cover. Your son, seeing his condition, and that the effort on the part of two men to carry him in had ended in one of them being shot, himself left his trench, and with the help of the unwounded man, brought Hemingway into the trench under a heavy fire.

During the journey the man with him was wounded in the foot, but got into the trench. Angus then went back and fetched in the other man who had been wounded. I have forwarded a recommendation in his case for the Victoria Cross, and the Brigadier has sent in one and supported it. We sincerely hope he may be awarded it, but there is always a chance that he may only be awarded an honour of lesser degree. I should like to tell you that I have previously brought his name to the notice of the General for gallant conduct at Helles on 7 January.

Buchanan's wound was not quite as insignificant as his CO made out: he had to be evacuated from the theatre of operations and sent to India for hospital treatment. Furthermore, he was not able to rejoin the battalion in Mesopotamia until 1 August. Hemingway, meanwhile, had died from his wounds on 6 April 1916, the day after being rescued: he is commemorated on the Basra memorial, now situated in southern Iraq.

On 24 September 1916, while the battalion was moving from Sheikh Sa'ad to Amara, Buchanan was again evacuated, although it is unclear whether this resulted from problems with his previous wound or whether he had again been wounded in action.

His evacuation, however, came just two days before the official announcement of his VC in the *London Gazette*. The news was warmly received in his home town of Coleford: the bell in the church tower rang out in tribute and the announcement relating to his VC was also flashed up on the screen of his local cinema during a screening of the recently released film of the Battle of the Somme.

On 13 February 1917, Buchanan was wounded for what seems to have been the fourth time – on this occasion far more seriously than previously. While taking part in fighting after having advanced from a temporary trench near Kut, a sniper's bullet hit Buchanan's right temple. He received immediate attention on the battlefield before being evacuated to a clearing station. Eventually, he was taken to a hospital in India where surgeons saved his life, but not his sight. From then onwards, Buchanan was blind in both eyes. Throughout his ordeal, he was cared for attentively by his batman, Private Perry, whom Buchanan later insisted had saved his life. On 2 September 1917, as a result of his serious injuries, Buchanan relinquished his commission but retained his rank of captain.

He was presented with his VC on 8 November 1917 at Durdham Down, Bristol. A crowd estimated at 60,000 strong had gathered for the investiture by George V of 127 recipients of gallantry medals and other honours. Each decorated man was clapped as he approached the royal dais, which was draped in imperial purple and bore gilded lions' heads. However, the loudest round of applause, from soldiers and civilians alike, was reserved for a uniformed officer – Buchanan – who had to be led to and from the dais by a uniformed chaperone who kept a firm grip on the man's left arm.

At the investiture, Buchanan had both the VC and the MC pinned on his chest by The King. It is believed that the man at his side may have been his batman, Private Perry, but this has never been confirmed. The very next day Buchanan appeared in his home town of Coleford, where he received a hero's welcome. He was also presented with a gold watch inscribed in Braille with the words: 'A Tribute to Captain Buchanan, VC, MC, by Dean Foresters, 9th November 1917.'

After returning from the war, Buchanan attended St Dunstan's hospital, supported by the charity Blind Veterans UK, where he learned Braille and typewriting, and where a fund-raising postcard, costing 1d and bearing a drawing of him sporting his VC, was issued in his honour. Next, Buchanan returned to Oxford where he studied for a degree in law and became a member of his college rowing eight. In those days, text books were not in Braille so they all had to be read to him by tutors and fellow students.

After gaining his BA and MA in October 1921 and then qualifying as a solicitor, he started a practice in his home town with another solicitor, although eventually Buchanan ran it on his own. Because of his disability, he did not accept criminal work and instead specialised in conveyancing and estate work. He enjoyed accompanied walking holidays throughout the UK, as well as Gilbert and Sullivan operettas, and he was vice-chairman of Coleford British Legion.

Buchanan's friends said that he never complained about his disability and remained both cheerful and determined to lead as normal a life as possible: he was anxious not to be a burden on his family and friends and saw his loss of sight as a challenge rather than a serious handicap. Buchanan was considered to be the best salmon fisherman in the area and had a detailed knowledge of the River Wye. He also played bridge, using Braille playing cards.

Buchanan, who never married, was fêted nationally as a hero long after the war ended. In 1929, he attended The Prince of Wales's dinner in the Royal Gallery of the House of Lords. After a surprisingly fulfilled life, he was taken ill at work one day and died a few hours later in Gloucester Royal Infirmary on 1 March 1944, aged forty-nine. He was buried, with full military honours, at Coleford Church. His gravestone said he 'died of old wounds', having never fully recovered from his wartime injuries.

Two days after his death, an 'obituary letter' appeared in *The Times* which began: 'Few men have faced adversity with greater cheerfulness and patience than Angus Buchanan.' The letter also praised his 'fortitude', and stated:

In walks in the pleasant countryside around Oxford or in Monmouthshire, I came to understand how cheerfulness can overcome difficulties. Never a murmur about his afflictions, but always a determination to lead a normal life and in it to share with his friends their pleasures and pains. For him there was no such thing as an obstacle in his path.

Furthermore, a colleague of Buchanan's who had worked as a clerk in his solicitor's office, said: 'He is a shining example to the people of Coleford as to what can be done in triumphing over affliction, and making a positive contribution to life and the district and his country.'

This quote and other material in this write-up comes from an excellent tribute to Buchanan in Gerald Gliddon's book, *VCs of the First World War: The Sideshows*. There is an equally splendid, and even more detailed, write-up on Buchanan's life and career by W. Alister Williams in his book *Heart of a Dragon: The VCs of Wales and the Welsh Regiments 1914–82*.

Buchanan is commemorated at several locations: his name is listed at Harvard Chapel, Brecon Cathedral, Wales; there is a memorial tablet at St John's Church, Coleford; the Buchanan Memorial recreation ground, purchased in 1919 as a tribute to the town's hero, is named after him; and Buchanan Close in Monmouth, Gwent, is also named after him.

I purchased Buchanan's medals privately in 2013 and I feel privileged to be the custodian of the decorations belonging to such a courageous and spirited man. I was particularly delighted to become the owner of the Buchanan medal group because, as a philanthropist and for personal reasons, I have long supported charities for blind and partially sighted people. My own mother, Rene, who has macular degeneration, has formed a local group for people with sight loss to help each other through this difficult period in their lives.

Recently, I discovered that there is not only a wonderful photograph of Buchanan receiving his medals from The King at his November 1917 investiture, but the event was also filmed. The recording can be viewed on the internet on the British Pathé website. In the footage, Buchanan can be seen receiving his medals from George V, saluting The King and then being led down the steps from the royal dais by his chaperone.

One eyewitness said:

> The investiture was that of a hero who has been sorely stricken in performing deeds of the utmost gallantry ... Unhappily, Capt Buchanan is now blind, and had to be led to the dais. After decorating him, His Majesty kept him for some time in sympathetic conversation. The huge assembly also showed their sympathy with the gallant officer, according him a special ovation.

PRIVATE WILLIAM BOYNTON BUTLER

Army: The Prince of Wales's Own (West Yorkshire Regiment)
DATE OF BRAVERY: 6 AUGUST 1917
GAZETTED: 17 OCTOBER 1917
Special feature of the VC: An extremely fine award for unselfish gallantry on the Western Front.

William Boynton Butler was born in Armley, Leeds, Yorkshire, on 20 November 1894. He was the son of William Boynton, a colliery worker, and his wife Caroline (*née* Butler). In fact, his parents married shortly after his birth, by which point he had been given his mother's surname as his own surname and his father's surname as his second Christian name. William Butler's childhood was spent at his family's modest home in Hunslet Carr, Leeds, where he lived with his parents and his one brother and three sisters. He was educated locally at St Oswald's School in Hunslet, which he left around 1907, aged about twelve.

Butler, who was quiet and unassuming, spent some seven years 'down the pit' as a miner before enlisting into the 17th Battalion, West Yorkshire Regiment, in Leeds on 9 January 1915, having previously been turned down for the military on the grounds that he was too short. Once in the Army, Butler was attached to a trench mortar battery and was trained at Ilkley, Yorkshire.

By June 1916, he was serving on the Western Front attached to the 106th Trench Mortar Battery (also known as a Stokes mortar battery after its type of mortar). On 6 August 1917, Butler was in charge of a mortar on the British line east of L'Empire, France. His precise position was between Cambrai and St Quentin, some 60 miles to the south of the Third Battle of Ypres, which had commenced in Flanders on 31 July – exactly a week earlier.

In fact, on 5 August the 17th West Yorkshires had been relieved from their frontline position by the 19th Durham Light Infantry, returning to billets at L'Empire. However, the next day was misty and the enemy, apparently taking advantage of the favourable weather conditions, successfully raided Guillemont Farm at around 3.30 a.m. with a force of some 150 troops. Within forty-five minutes, the West Yorkshires had 'stood to' and during the night and the following day they supplied working parties.

It was during heavy fighting on 6 August that Butler showed such quick thinking and bravery that he was later awarded the VC. His citation, published on 17 October 1917, takes up the story:

> For most conspicuous bravery when in charge of a Stokes gun in trenches which were being heavily shelled. Suddenly one of the fly-off levers of a Stokes shell came off and fired the shell in the emplacement. Private Butler picked up the shell and jumped to the entrance of the emplacement, which at that moment a party of infantry were passing. He shouted to them to hurry past as the shell was going off, and turning round, placed himself between the party of men and the live shell and so held it till they were out of danger.

He then threw the shell on to the parados [a protective, elevated area of earth], and took cover in the bottom of the trench. The shell exploded almost on leaving his hand, greatly damaging the trench. By extreme good luck Private Butler was contused only. Undoubtedly his great presence of mind and disregard of his own life saved the lives of the officer and men in the emplacement and the party which was passing at the time.

By 10.30 p.m. the following day, the 17th West Yorkshires were relieved once again, this time by the 18th Highland Light Infantry. Weeks later, Butler spoke about his 'accident' to the press, describing how the shell had been fired into the emplacement.

I picked it up and showed it to my mate. 'It's going off,' I said. 'I know it is,' he replied, and stopped still and never shifted. I hardly knew what I did, but I jumped to the entrance of the emplacement with the shell, which was an eleven-pounder, and there I saw a party of infantry passing.

I shouted to them to get out of the way, and they did so quickly. Those on the right rushed away, and a man turned about a dozen men back with him. I then threw the shell on to the parados. Not being too far over, it fell back to the bottom of the trench and burst. It damaged the trench, but didn't injure any of the men.

Within a month of the incident, word had spread that Butler was in line for a gallantry medal for his courage and his Commanding Officer wrote to Butler's mother, Caroline, praising his courage. In a letter to his parents written in September, Butler was extremely understated about his bravery:

I hope the decoration they say I am going to receive comes through before then [mid-October] so that I shall have a bit of something to show for my service. Well, it will only be for what other men

have done, or what is being done every week of the year. It will be
a surprise to you, I know, but never mind, accidents will happen.

It appears Butler was more seriously wounded at some point after
his VC action but, following medical treatment, he was back with
his battalion on 18 November 1917.

As stated, his VC was announced in the *London Gazette* on 17 October 1917 and Butler received it from George V at an investiture
at Buckingham Palace on 5 December 1917, when his parents were
present. The next day he was the guest of honour at a civic reception
in Leeds when the Lord Mayor delivered a speech about his gallantry.
On the same day, he visited his old school, St Oswald's, where he
was presented with a china clock from the citizens of Leeds. He also
received a gold medal from a Leeds man and £300 from other well-
wishers that was to be invested.

On 7 February 1920, Butler married Clara Johnson at Hunslet Reg-
istry Office, Leeds, and the couple went on to have a daughter. It is
understood that Butler was given a medical discharge from the Army
in 1921. After that, he worked for the North East Gas Board, while
living in Belle Isle Road, Leeds. George Sanders, another VC recipient, worked for the same gas board and the two men became friends.

For the rest of his life, Butler was an enthusiastic supporter of his
regimental association and also the Victoria Cross and George Cross
Association, attending many events. In 1940, after the outbreak of
the Second World War, he served in the Home Guard along with his
friend and workmate George Sanders. After the war, Butler attended
the Victory Parade of June 1946. During the final years of his life,
he suffered from poor health and he died in his home city of Leeds
on 25 March 1972, aged seventy-seven. Butler was given a full military funeral four days later and was buried in Hunslet Cemetery,
Leeds (originally he had an unmarked grave but this was rectified in
1994). Butler's name is one of seventeen VC holders on the memorial outside the Henry Moore Institute in Leeds.

CAPTAIN NOEL GODFREY CHAVASSE

Army: Royal Army Medical Corps, attached to 1/10th (Scottish)
Battalion, The King's (Liverpool Regiment)
DATES OF BRAVERY: 9 AUGUST 1916 AND (BAR) 31 JULY/
2 AUGUST 1917
GAZETTED: 26 OCTOBER 1916 AND (BAR) 14 SEPTEMBER
1917
Special feature of the VC: one of only three VCs and Bars in existence and the
only VC and Bar of the Great War.

Noel Godfrey Chavasse, the younger of identical twin boys by some twenty minutes, was born in the vicarage at St Peter-le-Bailey, Oxford, on 9 November 1884. He was the son of the Revd Francis Chavasse and his wife Edith (*née* Maude). At the time of the twins' births, the Revd Chavasse was the Rector of St Peter-le-Bailey and Principal of Wycliffe Hall, Oxford. The twins, however, were so small and weak at birth that their christening, by their father, was delayed until 29 December 1884. While still only a few months old, both twins were struck down by typhoid and their parents had them photographed in case they did not recover.

Noel was eventually one of seven children born to the couple, who included twin girls born two years after the twin boys. For a time, Noel and Christopher (his twin) were educated at home by a governess and tutor but, aged twelve, they attended Magdalen College School in Oxford. When the Revd Chavasse became Bishop of Liverpool in 1900, the family moved to the city and the twins were educated at Liverpool College School. In 1907, Noel graduated with a first in natural sciences from Trinity College, Oxford (Christopher also studied at the same college). Afterwards, Noel stayed on at Oxford to study medicine. While at university, Chavasse was a talented sportsman, earning 'blues' for athletics and lacrosse. Indeed, he and Christopher represented Britain in the 1908 Olympics, both running the 400 metres at the London event. After qualifying as a doctor in the summer of 1912, Noel Chavasse became house physician at the Royal Southern Hospital, Liverpool, and the following year he was appointed house surgeon at the same hospital.

As war loomed, Chavasse was commissioned as a lieutenant into the Royal Army Medical Corps (RAMC) and, after the outbreak of hostilities, he served in France and Belgium, where he was attached to the 10th King's (Liverpool Scottish) Regiment.

Chavasse travelled to France and, in a letter home, dated 13 January 1915, he provided a vivid description of the brutality and misery of life in the trenches. He wrote:

> Tell it not in gath [keep the information to yourself], but we are now only about 350 fighting strength. We are melting like a snowball in the sun, but we have stopped a little now because we have come down from a tough fibre. Our casualties are not great. Only about fourteen killed and thirty wounded, but exposure in the wet and muddy trenches has been more deadly than the enemy's guns. As a matter of fact the sickness is not serious. Men leave us when they get a chill and their temperature goes over 100 Fah [Fahrenheit]. I have only sent one man away with pneumonia and he has since returned well. Most of the men are knocked out with rheumatism and lumbago and by chilled and swollen feet that come after a man had been knee deep in the filthy slush for forty-eight hours in the trenches. We have also had an epidemic of diarrhoea which sent several away, but this cleared up with castor oil. The Christmas parcels caused a good deal of indigestion too.

Initially at least, Chavasse and the men of the Liverpool Scottish were not in the thick of the fighting. In a letter dated 21 February 1915, he began:

> Since leaving home I have had what is known here as a 'cushy' time, that is, things have been pretty easy and comfortable. We have been

lucky enough to have missed a spell of the trenches, and we have not been up to the firing line since I left you.

However, within a month this changed and the reality of war became apparent. In a letter home, dated 1 March 1915, Chavasse informed his parents:

> I had a grim job the other day. A very wet trench was being drained and the diggers came upon a dead leg which stopped [i.e. blocked] the drain, so I volunteered to take up two sanitary policemen and dig up our unknown friend and dispose of him in a grave where he would impede nothing. I gave my men hot cocoa, took them up, and we dug him out. They stuck it very well, and rather enjoyed the horror of it all. The poor fellow turned out to be an Englishman and a Corporal. He had been dead I should say three months and was rather horrible. He now lies in a grave further back, and I have had a Cross made for him and put on it 'Here lies an Englishman who died for his country'.

As the letters continued, Chavasse told how he was constantly treating severely wounded and dying men, several of whom remained alive for many hours, or even days, despite horrendous head injuries.

Chavasse often wrote about the sympathy he felt towards those men who were suffering from shell-shock, some of whom were sentenced to death for cowardice. In a letter dated 16 March 1915, he wrote:

> Like all Officers I have met the strain and constant, though often sub-conscious, tension of trench warfare [which] is wearing out his [a soldier's] nerves. The bravest fellows about after six months feel themselves getting jumpy, and constantly have to keep a hold upon themselves. I am very sorry for them.

Chavasse was constantly apologising to his parents for his lack of letters home, though in reality he was a prodigious letter-writer and typically sent home one letter every week, usually written on a Sunday. He constantly put a brave and positive face on even the worst of news. For example, on 16 May 1915, he wrote:

> Today things have been gloriously slack. The great [enemy] 'push' for Calais seems to have failed. Poisonous gases have not been used lately, but they have now poisoned the streams. A little stream that runs through our village from the direction of the German lines has been found with definite traces of arsenic in it. It is rather pitiful is it not? I think it shows they must be getting to the end of their tether when they begin to hit below the belt in this fashion. I am still up in my dressing station and all is the same except that the country is greener and more lovely every day. It's a real pleasure to live.

The pressures on Chavasse were immense but his letters home never reflected any sense of self-pity. In a letter to his parents dated 31 May 1915, he mentioned in passing: 'I am now in the proud position of being the only regimental doctor who had not broken down.' He added:

> I am still going strong. I am very glad I am so fit because I have tremendous attachment to the regiment, and could not bear to leave it. As for the war itself it is beginning to bore me a bit, and I shall not be sorry when it is over.

In the same letter, Chavasse was critical of workers at home who went on strike over pay, saying:

> the striking of munition workers for a halfpenny extra a day while poor jaded and terrified boys of eighteen are shot for shirking the cruel hardships of winter trenches, fills us with dismay and rage.

Why should trench exhausted men be driven to collapse, while boozy
and cushy slackers at home are only pampered?

At the same time we have a feeling that Germany is very hard
pushed, and that with proper munitions we shall soon win.

At some point, Chavasse travelled on to Belgium where, in the
St Eloi sector, he was kept busy treating the wounded and also writing letters of condolence to the families of dead and wounded British
soldiers. At this time, Chavasse was renowned for always putting
the needs of his men before his own safety, and also for making full
use of his athletic prowess. An unnamed soldier, who witnessed this
incident, wrote:

While on duty as a signaller at Battalion H.Q., I received a telephone message from the frontline, 'Man severely wounded in head,
could doctor come up at once?' In daylight, only the communication trench was used, and it took at least 20 minutes to reach the
front line.

To my surprise, a few minutes after giving the doctor the message, the front line sent word, 'O.K., the Doctor is here.' Instead of
using the communication trench, he [Chavasse] had sprinted up the
road – in full view of the enemy – in order to reach the wounded
man in the shortest possible time.

His battalion saw action in June 1915 at Hooge, near Ypres, where
Chavasse continually went into no-man's land for nearly forty-eight
hours until he was satisfied that there were no more wounded men
who needed treatment. He was awarded the Military Cross (MC) for
his heroic efforts and, shortly afterwards, he asked one of his sisters
to buy 1,000 pairs of socks and other comforts out of his own money
for the battalion.

In another letter home, Chavasse gave an insight into his difficult
and dangerous role:

Last night I had a bad but necessary job. I had to crawl out behind part of the trench and bury three poor Englishmen who had been killed by a shell. I am going out after another tonight. This is the seamy side of war, but all is repaired in the feeling of comradeship and friendship made out here. It is a fine life and a man's job, but I think we shall all be glad to get home again.

The first member of the Chavasse family to die in the Great War was Captain Frank Chavasse, Noel's cousin, who was killed, aged thirty, while serving in Aden on 7 June 1915. Noel wrote home to his family saying: 'I saw also that 2 officers had been killed but did not know it was poor Frank's hard fate to be one of them.'

As the regiment's doctor, Chavasse had to treat those wounded by enemy fire but also those who shot themselves to get out of fighting at the front. In a letter home dated 24 September 1915, he wrote:

Today a poor fellow was brought to me with a bad wound in the leg – most of his calf shot away … He comes from a first class Highland Battalion, and crawled into a dug-out where I am afraid he shot himself (he said he was cleaning his rifle, they all say that). When he gets well the poor fellow will be court-martialled or given penal servitude I fear. It seems like tending a dead man but it cannot be helped. He seems a poor specimen of humanity.

In a following letter home written just four days later – 28 September 1915 – Chavasse wrote of his frustrations at the terrible loss of life during trench warfare:

I have been the witness of as gallant a charge as ever took place, which has ended, so far as we are concerned, in our line here being exactly the same as it was before; but two regiments at least are cut to pieces. We cannot yet judge the full loss of life. What good it has or could of [have] done, only those who have full information of the whole battle-line can tell. Probably our show was only a little diversion to attract attention from the really big issues at stake further south.

I doubt if much attention will be paid to it in dispatches; yet it was the biggest thing that has happened since we came out into this tortured spot, and as usual everybody responded to the call of duty, and blood was poured out like water, and lives cast away as carelessly as old boots. I am sick of seeing men sent out to die in the mud which is the mould of former battalions 'gone under'; but it will always be a delightful honour to lend a hand to the wounded heroes, and so in spite of [it] all, in a selfish sense, this year has been the happiest of my life.

One of Chavasse's many duties was to help arrange burials for those killed in battle, or by snipers and stray shells. Judging from his letter home of 22 October 1915, it was a role he took very seriously:

We bring our dead about five miles behind the firing line now, and they are buried by a Chaplain. I have a stretcher bearer who is a carpenter, and he makes very good Crosses. To-day I am sending up a Cross within 300 yards of the firing line to mark the grave of one of our poor men who was killed on June 6th. I visited his grave a few days ago, and found his Cross broken by a shell. As it is a lonely grave we are very keen to mark them as well as possible.

In the same letter, Chavasse railed against those who deprived the frontline troops of supplies.

The trench men are splendid. The Base people are more than kind, but the people between are really very selfish. When a consignment of coke comes to the wagon line only a small percentage comes to the firing line, that our cushy friends in the wagon line should ever be a bit cold so that the men who are enduring the tenseness and hardships and sometimes horrors of the trenches should be warm could never be thought of for a minute. It fairly makes me sick.

In a PS to Chavasse's letter home of 16 November 1915, he told his father, who was Bishop of Liverpool at the time: 'I want some good sermons to read on Sunday.' As Christmas 1915 approached, the conditions endured by men on the frontline were horrific, and many were suffering from trench foot. In another letter home dated 17 December 1915, Chavasse wrote:

> The whole of our seven days in the trenches was wretched. It rained nearly all the time. The trenches were swamped. Communications trenches in parts were nearly up to the waist [in water and mud] in places, and we had to wade round them for the Huns are not so friendly as they used to be. The dug-outs collapsed and the men were much exposed to the weather.

Chavasse's letter home written on Boxing Day 1915 stated:

> Christmas day was very quiet. Hostilities seemed to stop by mutual consent. No one seemed to have the heart to try to kill or maim another on that day, but as far as I know there was no fraternising [with the enemy]. That had to be firmly put down. I think it is a great tribute to the very firm though hidden hold which Christianity has on every heart that war had to cease on Christmas Day. We in the village had Holy Communion at the ambulance ... Our fat useless lump of a padre had thought fit to leave his neglected flock for Christmas tide, and has gone on leave, and is not missed. Some of these padres have a very limited sense of their opportunities. Their great idea is to have a Service on Sunday at which they pray and preach vigorously, but after which they think their work is over unless they are called to conduct a funeral.

Chavasse made sure the men had a Christmas stocking too, with dry socks, cigarettes, sweets and 'I gave every man a bottle of sauce or pickles to make the Christmas dinner taste more festive...'

Another tragedy for the Chavasse family came on 12 March 1916 when Arthur Chavasse, the son of Sir Thomas Chavasse and the twin boys' cousin, died of pneumonia at the front. Arthur Chavasse, who was a brilliant young doctor, had his mother and sister, who had come over from Britain to the Continent, with him during his final few hours.

By early May 1916, Chavasse was looking forward to his impending leave but when he returned from Britain to France at the end of the month his thoughts turned to what might happen to his estate in the event of his death. His first cousin, Gladys Chavasse, had accepted his marriage proposal the previous month. In a letter home to his parents dated 27 May 1916, he wrote:

> I should like to ask your advice about making a will. Should I leave my money in the bank to Gladys, or should I give it to Chris [his twin brother] or to Aylmer [a young relative] for his education. It all comes to you, but I could tell you how [I] should like to portion it out?

In June 1916, Chavasse returned to Britain in order to be presented with his MC. Those present at the family party to mark the event included Gladys Chavasse. On 27 July 1916, and by this point with Chavasse back in France, the battalion was moved to trenches in front of Guillemont. Despite being unable to reconnoitre the enemy positions, the men were still ordered to attack at 4.20 a.m. on 9 August. Not surprisingly, within a few hours they had sustained 189 casualties out of 600 men. Chavasse attended to the wounded all day under heavy fire, frequently in view of the enemy, while during the night, he searched for injured men directly in front of enemy lines.

The next day, he recruited a stretcher-bearer and, under heavy shell-fire, carried a critically injured man 500 yards to safety. On the return journey, Chavasse was himself wounded but it did not stop him from further sterling deeds that same night. Helped by twenty volunteers, he rescued three more wounded men from a shell-hole just 25 yards from the enemy trenches. He also buried the bodies of two officers and collected numerous identity discs from dead soldiers. It was estimated that during those two days, Chavasse saved the lives of some twenty seriously wounded men as well as treating the countless 'ordinary' cases that passed through his hands.

Chavasse's parents heard through official channels that he had been wounded but, almost immediately, they received a letter from their son playing down the injury. In the short note dated 11 August 1916, which made no mention of his own astonishing bravery just two days earlier, he told them:

> Don't be in the least upset if you hear that I am wounded. It is absolutely nothing. The merest particle of shell just pricked me. I did not know about it until I undressed at night, but as I was very dizzy at the time I went to the Field Ambulance to get a tetanus injection, and when I had that I had to be entered in the visitors' book, and that started the mischief. I am not even inconvenienced. With much love to all at home.

In a letter to his parents dated 20 August 1916, Chavasse revealed that 'without any asking on my part I was suddenly sent home on eight days' sick leave. My leave started this morning...' Still playing down his injuries, he wrote: 'I am going to see a Birmingham dentist and surgeon to-morrow. This I promised my Colonel I would do, although my so-called wound is all right and healed up. Still it is my duty to use my privilege to get well as fast as I can.'

The Bishop of Liverpool was tipped off, in a letter, by a senior military contact that his son had been recommended for the VC and he had passed this news on to his son. In his reply to his parents' letter, Chavasse wrote:

> First, I must thank father very much for the letter and the too good news. I fear that honour is not given as easily as all that, and recommending is not getting, so I shall adopt the attitude of doubting Thomas – until I see it in print I shall not believe. If it will give me a bit of extra leave it will be worth having.

Indeed, Chavasse seemed more excited by other more practical improvements than the possibility that he was going to be awarded the VC: 'We have very large Thermos flasks now, about as big as milk cans, which will keep soup or tea scalding hot for about twelve hours. They are a great blessing.'

Chavasse was awarded his VC 'for most conspicuous bravery and devotion to duty' and his citation, announced in the *London Gazette* on 26 October 1916, concluded: 'His courage and self-sacrifice were beyond praise.'

The *Liverpool Daily Post & Mercury* said of the city's local hero:

> Few men have inspired such wonderful affection for themselves amongst the ranks of their colleagues. Letters from the Front have constantly told how eager he was, how ready to expose himself to dangers beyond those called for in the discharge of his duties, and how many a wounded soldier has brightened under the radiance of his cheery disposition ... His battalion almost regard him as their mascot.

A Canadian machine-gunner told the paper:

> I was up in the line that day, and the men were talking a lot about the fine courage of Captain Chavasse. It was absolute hell all day ... Hell would have been heaven compared to the place he was in, but

he never troubled about it. It's men like him that make one feel that the spirit of old is still alive in our midst.

The regional paper also quoted an anonymous stretcher-bearer who said:

At times it was absolutely impossible to stand up without being hit ... The Captain took no more notice of the enemy's fire than he would of a few raindrops, and even when the bullets were whistling all round he didn't get in the least bit flurried in his work. He made us all feel that it was an honour to work with him.

The compassion that Chavasse had for soldiers suffering from shell-shock was highlighted by the regimental historian who wrote of Chavasse:

The Doctor had a genius for picking out those men who were near a breakdown, either in nerve or general health, but not yet so run down as to be hospital cases. Rather than send them into the trenches where their collapse sooner or later was inevitable, he kept them at his aid post as light-duty men, where in comparative comfort they had a chance to rest and recover.

On 28 October 1916, Chavasse's fellow officers threw a dinner in his honour to celebrate his VC. Chavasse, however, could be extremely outspoken and during the event upset both the RAMC Field Ambulance Service and the medical services for their alleged failings in dealings with wounded and sick troops.

A letter home dated 10 January 1917 revealed that Chavasse had not written for some time because 'I have been up to the eyes in work'. He revealed he had been on a week-long course on sanitation, adding: 'During our stay they defined to us the duties of a Regimental Medical Officer, and said that his job was "the cure and comfort of his troops" – a tall order but quite correct. But if one tries to carry it out conscientiously one never goes to bed at all.'

Chavasse received his VC from George V at an investiture at Buckingham Palace on 5 February 1917. Once again, there was a family party that Gladys, his fiancée, attended. At the event, Noel Chavasse was deeply moved and inspired by The King, later telling Gladys: 'What a man! I could readily die for him.'

In a letter to his parents dated the day after his investiture, and written from Boulogne, he said: 'The investiture passed off all right. The King seemed to be quite sincere and was certainly very kind. Altogether there were seven of us [VC recipients]. Four being N.C.O.s and men, and they had really performed miracles.' When Chavasse had been about to return to the Continent, Gladys gave him a terrier, called Jelly or Jell, which he smuggled back with him against military regulations. Gladys had intended that Jell would be good company and a rat-catcher. In Chavasse's letter home of 6 February, Jell gets a mention: 'I have taken a jolly nice little fox terrier with me who will, I hope, help to settle the rat question in the trenches.' In fact, Jell ran away from the vermin that he was supposed to kill.

A letter home dated 14 March 1917 revealed that both Chavasse and the men of his battalion/regiment were finally feeling the pressure of their tough regime. He wrote:

> There has been so much to do and oversee that if I am not going round until dark I feel I have shirked my work. What I always feel and that rather oppressively is that if I get at all slack so many people suffer needlessly. The Battalion is being worked very hard now, I suppose as a military necessity, and, of course, if it must be it is all right; but we are using up our human material and wearing it out rather badly just now in our sector of the line. The men are being pushed exhausted and without respite, and good fellows are beginning to crack up. Thank goodness winter is over, and the men won't have to face exposure as well as overwork.

During the spring, Chavasse repeatedly told his parents he was having an 'easy time' of it. On 25 June, he wrote reassuringly:

> We are right back now well behind the line. I can't even hear the guns. We hope to be here about a month, and the men are very cheery about it and the sickness is going down. I have got a very good sick billet. It is a completely furnished house, a regular home from home, and the men love it. I think they like best the clock which ticks away and chimes.

On 2 July 1917, Chavasse wrote to his parents telling them of his plans to marry and of his pride in being a VC recipient:

> I am well rested now and feel very well. I don't think I can get leave just yet, but hope to get some about September. I am very keen on leave for I want to settle up things. I am thinking that if the war does not get on any quicker, I shall take time by the forelock and get married about Christmas. I could probably get leave for about a month then. What is your candid opinion of it? Gladys wants it very badly, and I think aunt Frances would like it. I should like it for a lot of reasons but shall feel rather a fool after the war as a married man without a job. Still it is a bit pathetic to have to leave a bronze cross to a nephew or cousin twice removed. I don't think I really earned it as many have done but deep in me I prize it more than I can say.

This letter, which was one of, if not the, last one to his parents, was signed, as usual: 'Always your loving [son], Noel.'

By the end of July 1917, the battalion had been moved to Belgian trenches near Wieltje, situated to the north-east of Ypres. Preparations were made for what would become the third Battle of Ypres – an attempt to recapture the infamous Passchendaele Ridge. The new offensive began on 31 July and the Liverpool Scottish, poorly protected against the enemy's mustard gas, lost two officers and 141 other ranks.

On the first evening of the battle, Chavasse received a nasty head wound from a shell splinter: his skull may even have been fractured. He had his injury bandaged but he refused to be evacuated. Time and again, under heavy fire and in appalling weather, he went out into no-man's land to search for and attend to the wounded. It is believed that he received two additional wounds during this time, one of them serious enough to have him removed from the battle-field. However, again he refused to be evacuated, insisting that he would not leave his comrades. With virtually no food, in great pain and desperately weary, he undoubtedly saved numerous lives until, in the early hours of 2 August, he was finally taking a rest at his first aid post when it was struck by a shell.

Everyone in the post was either killed or wounded. Chavasse himself suffered at least six injuries but he crawled for half a mile to get help for the others. He was taken through Ypres to the 46th Field Ambulance and then on to the 32nd Casualty Clearing Station, but his face was unrecognisable and he had a serious wound to the abdomen.

After an operation on the latter injury, he found the strength to dictate a letter to Gladys, in which he explained why he had carried on working in spite of his injuries. He told one of his nurses, Sister Leedam: 'Give her my love. Tell her duty called and called me to obey.' He had some death-bed thoughts for his father too: 'Poor dear father, he loves his boys, and we are all causing him a great deal of pain, with all his hard work, but cheer him, Sister, tell him I am quite happy.'

Noel Chavasse died between 1 p.m. and 2 p.m. on 4 August 1917, the third anniversary of the outbreak of the war. He was thirty-two years old. A telegram informed his devoted parents of the sad news.

Gladys Chavasse was distraught when she heard the news: the couple had intended to get married later that month in France, since it was impossible for Chavasse to come back to Britain. A memorial service was held in Chavasse's honour in the Parish Church of St Nicholas on Merseyside on 29 August. During August, Chavasse's parents were inundated with letters praising their lost son. Brigadier-General L. G. Wilkinson, who commanded the 166th Brigade until April 1917, wrote:

> I constantly met your son and appreciated his work. He was quite
> the most gallant and modest man I have ever met, and I should think
> the best-liked. What he did for his battalion of Liverpool Scottish
> was wonderful, and his loss to them is irreparable. I do not believe
> a man of more noble character exists.

Sir Henry Willink, who knew both the Chavasse twins from before the war as well as from the battlefield, wrote to his own mother at the time:

> I am awfully sorry about Noel Chavasse. He was wounded once and
> went on: he was wounded twice and went on: he was wounded thrice
> and went on: to the fourth he succumbed, I think next day. He is
> said to have earned the V.C. four times that day. His family may feel
> that in him England has lost one of the most saintly and one of the
> most devotedly gallant of her sons. He was a most wonderful chap.

There were full and affectionate obituaries of Chavasse in both the *British Medical Journal* and the *Liverpool Diocesan Gazette*, while his local papers in Liverpool were full of praise for his bravery.

Chavasse's parents were so inundated with letters of sympathy that they were forced to send a stock reply in a lengthy, two-page typed letter. Dated 20 August 1917, it began:

> It is quite impossible for us to reply with our own hand to the many
> hundreds of friends who have written with such wonderful kindness

to express their sympathy, and to assure us of their prayers in our present great sorrow. We can only send a printed letter of heartfelt gratitude; which seems a poor and cold return for such a wealth of affection and comfort as we have received.

In the assurance that our most dear boy is with Christ, that he laid down his life for others and that God cannot make a mistake, lie our strength and our hope. 'In God's Will is our Peace.' We know that He has our son, and that one day He will place us again at his side.

The letter then went on to give an extremely detailed account of the events leading up to Chavasse's death as given to them by their son, Bernard. The letter ended with a description of Chavasse's death:

All that skilful surgery and devoted nursing could do, was done – and at first he seemed to rally. But he was literally worn out, and he passed away at 2 p.m. on August 4th. He was conscious throughout, though dazed, and morphia was given freely. He did not suffer any great pain. His main idea seemed to be a quiet determination to pull through, if possible. He received the Holy Communion and to the Sister in charge said more than once that 'he was going home to his mother and his betrothed…'

'He asked life of Thee and Thou gavest him long life, even length of days for ever and ever.'

'Greater love hath no man than this that a man lay down his life for his friends.'

Again we thank you with all our heart for your sympathy and your prayers.

Yours ever faithfully.

It was signed by both of Chavasse's parents.

The Bar to Chavasse's VC – the equivalent of a second VC – was announced on 14 September 1917, when the citation praised his 'extraordinary energy and inspiring example'.

Among those serving with him, Chavasse had been known affectionately as simply 'the Doc', and he was hugely respected and admired. The Regimental Historian of the Liverpool Scottish wrote:

> It is difficult to find words to express all that the Doc's life and example meant to the Liverpool Scottish. There was never a man who was better loved by his officers and men alike: there never was a man who gave himself more unsparingly in the service of others. His bravery was not the reckless, flamboyant type but the far finer bravery that sprang from his determination that nothing should stand in the way of whatever he considered his duty.

Chavasse's Bar to his VC was presented to his father by Lieutenant-General Sir William Campbell, General Officer Commanding Western Command. On 29 June 1920, at the British Medical Association conference, Cambridge, the chairman of the BMA presented a gold medal, its highest award, to the Bishop of Liverpool to commemorate his heroic son.

Chavasse was the only individual to be awarded the VC and Bar during the Great War and he is one of only three men in the decoration's 160-year history to be awarded a 'double VC'. The first man to be awarded a VC and Bar was Lieutenant-Colonel Arthur Martin-Leake. He was awarded his first VC in May 1902, while serving as a surgeon-captain during the Second Anglo-Boer War. He was awarded his second VC in February 1915 for bravery during the First World War while serving as a lieutenant in the RAMC. In both cases, Martin-Leake rescued and treated wounded soldiers under a heavy fire: during his first VC action, he was shot three times.

The third man to be awarded the VC and Bar was Captain Charles Upham, the only frontline soldier to receive the double award. Upham, a New Zealander, was awarded his first VC in October 1941 while serving as a lieutenant with the New Zealand Military Forces.

He was serving in Crete, Greece, in May 1941 when in battle, according to his citation, he 'performed a series of remarkable exploits, showing outstanding leadership, tactical skill and utter indifference to danger'. Upham was awarded his second VC in September 1945 for bravery in Egypt back in July 1942 when, thanks to his bravery and leadership, his raiding party defeated a far larger enemy force. Upham was eventually captured and spent the rest of the war as prisoner. After several escape attempts, he was held in Colditz Castle.

Chavasse is buried in the Brandhoek New Military Cemetery, Belgium, where his headstone bears a representation of two VCs. The wonderfully apt inscription in the white stone, chosen by his father, reads: 'Greater love hath no man than this, that a man lay down his life for his friends.' It is a famous quote from the Gospel According to St John.

Gladys Chavasse is understood to have visited Chavasse's grave several times and each year she marked the anniversary of his death with an 'In Memoriam' notice in *The Times*. She also kept a photograph of him, his Officer's Advance Book, his writing case and his miniature VC until her death in 1962, when she was fatally struck by a car while holidaying in France.

Christopher Chavasse, who was awarded the MC for his own bravery during the Great War, apparently claimed that Gladys had first been led to her fiancé's grave by Jell, the abandoned terrier she had given him during the war. Christopher, who survived the war, gave an insight into his own loss in a letter, written in 1961, to a woman whose identical twin sister had just died. Christopher, who was seventy-six when he penned his letter, said:

> Then, also as an identical twin, how truly I can sympathise with you, as I still mourn my Noel every day of my life, and have done so for 44 years, and shall do till I see him again – quite soon now.
>
> Our bereavement is really as poignant as that of a husband or

wife of a marriage that has been one of the closest union, when (as must happen) one or the other dies first. The rest of life must remain clouded: and we would not have it otherwise, for the measure of our loss is the measure of our love. But that does not mean that life holds nothing for us. We have our lives to live for God; and, in his mercy, time is a great Healer, and (though the ache may always be there) life can be happy and useful, as long as we do not sit and mope, but try to be of service and make other people happy.

Furthermore, Christopher Chavasse added in his letter that he had known his twin brother had died through some kind of telepathy:

My loss of my twin was like amputation – I felt half of me had gone, for we were extremely close, so that I knew (I have proof of this) when he died, though he was 80 miles from me on the battle-front, and the news did not reach me until he had been dead a week.

Christopher Chavasse, who was Bishop of Rochester until 1960, died in March 1962, aged seventy-seven.

In 1963, the year after Christopher's death, Selwyn Gummer published a splendid book entitled *The Chavasse Twins*. In his book, Gummer stressed, quite accurately, that Noel Chavasse was not a conventional military hero.

On the contrary he was a profoundly Christian man whose love for his fellows made him *unconscious* of danger. He was no swashbuckler challenging the enemy's might: he was a doctor ministering to his patients where they were. The fact that they lay in open country under heavy fire was irrelevant. They needed his help and he was among them as one who serves.

Gummer, who was also a close friend of Christopher Chavasse, added: 'If the measure of a man is his stature in death, the Chavasse twins were giants.'

Since his death, Noel Chavasse has had at least sixteen memorials dedicated to his memory, including one in Liverpool Cathedral, and this total of memorials is greater than for any other VC holder in the world. In 2009, a magnificent bronze statue, depicting him aiding a wounded soldier with the assistance of a stretcher-bearer, was unveiled in Liverpool's Abercromby Square. It was commissioned by the Noel Chavasse VC Memorial Association and Ann Clayton, who penned a splendid biography of him and played a prominent role in bringing this about.

Decades ago, Chavasse's gallantry and service medals were left by his family to St Peter's College, Oxford. However, in 2009, after lengthy private negotiations, the college took the decision to sell his medal group to me. A report in the *Sunday Telegraph* quoted college sources as saying the price was 'close to £1.5 million', which easily topped the previous world record for a medal, rumoured to be a similar private sale worth £1 million. I have never confirmed or denied this figure because the details of the deal were confidential.

I was thrilled to add the Chavasse medals to my collection, along with the wonderful archive of family letters written before and during the war. I was especially glad that the money I paid for the group of medals was going towards academic purposes: indeed this encouraged me to pay what I have suggested was a 'non-commercial' price for this unique group of medals.

I had long felt that my VC collection would never be truly complete until it contained one of the only three VCs and Bars. In many ways, I look upon the Chavasse decorations as the ultimate group of gallantry medals. I am immensely proud to be their custodian and to know that they are now on public display at the Imperial War Museum, London.

SECOND LIEUTENANT (LATER CAPTAIN) MONTAGU SHADWORTH SEYMOUR MOORE

Army: The Hampshire Regiment
DATE OF BRAVERY: 20 AUGUST 1917
GAZETTED: 8 NOVEMBER 1917
Special feature of the VC: an exceptional award for daring and sustained bravery near Ypres, Belgium.

Montagu Shadworth Seymour Moore was born in Worthing, Sussex, on 9 October 1896. He was the elder son (there was also a daughter) of Frederick Moore, a barrister who had earlier served in the Army, and his wife Gertrude (*née* Guscotte). Moore was educated at Bedford Grammar School where, because of his limitations as an academic student, one of his teachers described him as 'a dud'. He later had a year's private tuition while his family lived in Bournemouth, Hampshire, followed by classes at the town's Municipal College. His education was completed at the Royal Military College, Sandhurst.

In August 1916, and aged nineteen, Moore was commissioned as a second lieutenant into the Hampshire Regiment. Within a month, he had been despatched to France with the regiment's 15th Battalion. Moore was a prolific letter writer, often signing off his letters 'Cheer oh. Keep smiling. Monty.' In a letter home dated 5 November 1916 and addressed to 'Dear Old Dad', he revealed his daring nature as well as providing an insight to the appalling conditions offered by what he accurately described as 'trench warfare'. He wrote:

> One night I crawled out across 'no man's land' up to the Boche
> [German] wire 60 yards away, it was most exciting. I discovered
> the position of a machine gun that was causing a lot of trouble.
> When I got back, I put the Lewis gun team on to that spot & they
> cleared them out. I think their Boche gun was put out of action ...
> The rats up in the trenches are awful, thousands of them. We also

had several cats which used to play with the wind vanes on top of the parapet, it is a most extraordinary life, you cannot imagine it, all is peace and quietness most of the day as far at the Boches go, only 40 to 150 yards away…

In another letter home to his father dated 18 November 1916, he provided a vivid account of coming under heavy enemy fire.

We have been up in reserve these last few days, working parties day and night, owing to the foolishness of another Regt. Boche spotted them & put about 20 shells all around our place, one pitched 10 yds behind our house, brought in the roof a bit, but no damage was done. Another exploded in the midst of a small party, killing 4 & wounding about 5 one man being blown to pieces, quite a lively morning, that Regt lost about 20 through that little show.

Then, in the equivalent of a scribbled PS, he added: 'What is all this about 40 zepps over London & 2000 casualties, any truth in it.[?]' It was at a time when the Germans had been using Zeppelin airships to attack the capital and other targets.

In a letter to his mother – 'Dear Old Mum' – also written on 18 November 1916, he revealed he had been appointed 'ADC' (Aide-de-Camp) to the Brigade General on a month's trial: 'seems a good stunt, but there will be no chance of straffing [*sic*] Boche, which seems a pity'. In various letters, he repeatedly thanked his parents for sending him luxuries such as cigarettes, socks, shortbread, chocolate and sweets.

After a short spell at Brigade Headquarters, he was transferred to the 1st Battalion of his regiment in January 1917. In a letter home to his mother dated 22 March 1917, he wrote:

Leave has gone West for the summer so there it is [,] beastly unfair I call it. The news [from the front] is of course very good indeed [,] things seem to be going as they should do, this year will no doubt make a difference in things & possibly finish it.

Although his letters were usually upbeat, he could, unsurprisingly, get disheartened by his time on the frontline and by his lack of leave. In a letter home to his father dated 17 April 1917, he wrote of France: 'Rain & heavy wind, awful country this. I never want to see it again.'

Moore was back with his original battalion, the 15th, in time for the operations at Messines, Belgium, on 7 June. During the advance, Moore was wounded in the leg by shrapnel. In a letter to his father dated 10 June 1917, he informed his parents that he had been injured.

> I got a small piece in the leg, not serious enough for Blighty and I fear, worse luck, chaps who did not go over the top were going on leave, sounds strange but it is so, that is how the Army treats you [,] just about fed up with it.

However, Moore had to go to hospital, because his letter home of 19 June 1917 was addressed from 'No 3 British General Hospital, B.E.F. [British Expeditionary Force]'. His letter began:

> Just a note to tell you I am going along quite well, it is only a small piece in, you see a whizz-bang burst at my side & a large piece caught me on the leg, knocking me some yards, bruising it badly & leaving a small piece in. I had to come back, not being able to walk much, it is now healing up and they are not going to worry about the piece.

Within three months of being wounded, and having taken some leave, he was back with his battalion, and during September and October he served in the Flanders region of Belgium. The second phase of the Third Battle of Ypres began on 20 September 1917 and, in what became known as the Battle of Menin Road Ridge, the British 2nd and 5th Armies were able to capture the main ridge east of Ypres before a deterioration in the weather. However, south of the Menin Road, the British forces had fared badly: after an assault by several regiments had failed, the 15th Hampshires were ordered at 6 p.m. to take, in a renewed assault, Tower Trench, a German strongpoint west of Gheluvelt. Because of the pillboxes that surrounded the stronghold, it had been nicknamed 'Tower Hamlets' by the British troops.

In a letter home to his mother dated 24 September 1917, Moore wrote of his involvement in the battle:

> Dad was right when he said I was coming back to hell. Well I have been through a hell I hope never to face again…
>
> To cut a long tale short I got over under a heavy rifle fire & machine gun fire through TOWER HAMLETS and in his [the enemy's] line with 4 men and 1 sergt captured 8 prisoners, 2 machine guns and 1 light field gun. Well, I stayed there until the rest of my men came up, dug in and held off the Boche, that night [20–21 September] he bombed us but we drove him off. The next morning, our guns put a most deadly barrage on us thinking we were all gone, it was a most awful time, finally, I was left with 10 men. In the afternoon, he [the enemy] counter-attacked, but I spotted it and got the S.O.S. up. Once again the guns opened and fairly pasted our dug-out. All that night 21–22 Sept, first a Boche barrage and then ours, my hat, it was awful. Well in the early morning mist I cleared out with my men, being absolutely usless [*sic*] staying there any longer, got back greatly to the astonishment of the General & CO [,] they had given me up as dead long ago, and fairly fell on my neck. Well, I got a hat for you, a most beautiful pair of glasses worth £15, 2 watches and several other odds and ends.

In fact, on 20 September, in the opening British attack that had begun at 5.40 a.m., the enemy had initially taken a heavy toll on the British forces. All four company commanders from the 15th Hampshires were among the many officers killed or wounded, and the 11th

Royal West Kents and the 12th East Surreys also took heavy casualties. So when Lieutenant-Colonel Cecil Cary-Barnard, the commander of the 15th Hampshires, was told, at 5 p.m., to renew the assault in an hour's time with his battalion and the West Kents, he, in fact, had very few men at his disposal. He later recalled: 'There were no West Kents in our area ... and the only thing to do was to take what men I could spare for the attack.' His solution was to instruct Second Lieutenant Moore, who had only been back with his regiment for a fortnight after being wounded at Messines, to lead the renewed assault across 400 yards of open ground, exposed to a deadly fire.

As Moore stated, both his commanders and his comrades were astonished to see him and a handful of men emerge from the early-morning mist at 7 a.m. on 22 September. They had long given the party up for dead after witnessing that they had been cut off since around 10 a.m. on 21 September with no chance of reaching them. In fact, Cary-Barnard had seen a massive German force preparing to attack Moore's position but he had been powerless to intervene. In the end, the CO simply watched as the enemy launched a terrifying assault on Moore's position and he feared the worst.

Cary-Barnard later calculated that most of the estimated 120-strong force that took part in Moore's attack – the second one – were killed or wounded. All told, he said that of 375 men who went into action that day, only 129 came out. As Stephen Snelling points out in his book *VCs of the First World War: Passchendaele 1917*, this is at variance to the regimental history that recorded six officers and eighty-three men killed or missing, and seven officers and 251 men wounded. Snelling concludes that 'either way the Hampshires' losses were grievous'.

The immediate result of Moore's bravery was that he was elevated to company commander with the rank of temporary lieutenant, acting captain, for what his CO described as a 'most extraordinary' action. In a letter home to his father dated 25 September 1917, he wrote: 'Just a short note to tell you I am now the proud owner of 3 pips...'

In the aftermath of his bravery, Moore was irritated that some press reports had not given his regiment full credit for their bravery. In the letter to his father dated 25 September 1917, he asked him to 'tell the papers it was the Hampshire Regt who did all the work and not the DLI [Durham Light Infantry], who left me in the lurch with 10 men and no rifles'. In another letter to his father dated 29 September 1917, Moore stated: 'I lost all my pals (nearly) on that last push... [then he lists fourteen men who were killed or wounded]. In fact I was the only one who came out without a scratch. Damn fine piece of luck, don't you think. [?]' In a letter home to his mother dated 1 October 1917, he confided that he had shot dead some of the men that he had taken prisoner. In an admission that would probably result in prosecution under modern-day international laws, he said:

> I captured 8 prisoners & shot 3 with my revolver. That was a day, Sept 20th, shall never forget it. All with their hands up, 'Shoot' I yelled & over they went like nine pins. No quarter was given to that little lot. The prisoners were taken later on from a dug-out, the one I was in through our barrage.

During the Great War, such shooting of prisoners was far from unheard of: both sides sometimes took a swift revenge on men who, just moments earlier, had been trying to kill them and their comrades.

In a letter to his sister dated 7 October 1916, Moore provided more details of the battle and the capture of prisoners:

> Did I tell you about clearing the dugout[?] Got up there and found a large concrete dug-out, full of Boche. In went one bomb, no result, 1 more, that was a dud, another one[,] that was a dud too and in went a 4th that bust my hat. There was a yell from inside, 'Kamerad, merci etc'. Out they came 8 of the beauties, hands full of souvenirs, which I carefully collected afterwards and lost. I was

standing at that time next to an officer when, crack & down he went with a bullet through his head, evidently meant for me, then we spent 36 hours in our own barrage. Very good for the nerves I can assure you.

On 8 October, Moore responded to his father's desire for more information on the two-day battle, which had become a major talking point in Belgium and back home:

I took 120 men & 2 officers with me. 4 men, 1 sergt and myself alone reached our objective, the remainder hung back in shell-holes until brought up ½ hour later, both officers were knocked out & only about 25 men reached that line. During that period of ½ hour, my sergt & myself cleared the dug-out as already described & then we crept into shell-holes & waited for what might turn up. The prisoners were sent back. The only wounded that ever got back were those who could look after themselves & a few who were found that night. Reinforcements came up making my party up to 70 odd. I left on the morning of Sept 22nd with 9 men and 1 wounded corporal who we assisted back. The guns had to be left behind, we all being too exhausted to carry any surplus kit or arms at all. The great point was that being there on Sept 21st the Boche failed to get through and so his whole advance was held up, mainly because he knew we were there but was unaware of our strength & had not got guts enough to risk it. According to the Div [Division] General, this saved the whole Div. If they had advanced our barrage would have just missed them & the whole line would have been lost. It is something to know I was of some use to them … It was just luck, anybody else would have done the same thing if they had been in my position.

Many comrades were full of praise for Moore's actions, including Second Lieutenant George Baker, who had been one of the two officers sent forward with reinforcements. He spoke of his pride at

Moore's actions and noted: 'To see Monty going up with a handful of men as coolly as if it were only a practice attack was a sight I shall never forget.'

Within a month of the action at Tower Hamlets, the first list of awards had been published rewarding the bravery of men in the unit. There were three Military Crosses (MCs), three Distinguished Conduct Medals (DCMs), twenty-eight Military Medals (MMs) and one Bar to an MM. At this point, Moore remained fairly confident that his own courage would still be recognised, telling his father in a letter home dated 22 October 1917: 'I am in for something good, only a rumour I expect, but [I] live in hopes.' Yet by 7 November, when he wrote to his sister Evelyn, he clearly feared he had been overlooked for an award. He said:

> Now don't go shouting all over the place about VCs etc, because it's most unlikely. It's strange that the whole batch got something except their leader, but it's just bad luck as usual, after all I didn't come out here for those things. My only thought is to get me some leave which they might have given me at least...

However, his waiting was soon over. Within twenty-four hours of writing those exasperated words, his VC was announced, accompanied by a detailed description of what had happened. The citation for his award, published on 8 November 1917, went some way to describing the full extent of his courage:

> For most conspicuous bravery in operations necessitating a fresh attack on a final objective which had not been captured.
>
> 2nd Lt. Moore at once volunteered for this duty and dashed forward at the head of some 70 men. They were met with heavy machine gun fire from a flank which caused severe casualties, with the result that he arrived at his objective – some 500 yards on – with only a Serjeant and four men. Nothing daunted, he at once bombed a large

dug-out and took twenty-eight prisoners, two machine guns and a light field gun.

Gradually more officers and men arrived, to the number of about 60. His position was entirely isolated as the troops on the right had not advanced, but he dug a trench and repelled bombing attacks throughout the night. The next morning he was forced to retire a short distance. When opportunity offered he at once reoccupied his position, re-armed his men with enemy rifles and bombs, most of theirs being smashed, and beat off more than one counter-attack.

2nd Lt. Moore held this post under continual shell fire for thirty-six hours until his force was reduced to ten men, out of six officers and 130 men who had started the operation. He eventually got away his wounded, and withdrew under cover of a thick mist.

As an example of dashing gallantry and cool determination this young officer's exploit would be difficult to surpass.

Moore's next letter to his sister, dated 10 November 1917, was full of joy and humour:

It has happened. You were quite right. It's the V.C. Well, I shall be home very shortly to buy up Bmth [Bournemouth] & we will go bust. Don't worry about money I have plenty to blue [sic]. Tell dad to bring out all that fizz he has got stored up.

Moore's name and photograph appeared in the newspapers, at least one of which reached him on the frontline. In a letter home dated 10 November 1917, he told his father: 'It certainly was a surprise to see my photo in the paper, not having had any announcement of the fact at all.' His investiture took place less than two weeks later when he received his VC from George V at Buckingham Palace on 21 November. In a letter home dated 10 December 1917, he informed his father than he had also received the French Croix de Guerre, saying 'not much to look at is it. [?]'

After his VC action, Moore's battalion was removed from the frontline and he spent time training drafts from a yeomanry unit. After promotion to acting captain, he served as a bombing instructor and, later, ADC to Lieutenant-General John Du Cane, the commander of XV Corps. After a short spell in early February 1918 with the 5th Army Infantry School, he was soon back in the thick of the action for, after the Germans launched their Spring Offensive on 21 March 1918, he was sent, along with his training unit, to try to halt the enemy advance.

Once again, Moore was at the heart of the fighting, writing home to his father on 2 April 1918: 'Had a very nasty four days holding up the Huns. Got buried once by a damn shell, fairly put the breeze up me but am still alive and living in hope of leave some time.' Two days later he wrote again to his father, saying: 'We expect a mail [delivery] tomorrow, the first for 9 days. We have had quite an experience [of] proper open warfare, a little better than those damn trenches but certainly more lively as regards bullets.' He survived the remainder of the war and ended it working again as an instructor.

Even after the war, Moore's military career remained filled with incident. In May 1919, he served with his regiment as part of the 238th Special Brigade in north Russia, where he was sent to Archangel to help with the withdrawal of Allied troops trapped by the Bolsheviks. In a letter home to his mother dated 25 June 1919, he described his involvement in a battle that cost the life of his friend, Captain D. T. Gorman, a recipient of the MC. 'Poor old Gorman (15th Bn with me) ... died 16 hours later having been brought back through that awful forest.'

After his return to Britain, he was transferred to the 1st Battalion and was despatched to Constantinople, joining the Army of the Black Sea. After being seconded to the Colonial Office for service in February 1921, he embarked on a new adventure – to East Africa: he was posted from March 1921 to the 2nd Battalion, King's African Rifles, in Tanganyika Territory, formerly German East Africa and now Tanzania. He travelled there with relish after learning the area was full of game. In October 1921, in a letter home, he indicated he was falling in love with Africa. 'This is a fine country and I like it immensely; game is very plentiful round here and have seen some fine sights already.'

On 1 September 1926, Moore retired from the Army with the rank of captain and took up a job as a ranger with the Tanganyika Game Department based in what would become the Serengeti National Park. Two years later, he accompanied The Prince of Wales on a shooting trip and in 1944 he was appointed chief game warden. By then he was married too: during leave in England in 1933, he had wed Audrey Penn Milton, from Torquay, and the couple went on to settle in the Serengeti and to have a son, Charles. Sharing her husband's love for Africa and its wildlife, she helped him to establish the Serengeti's formidable reputation as a game reserve. In 1951, and with his health suffering, he retired as chief game warden and went to settle in Kenya.

Moore, a no-nonsense colonialist who always spoke his mind, died from renal failure in Kiganjo, Nyeri, Kenya, on 9 September 1966, exactly a month short of his seventieth birthday. He was cremated at Langata Cemetery, Kenya, and his ashes were scattered in both Nairobi National Park, Kenya, and the Serengeti National Park, Tanzania. There is a memorial plaque to Moore at Bedford School (formerly Bedford Grammar School).

ACTING LIEUTENANT-COLONEL (LATER BRIGADIER-GENERAL) LEWIS PUGH EVANS

Army: Royal Highlanders (the Black Watch), attached 1st Battalion, the Lincolnshire Regiment

DATE OF BRAVERY: 4 OCTOBER 1917

GAZETTED: 26 NOVEMBER 1917

Special feature of the VC: the recipient was Wales's most decorated officer of the Great War.

Lewis Pugh Evans was born in Llanilar, near Aberystwyth, Cardiganshire, on 3 January 1881; the family home at nearby Llanbadarn was being rebuilt at the time. He was from a wealthy and respected Welsh-speaking family that claimed descent from one of the royal tribes of Wales. His father, Sir Griffith Evans, was a distinguished barrister and, despite having first studied medicine, he switched to law and was called to the Bar at Lincoln's Inn in 1867. Later in life, Sir Griffith was a Justice of the Peace and Deputy-Lieutenant of Cardiganshire, and spent some time in India where he became a member of the Viceroy's Legislative Council. Lewis Evans was one of six children born to Sir Griffith and his wife, Emelia (*née* Hills and from a strong military family), and he was the middle of three sons who all served in the military. He enjoyed a classic officer's education, attending Eton before the Royal Military College, Sandhurst, from early 1899. At Eton, one of his tutors said that 'he has plenty of spirit and will do well when he gets a bit bigger!'

Evans had hoped for a commission in the Royal Welsh Fusiliers, but, in fact, was commissioned as a second lieutenant into the Royal Highlanders (the Black Watch), a Scottish regiment, in December 1899. This was because the Black Watch had suffered heavy losses at the Battle of Magersfontein at the start of the Second Anglo-Boer War from 1899 to 1902, and the regiment was therefore in need of junior officers. During his service in South Africa, Evans was present at several of the larger battles and was promoted to lieutenant in May 1901. However, he was also taken prisoner by the Boers at one point in the conflict. Evans next served in India, where he remained until 1909 despite almost dying at one point from enteric fever. He picked up the nickname of 'Curly' as a result of his wavy, fair hair. At some point, too, he developed a passion for flying, taking private lessons while at the Staff College in Camberley, Surrey, and, as a 32-year-old captain, going solo to pass his pilot's test 'in excellent fashion' on 20 August 1913.

After the outbreak of the Great War in August 1914, Evans's

flying experience meant he found himself, somewhat reluctantly, serving with the fledgling Royal Flying Corps. He did not relish the conflict, saying he had 'no thirst for war ... only a desire to be there if it must take place'. For the early weeks of the conflict, however, he found himself posted to Netheravon, Wiltshire, where he had a desk job that involved helping to arrange for the movement of Britain's early military aircraft overseas. Evans failed in his attempts to get a posting to his old regiment, but he did succeed in his attempts to see action: he was posted to 3 Squadron to act as an observer. Here he took part in numerous reconnaissance missions in the early Bleriot two-seaters and other similar aircraft.

Flying was still in its infancy (the first powered flight by the Wright brothers had taken place as recently as December 1903) and flying was a dangerous enough 'sport' even without the added dangers provided by the war. In October 1914, Evans was returning from a reconnaissance flight with his pilot, Sergeant Reggie Carr, when they had a narrow scrape with death. In a letter to his then fiancée, Dorothea Pryse-Rice, Evans recounted:

> We had a bit of luck yesterday. We were just coming home ... after being out 2½ hours, coming up to the German lines when the engine stopped.
>
> Fortunately we were about 5,000 feet up and had the wind behind us and we fetched up just inside the French lines. I was not certain whether we had made it or not, though I knew we were clear of the German trenches, and we made for a wood.
>
> I was just off to question a ploughman when up came some French infantry, which was a great relief ... The Frenchmen very kindly insisted on pulling the machine under cover for they said we were within sight of the German guns, and so no doubt we would have been on a clear day, but it was misty and they did not see us.
>
> Sgt Carr got his engine right in no time and we got off home ... I returned to camp, had an excellent lunch on curried bullied beef

[and] slept under the lee of a gorse bush for an hour and a half. It is extraordinary how sleepy three hours of constant watching at speeds of 60 miles an hour makes you.

When Evans and Carr moved on to be attached to the 5th Division, they again carried out observation work flying, on average, six or seven hours a day. Aerial combat at this stage could hardly have been more primitive, as Evans explained again in another letter to his future wife: 'We all carry rifles and, most of us, a revolver as well. We ... exchange shots with a German machine from time to time but the prospects of either of us hitting the other are slight.' At this point too, bombs were dropped by hand.

It was, perhaps, his lack of contact with the enemy that made Evans continue to push for a return to his old regiment. On 13 December 1914, he got his wish when he was appointed as a company commander in the 1st Battalion, the Black Watch. Trench warfare was very different from the life of an airman, as he noted in a letter home: 'It's a rough life for one is in a constant state of filth and one is seldom dry.'

By the spring of 1915, Evans was promoted to the staff of a brigade commanded by Brigadier-General Colin Ballard, his brother-in-law. In mid June, he was in the thick of the action during the Battle of Hooge in Belgium when a British attack in the Ypres Salient went badly wrong. For his bravery, he was awarded the Distinguished Service Order (DSO) when his citation, announced the following month, stated: 'For conspicuous gallantry and devotion to duty on June 16th, 1915, at Hooge, when, after troops had become much mixed up, he continually moved up and down the firing line under heavy fire from 10 a.m. until midnight reorganising units and bringing back their reports.'

An account of Evans's relentless bravery from his brother-in-law suggests this citation was somewhat understated. Ballard described Evans as 'quite the hero of the day', adding:

> From 11 am to midnight, he never stopped and as a question of physical endurance I cannot understand how he did it ... Besides that he was under appalling fire the whole time. Every time he went out it seemed impossible that he could return unhurt. It was nothing but the goodness of God that he had not a scratch on him.

Typically, Evans dismissed his bravery as 'a stiff 36 hours' and was more concerned by the wisdom or otherwise of such an attack on the enemy as 'one always feels the few hundred yards gained and the few hundred prisoners captured have been paid for over-heavily'.

On 1 September 1915, Evans was promoted to major and the next eighteen months were spent away from the frontline on staff duties. However, on 23 March 1917, he was promoted to acting lieutenant-colonel and given his first battalion command with the 1st Lincolnshire Regiment, part of the 62nd Brigade, 21st Division.

On 3 October 1917, by which point the Third Battle of Ypres had been raging for weeks, he and his men moved into position for a major assault the next morning. Evans and his men were positioned near the south-west corner of Polygon Wood, close to the Menin Road. After a fierce bombardment early on 4 October, Evans learned that his battalion, instead of being kept in reserve, would lead the attack on one of the main targets. With just an hour to prepare, the 1st Lincolns managed to get to their new positions with a mere five minutes to spare. Some time later, with the attack from A, B, C and D companies in full flow, an enemy pill-box which had been bypassed suddenly sprang to life, inflicting significant casualties. In the heat of battle, Evans again rose to the challenge, as the citation for his VC described:

> For most conspicuous bravery and leadership. Lt.-Col. Evans took his battalion in perfect order through a terrific enemy barrage, personally formed up all units, and led them to the assault. While a

strong machine gun emplacement was causing casualties, and the troops were working round the flank, Lt.-Col Evans rushed at it himself and by firing his revolver through the loophole, forced the garrison to capitulate.

After capturing the first objective, he was severely wounded in the shoulder, but refused to be bandaged, and re-formed the troops, pointed out all future objectives, and again led his battalion forward. Again badly wounded, he nevertheless continued to command until the second objective was won, and, after consolidation, collapsed from loss of blood. As there were numerous casualties, he refused assistance, and by his own efforts ultimately reached the Dressing Station.

His example of cool bravery stimulated in all ranks the highest valour and determination to win.

As he recovered from his wounds in hospital, Evans was aware of reports from the front that he had been heroic in battle. Conscious that his fiancée might have picked up on the rumours, he wrote her an indignant letter which he hoped would put the record straight and avoid disappointment to her and his family when no such VC was forthcoming. Evans wrote:

> I don't expect to get it for I did nothing deserving of it so the less said about it the better. I am sure I don't know what they can have said I did, certainly nothing I consider deserving of it, in fact I am the reverse of proud of myself for having come away with the wounds I had. In fact the feeling I had about the whole business was that every dog had its day but this one has certainly not been mine…

Evans concluded: 'Your would-be husband is no hero and you had better know the truth.'

Evans insisted in his letter that he had been an organiser rather than a participant, though in a separate letter to his brothers he admitted to 'drawing his pistol'. It appears, in fact, that at one point Evans had, by mistake and already wounded in the shoulder, come across a heavily armed enemy position with only his orderly to support him. Realising they were hopelessly outnumbered, he decided to try to bluff the enemy into surrendering. 'Throw down your rifles!' he shouted and was astonished, but delighted, when some forty Germans laid down their rifles. There is some confusion about what happened next. One version stated that, realising he did not have sufficient men to take them as PoW, he looked back at his own lines and raced towards them. Fearing an enemy charge, his comrades shot at him but, fortunately, these shots missed. Another version of the same story suggests that it was the surrendering Germans who had run towards the enemy lines and they were shot at because the British troops, unaware the enemy had put down their arms, feared they were under attack.

However, it was when Evans again pressed forward to attack the enemy that a bullet grazed his ribs: the second wound referred to in his VC citation. Interestingly, however, Evans later wrote a paper on military training in which he said it was wrong for a battalion commander to leave his headquarters to make a personal reconnaissance, citing his own VC action, in which he said he had made a tactical error, to support his argument.

Evans's part in the battle eventually ended when he ordered the reserve company forward before relinquishing his command. Only then did he walk back in order to receive much-needed medical treatment. He was far from the only casualty of his battalion: of nearly 600 men who had taken part in the initial attack, 230 were killed, wounded or missing.

Evans's VC was formally announced on 26 November 1917. By the New Year, he had recovered sufficiently from his wounds to attend his investiture at Buckingham Palace on 2 January 1918, when he received his VC from George V. The investiture took place the day before his thirty-seventh birthday and soon afterwards he was back on active service. Evans spent the final months of the Great

War commanding the 1st Battalion of his own regiment, the Black Watch, during the final assaults on the Hindenberg Line.

Once again, he served with distinction for, on 16 September 1918, he was awarded a Bar to his DSO when his citation detailed his bravery during the lengthy battle:

> For conspicuous gallantry and devotion to duty in a three days' battle. On the first day he was moving about everywhere in his forward area directing operations, the next day he personally conducted a reconnaissance for a counter-attack, which was carried out on the third day. It was largely due to his untiring energy and method that the enemy were checked and finally driven out of our forward system.

On 10 October 1918, while on leave only a month before Armistice Day, he married his fiancée at Holy Trinity Church, Sloane Square, London, and, after the Armistice, he operated from a base in Holland. By this point, Evans was a brigadier-general and had been generously decorated in addition to his VC, DSO and Bar, and an incredible seven Mentions in Despatches. He received the Croix de Guerre from France and the Order of Leopold from Belgium, along with the Companionship of the Order of St Michael and St George (CMG) for distinguished war service. As Stephen Snelling concludes, in a wonderful tribute to Evans in the August 2015 issue of *Britain at War* magazine: 'All in all, it was not a bad record for a soldier with "no thirst for war".'

Sadly, after the war, Evans suffered a number of family tragedies. His sister-in-law was killed in a railway accident in Devon and then, in 1921, his wife died, apparently from heart failure caused by influenza, aged just twenty-seven. By this point, the couple had a son called Griffith, named after Evans's father, but, having served as a captain in the Black Watch during the Second World War, Griffith too died early, aged just thirty, in 1950.

In January 1936, Evans acted as a pall-bearer at the funeral of George V and in 1945, on the death of his father, he inherited the family estate at Llanbadarn, near Aberystwyth. Evans, whose last decoration was to be made a Companion of the Order of the Bath (CB), attended the confirmation service of his younger grandson, Roger, on 30 November 1962. As he left the platform on Paddington railway station, he suffered a massive heart attack and died almost immediately. He was just eight days away from his eightieth birthday.

Evans had always been a reluctant hero and, at one point, had even considered declining his VC on the grounds he had been no braver than any other soldier at Polygon Wood. His grandson, Christopher, once said: 'He felt there had been many others more deserving of the award who had not got it.'

Evans was buried in Llanbadarn churchyard and there have been numerous memorials in his honour over the decades including, in 2001, the unveiling of a memorial in Llanbadarn village square.

ACTING CORPORAL (LATER WARRANT OFFICER) ALEXANDER PICTON BRERETON

Canadian Expeditionary Force: The Manitoba Regiment
DATE OF BRAVERY: 9 AUGUST 1918
GAZETTED: 27 SEPTEMBER 1918
Special feature of the VC: a splendid Great War award for charging an enemy machine-gun post alone to prevent it from annihilating his platoon.

Alexander Brereton was born in Oak River, Alexander, Manitoba, Canada, on 13 November 1892. He was the son of Cloudesley Brereton, a farmer, and his wife Annie (*née* Black). One of six children, four boys and two girls, he was educated in Oak River. He worked as a farm labourer and, later, a barber before enlisting into the 144th Battalion in January 1916.

In September 1916, Brereton embarked for the United Kingdom with the Canadian Expeditionary Force. In January 1917, he arrived in France and joined the 8th Battalion. His VC action took place on 9 August 1918, during the second day of the Battle of Amiens in France. On this day, the Allies continued their successful progress eastwards. As the British and French advanced, the Canadian Corps also made significant gains, including the capture of Warvillers.

His VC was awarded for gallantry during the final stages of the First World War – the day after the Allies launched their famous Hundred Days Offensive. Brereton's platoon was ambushed on 9 August 1918 at Hatchet Wood, near Warvillers and east of Amiens. Machine-gunners threatened to wipe out the entire platoon but, as the *London Gazette* of 27 September 1918 explained, Brereton, aged twenty-five, then went into action:

> For most conspicuous bravery during an attack, when a line of hostile machine guns opened fire suddenly on his platoon, which was in an exposed position, and no cover available. This gallant N.C.O. at once appreciated the critical situation, and realised that unless something was done at once his platoon would be annihilated. On his own initiative, and without a moment's delay and alone, he sprang forward and reached one of the hostile machine-gun posts, where he shot the man operating the machine-gun and bayonetted the next man who attempted to operate it, whereupon nine others surrendered to him.
>
> Cpl. Brereton's action was a splendid example of resource and bravery, and not only undoubtedly saved many of his comrades' lives, but also inspired his platoon to charge and capture the five remaining posts.

As the Great War drew to a close, Brereton was presented with his VC by George V at an investiture at Buckingham Palace on 24 October 1918. Also present at the investiture was Sergeant Frederick

Coppins, from the same regiment as Brereton, who was awarded the VC for his bravery during the same action. As a 24-year-old corporal, Coppins had also been met by machine-gun fire and, like Brereton, he and his men had no cover. Coppins called on four men to follow him and they rushed straight for the machine-guns. The four men were killed and Coppins was wounded but he nevertheless reached the enemy alone, killed the operator of the first machine-gun and three of the crew before capturing four other surrendering soldiers. His citation stated: 'Cpl. Coppins, by this act of outstanding valour, was the means of saving many lives of the men of his platoon, and enabled the advance to be continued.'

After war ended, Brereton returned to Canada where he received a hero's welcome from family and friends before being discharged in 1919. Brereton farmed land at Elnora, Alberta, where he eventually acquired 640 acres of land on which he lived and worked. In June 1925, he married Mary McPhee and the couple went on to have a son and two daughters.

In June 1939, Brereton was presented to George VI and Queen Elizabeth during their visit to Edmonton, Canada. He resumed his military service, aged forty-six, after the outbreak of the Second World War, serving as a company quartermaster sergeant at Red Deer Training Camp, Alberta. He was discharged in 1944 and ran a butcher's shop and, later, a general store before returning to farming in Elnora. However, by this time his son, Mac, had taken on most of the responsibility for running the farm where he built up a splendid herd of Aberdeen Angus cattle.

In May 1976, Brereton was admitted to hospital suffering from heart problems. He died at Colonel Belcher Hospital, Calgary, on 11 June 1976, aged eighty-three. He was buried in Elnora Cemetery four days later, following a funeral service at Knox United Church, Three Hills. His wife, Mary, had died four years earlier. A Royal Canadian Legion post at Elnora has been named in Brereton's honour and there is a portrait of him at the Canadian War Museum in Ottawa.

PRIVATE (LATER LIEUTENANT)
THOMAS FASTI DINESEN

Canadian Expeditionary Force: The Quebec Regiment (the Royal
Highlanders of Canada)

DATE OF BRAVERY: 12 AUGUST 1918

GAZETTED: 26 OCTOBER 1918

Special feature of the VC: a very fine award to one of the very few
non-British/Commonwealth recipients of the VC. The medal group also
has a unique Croix de Guerre to a Dane. Dinesen was the brother of
Karen Blixen, of Out of Africa *fame.*

Thomas Fasti Dinesen was born in Rungsted, near Copenhagen, the capital of Denmark, on 9 August 1892. He was the son of Captain Adolph Dinesen and his wife Ingeborg (*née* Westenholz). Thomas Dinesen came from a wealthy, aristocratic, military family and his grandfather, as well as his father, served as officers in the Danish Army. His sister was Izak Dinesen (later Baroness Karen Blixen), the author of *Out of Africa* (in the film of the same name she is played by Meryl Streep) and other works. Dinesen was educated at Rungsted State School and the Polytechnical School, Copenhagen.

Before the war, he worked as an engineer and in 1914 he became a member of the Academic Rifle Corps in which he established himself as a first-class shot. After the outbreak of the Great War in August 1914, he tried to join the French and British Armies but they would only accept their own nationals. In his book about his wartime experiences, *Merry Hell! A Dane with the Canadians*, Dinesen wrote:

> But from the very first day of August [1914] I knew that, sooner
> or later, I should have to leave everything and go in search of the
> real war. There was – in my set, anyhow – a firm conviction [that]
> the future of humanity, the continuance of civilization, the sal-
> vation of the world, depended on the subjugation of Germany.

> The Prussian militarists had, in accordance with a prearranged and
> carefully-laid plan, let loose the demons of war over Europe; but now
> all civilized nations were fighting against them and soon the day
> of victory would dawn. The tyranny of Prussia should and would
> be crushed...

In April 1917, with Denmark still neutral and with Dinesen desperate to fight the Germans, he sailed to America where once again he was foiled, being unable to enlist into the US Forces. He finally succeeded in getting accepted for military service when he went to the New York recruiting office of the Canadian Army in June 1917. He enlisted as a private into the Royal Highlanders of Canada and was posted to Guy Street Barracks, Montreal. Three months later, he was posted to the UK where he underwent training at Bramshott and Aldershot, both in Hampshire. In March 1918, Dinesen travelled to France with his battalion where he volunteered for numerous trench raids, even though he initially took part in no major battles. During their early days on the frontline, Dinesen and his comrades were subjected to both gas and shell attacks. In *Merry Hell!* he wrote:

> *Hizzz-Crash!!* the shells are bursting both in front and behind our
> hiding-place; the very ground is trembling and we too tremble.
> Our hair is standing on end – but – are we scared? Are we down-
> hearted? No!! We hurl all sorts of execrations towards the shells
> flying above us, though our voices are lost in the din of the explosions.

In May 1918, during a spell behind the frontline, Dinesen and his comrade were chosen to take part in a Non-Commissioned Officer (NCO) training course, which took up most of June until Dinesen returned to the frontline in early July. At times, he bemoaned his lowly rank, writing in *Merry Hell!*: 'I wish I were an officer and could get a chance to follow events! A private soldier is moved about like a tethered cow. One thing, however, is certain: there is a big attack being prepared, but when is it coming off – and where – and how?'

During the eventual offensive, all hell was let loose, as Dinesen noted in his book:

> The whole of the western horizon bursts into flame as if the earth had opened. Thousands of guns are roaring at once; the shells howl and hiss right over our heads, and our knees give way under us ... every sense is drowned in the paralysing roar of those first minutes.

In *Merry Hell!* Dinesen related how he had been told by a friendly officer, Captain Grafftey, that the 42nd Battalion's objective would be to take the town of Parvillers. Dinesen wrote modestly about his own part in the fighting and his VC but he did describe some of the action:

> I turn a corner quickly – two grey Germans stand straight in front of me ... Two red flashes straight into my face – done for already! – but they haven't hit me, so now it's my turn. A snap-shot at one of the two, and the other disappears round a corner. The road is free! 'Come on boys, give them hell!' At the next corner a shower of rifle bullets and 'sticks' [bombs] whizz past my head from a machine-gun-post...I fire away madly till my magazine is empty; then I fling down the rifle and hurl my bombs at them – the trench is chock-full of dust and smoke.

Dinesen was awarded the VC for his courage displayed during the Battle of Amiens on 12 August 1918, three days after his twenty-sixth birthday. His citation announced in the *London Gazette* on 16 October 1918 read:

> For most conspicuous and continuous bravery displayed dur-ing ten hours of hand-to-hand fighting which led to the capture

of over a mile of strongly garrisoned and stubbornly defended enemy trenches.

Five times in succession he rushed forward alone and single-handed put hostile machine guns out of action, accounting for twelve of the enemy with bomb and bayonet. His sustained valour and resourcefulness inspired his comrades at a very critical stage of the action, and were an example to all.

On 21 August 1918, during more heavy fighting, Dinesen displayed yet more bravery that led to the award of the French Croix de Guerre. His other decorations included the Knight's Cross of the Order of Dannebrog from the King of Denmark. Dinesen was promoted to acting corporal in August 1918 and then spent a month at an officers' school. On 5 November, he was commissioned as a lieutenant and, six days later, when the war ended, he was based at Mons, Belgium. Dinesen received his VC from George V at an investiture at Buckingham Palace on 13 December 1918. Of his investiture, he said: 'The King said a few gracious words to each of us as he pinned the Cross on our breasts. We saluted and stepped back...' He was demobbed in January 1919, still with the rank of lieutenant. Dinesen wrote: 'We won the war ... I got off without a scratch, with all my aspirations and dreams fulfilled. And they rewarded me, into the bargain!'

Dinesen's sister Karen explained in a letter written in December 1918 that her brother's bravery, and the recognition from the British King, in some measure saved her own reputation in the community of British colonials among whom she lived in British East Africa. According to Blixen, she had inadvertently alienated many of her neighbours by helping to buy horses for a German officer whom she met on a ship while sailing to Kenya for the first time. Only months later this officer, General Paul Emil von Lettow-Vorbeck, was named commander of the German forces in East Africa. As part of this military role, Lettow-Vorbeck waged a campaign against Blixen's

English neighbours. Blixen noted the suspicion and resentment that this aroused in her fellow colonists subsided only after her brother was awarded the VC in 1918.

From 1920 to 1925, Dinesen lived in Kenya, working as a farmer and civil engineer. In the aftermath of the war, he helped his sister (whom he, and most of their Danish friends, called 'Tanne') manage her coffee farm in the Ngong hills, south-west of Nairobi. From 1925 onwards, and having returned to live in Denmark, Dinesen farmed an estate in Jutland. He married Joanna Lindhardt, the daughter of the Lutheran Dean of Arhus, in Denmark, in April 1926 and the couple went on to have two daughters. Dinesen was also an enthusiastic author and he penned several books, including a biography of his famous sister. Dinesen died in Leerbaek, Denmark, on 10 March 1979, aged eighty-six, and is buried in the family plot at Horsholm Cemetery, Rungsted, near Copenhagen.

In November 2014, I had the hugely enjoyable task of co-hosting a charity gala dinner at which HRH The Duke of Cambridge was the guest of honour. Prince William had become a loyal supporter of SkillForce and so it was a real honour to welcome him to the event – in his role as patron of the charity – to mark our tenth anniversary. I tend to launch and support charities involved in areas in which I have a real interest and SkillForce most certainly centres on two of my passions: education and the military. SkillForce inspires young people to achieve at school and succeed in life using the values of Armed Forces' personnel.

Before the dinner, I showed Prince William the Lord Ashcroft Gallery at the IWM, which is the home to my collection of VCs and George Crosses (GCs), and to similar awards in the care of the museum. The Duke of Cambridge was enthusiastic to learn about the stories behind some of the medals and he seized on one VC in particular from my collection: the decoration awarded to Dinesen. As such, I was able to give him a brief account of the Dane's astonishing bravery in the final months of the Great War.

MICHAEL ASHCROFT

ACTING LIEUTENANT-COLONEL
BERNARD WILLIAM VANN

Army: The Nottinghamshire and Derbyshire Regiment (the Sherwood Foresters)

DATE OF BRAVERY: 29 SEPTEMBER 1918

GAZETTED: 14 DECEMBER 1918

Special feature of the VC: the only recipient of the decoration who, although an ordained clergyman, fought as a combatant soldier.

Bernard William Vann was born in Rushden, Northamptonshire, on 9 July 1887. He was the son of a headmaster, Alfred Vann, and his wife Hannah (*née* Simpson), who was also a teacher. The fourth of five boys, Bernard attended his father's school, South End Elementary School in Rushden, where his mother also taught. Afterwards, he attended Chichele College, Higham Ferrers, Northamptonshire, where his father was by then headmaster. Vann Jr was both academic and sporty, captaining the football, hockey and cricket teams. After leaving school, he worked for a time as a teacher at Ashby-de-la-Zouch Grammar School and developed his football talents, playing centre forward for Northampton Town (he later played for Burton United and Derby County). Relentlessly ambitious, he attended Jesus College, Cambridge, from 1907, where he was a hockey blue and a talented football player. He also earned a reputation for delivering passionate speeches, although they could sometimes be somewhat chaotic in nature.

After graduating in 1910, Vann was ordained as a deacon on 22 September 1911 at St Barnabas, New Humberstone, near Leicester, by the Bishop of Peterborough. After this short-lived post, he was the curate at St Saviour's, Leicester, for two years until appointed as chaplain and an assistant master at Wellingborough School, Northamptonshire, from January 1913 to August 1914. Following the outbreak of the First World War in August 1914, he applied for an Army chaplaincy but, impatient at the delay in being accepted, enlisted instead as a private soldier into the 1/28th Battalion (County of London Regiment) (The Artists Rifles) in late August. Days later, on 1 September 1914, Vann was commissioned into the Sherwood Foresters as a second lieutenant.

The Revd A. E. W. Manvell, the vicar of St Barnabas in Wellingborough, told a local journalist: 'As soon as I heard that Vann had enlisted, I thought he would either get killed or win the VC, because there is nothing that would keep him back. He does not know what fear is.'

Vann arrived in France in February 1915 and, at Kemmel on 24 April, the small advance trench that he was in was blown up, causing him to be badly bruised and buried for a short time. However, he not only dug himself out, but then organised the defence and, under heavy fire, rescued others who were buried. Two days later, he was promoted to lieutenant.

He was made a temporary captain on 6 June and, on 15 August, he was awarded the Military Cross (MC) for his bravery over the previous months. His citation read:

> At Kemmel on 24 April 1915, when a small advance trench which he occupied was blown in and he himself wounded and half buried, he showed the greatest determination in organising the defence and rescuing buried men under heavy fire, although wounded and severely bruised he refused to leave his post until directly ordered to do so.
>
> At Ypres on 31 July 1915, and subsequent days, he ably assisted another officer to hold the left trench of the line, setting a fine example to those around him.
>
> On various occasions he has led patrols up to the enemy's trenches and obtained valuable information.

In October 1915, Vann took part in the Battle of Loos that, by then, had already claimed the life of one of his brothers, Captain Arthur Vann. In fact, Bernard Vann was badly wounded by a bullet that passed through his left arm during fighting in October that resulted from a British attack on the Hohenzollern Redoubt. However, he continued throwing grenades until ordered from the battlefield.

In June 1916, Vann was promoted to substantive captain and, later the same month, to acting major. In September, he took part in a daring raid on enemy trenches. When he came across a dug-out full of enemy soldiers at Blairville, he ordered them out. As two soldiers came at him with fixed bayonets, he killed one, wounded another and the rest of the party surrendered. For this action, he was awarded a Bar to his MC that was announced on 14 November 1916 when his citation read: 'For conspicuous gallantry in action. He led a daring raid against the enemy's trenches, himself taking five prisoners and displaying great courage and determination. He has on many occasions done fine work.'

For several months in 1917, Vann was back in the UK recuperating from neuritis (the inflamation of a nerve or the whole nervous system). In the same year, he was awarded the French Croix de Guerre. Far from renouncing his priesthood as a soldier, Vann was involved in religious work on the frontline and, even when commanding his battalion, he sometimes gave Holy Communion to sick or wounded soldiers.

In late September 1918, by then with the rank of acting lieutenant-colonel and having been wounded in battle no fewer than four times, Vann took part in the attack for which he was awarded the VC. At the time, he was commanding the 1/6th Sherwood Foresters.

The citation for his VC stated:

> For most conspicuous bravery, devotion to duty and fine leadership during the attack at Bellenglise and Lehaucourt on September 29th, 1918.
>
> He led his battalion with great skill across the Canal du Nord through a very thick fog and under heavy fire from field and machine guns.
>
> On reaching the high ground above Bellenglise the whole attack was held up by fire of all descriptions from the front and right flank.

> Realising that everything depended on the advance going for-
> ward with the barrage, Col. Vann rushed up to the firing line and
> with the greatest gallantry led the line forward. By his prompt action
> and absolute contempt for danger the whole situation was changed,
> the men were encouraged and the line swept forward.
>
> Later, he rushed a field-gun single-handed and knocked out three
> of the detachment. The success of the day was in no small degree due
> to the splendid gallantry and fine leadership displayed by this officer.

The British assault had been successful, but at a price. During the
capture of Ramicourt–Montbrehain on 29 September, 1,500 enemy
prisoners were captured but four British officers and twenty-five
other ranks were killed, with 109 men wounded and eight missing.

Vann's VC was announced in the *London Gazette* on 14 December
1918, just over a month after the war ended. However, by then it was
a posthumous award because Vann had been killed, aged thirty-one,
by a sniper near Ramicourt on 3 October 1918, when leading his
battalion in another attack.

After Vann's death, a fellow officer wrote in *The Times*:

> I can think of him only as a fighter, not merely against the enemy
> in the field, but a fighter against everything and everybody that
> was not an influence for good to his men ... His many friends will
> rejoice that the constant gallantry and magnificent example of this
> fine Christian gentleman has been recognised by the highest award
> the country can bestow.

Many clergymen served during the two world wars but strictly as
non-combatants, whereas Vann served as a frontline officer. To this
day, he remains the only clergyman to receive the VC for his actions
as a combatant soldier.

Vann left a widow, Doris (*née* Strange-Beck), a Canadian nurse
whom he had met in Paris and married at St Paul's Church in

Knightsbridge, London, on 27 December 1916. Their son Bernard Geoffrey was born on 2 June 1919 but, of course, Vann never lived to see him. Doris received her late husband's VC from George V at an investiture at Buckingham Palace on 26 November 1919. As well as his VC, she received her late husband's damaged chalice and his Bible in a small, leather case. Vann's son went on to become a lieutenant-commander in the Royal Navy and he died in 1994.

Vann is buried in the Bellicourt British Cemetery in France where the inscription on his headstone, which was composed by the Bishop of Peterborough, who had ordained Vann, reads: 'A Great Priest Who In His Days Pleased God.' Additionally, his name appears on several memorials including, along with the name of his brother who died at the Battle of Loos, on the Coates War Memorial in Gloucestershire. In 2006 a Blue Plaque was unveiled at Vann's birthplace – 46 High Street, Rushden – by his grandson.

In 2014, to mark the centenary of the start of the Great War, a BBC radio documentary was aired which was presented by Revd Richard Coles, the vicar of St Mary's in Finedon, Northamptonshire, who had given up his career as a pop star in The Communards to become a priest. Revd Coles, who wanted to go in search of the 'real' Bernard Vann, was full of admiration for the VC recipient. 'I don't think he could have asked for a more honourable death. That is a warrior's death.' However, he conceded that Vann must have struggled to reconcile his Christian beliefs and his role as a frontline soldier: 'There would have been tensions. But he was convinced of the righteousness of this war and the British cause.'

Gallipoli

In early 1915, the war on the Western Front was not going well for the Allies: fighting was bogged down, casualties were high and all the signs were that it would not be the short conflict that most had predicted. Winston Churchill, the Secretary of State for War, and others thought it would be advantageous to open a second front in the East. This, it was thought, would distract the Germans on the Western Front, possibly knock Turkey out of the war, and enable the Allies to prop up Russia. It was therefore decided to land an expeditionary force on the Gallipoli peninsula in the Dardanelles.

CAPTAIN (LATER MAJOR)
RICHARD RAYMOND WILLIS

Army: The Lancashire Fusiliers
DATE OF BRAVERY: 25 APRIL 1915
GAZETTED: 24 AUGUST 1915
Special feature of the VC: one of the famous 'Six Before Breakfast' awards for the ill-fated Gallipoli landings.

Richard Raymond Willis was born in Woking, Surrey, on 13 October 1876. He was the son of Richard Willis, a merchant, and his wife Marion (*née* Godfrey). Richard Willis Jr was educated at Totnes Grammar School, Devon, and Harrow School, Middlesex, before attending the Royal Military College, Sandhurst. On 20 February 1897, he was gazetted into the Lancashire Fusiliers as a second lieutenant.

Shortly afterwards, Willis joined the 2nd Battalion of the regiment in Quetta, India, although he had to return home in order to recover from enteric fever. In January 1898, he travelled with his battalion to Egypt, where it was part of Kitchener's Army tasked with the reconquest of the Sudan. Willis was promoted to lieutenant in July 1898 and on 2 September of that year took part in the Battle of Omdurman when a smaller, but better equipped, British/Egyptian force won a major battle against Abdullah al-Taashi's troops.

Willis was promoted to captain in 1900 and transferred to the 1st

Battalion. From July 1900 until 1915, he commanded C Company as he and his men served in Crete, Malta, Gibraltar and Alexandria (Egypt). He was a talented sportsman, representing the battalion at polo and hockey, as well as being a champion shot with a revolver, a gifted linguist and a musician. Willis married Maude Temple, the daughter of an Army officer, in Marylebone, central London, on 10 July 1907, and the couple went on to have a daughter and two sons. From January 1901, Willis was an enthusiastic Freemason and he initiated the St John and St Paul Lodge in Valletta, Malta.

From 1907, he was in India but, after the outbreak of the Great War in August 1914, the 1st Battalion arrived back in the UK that Christmas Day. On 28 March 1915, the battalion arrived in Alexandria to prepare for their part in the Gallipoli campaign, in which the Lancashire Fusiliers would play a key role from the start.

On 25 April 1915, while two companies from the 2nd Battalion landed at X Beach north of Cape Tekke, four companies from the 1st Battalion were ordered to land at W Beach. A small, sandy cove between Cape Helles and Tekke Burnu, it was so well defended that the Turks may have regarded it as impregnable to an attack from open boats. Nevertheless, it was decided to launch an offensive at 6 a.m.: worse still, the defenders knew exactly when it was coming because, as was customary throughout the First World War, the attack was preceded by a sustained naval bombardment by heavy guns which ceased just before the assault began. As a result, there was no element of surprise to aid the British troops in the biggest amphibious landing of the war.

Captain Willis, who led his beloved C Company during the attack, was one of several survivors to provide a vivid description of the events that day:

> Not a sign of life was to be seen on the Peninsula in front of us. It might have been a deserted land we were nearing in our little boats. Then crack! ... The signal for the massacre had been given:

rapid fire, machine-guns and deadly accurate sniping opened from the cliffs above, and soon the casualties included the rest of the crew and many men…

The timing of the ambush was perfect; we were completely exposed and helpless in our slow-moving boats, just target practice for the concealed Turks, and within a few minutes only half of the thirty men in my boat were left alive. We were now 100 yards from the shore, and I gave the order 'overboard'. We scrambled out into some four feet of water and some of the boats with their cargo of dead and wounded floated away on the currents still under fire from the snipers. With this unpromising start the advance began. Many were hit in the sea, and no response was possible, for the enemy was in trenches well above our heads.

We toiled through the water towards the sandy beach, but here another trap was awaiting us, for the Turks had cunningly concealed a trip wire just below the surface of the water and on the beach itself were a number of land mines, and a deep belt of rusty wire extended across the landing place. Machine-guns, hidden in caves at the end of the amphitheatre of cliffs, enfiladed this.

Our wretched men were ordered to wait behind this wire for the wire-cutters to cut a pathway through. They were shot in helpless batches while they waited, and could not even use their rifles in retaliation since the sand and the sea had clogged their action. One Turkish sniper in particular took a heavy toll at very close range until I forced open the bolt of a rifle with the heel of my boot and closed his career with the first shot, but the heap of empty cartridges round him testified to the damage he had done. Safety lay in movement, and isolated parties scrambled through the wire to cover. Among them was Sergeant Richards with a leg horribly twisted, but he managed somehow to get through.

Captain Clayton, who was killed in action six weeks later, also described desperate scenes:

There was tremendously strong barbed wire where my boat was landed. Men were being hit in the boats as they splashed ashore. I got up to my waist in water, tripped over a rock and went under, got up and made for the shore and lay down by the barbed wire. There was a man there before me shouting for wire-cutters. I got mine out, but could not make the slightest impression. The front of the wire was by now a thick mass of men, the majority of whom never moved again. The noise was ghastly and the sights horrible. I eventually crawled through the wire with great difficulty, as my pack kept catching on the wire, and got under a small mound which actually gave us protection. The weight of our packs tired us, so that we could only gasp for breath. After a little time we fixed bayonets and started up the cliffs right and left. On the right several were blown up by a mine [this later proved to be 'friendly fire' – a British naval shell]. When we started up the cliff, the enemy went, but when we got to the top they were ready and poured shots on us.

The Lancashire Fusiliers had started the day with twenty-seven officers and 1,002 other men. Twenty-four hours later a head count revealed just sixteen officers and 304 men. The *London Gazette* of 24 August 1915 reported that the Fusiliers

were met by a very deadly fire from hidden machine-guns which caused a great number of casualties. The survivors, however, rushed up to and cut the wire entanglements, not withstanding the terrific fire from the enemy, and after overcoming supreme difficulties, the cliffs were gained and the position maintained. Amongst the very gallant officers and men engaged in this most hazardous undertaking, Capt. Willis, Sergt. [Alfred] Richards and Private [William] Keneally have been selected by their comrades as having performed the most signal acts of bravery.

In a second, similar citation, delayed until 15 March 1917 because of discussions over how many VCs should be awarded for the single action, three other men were awarded the VC for bravery at W Beach after also being chosen by their comrades. These were Captain Cuthbert Bromley, Sergeant Frank Stubbs and Corporal John Grimshaw. Willis, Richards, Keneally, Bromley, Stubbs and Grimshaw soon became known as the 'Six Before Breakfast' VCs.

Willis, who was thirty-eight at the time of his VC action, had, in fact, been involved in heavy fighting in between the Gallipoli landings of 25 April and the announcement of his VC on 24 August. Twice in the fortnight following 25 April he escaped uninjured when men were killed just feet away from him. He then took part in an action on 28 April when he led an attack by a small force in the First Battle of Krithia, but he and his men had to withdraw. On 2 May, he was back in action on W Beach during a major attempt by the Turks to retake the position. On 4 June, after a brief spell of sick leave, he commanded D Company in an attack that was intended to break through the Turkish lines in front of Krithia. In a day of terrifying fighting at the Third Battle of Krithia, in which the 1st Battalion suffered more than 500 casualties, Willis was shot and wounded just below his heart. He was evacuated to Egypt and, later, to the UK.

Willis seemed embarrassed by his award of the VC and asked journalists to 'Please keep me out of it'. He did, however, assist an artist from the *Illustrated London News* with his recollections of the W Beach landings, and the painting that resulted from it depicted Willis as the central figure, with one hand cupped to his mouth shouting encouragement and the other clutching a walking stick high in the air. This resulted in him receiving the nickname of 'Walking Stick Willis' for the remainder of his military career. Much later, when asked what it was like to return to service after being badly injured, Willis replied: 'It is not pleasant, but by far the worst of it in my case is that all of my brother officers and most of my men are gone.'

Willis was promoted to major in September 1915 and he received his VC from George V at an investiture at Buckingham Palace on

21 December 1915. After recovering from his injuries, Willis was posted to the Western Front with the 2nd Battalion. He served both on the Somme and in the Ypres Salient with three other units: the 1st Royal Inniskilling Fusiliers, the 8th West Ridings and 6th York & Lancasters. In August 1916, he was made an acting lieutenant-colonel and in January 1917 he was appointed Commanding Officer of the 1st Battalion, Royal Inniskilling Fusiliers. In March 1917, he reverted to the rank of major and in April 1918 he was present during the German breakthrough on the Lys, when he was praised for his work in marshalling his men. At the end of the war, he returned to his regiment and was appointed second-in-command of the 2nd Battalion. Having commanded a unit in India for a short time, Willis retired on 26 November 1920 after more than twenty-three years of military service.

Willis became a teacher in 1923 and for the next six years he worked for the RAF Education Branch and, later, in private schools. Both his sons pursued Army careers – one was awarded the Military Cross (MC) – and they both eventually moved to Africa.

After the outbreak of the Second World War in September 1939, Willis volunteered to work as a training officer for the Army and was based at Aldershot, Hampshire. During the 'Blitz', he was injured while in London and needed hospital treatment. After he recovered, he resumed his teaching career in a prep school. Both his health and his finances suffered during the 1950s and, in 1957, he appealed in the press for a loan of £100, citing 'a desperate need'. In 1958 Willis moved into the Lilian Faithfull Home in Cheltenham, where he lived with his wife. He died at the home on 9 February 1966, aged eighty-nine. On 15 February 1966, he was cremated at Cheltenham Crematorium, where his ashes were scattered in the Garden of Remembrance.

Lieutenant-Colonel John Grimshaw, who had served under Willis at W Beach and who had also been awarded the VC for his bravery, paid a warm tribute to his former Commanding Officer in an obituary in the *Regimental Gazette*. Grimshaw said: 'I shall always remember him as my old Company Commander and the excellent example of courage and leadership that he always displayed which made one proud to serve under him. He was a great man who we will always remember.' At the time of Willis's death, Grimshaw was the only 'Six Before Breakfast' VC recipient left alive. A memorial plaque for Willis was unveiled at Cheltenham Crematorium nearly forty years after his death.

I purchased Willis's medal group privately in 2010 and this meant that I then possessed three of the 'Six Before Breakfast' VCs in my collection, having already bought Grimshaw's medal group privately in 1999 and Sergeant Alfred Richards's medals at a Spink auction in London in 2005. I felt hugely privileged to be the custodian of half of these legendary six VCs and even more delighted that they were on public display at the Imperial War Museum in London.

In 2014, ahead of the centenary of the Gallipoli landings, I was approached by the Fusilier Museum in Bury, Lancashire, to see if I would be willing to loan my medal groups to mark the centenary. The Fusilier Museum, which had in its own possession the VCs belonging to Sergeant Frank Stubbs and Private William Keneally, hoped to unite all six VCs the following year: 2015.

I readily agreed to loan my three medal groups and the Fusilier Museum carried out some good old-fashioned detective work in order to locate the sixth and final VC – that belonging to Major Cuthbert Bromley, from Seaford in East Sussex, who had been temporarily promoted from captain and was wounded in the landing. In an article for the *Sunday Telegraph*, published in February 2014, I wrote about the 'Six Before Breakfast' VCs and my delight at the prospect of all the VC awards being united for the first time in 100 years.

Before long, Colonel Brian Gorski, the chairman of the Fusilier Museum, who supervised the search for the VC, said: 'We are delighted to have found the missing medal. It's taken a lot of time and effort but we are hopeful that all six will be united as part of our centenary exhibition for Gallipoli.' The final VC was eventually tracked down to a member of the Bromley family and the owner agreed to loan it for the centenary celebrations.

The Bromleys had also kept letters that were sent from Bromley to his mother, Louise, during the war. One of them was dated 29 April 1915, just four days after the W Beach landing. It read, with considerable understatement:

> MY DEAREST MOTHER,
>
> I'm laid up with a bullet wound, nothing serious at all, clean through the flesh and I'm as fit as can be. The regiment suffered rather heavily in the recent fighting. I quite enjoyed myself and hope to be about again very shortly. Fondest love, Cuthbert.
>
> PS Writing bad is not due to wound but awkward position lying down.

W Beach was eventually renamed 'Lancashire Landing' in honour of the Lancashire Fusiliers. Rightly so, in my view, and the landing on those 350 yards of beach at dawn on 25 April 1915 remains one of the most courageous actions ever performed by British Armed Forces.

ACTING CORPORAL (LATER STAFF SERGEANT) WILLIAM COSGROVE

Army: The Royal Munster Fusiliers
DATE OF BRAVERY: 26 APRIL 1915
GAZETTED: 23 AUGUST 1915
Special feature of the VC: an award for quite exceptional gallantry during the Gallipoli landings.

William Cosgrove was born at Ballinookera, near the fishing village of Aghada, Co. Cork, Ireland, on 1 October 1888. He was one of five sons of Michael Cosgrove, a local farmer, and his wife, Mary (*née* Morrissey). At one point, Michael Cosgrove left his wife and children at home and travelled to Australia to seek work but he later returned to Ireland after the death, aged just thirteen, of his only daughter, Mary Catherine, who had contracted tuberculosis following a fall from her pony. William Cosgrove attended Ballinrostig School before becoming an apprentice butcher at Whitegate, on the edge of Cork harbour. Meanwhile, three of his four brothers had travelled to the United States in search of work and better opportunities.

As a young butcher, Cosgrove delivered meat to Fort Carlisle Army camp and this appears to have given him an interest in the military. In 1910, the quiet, shy young man enlisted into the Royal Munster Fusiliers. He served with his regiment in India and Burma but, after the outbreak of the First World War in August 1914, his unit returned to the UK in January 1915. In March of that year, his Coventry-based battalion was ordered to the Dardanelles. On 25 April, the troops began their landing on V beach near Cape Helles, Gallipoli, in the face of a murderous enemy fire. During the fierce two-day battle, his battalion took some 600 casualties: killed, missing and wounded.

Cosgrove, then twenty-six, a mountain of a man standing 6ft 6in. tall and weighing sixteen stone, was awarded his VC for extraordinary bravery on 26 April. The man known affectionately as the 'East Cork Giant' led his section in an attack on the Turkish positions. When they were stopped by 6ft-high posts and thick barbed wire, Cosgrove used his formidable frame and great strength to help his men break through. Using only his bare hands, he tore both the fence and its fence-posts down.

The *London Gazette* of 23 August 1915 stated:

> For most conspicuous bravery in the leading of his section with great dash during our attack from the beach to the east of Cape Helles, on the Turkish positions, on 26th April, 1915.
>
> Corporal Cosgrove on this occasion pulled down the posts of the

enemy's high wire entanglements single-handed, notwithstanding a terrific fire from both front and flanks, thereby greatly contributing to the successful clearing of the heights.

Cosgrove was severely wounded in the action and was evacuated to hospital for two operations. He spent time recuperating in the UK and, later, Ireland. Cosgrove, who was a colourful character with a delicious turn of phrase, described how he was well aware of the dangers that he faced after he and his comrades were tasked with cutting their way through the enemy wire:

> I thought, when I heard the work I was detailed for, that I would never again have the opportunity of a day's fighting. However, the work was there; it had to be done, for on its success rested the safety of many men, as well as the opportunity it would afford them of helping to throw back the Turks.
>
> Our job was to dash ahead, face the trenches bristling with rifles and machine-guns, and destroy the wire entanglements – that is, to cut them here and there with our pliers. Fifty men were detailed for the work; poor Sergeant-Major Bennett led us, but just as we made the dash – oh, such a storm of lead was concentrated on us, for the Turks knew of our intention.
>
> Our Sergeant-Major was killed – a bullet through the brain. I then took charge; shouted to the boys to come on. From the village near at hand there came a terrible fire to swell the murderous hail of bullets from the trenches. In the village they fired from doors and windows, and from that advantage they could comfortably take aim.
>
> The dash was quite 100 yards, and I don't know whether I ran or prayed the faster – I wanted to try and succeed in my work, and I also wanted to have the benefit of dying with a prayer in my mind. I can tell you it is not fortunately given to everyone to note the incidents that seem to be the last in your life, and you [are] never feeling better or stronger.

Well, some of us got close up to the wire and we started to cut it with pliers. You might as well try and snip Cloyne Round Tower with a lady's scissors, and you would not hurt yourself either. The wire was of great strength, strained as tight as fiddle-string, and so full of spikes and thorns that you could not get the cutters between.

'Heavens,' said I, 'we're done'; a moment later I threw the pliers from me. 'Pull them [the posts] up,' I roared. 'Put your arms around them and pull them out of the ground.' I dashed at the first one; heaved and strained, and then it came out into my arms; and same as you'd lift a child. I believe there was wild cheering when they saw what I was at, but I only heard the screech of the bullets and saw dust rising all around from where they hit.

I could not tell how many I pulled up. I did my best, and the boys that were left with me were every bit as good as myself, and I do wish they all got some recognition. When the wire was down the rest of the lads came on like 'devils', and not withstanding the pulverising fire, they reached the trenches. They met a brave honourable foe in the Turks, and I am sorry that such decent fighting men were brought into the row by such dirty tricksters as the Germans. They gave us great resistance, but we got to their trenches, and won about 200 yards length by 20 yards deep, and 700 yards from the shore…

Cosgrove was wounded in the fighting later in the day as he recalled with apparent relish:

A machine-gun sent some bullets into me, and strange, I was wounded before I reached the trench, though I did not realise it. When I got to the trench I did my own part, and later collapsed. One of the bullets struck me in the side, and passed clean through me. It struck the left hook of my tunic, then entered my body, took a couple of splinters off my backbone, but of course did not injure the spinal column, and passed out on my right side, knocking off the other belt hook. I was taken up feeling pretty bad, when I came to my senses,

and considered seriously wounded. I was removed to Malta Hospital, where there were two operations performed, and the splinters
of my backbone removed. I was about sixteen stone weight at the
Dardanelles, but I am now down in weight but not too used up...

Although Cosgrove was keen that his comrades were given credit
for their bravery, there was no doubt that he had led the way and
that the combination of his formidable courage and his immense
strength had made him a truly formidable adversary in battle. Burrowes Kelly, the ship's surgeon, wrote in his diary: 'The manner
in which the man worked out in the open will never be forgotten
by those who were fortunate enough to witness it.' Many others,
both on shore and aboard the *River Clyde*, also witnessed the full
extent of Cosgrove's gallantry and strength.

Cosgrove's VC was announced on 23 August 1915, two months
after those awarded to two other soldiers, Lieutenant-Colonel Charles
Doughty-Wylie and Captain Garth Walford, for their bravery on
V Beach. Cosgrove's award had been prompted by a recommendation from Second Lieutenant H. A. Brown, of the 1st Royal Munster
Fusiliers, that a 'most conspicuous act of bravery' had been displayed.
He said of Cosgrove: 'I personally consider he deserves the height
of praise for such a courageous act and was much impressed to see
him though wounded in the back leading his section shortly before
the enemy were driven from their trenches and the fort captured.'

Cosgrove never fully recovered from his injuries because not all
the shrapnel could be removed from his back during the two operations in Malta. He was promoted to sergeant in 1915 and took part
in recruiting in Ireland. He received his VC from George V at an
investiture at Buckingham Palace on 4 November 1916.

In 1922 the Royal Munster Fusiliers were disbanded (following
the creation of the Irish Free State) and Cosgrove transferred to the
Royal Northumberland Fusiliers. In 1928, he transferred to the 6th
(Burma) Battalion, University Training Corps, based in Rangoon,

Burma. Cosgrove was an expert shot despite his injuries and in two successive years he helped the Rangoon Training Corps to third place in the Imperial Universities' Shoot. In 1934, Cosgrove retired as a staff sergeant instructor after twenty-four years' service. As a result of his VC, Cosgrove was often the centre of attention, although he was a shy man who never wanted any fuss made of him.

After his retirement, Cosgrove, who never married, suffered from serious ill health. The splinters of shrapnel left in his back were painful and were slowly killing him. He was treated at the military wing of Millbank General Hospital in London for his injuries, including a serious muscle shrinkage, but he died there, with his brother Joseph at his bedside, on 14 July 1936, aged forty-seven.

In recognition of his outstanding career, Cosgrove was given a special send-off. On 17 July, his remains were brought into Cork Harbour in SS *Innisfallen* and 300 members of the Munster Comrades Association formed a guard of honour. Later that day, some of his former comrades shouldered his coffin to the family burial ground in Upper Aghada. A bugler played 'The Last Post' and one of the wreaths, from the Leinster Regiment Old Comrades Association, bore an inscription that read: 'In Loving Remembrance of a great Irish soldier.'

CAPTAIN GERALD ROBERT O'SULLIVAN

Army: Royal Inniskilling Fusiliers
DATES OF BRAVERY: 18/19 JUNE 1915 AND 1/2 JULY 1915
GAZETTED: 1 SEPTEMBER 1915
Special feature of the VC: a quite exceptional award for gallantry at Gallipoli.

Gerald Robert O'Sullivan was born in Frankfield, near Douglas, Co. Cork, Ireland, on 8 November 1888. He was the only son of Lieutenant-Colonel George O'Sullivan, of the Argyll and Sutherland

Highlanders, and his wife Charlotte (*née* Hiddingh), whose family originated from South Africa. Gerald O'Sullivan, who was widely known as 'Gerry'/'Jerry', was privately educated in Greenwich, south-east London; Wimbledon College, south-west London; and Southsea, Hampshire. During his school days, he earned a reputation on the sports field and in the classroom as a daring, but also a headstrong and rash, character. He had been destined for a career in the Royal Navy but early on he decided that he would instead join the Army. After leaving school in 1906 aged seventeen, he attended the Royal Military College, Sandhurst. He was commissioned into the Royal Inniskilling Fusiliers in May 1909 and joined the regiment's 2nd Battalion in Dublin, the city where he had spent some of his childhood.

In September 1909, O'Sullivan embarked for Tientsin, China: he was present during the Chinese rebellions of 1911 and 1913, although British troops did not take part in any fighting. In between these two stints in China, he served with the 1st Battalion of his regiment at Secunderabad, central India.

Shortly after the outbreak of the Great War in August 1914, O'Sullivan returned with his regiment to Britain: the 1st Inniskillings helped form the 29th Division that was destined to fight in the Dardanelles. By then with the rank of captain and serving as a company commander, he landed at X Beach, Gallipoli, on 25 April 1915. He served with distinction, but without mishap, for the first six weeks of the Gallipoli campaign. However, it was for two significant actions in mid-June and early July of 1915 that O'Sullivan was awarded the VC.

The date of 18 June 1915 marked the hundredth anniversary of the Duke of Wellington's victory at Waterloo and it did not go unrecognised among the British forces serving in the Gallipoli campaign. However, as Stephen Snelling noted in his book *VCs of the First World War: Gallipoli*: 'With little sense of history, the Turks had indeed contrived to spoil the party by launching a fierce assault on a recently captured extension of the British line at the eastern edge of Gully Ravine.' On 11 June, the British forces had succeeded in capturing 70 yards of 'Turkey Trench' that the enemy had held in fighting since 4 June. But on the evening of 18 June, the Turks tried to win back this ground and there was heavy shelling of the 2nd South Wales Borderers, manning the recently gained trench, from 6.30 p.m. The heavy bombardment was followed by an initial assault that was fended off. However, a second assault, launched shortly before 9 p.m., was more successful and the north-west sector of the trench was seized, with the enemy killing or wounding its occupants. After a senior officer was killed, the remaining South Wales Borderers fled, leaving 'Turkey Trench' back in enemy hands and a gap in the line. The immediate knock-on effect of the trench falling into enemy hands was that the Turks bombed an area occupied by B Company, the 1st Royal Inniskilling Fusiliers. British military commanders responded by issuing orders for the gap 'to be made good by force and to be maintained by force'.

Enter Captain O'Sullivan: he led A Company and a platoon from C Company as they moved forward to tackle the enemy. Armed mainly with modestly effective 'jam tin' bombs, they regained the battalion's lost fire-trench and, working with a party of South Wales Borderers, some thirty yards of 'Turkey Trench', all by 9.45 p.m. However, the Turks retaliated and seized back 20 yards of the crucial trench. As the battle raged this way and that, O'Sullivan called for assistance to fend off the Turkish assault. At the same time, he also resolutely refused to budge from the end of 'Turkey Trench', knowing how difficult it would be to establish another toe-end in the vital position. At 3.30 a.m. on 19 June, a party of South Wales Borderers launched a fresh offensive but this was thwarted. By then General W. R. Marshall, the General Officer Commanding (GOC) of 87th Brigade, was on the scene and, after discussions with his officers, yet another assault was planned. This attack was detailed in the Inniskillings' war diary:

4.30 a.m. Capt O'Sullivan with bomb party of about 6 men together
with SWB [South Wales Borderers] bomb party drove enemy down
Turkish sap. Enemy then endeavoured to evacuate sap by retiring
across the open, but were shot down by rapid fire from A and B Coys.
Remainder of enemy in Turkish Sap (13) taken prisoners.

This was an oversimplification of events: in fact, the battle was
still raging at dawn and it was not until 5.15 a.m. that 30 yards of
trench were in British hands and it was not until 10 a.m. that the
whole of 'Turkey Trench' was once again back in British control. The
fighting over the two days had been ferocious, leaving an estimated
200 Turks dead and some 175 British soldiers dead or missing.
According to the 87th Brigade's war diary, O'Sullivan had 'behaved
magnificently throughout' and was therefore recommended for the
VC. In the short term, however, he was treated for minor wounds
and Mentioned in Despatches.

On 28 June, O'Sullivan, aged twenty-six, was back in action
on the frontline when the Inniskillings played a significant role in
the Battle of Gully Ravine, south-west of Krithia, another part of
the Gallipoli peninsula. This had been an important day for the
British forces when they captured and consolidated two trenches,
J10 and J11, situated on the western edge of Gully Ravine. Anticipat-
ing that the Turks would try to seize back their lost ground, British
commanders were ordered to hold J11a 'at all costs' and a new trench
was dug in an attempt to strengthen the position. Digging for this
new trench – later known as 'Inniskillings Trench' – began during
darkness on the night of 30 June. The following evening, on 1 July,
the digging continued, but at around 9.30 p.m. events escalated as
the Turks launched a significant assault on the British positions.

The fighting throughout the night was reminiscent of the battle
for 'Turkey Trench' less than a fortnight earlier, in that the advances
by both sides went to and fro and the situation was often confused.
One of the best reports of the action that day came from Colonel

E. J. Buckley, in temporary command of the Inniskillings, who later wrote:

> Captain O'Sullivan took his Company down J11a (which was held by 1/2 [half] Company) with the intention of moving down J12 to the Birdcage where the left of B Company rested and then cover the retirement of what was left of that Company.
>
> Capt [H. S.] Edden moved his force in a direct line towards the Birdcage so as to be ready to support Capt O'Sullivan.
>
> On arriving at the junction of J11a and J12 Capt O'Sullivan found the situation changed as J12 was occupied by the Turks, who were in fact driving out the Gurkhas [2/10th Gurkha Rifles]. He decided to carry out his original plan to move down J12 to relieve B Company and to attack the Turks in J12 and recapture the trench.
>
> 'He immediately attacked, leading the storming party. Accompanied by Cpl [James] Somers, he advanced in the open along the parapet of the trench, bombing the interior as he regained it. The Turks bombed back and from where I was I could distinctly see the flashes of the Turkish bombs, generally two to Captain O'Sullivan's one. We had only the jam-pot bomb ... while the Turks had quite a useful bomb.
>
> Capt O'Sullivan cleared the trench as far as the Birdcage and, leaving a garrison in the trench, proceeded to disengage B Company, leaving Capt Edden to continue the attack on the Turks.

However, during the fighting O'Sullivan received a serious leg wound and eventually had to hand over the command of the Inniskillings on the ground to Captain Edden. Eventually, too, after further fighting, the British had to abandon J12, leaving the Turks to reoccupy the trench once again. The battle resulted in the Inniskillings having six men killed and thirty-seven, including O'Sullivan, wounded. 'Well done Inniskillings' read a telegraph received by Captain Edden at 9 a.m. on 2 July and sent by Major-General B. de Lisle (General Officer Commanding 29th Division). Three men had acquitted themselves superbly during the fighting: O'Sullivan, who was (again) recommended for the VC, Corporal Somers, who was promoted to sergeant in the field and also recommended for the VC, and Captain Edden, who was recommended for the Distinguished Service Order (DSO). However, Edden's award never materialised: he was, aged twenty-nine, killed in action on 21 August and his only formal recognition for his relentless bravery during the Gallipoli campaign was a posthumous Mention in Despatches. Both O'Sullivan and Somers were evacuated to Egypt and treated at a hospital in Cairo: the former was then sent back to Britain to recuperate from injuries to his back caused by bomb splinters, while the former made a rapid recovery from his serious leg wounds and remained in Egypt. Both men were subsequently awarded the VC for their bravery at Gully Ravine.

However, O'Sullivan's VC was also to be a posthumous award: he had reported back to his battalion on 11 August having been away for less than six weeks. This coincided with the 29th Division's move to Suvla Bay, where it was hoped there would be a big offensive against the Turks in the northern sector of the country.

On 21 August, and having recently been told of his VC award, O'Sullivan and his depleted Inniskillings were given the task of seizing Hill 70 (also known as Scimitar Hill) as part of a major attack that day. Amid chaotic scenes, O'Sullivan's leadership skills were matched only by his courage as he led his men through a hail of heavy fire up onto the crest of Hill 70. When the party was forced back by artillery fire, he regrouped his men fully some 400 yards beneath the hilltop and urged them to make 'one more charge for the honour of the Old Regiment'. Fifty men charged forwards but they were, yet again, struck by a hail of bullets and one by one they were killed or wounded, and the survivors had to retreat. O'Sullivan was missing in action, and a private witnessed him being killed outright by a bullet to the head.

The Commanding Officer of the regiment said in a letter to Charlotte O'Sullivan, the heroic captain's mother:

Acting Lieutenant-Colonel (later Brigadier-General) Lewis Pugh Evans was Wales's most decorated officer of the Great War. He was awarded his VC in November 1917 for bravery the previous month in Belgium, when he led his battalion through a terrific enemy barrage and personally attacked a machine-gun post. He also received the DSO & Bar, amongst many other honours.

Private (later Lieutenant) Thomas Dinesen, a Dane fighting with the Canadian Expeditionary Force, was awarded the VC in October 1918 for bravery in August of that year. The brother of Karen Blixen, the authoress of *Out of Africa* fame, Dinesen was decorated for his part in ten hours of hand-to-hand fighting in France and is one of only a handful of foreign VC recipients.

Acting Lieutenant-Colonel Bernard Vann was the only recipient of the VC who, although an ordained clergyman, fought as a combatant soldier. His decoration was announced in December 1918 for gallantry in September of that year, when he led his men, skilfully and under a heavy fire, across the Canal du Nord, France. He was killed in action four days later.

Captain (later Major) Richard Willis was awarded the VC in August 1915 and became one of the famous 'Six Before Breakfast' decorations for the ill-fated Gallipoli landings in April that year. I feel privileged to be the custodian of three of these six iconic VCs that were awarded to the Lancashire Fusiliers for gallantry on that fateful morning.

Acting Corporal (later Staff Sergeant) William Cosgrove was awarded the VC in August 1915 for quite exceptional bravery the day after the Gallipoli landings. Under a heavy fire, the giant Irishman used his immense strength to rip heavy posts and thick barbed wire out of the way with his bare hands to enable him and his comrades to advance inland near Cape Helles.

Captain Gerald O'Sullivan was awarded the VC in September 1915 for two acts of outstanding bravery in Gallipoli in June and July of that year. In the second incident, he led a party of bomb-throwers that successfully recaptured a trench. He was wounded and, although he survived, he was killed in action soon afterwards on 21 August 1915.

Private David Ross Lauder was the first member of the Royal Scots Fusiliers to receive the VC for bravery during the Great War. His award was announced in January 1917 for unselfish bravery in Gallipoli in August 1915, when he threw a live bomb which failed to clear the parapet and landed instead amongst him and his comrades. As he tried to smother the blast with his foot, the bomb blew it off, but the rest of his party escaped uninjured.

Acting Lieutenant-Colonel Edward Henderson was awarded a posthumous VC in June 1917 for outstanding bravery in Mesopotamia in January of that year. His decoration came after he led a counter-attack against the enemy and, despite being wounded twice, then led a bayonet charge. After receiving two more wounds, he died later that day.

LEFT Sergeant (later Battery Sergeant-Major) Thomas Steele was awarded the VC in June 1917 for exceptional bravery in Mesopotamia in February that year. His decoration came after he fought tenaciously to keep the line intact despite two fierce enemy counter-attacks. Steele was seriously wounded in the second attack but survived.

BELOW LEFT An image of Seaman (later Petty Officer) George Samson appears on a cigarette card after the award of his VC for the Gallipoli campaign. His decoration, the first VC to the Royal Naval Reserve, was announced in August 1915 for bravery in April that year during the landing at V Beach, Cape Helles, where he received no fewer than nineteen wounds.

BELOW RIGHT The bravery of Commander Loftus Jones made front-page news in the *Daily Sketch* and eventually resulted in arguably the finest Royal Navy VC of the Great War. Jones's VC was announced in March 1917 for outstanding and relentless bravery in May the previous year during the Battle of Jutland, when he continued to command his ship even after his right leg had been blown off.

Skipper (later Chief Skipper) Joseph Watt was awarded the VC for astonishing bravery in taking on an Austrian cruiser in his insignificant little drifter armed with only a puny six-pounder gun. A fisherman serving in the Royal Naval Reserve, he received his VC in August 1917 for the action in May that year in the Adriatic.

A remarkable photograph taken inside his submarine shows Lieutenant-Commander Geoffrey Saxton White (believed to be the unique image of a Great War submarine commander at the periscope). He was awarded his VC – one of only five to submariners during the Great War – in May 1919 for bravery in January the previous year, when his submarine *E14* was destroyed by the enemy after a gallant defence in which he himself was killed.

The multi-decorated Major (later Group Captain) Lionel Rees was awarded his VC for gallantry in the air on the iconic first day of the Battle of the Somme. His decoration was announced in August 1916, a month after he was wounded in a dramatic air battle over France before landing his aircraft safely.

Lieutenant (later Flight Lieutenant) Alan Jerrard was awarded the VC in May 1918 for bravery in attacking enemy aircraft near Mansue, Italy. Jerrard is believed to have shot down three enemy aircraft and attacked an aerodrome before being shot down himself. He was known as the 'Pyjama VC' because he was taken as a PoW wearing only his nightclothes beneath his flying suit; his award was the unique flying VC for the Italian Front.

Acting Captain (later Flight Lieutenant) Andrew Beauchamp Proctor was awarded the VC in November 1918 after achieving fifty-four confirmed 'kills', all earlier that year. This South African pilot's astonishing medal group – the VC, DSO, MC & Bar, DFC – became the landmark 200th VC in my collection.

The magnificent multiple gallantry group awarded to Acting Captain (later Flight Lieutenant) Andrew Beauchamp Proctor, VC, DSO, MC & Bar, DFC, the sixth highest-scoring Allied fighter ace of the Great War. He was killed in a peacetime flying accident in 1921.

Second Lieutenant (later Captain) Richard Annand was awarded the Army's first VC of the Second World War in August 1940 for bravery during the battle to save France in May that year. He was known as the 'wheelbarrow VC' after rescuing his wounded batman – using a wheelbarrow – despite being injured himself.

Havildar (later Subadar-Major and Honorary Captain) Gaje Ghale, a Gurkha serving in the Indian Army, was awarded the VC in September 1943 for outstanding bravery during the Burma campaign in May that year. His decoration was for leading a daring and skilful attack on a well-defended enemy position in the jungle, despite being wounded in the battle.

Company Sergeant-Major Peter Wright, accompanied by his fiancée (and future wife) Mollie and his mother Florence, at his investiture at Buckingham Palace in September 1944. He had received the VC for bravery at Salerno, Italy a year earlier. Originally awarded a DCM for the action, this lesser decoration was uniquely upgraded to the VC upon the specific insistence of George VI.

Jemadar Adbul Hafiz, Indian Army, was awarded a posthumous VC in July 1944 for bravery in April of that year. He was fatally wounded after carrying out a daring attack on a steep enemy position north of Imphal, India, during which he killed several Japanese soldiers.

Lieutenant (later Major Sir) Tasker Watkins was one of the handful of immediate post D-Day VCs. His decoration was announced in November 1944 for courage in August that year, when, after his company came under a murderous fire, he led a successful bayonet charge on the enemy before also personally silencing a machine-gun post.

JEMADAR RAM SARUP SINGH.
Jemadar Ram Sarup Singh, 1st Punjab Regiment, was posthumously awarded the V.C. in February 1945 for his courage on October 25, 1944. He was in charge of a platoon in Burma which was ordered to put in a diversionary attack. He led charges until he fell mortally wounded.

ABOVE An unidentified newspaper cutting announces the posthumous award of the VC to Acting Subadar Ram Sarup Singh, Indian Army. His decoration was announced in February 1945 for 'cool bravery' during the Burma campaign in October the previous year, when he killed six of the enemy before being mortally wounded in the assault.

RIGHT Corporal (later Company Sergeant-Major) Edward Chapman meets the Queen on 9 July 1953 during her Coronation Tour of Wales. He had been awarded his VC in July 1945 for bravery in April, the final month of the war in Europe, when he thwarted an enemy ambush close to the Dortmund-Ems canal in Germany.

ABOVE Commander (later Rear-Admiral Sir) Anthony Miers, one of the most able submariners of the Second World War, was one of three submarine commanders to be awarded the VC for actions in the Mediterranean. His award was announced in July 1942 for bravery in March that year, when, in command of HM Submarine *Torbay*, he boldly penetrated the enemy defences at Corfu Harbour and torpedoed two transports; whilst in the harbour, he had to surface in a full moon in the midst of the enemy to recharge the submarine's batteries.

LEFT Wing Commander Hugh Malcolm was awarded a posthumous VC in April 1943 for outstanding bravery in November and December the previous year. On 4 December 1942, he led a suicidal sortie to support Army units in a battle area but, without fighter support, his and eight other aircraft were shot down one by one over north Africa.

It seems tolerably certain that he was killed, and killed outright by being hit in the head as the assaulting line reached the furthest line of the enemy's trenches on the 21st of August. He was seen to fall in the trench wounded, as was thought for some days, but a private who got back and says he was next to your son, is positive that he was killed outright.

As the O'Sullivans grieved over their son's death in Co. Cork, there were contrastingly joyous scenes on 28 August 1915 in another part of Ireland over the imminent award of the VC to the newly pro-moted Sergeant Somers. In his excellent write-up on the award of the two VCs to O'Sullivan and Somers, Stephen Snelling writes in his book *VCs of the First World War: Gallipoli*:

Seven days after O'Sullivan's last charge, a train pulled into the small country town of Cloughjordan, in County Tipperary. The station was a sea of cheering people, and above the din a band welcomed home their conquering hero. News of Sergeant Somers' VC recommend-ation had leaked out, prompting a wave of premature celebrations in which the young NCO [Non-Commissioned Officer] was show-ered with praise and gifts, including a cheque for fifty guineas. On 1 September *The London Gazette* announced what the citizens of Cloughjordan had taken for granted, that No. 10512, Sgt. James Somers, had won the Victoria Cross.

O'Sullivan's VC was announced on the same day – 1 September 1915 – when his citation highlighted his bravery at 'Turkey Trench' as well as Gully Ravine. O'Sullivan's decoration was posted to his mother in September 1915.

O'Sullivan has no known grave but his name is listed on both the Helles Memorial, Gallipoli, and the Dorchester War Memorial in Dorset. Additionally, his name is on the regimental plaque in St Anne's Cathedral in Belfast, Northern Ireland.

PRIVATE DAVID ROSS LAUDER

Army: The Royal Scots Fusiliers

DATE OF BRAVERY: 13 AUGUST 1915

GAZETTED: 13 JANUARY 1917

Special feature of the VC: the first member of the Royal Scots Fusiliers to receive the award for the Great War. A splendid Gallipoli VC for saving life among his comrades.

David Ross Lauder was born in Easter Glentore, near Airdrie, Scotland, on 31 January 1894. He was the son of Angus Lauder, a tailor, and his wife Marion (*née* Crawford). Little is known of his early life and education but, after leaving school, he worked as a carter and he served in the 4th Battalion, the Royal Scots Fusiliers (Territorial Force). In February 1913, he married Dorina McGuigan, a coalminer's daughter. Lauder was mobilised in August 1914, aged twenty. After training with the 52nd Division, he and his comrades in the 4th Battalion, the Royal Scots Fusiliers, were despatched to Gallipoli, Turkey. Even before they set foot on the frontline in the early summer of 1915, the battalion, a territorial unit recruited from Ayrshire, was involved in two major incidents.

As they were on their way to their embarkation point, a troop train carrying members of the 52nd Division crashed outside the Quintinshill signal box near Gretna Green in Dumfriesshire. The five-train accident on 22 May 1915 claimed the lives of some 227 men and injured more than 200 others. To this day, the Quintinshill rail disaster remains the worst and one of the most controversial rail crashes in British history.

Next came an accident in which the SS *Reindeer*, sailing from Mudros to Helles and transporting Lauder and his comrades, collided with SS *Immingham*. *Immingham*, which was returning without troops, sank immediately but *Reindeer* limped back to Mudros. The Royal Scots did not lose any men in either incident but it was June 1915 before they finally arrived in Gallipoli.

On 12 July 1915, the 1/4th Royal Scots Fusiliers were involved in an action at Achi Baba Nullah when they lost all but one of their officers and half their rank and file, killed or wounded. In fact, an ill-fated charge on three lines of Turkish trenches cost the lives of several of Lauder's friends and left a deep impression on him.

It was for bravery at The Vineyard, south-west of Krithia, Gallipoli, just a month later, that Lauder, then aged twenty-one, was awarded the VC. In a diversionary attack to coincide with the Allied landing at Suvla Bay on the night of 6 August, the 88th Brigade had captured a small vineyard, which became known simply as The Vineyard. On the night of 12 August, the Turks had launched a heavy bombardment of the British forces, causing many casualties, in an attempt to recapture the lost ground. The 9th Manchesters, who had made heavy gains over the previous four days, had been forced to give up ground that they had previously taken.

By the morning of 13 August, the fighting was still fierce, with both sides moving forward, then being forced back again. At around 11.30 a.m., the 1/4th Royal Scots Fusiliers started replacing the exhausted Manchesters. A party of Scots was sent ahead to reconnoitre the area but they were confronted by an advancing Turkish force moving along a communication trench. However, despite more casualties, the Turks were eventually driven out and half of The Vineyard was re-secured.

By late afternoon on the 13th, the battle was drawing to a close although Lauder and his comrades continued throwing large numbers of bombs to prevent the Turks from advancing and interfering with the building work of a permanent barricade that the British were constructing. To amuse themselves, the men were keeping a record of just how many bombs they had each thrown over the lip of the sap. Lauder's own tally was 200-plus when disaster struck.

Lauder's citation for his VC, which like others from the period gave no details of the location or date of the incident, takes up the story:

> For most conspicuous bravery when with a bombing party retaking a sap.
>
> Pte. Lauder threw a bomb, which failed to clear the parapet and fell amongst the bombing party. There was no time to smother the bomb, and Pte. Lauder at once put his foot on it, thereby localising the explosion. His foot was blown off, but the remainder of the party through this act of sacrifice escaped unhurt.

Lauder's bravery had prevented nine comrades, including an officer, being killed or badly wounded. He later recalled the moment when it all went wrong:

> I threw a bomb that fell short. I saw it slip down the parapet and roll towards the bombing party. A three second fuse does not allow you very long for thinking. I recognised the fault as mine and the only course that seemed open to me was to minimise the explosion as much as possible. So I put my right foot on it. The explosion was terrific and the concussion was awful. My foot was clean blown away, but, thank goodness, my comrades were saved.

Lauder remained conscious after the accident and was carried back to his battalion's fire trench where he received medical attention. His self-sacrifice was hugely appreciated and admired by those who had been with him and Captain J. Bryce wrote home telling his family it was the pluckiest action that he had witnessed while in Gallipoli. Lauder was later transferred to Malta for further medical treatment before returning to the UK. He was eventually fitted with an artificial lower leg – from just below the knee – and he learned to walk well with it. However, he continued to be troubled by his injuries and shrapnel remained in his hands for the rest of his life.

His VC was not announced until 13 January 1917, nearly a year and a half after the action. In the same month, he was discharged from the Army and he went to work in a munitions factory in Parkhead,

Glasgow. He also lived in Glasgow with his wife and, eventually, their three sons and three daughters.

Lauder received his award from George V at an investiture at Buckingham Palace on 3 March 1917 – he was Scotland's only VC from the Gallipoli Campaign. Britain's ally Serbia was also so impressed by his bravery that the nation awarded him its prestigious Medal for Bravery.

After the Great War ended in November 1918, Lauder worked for the General Post Office as a telephone operator, eventually becoming a supervisor at its Pitt Street Exchange in Glasgow. In February 1920, he became a Freemason. After divorcing his first wife, he married Rachel Bates, the daughter of a chemical worker, in Guthrie Memorial Church, Glasgow, in August 1929. The couple went on to have five children (although two died in infancy), meaning that Lauder had fathered eleven children in total.

In April 1937, Lauder was a passenger in a tramcar when it jumped the rails and collided with a bus in Hope Street, Glasgow. Lauder was cut and dazed in the crash but he nevertheless helped those more seriously injured to get out of the wreckage. Once his rescue mission was completed, he calmly reported for work. During the Second World War, Lauder combined his night work as a switchboard operator with being a part-time air-raid warden by day. It is also understood that for a time he served in the Home Guard. In 1960, Lauder retired from his General Post Office job but he continued to work part time as a night watchman for a local bakery.

Lauder died at his home in Cranhill, Glasgow, on 4 June 1972, aged seventy-eight. On 7 June, former comrades, including senior officers, joined family and friends at his funeral, where a piper from the Royal Highland Fusiliers (the successors to his regiment) played a lament. After being cremated, his ashes were scattered in the 'June Avenue of Trees' at the Garden of Remembrance, Daldowie Crematorium, Broomhouse, Glasgow. Lauder's name is one of the fourteen Lanarkshire VC recipients on a granite memorial arch in Hamilton town square, Lanarkshire, that was unveiled in April 2002.

The Middle East

The Middle East theatre of the war was fought between the Allied Powers, mainly forces from Britain and the Russian Empire, versus the Central Powers, mostly forces from the Ottoman Empire. The Ottoman Empire, in military terms, was a weak link for the Central Powers (with the exception of the Gallipoli Campaign). Its army was large but often ineffective and it would probably have been defeated in mid-1915 without being propped up by Germany.

The Ottoman Empire's entry into the Great War on 29 October 1914 – the result of a secret pact with Germany – saw a number of campaigns in the Middle East. These included the Caucasus Campaign, the Dardanelles Campaign (known in Australia and New Zealand as the Gallipoli Campaign), the Mesopotamian Campaign, the Sinai and Palestine Campaigns, and the Arabia and Southern Arabia Campaigns. The Allied Powers gradually assumed control in these areas as the war progressed.

ACTING LIEUTENANT-COLONEL EDWARD ELERS DELAVAL HENDERSON

Army: The North Staffordshire Regiment, attached the Royal Warwickshire Regiment

DATE OF BRAVERY: 25 JANUARY 1917

GAZETTED: 8 JUNE 1917

Special feature of the VC: an outstanding award for exceptional bravery in Mesopotamia (now Iraq).

Edward Elers Delaval Henderson was born in Shimla, India, on 2 October 1878. He was the son of Major-General Philip Durham Henderson, formerly of the Madras Cavalry, and his wife Rosana, who was herself from a formidable military family and whose father had also served as an officer in the Madras Cavalry. After being educated at St Paul's School in London, Henderson Jr embarked on a career as a tea planter in India.

However, he had long wanted to be a soldier and on 7 May 1900 he joined the 5th (Militia) Battalion, the Worcester Regiment, because, aged twenty-one, he was too old to attend the Royal Military College, Sandhurst. He transferred to the West India Regiment as a second lieutenant in December of the same year. From 1901 to 1905, he served in West Africa and, during that time, he was promoted – in February 1902 – to lieutenant. From July 1905 to February 1907, Henderson served with his regiment in Jamaica.

In May 1908, and on the disbandment of the West India Regiment, Henderson was transferred to the North Staffordshire Regiment. In March 1909, he was promoted to captain and before the outbreak of the Great War he served in Peshawar (now Pakistan), on the North-West Frontier, India and West Africa (again). In the meantime, on 2 February 1910, he married Madeline Fish, the daughter of a Royal Fusiliers officer, at All Saints Church, Knightsbridge, west London.

After the outbreak of the Great War in August 1914, Henderson was soon in action with his regiment, serving with the 3rd Battalion. Next, he served with the 7th North Staffordshires in 39th Brigade, 13th Division, which arrived in Gallipoli in July 1915. During one sustained attack by the Turks on 19 July, Henderson was one of three officers wounded (another officer was killed and nineteen more men also injured).

Having recovered from his wounds, Henderson was promoted to major on 1 September 1915. As part of the 13th Division, he was given command of the 9th Worcesters, part of 39th Brigade. On 24 January 1916, the division left Gallipoli for Egypt and a month or so later the Worcesters moved on to Mesopotamia (now Iraq). After Henderson was relieved of his command of the Worcesters by the return of a more senior officer, he spent just ten days with the 38th Brigade during which he commanded the 6th King's Own Royal Regiment. In July 1916, he was promoted to acting lieutenant-colonel and became Commanding Officer of the 9th

Royal Warwickshires, a unit that for two months was brigaded with the 7th Battalion, the North Staffordshires.

On 14 December 1916, Lieutenant-General Sir Stanley Maude, who in July of that year had been appointed British commander in Mesopotamia, launched the second phase of his campaign in the area. Some British troops attacked Turkish positions around Kut-el-Amara, while others advanced to reach the Hai, a river that flowed north to join the River Tigris opposite Kut. On 25 January 1917, the British tried to strengthen their position by attacking the Hai salient, near Kut. After initial gains on the west bank of Hai, the 39th Brigade was driven back. It was at this stage, around 11.30 p.m., that the 9th Warwickshires, led by Henderson, moved into action. The citation for Henderson's VC (in which his third Christian name is misspelled) reveals the full extent of his bravery as he led his men across some 500 yards of open ground in order to recapture ground lost by the North Staffordshires:

> For most conspicuous bravery, leadership and personal example when in command of his battalion.
>
> Lt.-Col. Henderson brought his battalion up to our two front-line trenches, which were under intense fire, and his battalion had suffered heavy casualties when the enemy made a heavy counter-attack, and succeeded in penetrating our line in several places, the situation becoming critical.
>
> Although shot through the arm, Lt.-Col. Henderson jumped onto the parapet and advanced alone some distance in front of his battalion, cheering them on under the most intense fire over 500 yards of open ground.
>
> Again wounded, he nevertheless continued to lead his men on in the most gallant manner, finally capturing the position by a bayonet charge.
>
> He was again twice wounded, and died when he was eventually brought in.

The man who went out in the heaviest of fire to rescue his CO was Temporary Lieutenant Robert Phillips, aged twenty-one. With the help of a comrade, Phillips managed to bring Henderson back to Allied lines, but his life could not be saved. Phillips, too, was awarded the VC on the same day that Henderson's posthumous award was announced on 8 June 1917. Phillips's citation ended: 'He showed sustained courage in its very highest form, and throughout he had but little chance of ever getting back alive.' However, he survived both the action and the war.

Henderson, who left a widow and a son, had died aged thirty-eight. His widow, from Camberley, Surrey, received his posthumous VC from George V at an investiture at Buckingham Palace on 20 October 1917. Henderson's name is on a wall in the Amara War Cemetery, some 150 miles south of Baghdad in modern-day Iraq, and there is a memorial in his honour at the Garrison Church, Whittington Barracks, Lichfield, Staffordshire.

SERGEANT (LATER BATTERY SERGEANT-MAJOR) THOMAS STEELE

Army: The Seaforth Highlanders
DATE OF BRAVERY: 22 FEBRUARY 1917
GAZETTED: 8 JUNE 1917
Special feature of the VC: an award for exceptional bravery in Mesopotamia (now Iraq).

Thomas Steele was born in Claytons, Saddleworth, Lancashire, on 6 February 1891. Of Scottish descent, he was one of four children and the eldest of three sons born to Harry Steele, a cotton worker, and his wife Elizabeth (*née* Mitchell). Thomas Steele was educated at Austerlands Day School in Saddleworth and also attended Shelderslow Sunday School. After leaving school, Steele worked as a bobbin carrier at Rome Mill, Saddleworth, a low-paid job in the cotton industry that involved carrying spools of thread to the looms ready for use by the weavers.

On 22 August 1911 Steele enlisted into the 1st Battalion, Seaforth Highlanders, aged twenty. Serving as a private, he was despatched to India, where he was stationed from December 1912. At the outbreak of the Great War in August 1914, Steele, by then a lance-corporal, was still in India, based with his battalion at Agra. On 20 September 1914, he left with the 7th (Meerut) Division as part of the Indian Expeditionary Force. On 12 October, Steele and his comrades arrived at Marseilles, southern France, ready for service on the Western Front as part of 19th Brigade.

Over the next few months, Steele was repeatedly in the thick of the action, serving in the retreat from Mons, as well as at Ypres, La Bassée and Neuve Chapelle. On 1 June 1915, he was promoted to corporal and in September that year he took part in the Battle of Loos. In October 1915, he was promoted to lance-sergeant and the next month, after being given twenty-four hours leave, he left France with the 7th (Meerut) Divison for Mesopotamia (now Iraq). As part of the 19th Indian Brigade, the Seaforths were tasked with trying to relieve General Townsend's beleaguered force at Kut-el-Amara. Further promotion followed for Steele in January 1917, when he was elevated to sergeant. During his time in Mesopotamia, he suffered bouts of ill health, notably malaria, but this did not prevent him from once again being in the thick of the fighting.

By February 1917, the south bank of the Tigris had been largely cleared of enemy fighters, but the Turks remained well entrenched along the north bank, from Sanna-i-Yat east of Kut-el-Amara to the Shumran peninsula to its west. Lieutenant-General Sir Stanley Maude devised a plan to attack the Turks on both fronts, but the initial attack on Sanna-i-Yat on 17 February failed to achieve any breakthrough. On 22 February, he launched another attack in the same area, with the intention of drawing enemy soldiers away from Shumran so that British troops could cross the river from the south bank. During intensive fighting, which followed a heavy bombardment of the enemy, the first two lines of Turkish trenches were seized. Although the enemy counter-attacked and temporarily regained some of their trenches, they were eventually driven out again.

It was during this fighting that Steele showed such exceptional bravery that he was, in the words of his letter home to his parents, 'recommended for something'. That 'something' was none other than the VC, with his award being announced on 8 June 1917, when his detailed citation stated:

> For most conspicuous bravery and devotion to duty.
>
> At a critical moment when a strong enemy counter-attack had temporarily regained some of the captured trenches, Sjt. Steele rushed forward and assisted a comrade to carry a machine gun into position. He kept the gun in action till relieved, being mainly instrumental in keeping the remainder of the line intact.
>
> Some hours later another strong attack enabled the enemy to reoccupy a portion of the captured trenches. Again Sjt. Steele showed the greatest bravery, and by personal valour and example was able to rally troops who were wavering. He encouraged them to remain in their trenches and led a number of them forward, thus greatly helping to re-establish our line. On this occasion he was severely wounded.
>
> These acts of valour were performed under heavy artillery and rifle fire.

Steele, by then aged twenty-six, received no fewer than twelve separate wounds during his VC action and was treated for his severe injuries in Malpa hospital, India. The *Oldham Evening Chronicle* quickly picked up on its local hero, publishing an article in which they described him as 'a gallant sergeant ... of a most retiring disposition'. The paper's report said 'his father received a telegram from the sergeant's battalion headquarters last evening telling him of the award and asking him to send at once a photograph of Thomas who by the way has been offered a commission'. During Steele's VC action, he had been greatly helped to encourage the Indian troops by Private Joseph Winder, who was awarded the Distinguished Conduct Medal (DCM) and the French Médaille Militaire.

Thomas was not the only member of the Steele family to serve with credit during the Great War: his middle brother, Samuel, served with the Royal Scots and, having been wounded, was in hospital in Cardiff at the time of Thomas's VC award, while the youngest brother, William, served with the Highland Light Infantry.

Despite the severity of his injuries, Thomas Steele was soon back on the frontline and on 15 August 1917 he was Mentioned in Despatches by General Sir Frederick Maude for further gallantry in Mesopotamia. In January 1918, Steele left the Persian Gulf region and from then until February 1919 he served in Egypt and Palestine. He was transferred to the Regular Army Reserve in March 1919 and his investiture by George V took place at Buckingham Palace on 10 April 1919. For the remainder of his life, he was a keen supporter of Victoria Cross and George Cross Association events, including attending the Buckingham Palace garden party of June 1920.

On 9 April 1921, Steele briefly rejoined the Army only to be transferred to the Regular Army Reserve less than two months later. On 8 June 1922, he got married in his home county of Lancashire to Bertha McCready. Steele played rugby league to a high standard: he played three matches as a professional for Broughton, one of rugby league's founding clubs, and enjoyed a distinguished career as an amateur with his local club, Healey Street.

At some point in the late 1920s, the Steeles moved to Leicestershire, where he worked for Central Motors of Leicester and also apparently as a wholesale fruiterer. During this time, he maintained his links to the military, enlisting in the Leicester Regiment

(Territorials) on 29 March 1932, after which he became a sergeant with C Company.

Just before the outbreak of the Second World War, Steele was called up and he served as a battalion sergeant-major with the Royal Artillery (Territorials). In 1941, and by then aged fifty, Steele was posted to Leicester, where he served in the Home Guard before being discharged in April 1942. After the war, he continued to live in Leicestershire, working first as a telephone clerk and then with a car sales firm. He retired in 1956, aged sixty-five. In his retirement, he continued to attend VC and GC events on a regular basis.

In December 1977 and following the death of his wife, Steele returned to his Lancashire roots, living with his sister-in-law in Saddleworth. He died at his home on 11 July 1978, aged eighty-seven, and was cremated six days later at Hollinwood Crematorium, Oldham.

In October 2003, Steele was one of three Great War VC recipients from Oldham who were honoured with a commemorative Blue Plaque. This was unveiled by Councillor Valerie Sedgwick, the Mayor of Oldham, following a service at the local parish church.

North Waziristan,
India, 1919

There were numerous trouble-spots around the world in the aftermath of the Great War as a result of everything from political revolution to social collapse. The transition from war to peace and the demobilsation of hundreds of thousands of men, many of them traumatised by years of fighting, caused troubles of their own to the losers and victors alike.

In May 1919, the outbreak of the Third Afghan War was caused by unrest among the Wazirs and Mahsuds on the North-West Frontier. On 21 October 1919, a British convoy was attacked near Khajuri Post, some 10 miles west of Bannu in Northern Waziristan.

TEMPORARY CAPTAIN HENRY JOHN ANDREWS

Indian Army: Indian Medical Service

DATE OF BRAVERY: 21 OCTOBER 1919

GAZETTED: 9 SEPTEMBER 1920

Special feature of the VC: an extremely rare inter-war award and a very rare 'Salvation Army VC'.

Henry Andrews was born in London in 1873 (more precise details of his birth are not known). His father was the foreman in a cardboard box factory and his mother died shortly after her son's birth. Both his parents were members of The Salvation Army and his mother's dying wish was that baby Henry (who became known as 'Harry') should be cared for by Bramwell Booth, the first chief-of-staff and the second general (or head) of The Salvation Army. This wish was complied with although Booth asked his sister, Emma, to help him with the task. In her book *It Began With Andrews: The Saga of a Medical Mission*, Miriam M. Richards writes: 'When he [Booth] promised to care for a dying mother's baby boy he was not to know that he was cherishing a seed from which would spring a vital harvest in the field of medical mission work.'

Andrews's early care and education came at The Salvation Army Nursery at Clapton, London, when Emma Booth was the principal of the Officers' Training Home. As a youth of fifteen, he accompanied the woman he called his 'mother' when, having got married, Booth went with her husband, Commissioner Booth-Tucker, to India. Andrews was destined to become The Salvation Army's first 'medical man' in India, eventually serving there for almost thirty years. His work started within months of him arriving in Bombay even though, at the time, he was a teenager and completely unqualified for any kind of medical work. A chance meeting with an Indian boy suffering from acute toothache led to him reading a dental manual and then using sterilised forceps to remove a decaying tooth.

The grateful youngster christened his young healer 'the little doctor' and, after returning to his village, word soon spread that Andrews was willing and able to treat those suffering from ailments at his 'office': a small room equipped with a grass mat (on which he slept at night), a floor-level 'sink', a table and shelves that were soon crammed with various lotions and potions that he used to treat malaria, cholera and those other diseases that were rife in India. As his workload grew, the Indians soon gave him an alternative name to 'little doctor': that of 'Dr Sikundar' (sometimes spelled 'Sekunder') in honour of a Sikh of that name who had, in turn, been known as 'The Brave One'.

Aged only seventeen, Andrews unsurprisingly became an officer in The Salvation Army and, as his amateur medical work increased, he eventually received formal training as a pharmacist. Additionally, he was appointed to assist Major William Stevens at The Salvation Army's Indian headquarters at Nagercoil and during the 1893 cholera outbreak in Travancore, India, Andrews worked tirelessly to help the sick and dying. Miriam R. Richards writes: 'To see suffering was to him a call to try to remedy it.' On his return to the UK in 1896, Andrews received further training as a dresser of injuries and wounds. However, he was keen to return to India and he was soon back in his adopted 'homeland' later that year to assist in the establishment of the Catherine Booth Hospital in Nagercoil. Some four years later, he was transferred to Anand in Gujarat where he helped establish the Emery Hospital. In October 1899, Andrews had got married in India – in Nagercoil – to Gena Smith, who had shared his childhood home in the Clapton nursery established by his 'mother'. Later, Andrews underwent yet more medical training in the USA, graduating from the University of Chicago in 1910, before returning to India in 1912, based at Moradabad.

In his book *The History of the Salvation Army Volume III 1883–1953*, Robert Sandall noted that, after the outbreak of the Great War in August 1914, The Salvation Army placed this hospital (Moradabad) at the disposal of the government together with Dr Andrews and his staff. Sandall writes: 'By then, it had become one of the best and most fully equipped in the country. At the conclusion of the war the hospital reverted to its original purposes.'

Once the war began in earnest, Andrews, who was by then a lieutenant-colonel in The Salvation Army, volunteered several times for active service but he was turned down because of his superlative work as a hospital commandant. However, in June 1917, he was finally commissioned as a lieutenant in the Indian Medical Service and a year later he was promoted to acting captain.

In June 1918, he was made an MBE and soon afterwards he was permitted to relinquish his hospital post in order to head to the North-West Frontier, where problems continued. On 21 October 1919, Andrews, by then aged forty-six, was serving at Khajuri Post, Waziristan, India (now Pakistan). The citation for his VC, announced on 9 September 1920, provides an account of what happened, although the date for his action is incorrect by a single day:

> For most conspicuous bravery and devotion to duty on, the 22nd October, 1919, when as Senior Medical Officer in charge of Khajuri Post (Waziristan) he heard that a convoy had been attacked in the vicinity of the post, and that men had been wounded. He at once took out an Aid Post to the scene of action and, approaching under heavy fire, established an Aid Post under conditions which afforded some protection to the wounded but not to himself.
>
> Subsequently he was compelled to move his Aid Post to another position, and continued most devotedly to attend to the wounded.
>
> Finally, when a Ford van was available to remove the wounded, he showed the utmost disregard of danger in collecting the wounded under fire and in placing them in the van, and was eventually killed whilst himself stepping into the van on the completion of his task.

In his Foreword to Miriam R. Richards book, Sir John 'Jackie' Smyth, himself a VC recipient and later the President of the Victoria

Cross and George Cross Association, told how he had been present during the action for which Andrews received his posthumous VC. He wrote:

> Temporary Captain Henry John Andrews, M.B.E., had been an officer in The Salvation Army for over thirty years and was therefore not a young man at this time. He was a Senior Medical Officer at Khajuri Post at one end of the Shinki Pass, which was an important defended post on the lines of communication within the area of the 43rd Infantry Brigade of which I was Brigade Major. A very long and important animal transport convoy, over seven miles in length, was on its way up the line. A raiding party of about a hundred Mahsuds, the toughest of all the North-West Frontier tribesmen, had come down the night before and hidden themselves amongst the rocks at the side of the road. They waited until the head of the convoy had reached Khajuri Post and then opened fire, creating great havoc and causing a large number of casualties in men and animals.
>
> But the officer commanding Khajuri Post had telephoned to Brigade Headquarters and the Brigade Commander sent me off at once with 300 Indian soldiers of the 9th Jats in Ford vans with two rather antiquated armoured cars. On our arrival a very hectic engagement took place in which the Mahsuds were eventually routed. Captain Andrews, quite regardless of his own danger, had only one thought – to collect the wounded, dress them quickly and send them off to safety in some of our Ford vans, which I had put at his disposal. He seemed to bear a charmed life as a number of his assistants were killed or wounded. Just as he was about to step into the last van, however, he was killed.
>
> I brought his gallantry to the notice of my Brigadier and he was awarded a well-deserved posthumous Victoria Cross.
>
> Captain Andrews had acted in accordance with the highest traditions of the Indian Medical Service and also of The Salvation Army.

A further account of Andrews's courage that day is provided by Catherine Baird in her booklet *'Little Doctor', V.C. (Harry Andrews)*. She described how, on 21 October 1919, Andrews was determined to go out to help the wounded regardless of the risks to his personal safety.

> Making quick, thorough preparations he went out, dodging bursting shells and stumbling over thick shrubs while the whistling of shells announced their passage through the night. Near a great boulder he built a shelter for the wounded, as sturdy as the urgency of the occasion would allow. He himself had no cover. As the fighting grew more desperate, the shelter had to be moved to another position, but the doctor remained where the danger was most acute. His wiry figure could be seen running here and there, stooping over inert bodies, working swiftly so that, as soon as an ambulance was available, as many as possible could be collected from amid the flying bullets and sent off to safety.
>
> As he slid the last stretcher into its place, a burst of gunfire cracked sharply. The ambulance moved out of a cloud of smoke and started on its way to safety. But the 'little doctor' lay still, among the dead, as one overcome with weariness might lie, having fallen asleep at his work.

Andrews, who died aged forty-six, had, in the phrase favoured by The Salvation Army for those who have died, been 'promoted to Glory'. He was buried at Bannu Cemetery, India (now Pakistan), and his posthumous VC was presented to his widow by George V at an investiture at Buckingham Palace on 2 November 1920. His name is commemorated on the Delhi Memorial (India Gate) and there is a painting of him by Joan Fairfax Whiteside at the Regimental Headquarters of the Royal Army Medical Corps in Camberley, Surrey.

The final word on the remarkable life of Harry Andrews, a man who devoted his life to serving others, should go to a posthumous tribute published in the *British Medical Journal*. It said:

He was energetic, brimful of vitality, extremely modest, quiet, thorough and reliable, completely unselfish ... His goodness infected all those around him ... a man with broad human sympathies, and a splendid type of medical missionary in India ... good operator ... crowds of people flocked from various parts to be treated by him. He designed and supervised the construction of the Salvation Army hospital at Moradabad ... model of what a district hospital should be in India ... well organized and administered ... For such a man the future life could have no cause for apprehension, and we may be certain that he was welcomed to the other world with the words, 'Well done, thou good and faithful servant'.

6

THE FIRST WORLD WAR: NAVAL AND AIR VCS

The Royal Navy

The Royal Navy is the oldest of the British armed services and it is therefore the most senior. From the late seventeenth century to the Great War and beyond, it was the most powerful navy in the world. This meant that, during the First World War, enemy countries were reluctant to take on the Royal Navy in a head-to-head battle – and were even more circumspect about any attempt to invade Britain. The Royal Navy sought to blockade the enemy's ports, thereby strangling its trade, as well as keeping its fleet in harbour, out of harm's way. If enemy ships did get out to sea, the aim was to destroy them.

The Royal Navy played a vital role in the war. It kept the United Kingdom supplied with food, raw materials and arms and, despite setbacks, defeated the German campaigns of unrestricted submarine warfare. It was heavily committed in the Dardanelles Campaign against the Ottoman Empire. Furthermore, the Royal Navy fought several battles against the enemy, notably the Battle of Heligoland Bight, the Battle of Coronel and the Battle of the Falkland Islands all in 1914, the Battle of Dogger Bank in 1915 and the Battle of Jutland. This latter battle, in the North Sea in 1916, was the best-known naval confrontation of the war and, though costly, prevented the German High Seas Fleet from taking further serious action.

SEAMAN (LATER PETTY OFFICER)
GEORGE MCKENZIE SAMSON
Royal Naval Reserve
DATE OF BRAVERY: 25 APRIL 1915
GAZETTED: 16 AUGUST 1915
Special feature of the VC: a superb Gallipoli campaign VC – and the first
to the Royal Naval Reserve – gained during the landing at V Beach, Cape
Helles.

George McKenzie Samson was born in Carnoustie, Forfarshire (now Fife), Scotland, on 7 January 1889. He was the second son – and one of nine children – of David Samson, a shoemaker, and his wife Catherine (*née* Lawson). A restless soul, he was educated at Carnoustie School, where he often played truant. After leaving school, he went to work on his uncle's farm in Arbroath but he ran away determined to embark on a life at sea, although he was initially rejected on the grounds of his youth. Aged seventeen, he was employed by a Forfarshire cattle dealer to take thirty prize bulls to Argentina. Once that mission was completed, Samson travelled inland and found work as a cowboy on a cattle ranch. A year later, he returned home and enlisted into The King's Own Scottish Borderers, but bought himself out after basic training in favour of returning to sea, this time on a whaling trip to Greenland.

As a merchant seaman, he had experienced many adventures, including a voyage from Leith to Smyrna, Turkey, where, in 1912 and then aged twenty-three, he worked at the gas works prior to becoming a fireman on the railway line between Smyrna and Adana. He said of his work in Turkey: 'This life suited me excellently and even better so when, after becoming acquainted with the line, I was promoted to the position of driver. I was the youngest driver in the service, and I think it was my nerve and confidence which got me on.'

Like many merchant seamen at the time, Samson enrolled into the Royal Naval Reserve and, after the Great War broke out in

August 1914, he headed for Port Said, Egypt, and then for Malta, where he joined HMS *Hussar*. It was in this ship that he found his way to the Dardanelles in 1915. In a letter home written in early 1915 Samson said:

> We are having awful weather here, and the ship has been trying to stand on her head for the last fortnight, but has not managed it yet. The cold is much worse than the Germans, the only difference being that you can feel the cold and not see it, and see the Germans not feel them. We are all very anxious to have another go at them and get it finished.

As a result of his earlier travels, Samson could speak both Greek and Turkish so he was regularly called upon to act as an interpreter for Rear-Admiral Rosslyn Wemyss. His linguistic talents also enabled him to join Commander Edward Unwin's flat-bottomed steam hopper, the *Argyll*, for the forthcoming landings at V Beach.

V Beach was some 300 yards long and was dominated by Seddel-Bahr, an old fort, at its eastern end. On 25 April 1915, it was the landing place allotted to the Dublin Fusiliers and the Munster Fusiliers as part of the landings across the peninsula. The plan was that, after the initial landings, more troops would be brought in aboard SS *River Clyde*, a specially modified old collier. The intention was to run her aground just offshore, with the gap between the *River Clyde* and the shore to be bridged by *Argyll*.

The assault was scheduled to take place at dawn: on board the steamship, Unwin was accompanied by Samson, Midshipman George Drewry and six Greek seamen, who all clambered aboard at 5 a.m. Tragically, events did not go to plan after the incoming force at V Beach was met by a murderous enemy fire and *Argyll* grounded too far from the *River Clyde* to be of any immediate use. Unwin himself leapt into the water and with Able Seaman William Williams, who had been aboard the *River Clyde*, dragged the lighters – large, flat-bottom barges – forward to form a pontoon bridge to the shore via a shoal of rocks which jutted out into the sea from the fort. With nothing to attach the mooring ropes to, Unwin and Williams stood in the water holding the ropes to keep the two craft in place. As the Munsters started to land, they faced a hail of bullets and many men fell instantly, dead and wounded. When Williams was fatally wounded by a Turkish shell, the link to the shore was cut until Midshipmen Drewry and Wilfred St Aubyn Malleson, along with Samson, were able to form a bridge of lighters between the *River Clyde* and *Argyll*.

Drewry later provided a detailed account of the terrifying events that morning:

> Shells began to fall round us thick but did not hit us. We were half a mile from the beach and we were told not yet, so we took a turn round two ships. At last, we had a signal at 6 am and in we dashed, Unwin on the bridge and I at the helm of the hopper ... At 6.10 am the ship struck, very easily she brought up, and ... grounded on her port bow. Then the fun began, picket boats towed lifeboats full of soldiers inshore and slipped them as the water shoaled and they rowed the rest of the way, the soldiers jumped out as the boats beached and they died, almost all of them wiped out with the boats' crews...
>
> And it was under such desperate circumstances that Samson commenced his gallant work, bringing back wounded from the beach, and repairing the pontoon of boats and lighters started by Unwin and Leading Seaman Williams, the water now red with blood and whipped by devastating enemy fire – even so, he left the steam hopper on 30 occasions.

In another account, Unwin stated:

> Seeing what an awful fiasco had occurred I dashed over the side and got hold of the lighters which I had been towing astern and which

had shot ahead by their impetus when we took the beach, then I got under the bow and found Williams with me. I had told him the night before to keep with me, and he did so literally.

We got them connected to the bows and then proceeded to connect to the beach but we had nothing to secure so we had to hold on to the rope ourselves, and when we had got the lighters near enough to the shore I sung out to the troops to come out, and they soon began to come out.

The Turks seemed to concentrate on the lighters more than on the *River Clyde*, and it was on the lighters and on the reef that the greatest number of dead and wounded lay, of course many fell into the water and were drowned. We were literally standing in blood. For an hour we held on and thinking I could be of more use elsewhere I asked Williams if he could hang on without me but he said he was nearly done and he couldn't.

Just then a 6in shell fell alongside us (I have it in my field at home). Williams said to me: 'what ever is that?' I told him and almost immediately I heard a thud and looked around and Williams said 'a shell has hit me'. I caught hold of him and, as I couldn't let him drown, I tried to get him on to the lighter and then, for the first time, I saw Drewry, who with somebody else helped me and I remember no more till I found myself stripped in my cabin in blankets.

Samson himself said:

The hail of bullets from the Turkish rifles was beginning to take its terrible toll, and I soon found fresh duties to perform – that of carrying the wounded from the shore to the hopper, from which they were, as soon as it was possible, transferred to the *River Clyde* … I cannot say that I felt quite as cool as I may have looked. I am not a very excitable sort when there is serious trouble about. It takes a good deal to disturb me, but I can say without hesitation that this was the 'goods' for excitement.

> During these first dark hours ... I had many narrow escapes just the same, of course, as my companions ... Bullets were whizzing about our heads every few minutes, and we were soon aware of the fact that machine-guns were in operation ... Men were falling down like ninepins quite near us, and perhaps it was only the thought that we must give them a helping hand that made us forget our own danger.

Samson continued:

> This time I began to think that any moment would be my last. Indeed, it became so hot that I finally decided to make a bold bid for safety. I began to roll over towards the side of the little vessel. There was no rail, and the fact was very much in my favour, for I was able to keep low down all the time. Bullets were flying all about the deck; once again I seemed to bear a charmed life ... When I reached the side of the hopper I gave myself a big lurch, and fell into the sea. The sea was extremely choppy but ... I was a good swimmer, and I did not find the slightest difficulty in getting back to the ship.

At around 1.30 p.m. on the following day, with the beach-head more or less secure, Samson, already wounded and having been on the go without a break for some thirty hours, was hit by a burst of enemy machine-gun fire. He suffered multiple hits on his left side, but dragged himself back to his feet, only to be hit yet again. By the time he had been brought before the *River Clyde*'s surgeon, Dr P. Burrowes Kelly, it was touch and go whether he would pull through, with nineteen separate wounds to his body. Later Burrowes Kelly said: 'He was in great agony when I saw him and, whether he lived or died, I knew he had won the VC.'

On 16 August 1915, Unwin, Malleson, Williams, Drewry and Samson were all awarded the VC for their bravery at V Beach. The

VC for a sixth man involved in the same action, Sub-Lieutenant Arthur Tisdall, was announced later, on 31 March 1916, and was awarded for his gallantry in rescuing wounded soldiers from the shore in a small boat.

Samson's wounds were initially treated at a hospital in Port Said but he was later transferred to the RN Hospital Haslar in Gosport, Hampshire. While he was back in Scotland recovering from his wounds, and staying at his father's convalescent home in Aboyne, surgeons had only been able to extract four of the suspected nineteen bullets in his body. Soon afterwards, he returned in triumph to his home town, Carnoustie, where he was the star guest at an impromptu reception, the crowds cheering him as he made his way through the streets. It was a rather different reaction to the one given him by a clergyman who had shared the same railway compartment as Samson earlier that day. With Samson yet to receive his new uniform and in civilian clothes, the clergyman announced in a loud voice, 'Look at that fine-looking young fellow. He ought to be serving his country instead of being a slacker.' Samson's investiture took place at Buckingham Palace on 5 October 1915 when he received his VC from George V. He married Catherine Glass on 31 December 1915 at the Huntly Arms Hotel in Aboyne, near Aberdeen, and the couple went on to have two sons and a daughter.

After being promoted to chief petty officer, Samson was granted one year's sick leave in June 1916. Sadly, however, much of this time was spent in assorted hospitals and he was discharged from the Royal Naval Reserve in 1917. He was still on the sick list at Invergordon, Scotland, when he was presented with his French Médaille Militaire as late as 1918. Even after the Great War ended, Samson remained determined to return to active service and made an unsuccessful application to join the North Russia Expeditionary Force in 1919, presenting himself at the Dundee recruiting office in his chief petty officer's uniform, complete with VC and French Médaille Militaire ribands.

Eventually Samson decided to revive his career in the Merchant Navy, sailing out of Dundee as quartermaster of the tanker *Dosina* in early 1922. Unfortunately, he fell ill during a voyage to the Gulf of Mexico in early 1923. Transferred to the SS *Strombus*, bound for Bermuda, he died from double pneumonia on 23 February, aged thirty-four, still carrying thirteen pieces of shrapnel from his wartime injuries.

Samson was buried with full honours in the military section of St George's Methodist Cemetery. However, but for the splendid work of L. N. Tucker, the founder of the island's Sailors' Home, Samson would have ended up in an unmarked grave. Tucker said:

> I remember one year a ship came to Bermuda with a dead sailor … The captain of the ship dropped the body ashore, and without waiting went back to his ship. I later called the captain on the radio and asked him for the man's papers. He replied that they were on the body, so I went through his clothes and found out that he had been awarded the Victoria Cross … during the First World War. I rang Admiralty House and got hold of the flag lieutenant. He told me that he would check the records and sure enough the man had been awarded the VC. I received a call later from the lieutenant telling me that he would send down three petty officers and a commanding officer for the funeral, and would also arrange for a gun-carriage. Next day the whole army turned out. It was one of the biggest funerals that ever took place.

A road – Samson Close – is named after the VC recipient in Gosport, Hampshire. I am fortunate enough also to own the VCs awarded to both Wilfred Malleson and William Williams, meaning that my collection now has three of the six VCs awarded for astonishing bravery during the landings at V Beach.

COMMANDER LOFTUS WILLIAM JONES

Royal Navy

DATE OF BRAVERY: 31 MAY 1916

GAZETTED: 6 MARCH 1917

Special feature of the VC: arguably the finest Royal Navy VC of the Great War and one of four for the Battle of Jutland.

Loftus William Jones was born in Southsea, Hampshire, on 13 November 1879 into a family with a strong naval tradition. He was the second son of Admiral Loftus Jones and his wife Gertrude (*née* Gray). With his father being such a senior Royal Navy officer, it was not surprising that 'Willie', as he was affectionately known in his family, followed him into the senior service. Indeed, of the four brothers in the family, three served in the Royal Navy (the fourth breaking with tradition and entering the Indian Army).

After being educated at Eastman's Royal Naval Academy in Fareham, Hampshire – which the young Jones never warmed to – he rose quickly through the officer ranks and, aged just twenty-three, was given his first command: the destroyer HMS *Sparrowhawk* in 1903. Later the same year, he was given the command of the gunboat *Sandpiper*, a role he fulfilled for two years, and several other commands followed in the decade or so leading up to the Great War.

On 13 January 1910, Jones married Margaret Dampney in Holy Trinity Church, Exmouth, Devon. In June 1914, Jones was promoted to commander. Following the outbreak of the First World War in August 1914, Jones was initially captaining the destroyer *Linnet*, which, along with three other destroyers, sank the German minelayer *Königin Luise* as early as 5 August 1914 in the first British action of the war. When Jones's wife Margaret gave birth to the couple's daughter that year, she was named Linnette after her father's ship, although with a different, more feminine, spelling. From 9 October 1914, Jones commanded HMS *Shark*, another destroyer that, late in

December 1914, clashed with the German High Seas Fleet, aggressively pursuing and helping to see off the superior force.

At 2 p.m. on 31 May 1916, HMS *Shark*, captained by Jones, was providing protection from enemy submarines, along with three other destroyers and two light cruisers, for Vice-Admiral (later Admiral of the Fleet) Sir David Beatty's Third Battle Cruiser Squadron as it headed south in the North Sea ahead of the British battle fleet. The Battle of Jutland was about to begin.

At 2.20 p.m., messages were received that German warships were at sea and the ships' companies were immediately ordered to 'action stations' as they proceeded, at full speed, to intercept the enemy. At 5.20 p.m., the first sounds of firing were heard and, some twenty minutes later, German destroyers and light cruisers appeared out of the haze. When ten German destroyers launched a torpedo attack on the Third Battle Cruiser Squadron, four British destroyers, including *Shark*, rapidly defused the threat.

Soon after the four destroyers had rejoined their two light cruisers, three German battle-cruisers appeared and opened fire on the six British ships. Under such intense fire, *Shark* was hit and a shell fragment destroyed the ship's helm on the bridge. Jones ordered the after steering gear to be manned and, along with the wounded coxswain and a signalman, he climbed down the bridge ladder and ran along the deck.

The enemy, whose bombardment was murderous, was using shrapnel, some of which struck Jones in the thigh and face, leaving him to stem the flow of blood with his hands. Meanwhile, the coxswain was hit a second time and lapsed into unconsciousness. Realising that *Shark* had been severely disabled by such a heavy fire, the captain of the *Acasta* brought his destroyer between the stricken vessel and the enemy ships. Jones was told by the signalman that his fellow captain had offered to assist. 'No, tell him to look after himself and not get sunk over us,' was the captain's firm and selfless reply.

As the Third British Battle Cruiser Squadron disappeared from sight, the enemy closed in on *Shark*: its after gun was put out of action almost immediately, and its crew killed or wounded, while the forward gun had already been blown away. The situation was worsening by the minute although, even in a hail of shrapnel, *Shark's* crew were desperately trying to load their final torpedo into the tube. Before it could be fired, the torpedo itself was struck by an enemy shell and exploded, causing heavy casualties and leaving only one gun in action. Petty Officer William Griffin, who had been wounded in the attack, later recalled the scene: 'On all sides there was chaos. Dead and dying lay everywhere around. The decks were a shambles. Great fragments of the ship's structure were strewn everywhere.'

Yet, still *Shark* was under a fearsome attack: some shells exploded on the ship itself and others fell into the sea, throwing vast amounts of water over the stricken destroyer. Unsurprisingly, the one surgeon on board was overwhelmed by his task. He, too, was wounded and he was last seen bandaging a man who had lost a hand when *Shark's* last torpedo was hit and exploded.

By then, the enemy was at close range and preparing for the 'kill'. Jones ordered the collision mats over the shot holes as desperate attempts were made to keep the ship afloat. When the crew of the last gun – amidships – was reduced to two men, *Shark's* bloodied captain stood beside it, calling the range. As one of the two men fell, weakened by loss of blood, the captain took his place.

Then, moments later, Jones was struck by a shell which blew off his right leg above the knee. As his men tied an improvised tourniquet – made from pieces of rope and wood – on his shattered leg, Jones continued to direct the firing of the gun. As the German destroyers closed in, and the captain feared his ship would be captured, Commander Jones ordered the ship to be scuttled. However, just at that moment *Shark's* gun fired another round so he countermanded his order by shouting, 'Fight the ship,' to encourage his men to carry on the battle.

At this point, Jones, weakened by his own loss of blood and in great pain, noticed that the main yard had been broken by a shot, and the ship's flag hung limp besides the mast. Despite the hopelessness of the situation, the captain, who wanted to retain his ship's integrity, ordered the flag to be re-hoisted and a crew member climbed the mast, detached the ensign and handed it down to a comrade, who attached it to a new set of halyards. 'That's good,' was the captain's only observation when he saw the flag flying defiantly once more.

The bows of *Shark* were already disappearing below the waves and other parts were awash with water as two German destroyers closed in to only a few hundred feet in order to finish off the stricken ship. 'Save yourselves,' was Jones's final order to his men, shortly before he was eased into the sea and floated clear of his ship with the help of a life-belt.

Some twenty survivors clambered on to two rafts and pieces of wreckage as two more torpedoes hit *Shark*, blasting the dead and wounded into the water. Her stern rose up and she sank, but with her ensign flying. Jones, who had been placed on one of the rafts and propped in a sitting position, smiled and said: 'It's no good, lads.'

Eventually, battle-cruisers swept past in pursuit of the enemy. Jones sought confirmation that they were British ships and, when told they were, whispered: 'That's good.' Minutes later his head fell forward as he took his final breath. Jones was aged thirty-six when he died.

Some of those who had made it on to the rafts also died from their injuries, or fell into the water and either drowned or died from the cold. Shortly after midnight, however, a flare fired from the other raft was spotted and six survivors from *Shark*'s 91-strong complement were eventually rescued by the Danish steamer, SS *Vidar*.

The heroism of Jones and his crew was soon headline news in Britain, and for days rival newspapers competed with each other to provide their readers with the best and most sensational account of events. 'Captain fought on though his leg was shot away', was one headline.

Shortly after his death, Jones's body was washed ashore off the coast of Sweden still in the life-belt that he had donned after being forced to leave his ship. On 24 June 1916, he was buried in Fiskebäckskil Churchyard, Vastra, Götaland. The funeral was attended by many local people and a monument was erected through subscriptions from local fishermen. Margaret Jones, Jones's widow, later received letters from the Admiralty with detailed information about her late husband's body and burial.

Margaret Jones subsequently made extensive inquiries into how her husband had perished during the Battle of Jutland. As Stephen Snelling puts it in his book *VCs of the First World War: The Naval VCs*: 'Motivated, no doubt, by a desire to have her husband's well-publicised heroism officially recognised, she set about visiting and interviewing as many of *Shark*'s survivors as she could find.' She discovered that one of her husband's last acts on his raft had been to say, 'Let's have a song, lads.' The first lieutenant started singing, 'Nearer, my God, to thee', and the survivors sang until they were exhausted, as oil from the stricken ship covered the surface of the sea.

The results of Margaret Jones's research convinced the Royal Navy hierarchy that both Jones himself and other members of his crew were deserving of gallantry awards. Until his widow's involvement, Jones's name had simply appeared in the Jutland honours list on 15 September 1916 among those officers and men Mentioned in Despatches.

Jones's posthumous VC was announced on 6 March 1917 when his citation said the decoration was 'In recognition of his most conspicuous bravery and devotion to duty in the course of the Battle of Jutland. The full facts have only now been ascertained.' The six survivors from the ship, including Petty Officer Griffin, each received the Distinguished Service Medal (DSM).

Margaret Jones received her husband's VC from George V at Buckingham Palace on 31 March 1917. In 1920, accompanied by her daughter Linnette, she visited her husband's grave in Sweden and they were photographed beside it. In 1961, Jones's remains were transferred to the British War Graves Kviberg Cemetery in Gothenburg and his widow also retrieved some of his personal effects. In 1991,

Linnette Sheffield, by then married, returned to Sweden to attend a ceremony to mark the seventy-fifth anniversary of the Battle of Jutland and her father's heroic death. Earlier that year, she had loaned her father's VC to the Royal Naval Museum, Portsmouth, saying: 'I'm so proud of this medal but I did worry about being burgled.'

I purchased Jones's VC and service medals in 2013 in a private sale, along with a number of personal effects including his water-stained wristwatch, his smashed binoculars and the life-belt that he was wearing when he died. I am delighted that Jones's VC and his damaged watch have gone on public display at the Imperial War Museum. Over the years, many people have praised Jones's bravery but perhaps the greatest compliment to his courage came from Admiral Beatty, the Commander-in-Chief of the Grand Fleet during the war and later the first Earl Beatty. He said that: 'No finer act had been produced in the annals of His Majesty's Navy.'

SKIPPER (LATER CHIEF SKIPPER) JOSEPH WATT

Royal Naval Reserve

DATE OF BRAVERY: 15 MAY 1917

GAZETTED: 29 AUGUST 1917

Special feature of the VC: An astonishing award for bravery in taking on an Austrian cruiser in a drifter armed with a puny six-pounder gun.

Joseph Watt was born in the fishing village of Gardenstown near Banff, Scotland, on 25 June 1887. One of five children, he was the son of Joseph Watt, a fisherman, and his wife Helen (*née* Mair), and he was educated locally at Bracoden School, Gamrie. Sadly, his father died at sea, while fishing for haddock more than 20 miles off the coast, when Joseph Jr was just ten years old. Although his mother soon remarried and moved to nearby Broadsea, Watt was determined to follow his father's career and, after leaving school, he served an apprenticeship in the *White Daisy*, a fishing boat. Yet, like many fishermen of his generation, Watt never learned to swim. In 1907, he left home and became part-owner of the *Annie*, a Dundee-built steam drifter. Over the next five years, he earned a reputation as a daring fisherman who would go out into the North Sea in the wildest of storms.

After the outbreak of the Great War in the summer of 1914, Watt volunteered for the Patrol Service, and was commissioned as a skipper in the Royal Naval Reserve on 11 January 1915. After a few months of patrolling the North Sea, he was posted to Italy, one of hundreds of fishermen who had volunteered for similar services to their king and country. In the meantime, Watt had married: on 5 August 1915, to Jessie Ann Noble, a fisherman's daughter.

Once in Italy, Watt was appointed to the command of HM Drifter *Gowanlea*, an 87ft wooden vessel that had been completed the week that the war had begun. With its crew of nine and armed with a solitary six-pounder gun, the *Gowanlea* was part of a flotilla of commandeered steam drifters based in the heel of Italy. The crew, mainly Fraserburgh men, were a close-knit team, and included Fred Lamb, the boat's gunner, a cooper in civilian life known for his immense strength, and William Noble, the boat's engineer. Like most ships at the time, the crew had a mascot: a monkey that had been presented to them by local Italian sailors (the monkey was not a success and was soon replaced by a small terrier that proved more popular with the crew). As part of the so-called Otranto Barrage, the task of *Gowanlea* and her crew was to prevent Austrian submarines operating out of Cattaro, 140 miles to the north, entering the Mediterranean via the straits separating Italy from Albania. No fewer than 120 drifters provided a 24-hour net barrier across 44 miles of water, supported in their task by an Allied fleet of motor-launches, destroyers, cruisers and aircraft.

In January 1916, the routine pattern of patrol work was interrupted by the need to help evacuate the remnants of the Serbian

Army from Albania. Watt and his crew, who at this point were based in Brindisi, assisted in the evacuation of the Serbs from Valona to Corfu by helping to guard the transports from enemy U-boats. It was in recognition of this work that Watt was awarded the Serbian Gold Medal for Zealous Service.

For the remainder of the year, *Gowanlea* and her crew were back on patrol duties. On 22 December 1916, four enemy destroyers and a light cruiser from the Austro-Hungarian Navy attacked the barrage, taking the drifters by surprise. The *Gowanlea* was hit by an enemy shell that blew away the funnel. Watt gave the order to prepare to abandon ship, and as the lifeboat was being lowered, with their only compass aboard it, a second shell hit and sent the lifeboat down. A third shell then hit the boat at the waterline but, fortunately, the enemy was driven off by the timely arrival of six French destroyers. However, *Gowanlea* was a wreck and several members of her crew lay dying among the debris. The situation was desperate and, without their compass, the crew was lost. However, after steaming around, Watt sighted another patrol vessel and ordered more speed as the crew were below, fighting for their lives and trying to patch up the shell hole. Eventually, *Gowanlea* caught up with the other drifter and she was led back to the safety of the port. After being repaired, *Gowanlea* returned to her patrol duties in early 1917. Ominously, April suddenly saw a marked rise in the number of enemy submarine sightings even though a number were forced to turn back.

On the night of 14/15 May 1917, the Austro-Hungarian Navy launched an all-out attack on the Otranto Barrage, with the aim of wiping out so many Allied vessels that their U-boats would be able to access the Mediterranean and Allied shipping lanes. Nine ships, including light cruisers, sailed from Cattaro, confident of causing massive damage to the Allied flotilla because of their vastly superior size and guns.

The nine enemy ships separated before beginning their attack on the barrage at 3.15 a.m. At the time, forty-seven drifters were stretched across the straits in seven groups, with the *Gowanlea* on the far western side of the barrage. Watt was on board with a crew of eight and their dog. As soon as firing was heard, *Gowanlea* slipped her nets and made for the Italian coast. However, within minutes she ran into the *Novara*, one of the light cruisers taking part in the attack. When the two vessels were only 100 yards apart, the *Novara* signalled to the *Gowanlea* – by dipping her flags and blowing hard on her siren – to abandon ship. 'Surrender' was not, however, a word in Watt's personal vocabulary and the offer was refused. Instead, calling for full steam ahead, Watt encouraged his crew by shouting: 'Three cheers, lads, and let's fight to the finish!' As the *Gowanlea* made straight for the enemy ship, the drifter's gun team, comprising Fred Lamb and Edward Godbald, immediately opened fire with their six-pounder gun, with menacing accuracy.

The enemy response was both swift and predictable: they brought their nine 3.9-inch guns to bear on the *Gowanlea* and two shells caused instant and significant damage. One blast carried away the port railings and smashed the boat's bulwarks while the other plunged through the deck, disabled the gun, and detonated a box of ammunition. In the second explosion, Lamb was blown away from the gun and severely wounded, shattering his right leg and foot, and shell splinters struck him in the face and eyes. Two further shells landed on the drifter: Watt, whose cap had been ripped by shrapnel, narrowly escaped death when one of these shells struck the wheelhouse. But *Gowanlea* was able to limp away under her own steam, thanks to the efforts of William Noble, the ship's engineer. The *Novara* only moved on because she was convinced that the *Gowanlea* was sinking.

The raid lasted just over an hour, during which fourteen of the forty-seven drifters were sunk and several more damaged. As the cruisers withdrew, they left behind a scene of destruction and chaos. *Gowanlea*, despite being badly damaged, even joined in the rescue effort and managed to help the wounded from the drifter *Floandi* before making for port. Of *Floandi*'s crew of ten, four were killed and three, including the skipper, were wounded. One casualty from the *Gowanlea* was its terrier, who died three days later having never recovered from the shock of the raid.

In his book *VCs of the First World War: The Naval VCs*, Stephen Snelling examines the controversy surrounding the recommendation of so many awards for gallantry on the night of 14/15 May. Within a fortnight Rear-Admiral Mark Kerr, who commanded the British Adriatic Squadron, had recommended two awards of the VC: one to Skipper Watt and the other to Deckhand Lamb, who had kept to his gun despite having his leg and ankle shattered. Altogether there were 119 recommendations for gallantry awards, including forty-five proposals for the Conspicuous Gallantry Medal (CGM). However, in London, senior figures in the Admiralty were unhappy with the scale of the recommendations: they felt too many of the crews had surrendered too quickly and they felt the CGM was too high an award for the many who had stood their ground (at that point only 54 awards of the CGM had been made in the entire war). There was also a feeling that there should not be so many awards for what amounted to a 'rout' and so it was suggested that the numbers of awards should be significantly scaled down.

Watt's VC – the only one for the action – was announced on 29 August 1917 when the citation for his award gave a splendidly succinct summary of the day's events:

> For most conspicuous gallantry when the Allied Drifter line in the Straits of Otranto was attacked by Austrian light cruisers on the morning of the 15th May, 1917.
>
> When hailed by an Austrian cruiser at about 100 yards range and ordered to stop and abandon his drifter the 'Gowan Lea,' Skipper Watt ordered full speed ahead and called upon his crew to give three cheers and fight to the finish. The cruiser was then engaged, but after one round had been fired, a shot from the enemy disabled

the breech of the drifter's gun. The gun's crew, however, stuck to the gun, endeavouring to make it work, being under heavy fire all the time. After the cruiser had passed on Skipper Watt took the 'Gowan Lea' alongside the badly-damaged drifter 'Floandi' and assisted to remove the dead and wounded.

Watt, who was aged twenty-nine at the time of his VC action, was also rewarded with the Italian Al Valore Militare and the French Croix de Guerre. Lamb, the wounded gunner, was awarded the CGM and Noble, the engineer, and Godbald, the deck hand, were both awarded the Distinguished Service Medal (DSM).

In total, the action led to the award of one VC, two Distinguished Service Orders (DSOs); six Distinguished Service Crosses (DSCs); five CGMs; eighteen DSMs; and thirty-one Mentions in Despatches, together with several foreign awards. Admiral Sir John Jellicoe, the First Sea Lord, delivered a speech in praise of the crew of the *Gowanlea* and other small British ships: 'The enemy has been up against the grit of the British sailor. It is this spirit which will win the war and I hope win it quickly, but while you applaud this moment the spirit of the British sailor, never forget the duty of gratitude this country owes him.'

In Scotland, W. R. Melvin, the Fraserburgh poet, commemorated the gallantry of the crew with a poem, 'H.M. Drifter *Gowanlea*':

Four Hundred years have sped since first, Britannia ruled the wave,/ And history's page is crowded with, Deeds glorious and brave;/ But none outshine the story fine, Of Austrian cruisers three,/ That were faced and fought by a fishing boat, The drifter *Gowanlea*.

Neath the purple Adriatic night, Our Scotch minesweepers lay,/ When a Squadron of the foe swooped down, Like a vulture on its prey./ 'Surrender'! cried the Austrian chief; 'Surrender!, No not me;/ So there, that's flat!' bawled Skipper Watt, Of the drifter *Gowanlea*!

Then his crew gave three defiant cheers, As they made their pop-gun squirt;/ Why 'twas like ten men in armour Against one man in his shirt!/ The foe's broadside flamed across the tide, But the drifter – what cared she?/ With her six pound shot she answered hot, Did the tiny *Gowanlea!*

The wheelhouse smashed and her nose sore bashed And the bulwarks all afire,/ But the flag still flew, and no thought but do Or die was the crew's desire./ A ball came slap through the skipper's cap, 'I still keep my head', laughed he,/ 'And if down we go, then the world will know We died game on the *Gowanlea*'!

And bold Fred Lamb served his gun as calm, As if no darned foe was nigh./ Till a shell came along with a death-like song And mangled his leg and thigh./ 'That's one spar gone', said Fred with a groan, 'But I've still got my fists you see!'/ And he fought his gun till the foe did run From the drifter *Gowanlea!*

Who were those heroes of the main Who won such high renown?/ A cooper and a fisherman From a quiet Buchan town./ Spirit of Nelson and of Drake! Spirit of Victory!/ Ye are not dead while we've Joe and Fred And the drifter *Gowanlea.*

Watt fell ill shortly after his VC action and spent six weeks recuperating in hospital on Malta. After his release, he was promoted to chief skipper, backdated to the date of his action. He was also given a period of leave and allowed to return home. On learning of the news, Fraserburgh town council had planned a hero's welcome but Watt, forever shy of publicity, travelled home secretly, arriving back one evening in November 1917. The following day, attired in his fisherman's clothes, he went to relax down at the harbour. Although well known for his friendliness and cheerful disposition, he was extremely reluctant to discuss his VC action, prompting one journalist to describe him as 'a painfully modest man'. Watt's wife also learned nothing of his bravery from her husband. 'He refuses to tell me anything about it,' Helen Watt told a journalist.

Watt also felt that his gallantry had been greatly embellished by the press because of their desperation to create a war hero. He turned down one request for an interview saying: 'I have firmly made up my mind to say nothing about that. There has been too much said already and it should get a rest ... I'm ashamed to read the exaggerations that have been printed.'

Watt did, however, accept a gold watch and chain, given to him by George Walker, the owner of the *Gowanlea*, and some cash raised by local townspeople. His VC was presented to him by George V at an investiture at Buckingham Palace on 6 April 1918. Typical of the man, there is no record of him ever applying for, or receiving, his Great War service medals.

Watt's own drifter *Annie* was sunk clearing mines a few weeks after the November 1918 Armistice. However, he bought another vessel, the drifter *Bennachie*, named after Aberdeenshire's highest mountain, and returned to his first love – fishing at sea. Some time after the end of the Great War, Watt was visited on the *Bennachie* by HRH The Duke of Kent but, unaccustomed to receiving royal visitors, he forgot to remove his cap. His hugely valuable VC was kept in a small, cluttered drawer on his boat.

Watt had two children, a daughter and a son. During the Second World War he commanded a drifter serving with the Home Fleet, with a crew that included his son, who had been invalided home in 1940 after being wounded while serving with the Gordon Highlanders. Even in his fifties, Watt's fighting spirit remained undimmed because he told one journalist: 'Ah'm not allowed to go to sea to fecht [fight], they think ah'm tae auld.'

Joseph Watt, who was known locally as 'VC Joe', died from cancer at his home in Fraserburgh on 13 February 1955, aged sixty-seven. He was buried in Kirktown Cemetery, Fraserburgh, in the same plot as his wife and her parents.

The remarkable story of Watt's bravery received some welcome publicity in 2002 when pupils from his old school, Bracoden

Primary, looked into his story as part of a project set for them by Barbara Smith, their teacher. The pupils from the school, many of whom lived in Watt's home village of Gardenstown, then started to campaign for a permanent memorial for their local hero. Barbara Smith said at the time:

> I was fed up hearing about *Pop Idol* and the World Cup in class and decided they should learn something about a real hero. I am related to Joe Watt and I remembered my dad telling me about him when I was a child. The pupils really enjoyed the story and realised Gardenstown had its own hero and want him to be remembered for ever.

LIEUTENANT-COMMANDER GEOFFREY SAXTON WHITE

Royal Navy
DATE OF BRAVERY: 28 JANUARY 1918
GAZETTED: 24 MAY 1919
Special feature of the VC: one of only five VCs awarded to submariners during the Great War. It was also the first and only time that the VC has been awarded to two different captains of the same naval vessel.

Geoffrey Saxton White was born in Bromley, Kent, on 2 July 1886. He was the son of William White, a Justice of the Peace, and his wife Alice (*née* Saxton). White was educated at Parkfield School in Haywards Heath, Sussex, and Bradfield College, Berkshire. He joined HMS *Britannia* in May 1901, when still only fourteen, passing out later that year. In 1902, he served in the armoured cruiser HMS *Aboukir* and in November of that year he was made a midshipman. Over the next seven years, he had a variety of postings, travelling all over the world and, after the second of two promotions, he was made lieutenant in October 1908. In January 1909, he joined HMS

Mercury, a Portsmouth-based depot ship, for submarine training. Within two years he was given his first submarine command – HM Submarine *A11* in July 1911. This initial appointment – which was followed by a series of further submarine commands – came just a month after his wedding to Sybil Thomas in Plymouth, Devon (the couple went on to have two sons and a daughter).

In April 1914, just four months before the start of the Great War, White's first spell in submarines ended when he was transferred to the battleship HMS *Monarch*. This occupied him for the early part of the war but in May 1915 he returned to submarines when he was given the command of HM Submarine *D6*. In May 1916, he was given the command of HM Submarine *E14*, and in October that year he was promoted to lieutenant-commander. In December 1916, *E14* carried out patrols in the Mediterranean and the following year it was one of four submarines sent to Corfu to strengthen the so-called Otranto Barrage (see previous entry for Skipper Watt).

As soon as war began in August 1914, two powerful German navy ships, *Goeben* and *Breslau*, succeeded in escaping from the Mediterranean through the Dardanelles. They based themselves in Constantinople from where they made occasional forays into the Black Sea. There was huge concern in the Admiralty that *Goeben*, in particular, as a massive modern battlecruiser, would slip out of Constantinople and be able to wreak havoc in the Mediterranean and, possibly, beyond. Indeed, these acute fears were a forerunner to those experienced by the Royal Navy in the Second World War when it was desperately anxious that the *Bismarck*, the formidable enemy battleship, would slip out of northern Germany and cause mayhem among the North Atlantic convoys.

In November 1917, following the Bolshevik revolution, Russia withdrew from the war with the result that on 20 January 1918, *Goeben* and *Breslau* sailed through the Dardanelles with the intention of attacking the British naval base of Mudros on the Greek island of Lemnos. However, after successful attacks on two British ships, both

German ships struck mines and, while *Breslau* sank, *Goeben* limped back to the Dardanelles. Despite striking a second mine, *Goeben* would have made it back to safety were it not for the miscalculation of her commander who, as the ship neared Nagara Point, mistook a buoy and ran her aground. This presented the Royal Navy and the Royal Flying Corps with a heaven-sent opportunity to sink the renegade German ship.

After much careful planning, including failed air attacks, White and his crew of *E14* were tasked with attacking *Goeben*, and the submarine set sail from Imbros on 27 January on a dangerous journey through mined seas and enemy shore batteries. White and his men travelled by night to reach Nagara Point the next day. At 5.30 a.m. on 28 January, having negotiated a minefield safely, *E14* advanced beneath the waves but soon found her path obstructed by an unidentified object. White brought his submarine to the surface and climbed out to investigate, but only after giving strict instructions that the submarine must dive if attacked – leaving White himself to a certain death. White guided the submarine clear of the mysterious obstruction and returned inside, confident he now had his bearings.

It was light by 7 a.m., and White took a fix through his periscope. Nagara Point was clearly visible to him but there was no sign of *Goeben*: unbeknown to the British, the ship had been refloated some twenty-four hours before *E14* embarked on its ill-fated mission. White took the submarine further up the Straits in the hope of spotting his target but, with no sign of *Goeben*, he faced the unappealing prospect of a dangerous return journey on depleted submarine batteries.

At 8.45 a.m., White raised his periscope to take a fix and spotted a Turkish merchant ship within easy range. Perhaps to ease the disappointment of his failed mission, he decided to attack. However, just eleven seconds after the second torpedo left the submarine's bow tube, *E14* was rocked by a massive explosion. She was lifted up some 15 feet and the conning tower rose out of the water. Furthermore, the forward torpedo hatch sprung open, enabling hundreds of gallons of sea water to enter. To this day it is not known what caused the blast but a torpedo may have struck a mine or exploded prematurely.

Immediately after the blast, the shore batteries opened up on the stricken submarine, which received several hits. Nevertheless, White regained control of *E14* sufficiently to submerge and assess the damage. For the next two hours, she limped along – still submerged – towards the open sea, with White hopeful that all was not lost. Suddenly, a surge of water sent *E14* plunging to 165 feet and, with virtually no control of the submarine, White was forced to bring her back to the surface and run the inevitable gauntlet of guns from the shore. In a final attempt to guide his submarine and its crew, White climbed out onto the casing soon after she reached the surface. With the conning tower flooded and its hatch jammed, he was forced to emerge from the fore-hatch.

By then the situation was hopeless, as Petty Officer Perkins, who survived the debacle, later detailed:

> The captain was the first one up on deck, and then the navigator [Lieutenant Drew of the Royal Naval Reserve]. I followed to connect up the upper steering gear. We found the spindle to be shot in half. Orders were given to steer from below. We ran the gauntlet for half an hour, only a few shots hitting us ... The captain, seeing it was hopeless, ran towards the shore. His last words were, 'We are in the hands of God', and only a few seconds later I looked for him and saw his body, mangled by shellfire, roll into the water and go under. The last shell hit the starboard tank, killing all [in the area] I believe. By this time the submarine was close to the shore. Soon afterwards she sank...

The shore fire had come from batteries on Cape Helles and Kum Kale. Perkins was convinced that Lieutenant Drew had been killed by the same shell that claimed White's life. The Turks picked up only nine of *E14*'s 39-strong complement, including Perkins, and, after the war was over, they described the bravery of their commander and others.

White's VC was announced on 24 May 1919 when his citation ended: 'Lieutenant-Commander White turned [his submarine] towards the shore in order to give the crew a chance of being saved. He remained on deck the whole time himself until he was killed by a shell.' Two survivors, Able Seaman Reuben Mitchell and Signaller Charles Timbrell, were both awarded the Distinguished Service Medal (DSM) for their bravery in keeping a badly wounded comrade afloat until help arrived. Eight months later, on 22 January 1920, Petty Officer Perkins was also awarded the DSM, while Telegraphist William Prichard was awarded a Bar to his DSM.

White's VC meant that *E14* became the only vessel in the Royal Navy's history to have two of its commanders awarded Britain and the Commonwealth's ultimate gallantry award. Lieutenant-Commander Edward Boyle's VC had been announced on 21 May 1915 for his bravery in the Sea of Marmora, Turkey, in *E14* when he avoided enemy patrols and mines in rough weather to sink two Turkish gunboats and one large military transport ship.

White's body was never recovered from the sea: his widow received his VC from George V at an investiture at Buckingham Palace on 12 June 1919. White's name is remembered on both the Horley Memorial in Surrey and the Portsmouth Naval Memorial, Hampshire.

The Royal Flying Corps (RFC)/ Royal Air Force (RAF)

The Royal Flying Corps (RFC) was created by a Royal Warrant on 13 May 1912 and superseded the Air Battalion of the Royal Engineers. It was initially intended to have separate military and naval branches. Inter-service rivalry meant, however, that the Royal Navy was not keen to have naval aviation under the control of an Army corps so it formed its own Royal

Naval Air Service (RNAS). When war broke out in Europe in August 1914, the RFC had fewer than 1,400 men, the majority of whom went to France along with seventy-three aircraft and ninety-five support vehicles and a small number of manned balloons.

When war broke out, the airplane was initially viewed by the military as a vehicle for reconnaissance. In the early stages of the war, enemy pilots who saw each other in the air simply went about their reconnaissance duties. The more aggressive ones, however, were soon taking to the skies with revolvers, grenades, rifles and anything else they could get their hands on to attack enemy pilots and prevent them completing their task. Soon, machine-guns were converted for use in planes too and, even by 1915, the number of aerial combats was escalating rapidly. By 1916, aircraft became generally more sophisticated and, by the Battle of the Somme, the RFC had a marked aerial supremacy. It had 421 aircraft, fourteen balloon squadrons and four kite-balloon squadrons.

On 1 April 1918, the RFC and RNAS were amalgamated to form a new service, the Royal Air Force (RAF), which was controlled by a new Air Ministry. By August 1918, when the Allies began their push for victory, aircraft were playing a crucial role in supporting the ground offensive. By 1919, just a year after the end of the war, the RAF had 4,000 combat aircraft and 114,000 personnel.

MAJOR (LATER GROUP CAPTAIN) LIONEL WILMOT BRABAZON REES

Royal Flying Corps
DATE OF BRAVERY: 1 JULY 1916
GAZETTED: 5 AUGUST 1916
Special feature of the VC: an iconic VC for gallantry in the air on the first day of the Battle of the Somme.

Lionel Wilmot Brabazon Rees was born in Carnarvon, north Wales, on 31 July 1884. He was the son of Colonel Charles Rees, a solicitor and an officer in the Royal Welsh Fusiliers (Volunteer Force), and his wife Leonora (*née* Davids). He was educated at Elms Preparatory School in Colwall, Worcestershire, and Eastbourne College, Sussex. At Eastbourne College, he had a reputation as a fine sportsman but his write-up for the rugby first XV in 1901, when he was sixteen, suggests he could sometimes be too laid-back: 'One of the hardest workers in the team and a good player in other respects when once roused, but it takes an awful lot to rouse him.' After leaving school, he decided to pursue a military career and attended the Royal Military Academy (RMA), Woolwich, southeast London, as a gentleman cadet. On 23 December 1903 and aged nineteen, he was commissioned as a second lieutenant into the Royal Garrison Artillery, and quickly established himself as a superb shot.

Rees, who was promoted to lieutenant in 1906, spent some six years in west Africa from 1908 until the outbreak of the Great War, during which time he showed a great interest in and aptitude for the new 'sport' of flying. He gained his pilot's certificate in January 1913 after undertaking private lessons: in fact, he learned to fly at Bristol Flying School, Larkhill, Wiltshire. Shortly after the war began, he voluntarily transferred to the recently formed Royal Flying Corps (RFC).

After further training from 10 August 1914 and being promoted to captain, he was transferred to command a flight in No. 7 Squadron. In October 1914, he was ordered to Belgium to deliver stores to his new squadron and to set up an aircraft park. In January 1915, he survived a crash-landing in his two-seater Vickers aircraft and he had his first taste of war when he flew as an observer at the time when the British forces were involved in the retreat from Ostend. In February 1915, he was given command of a flight of No. 11 Squadron, based at Netheravon, near Bristol. By July of that year, the squadron was in France, stationed at Vert Galant, near Amiens, with eight aircraft, later increased to eleven.

During one mission, on the day after his arrival, Rees became involved in a dogfight with an enemy Fokker machine. Both pilots displayed immense skill and Rees's Vickers aircraft was hit and badly damaged, before Rees placed a burst of fire that sent the monoplane crashing to the ground behind enemy lines. This meant that Rees had become the first officially designated fighter pilot to take part in aerial combat, a notable achievement.

It was not long before Rees, who was shy and introverted, earned a reputation as a courageous and skilful pilot. A. J. Insall, an observer with No. 11 Squadron, was one of the many who admired him at close quarters:

> Captain Rees was one of those rare men who are born leaders, who never flap and who believe essentially in precept ... Rees it was, also, who taught us in No. 11 Squadron that our cardinal rule of behaviour on the battlefront must always adhere to the Flying Corps' watchword: 'Go in to the attack! Whenever you see the Hun, no matter where he is, be he alone or accompanied, go for him, and shoot him down.'

In the skies above Flanders, the Fokker aircraft soon began to gain ascendancy, leading to what was known as the 'Fokker scourge'. During the summer of 1915, Rees and his gunner, Flight Sergeant Hargreaves, repeatedly showed great courage in various encounters with enemy aircraft. This led to the award of a Military Cross (MC) for Rees and a Distinguished Conduct Medal (DCM) for his gunner. Rees's citation, announced on 29 October 1915, stated:

> For conspicuous gallantry and skill on several occasions, notably the following:
>
> On the 21st September 1915, when flying a machine with one machine gun, accompanied by Flight-Serjeant Hargreaves, he sighted a large German biplane with two machine guns 2,000 feet below

him. He spiralled down and dived at the enemy, who, having the faster machine, manoeuvred to get him broadside on and then opened fire. In spite of this Captain Rees pressed his attack and apparently succeeded in hitting the enemy's engine, for the machine made a quick turn, glided some distance and finally fell just inside the German lines near Herbecourt.

On 28th July, he attacked and drove down a hostile monoplane in spite of the fact that the main spar of his machine had been shot through and the rear spar shattered.

On 31st August, accompanied by Flight-Serjeant Hargreaves, he fought a German machine more powerful than his own for three-quarters of an hour, then returned for more ammunition and went out to attack again, finally bringing the enemy's machine down apparently wrecked.

The first action that led to Rees's MC took place on 21 September, four days after the start of the Battle of Loos, when he and Hargreaves had been ordered to photograph the German frontline trenches between Peronne and Esterre. Hargreaves, who had been responsible for taking the photographs as well as manning the Lewis gun in the forward cockpit, later wrote of his admiration for Rees in an article for *Popular Flying* magazine:

> Much credit was due to the masterly art of piloting by Captain Rees, who performed all sorts of misleading evolutions to the watchful eyes of 'Archies' [anti-aircraft fire] attendants.
>
> Without hitch or hindrance we shot every plate [photograph] successfully. Just after completion, and before I had time to collect the scattered plates from the floor of the nascelle [*sic* – a nacelle is casing to an aircraft's engine], Captain Rees drew my attention to a machine coming up from the German lines with the obvious intention of pushing us off or at least shaking our morale. My pilot immediately switched his engine off and glided down towards the German

machine. After dropping some 2,000 feet we were slightly above it and about 200 yards apart; we could clearly see that she was a new bus and vastly different from anything we had encountered before. The arrangement of the two fuselages with tractor screws and a nascelle with a propeller behind gave them an excellent distribution of gun power of which I believe they had three – one forward and two aft. They fired several bursts from about 200 yards to 100 yards range, but fortunately for us with no effect. When the range had slightly decreased I opened with half a drum, which must have resulted in some vital damage for the machine turned into a glide outwards and headed for their own lines, where she apparently crash landed.

The British duo successfully returned to base and the plates were duly delivered. Moreover, the 3rd Army Headquarters later stated that they were 'the finest series of photographs ever taken in France to that date'.

Some seven decades on, Gwilym Lewis, who, at the age of eighteen, had flown in Rees's squadron, was still full of praise for his CO:

Rees was a very competent commanding officer and a very experienced aviator. He was very senior to the rest of us in the squadron and full of guts. He was exciting to serve under, always keen to have a go at the enemy and an expert at his job. Unusually for a commanding officer at that time, he knew as much as anyone about engines and the rigging of aeroplanes, so it was no use anybody trying to pretend they had something wrong with their machine – he would have very quickly found them out.

After a short stint at the end of 1915 as the commander of the Central Flying School at Upavon, Wiltshire, which saw Rees promoted to major, he was soon back on operational duty. On 12 January 1916, Rees took command of the newly formed No. 32 Squadron. With the Fokker still ruling the skies, the new squadron was equipped with the nimble, single-seater DH.2 biplane. Rees, however, usually flew a Vickers Bullet, an advanced aircraft but one that did not have a good combat record. As a squadron commander, Rees was permitted to fly with his squadron but he was not allowed to cross the frontline and fly above enemy territory in case he was shot down and captured.

By 1 July 1916, the first day of the Battle of the Somme, No. 32 Squadron was based at Treizennes, France. At around 4.15 p.m., after acting as an escort for a bombing mission, Rees was in the air when he sighted a formation which he believed to be British bombers returning from a sortie. He made towards them to offer them protection on their home journey, only to discover that he was approaching around ten two-seater enemy bombers. By the time he realised his error, Rees courageously opted to turn defence into attack and fired on the first aircraft to come into range, hitting it so that it spiralled away out of control.

After turning and approaching the enemy again, he hit another enemy aircraft before coming under attack from up to five others who all missed their target. In continued fighting, Rees hit and damaged a third German aircraft before giving chase to yet two more.

However, one of the enemy aircraft closed in on Rees's machine with its gunner firing all the time, and the British pilot felt a sudden pain shoot through his thigh, meaning he was unable to use the rudder bar. By then, Rees had used all his plane's ammunition and so he drew his revolver and fired that at an enemy aircraft before turning for home. Rees made a successful landing before sitting on the grass and telling the ground crew that he needed to be taken to hospital.

An enemy bullet had narrowly missed an artery yet Rees was still annoyed that he had not been able to cause more damage to the enemy, telling medics he 'would have brought them all down, one after another, if I could have used my leg!'

Later, he gave a much more detailed and considered account of his extraordinary battle in the air:

As I got nearer, at about Annequin, the second machine turned out of the position and dived towards me firing his gun. I waited until he came within convenient range and fired one drum. This [sic] after about the 30th round I saw the top of his fuselage splinter between the pilot and the observer. The machine turned round and went home. This machine was marked with a big '3' and a small cross on the fuselage. I then went to attack a second machine. When he saw me he fired red Very's Lights [a pyrotechnic signal usually projected from a special pistol], and three more joined him. They fired an immense amount of ammunition but were so far away that they had no effect. The escort machines swooped down on to their own machines rather than me, and so shot past him and went out of action. When I got to a convenient position, I fired one drum. After about 30 rounds a big cloud of blue haze came out of the nascelle [sic] in front of the pilot. The machine turned and wobbled, and I last saw him down over the lines under [Allied] control. It looked either as if a cylinder was knocked off or else the petrol tank punctured. I then saw 5 [aircraft] close together. They opened fire at very long range. I closed, and fired one drum at very long range at the centre and the five dispersed in all directions. I then saw the leader and the two second machines going west. I overhauled them rapidly and, when I got near the lowest, he turned sharply to the left and dropped a bomb. He opened fire at long range. I closed, just as I was about to fire, a shot struck me in the leg putting the leg temporarily out of action. I fired another drum, but not having complete control of the rudder, I swept the machine backwards and forwards. I finished firing about ten yards away, and saw the observer sitting back firing straight up into the air, instead of at me. I grabbed my pistol but I dropped it on the floor of the nascelle and could not get at it again. I then recovered the use of my leg and saw the leader going towards the lines. I got within long range of him. He was firing an immense amount of ammunition. Just before he reached the

lines I gave him one more drum. Having finished my ammunition
I came home.

The men of the 22nd Anti-Aircraft Battery had witnessed the whole
aerial battle from the ground and could barely believe their eyes.
Word soon spread of Rees's bravery and Gwilym Lewis, who flew
with Rees and was quoted earlier in this write-up, told his parents
in a letter home: 'I told you he was the bravest man in the world ...
Of course everyone knows the Major is mad. I don't think he was
ever more happy in his life than attacking those Huns.'

Rees spent some six months in hospital but, despite walking
with a slight limp for the rest of his life, he soon resumed his military service. His VC – the original recommendation had, in fact,
been for a Distinguished Service Order (DSO) – was announced on
5 August 1916. On 15 December 1916, Rees received his decoration from George V at an investiture at Buckingham Palace. He
was promoted to lieutenant-colonel on 1 May 1917, shortly after
heading to America to act as an aviation adviser to the US Army.
On 7 March 1918, Rees was appointed to the command of No. 1
School of Aerial Fighting in Turnberry, Ayrshire, but he did not see
combat again because of his injured leg.

As the war drew to a close, he was, on 2 November 1918, awarded
the Air Force Cross (AFC) for services as a flying instructor, as well
as an OBE. The Great War formally ended nine days later but Rees
was determined to pursue a career in the recently formed RAF. This
meant he relinquished his Army rank and became a wing commander.

One of his early post-war appointments was as Assistant Commandant of RAF Cranwell in Lincolnshire. For thirteen years from
1918, Rees took up a number of senior positions both at home
and abroad before retiring in 1931 with the rank of group captain.
Unmarried and with no close family, Rees, in retirement, donated
his service pension to the RAF Benevolent Fund and his medal group
to his former school. Even this act of generosity was carried out in

the most modest of ways. In a letter to his old school dated 1 July 1931, he wrote: 'Dear Headmaster, At the end of the month I am retiring from the Service, and as I intend to live abroad, I shall not want again my medals, sword and aiguillettes [ornaments on a military uniform]. Would you care to have them, possibly to hang in a case in the Library or elsewhere? The College did a great deal for me, and possibly you might think that in this way I might work off some of the debt. I am yours sincerely...'

In retirement, Rees took up sailing, achieving a single-handed Atlantic crossing in the winter of 1933/34 in a 34ft yacht. Some believe that his 96-day crossing to the harbour of Nassau, in the Bahamas, was the very first single-handed Atlantic crossing. He spent the next few years sailing around the Caribbean but, between 1941 and 1942, Rees was briefly recalled for military service in the Second World War because of a shortage of experienced officers required for administrative posts.

In a superb tribute to Rees in his book *Heart of a Dragon: The VCs of Wales and the Welsh Regiment 1914–82*, W. Alister Williams ends his write-up of the pilot:

> In 1947, he caused considerable gossip amongst the white community in Nassau when he married Sylvia Williams, the eighteen-year-old daughter of a black family, on the island of Andros, where he lived the remainder of his life, all but forgotten, not only by the service which he did so much to establish, but also the land of his birth.

In fact, Rees, who was intelligent and well read, and his young wife, who was forty-five years his junior, went on to have two sons and a daughter. Rees, who battled leukaemia late in his life, died in the Princess Margaret Hospital in Nassau on 28 September 1955, aged seventy-one. He is buried at the Nassau War Cemetery for United Nations Airmen. There are several memorials in his honour including one at the RAF College, Cranwell, Lincolnshire, and the Royal Artillery Chapel at Woolwich, south-east London. His devotion to aviation was recognised many years later when someone who could not be kept away from his aircraft engine became known affectionately as a 'Rees'.

LIEUTENANT (LATER FLIGHT LIEUTENANT) ALAN JERRARD

Royal Flying Corps
DATE OF BRAVERY: 30 MARCH 1918
GAZETTED: 1 MAY 1918
Special feature of the VC: Jerrard was affectionately known as the 'Pyjama VC', the only Sopwith Camel VC and the unique air VC from the Italian Front.

Alan Jerrard was born in Lewisham, south London, on 3 December 1897. He was the son of Herbert Jerrard, a teacher, and his wife Jane (*née* Hobbs). Five years after Alan's birth, the family moved to the West Midlands because of his father's work: Herbert became the headmaster of Bishop Vesey's Grammar School in Sutton Coldfield. Jerrard Jr was first educated at his father's school, then Oundle School in Northamptonshire and, finally, Birmingham University.

After only a matter of months at university, however, he volunteered, in 1915, to join the Army. On 2 January 1916, Jerrard, a quiet and unassuming man, was commissioned as a second lieutenant into the South Staffordshire Regiment but he spent only a very short time as an infantry subaltern before applying to be transferred to the Royal Flying Corps. At the time, Britain was short of pilots and training was quick: having reported for initial training on 23 September 1916, he was posted to No. 59 Squadron based at RAF Narborough, Norfolk, on 5 December. Here, he fell ill as the unit was preparing for operations in France and he was therefore temporarily attached to No. 50 (Reserve) Squadron based at the same station.

Once fit again, he graduated as a RFC pilot on 14 June 1917. He showed above-average abilities in his further training and, on 2 July, he was promoted to lieutenant. Jerrard was then selected to fly single-seater aircraft and he was notified of his first operational posting, arriving at No. 19 Squadron, based at Liettres, France, on 24 July.

On 29 July 1917, Jerrard flew his first operational patrol and, after failing to see the enemy, he lost contact with his formation and had to land at Saint-Omer. His second operational patrol on 5 August was more eventful. Still inexperienced, he again lost contact with his formation and flew low to get his bearings. When he came across a large convoy of German transport vehicles, he raked the convoy with machine-gun fire, causing several vehicles to burst into flames. After climbing to 10,000 feet through fog and low cloud, his engine cut out and he was forced to crash-land his Spad A8830 into a railway embankment near Sainte-Marie-Cappel. Allied troops reached him and dug him out of the wreckage.

In his book *VCs of the First World War: The Air VCs*, Peter G. Cooksley writes:

> Alan was only semi-conscious and in pain when the soldiers reached him and it took some time with manfully applied intrenching tools, pickaxes and even their bare hands for them to dig the wrecked aircraft out of the railway bank into which the force of the blind impact had driven it. The balance sheet of Alan Jerrard's second sortie in France had not been favourable to the Allies – a pilot temporarily lost through facial injuries that included a broken nose, multiple fractures of the jaw and a multitude of less serious wounds, plus a valuable aircraft destroyed for a few German vehicles set ablaze.

After being invalided back to England, he was eventually declared fit for operational flying once again in the New Year. On 22 February

1918, Jerrard arrived with his new unit, 66 Squadron, which flew Sopwith Camels and was based in Italy. Just five days later, he claimed an enemy Berg single-seater Scout as shot down and out of control. Over the next month, he had more successes, shooting down an enemy observation balloon, claiming a pair of Berg Scouts (one crashed, the other damaged) and, finally, shooting down an Albatros Scout that also crashed.

On 30 March, Jerrard and two other pilots, one experienced and the other a novice, were given a sortie in their three Sopwith Camels. There are some discrepancies over exactly who did what next but essentially they found themselves in a massive dogfight with at least nineteen enemy aircraft over Mansuè, Italy. According to the British pilots (although their account was disputed by their Austro-Hungarian opponents), Jerrard shot down three enemy aircraft and the other two pilots shot down a further three between them. Jerrard also launched a courageous attack, flying as low as 50 feet, on an enemy aerodrome, successfully shooting up aircraft as they tried to take off.

Jerrard only retreated when ordered to do so by his patrol leader and he was then pursued by five enemy aircraft. However, by then wounded and with his aircraft damaged, he crash-landed west of Mansuè aerodrome, where he was captured and taken Prisoner of War (PoW). In his book, Cooksley once again paints a vivid picture of the scene with the Sopwith Camel in a meadow having lost both port wings in the crash and with the aircraft pointed nose down in the ground.

> When assistance arrived, Alan was found dazed and in shock, able only to sit with clasped hands and bowed head on the remains of his machine: mask, goggles and helmet discarded and flung on the ground in a heap, small wonder considering the effect of the fight. The Camel's wreckage had 163 bullet holes, nearly thirty in the fuel tank and half that number in the engine, circumstances with which

his victor hastily sympathized before taking Alan with every sign of
cordiality to Austrian Army Headquarters at Oderzo.

The officer who shot down Jerrard was Oberleutnant Benno Fiala
von Fernbrugg, an Austrian air ace, who, after landing his aircraft,
commandeered a car and drove to the crash site.

Although some of the precise facts of the mission were unclear
– shrouded, as they say, in the 'fog of war' – one thing was certain:
when Jerrard was captured he was wearing only his pyjamas beneath
his bulky flying overalls. On the morning of 30 March, the weather
had been unsuitable for flying and Jerrard thought he had been stood
down for the day. When he was suddenly ordered to 'scramble', he
had been asleep and had to dress rapidly, simply pulling on his overalls over his pyjamas. Jerrard's chivalrous captors had sympathy with
his predicament as a pyjama-clad prisoner and arranged for a note
to be dropped behind Allied lines, requesting various items to be
air-dropped for him. No. 66 Squadron arranged for two such pack-
ages for the twenty-year-old prisoner, containing everything from
his military uniform to cigarettes and other clothing.

A combat report led to Jerrard being recommended for the VC
and his award was announced on 1 May 1918, while he was still a
PoW. His citation described the dogfight and ended:

> Although apparently wounded, this very gallant officer turned repeat-
> edly, and attacked single-handed the pursuing machines, until he
> was eventually overwhelmed by numbers and driven to the ground.
>
> Lt. Jerrard had greatly distinguished himself on four previous
> occasions, within a period of twenty-three days, in destroying enemy
> machines, displaying bravery and ability of the very highest order.

As well as being known affectionately as the 'Pyjama VC', Jerrard
had the distinction of being the only air VC during the prolonged
campaign on the Italian Front. Furthermore, he was the only Sopwith

Camel fighter pilot to be awarded the VC: by the end of the Great War, the Sopwith Camel was as well known to the British public as the Spitfire was during the Second World War.

Jerrard remained a PoW at Salzburg until the end of the war, when he was repatriated back to England. He chose to stay in the RAF and, after his investiture by George V at Buckingham Palace on 5 April 1919, he served with the RAF Murmansk detachment in Russia. While still serving in the RAF, he married Eliza Woods in London in 1926.

Jerrard rose to the rank of flight lieutenant in the RAF but, due to ill health, retired from the service on 24 August 1933. In 1956, he lent his VC to an exhibition to mark the centenary of the award. Jerrard died at a nursing home in Lyme Regis, Dorset, on 14 May 1968, aged seventy. Three days later he was buried with full military honours and his ashes were later interred at Hillingdon, Uxbridge. His name is on a family grave in Hillingdon, on a memorial at Lewisham Civic Centre and on an RAF memorial at St Clement Danes, London.

ACTING CAPTAIN (LATER FLIGHT LIEUTENANT) ANDREW WEATHERBY BEAUCHAMP PROCTOR (BORN ANDREW FREDERICK WEATHERBY PROCTOR)

Royal Air Force

DATES OF BRAVERY: 8 AUGUST 1918 – 8 OCTOBER 1918

GAZETTED: 30 NOVEMBER 1918

Special feature of the VC: a quite exceptional group of awards for gallantry in the air to the Allies sixth-highest scoring ace of the Great War and South Africa's leading ace of the conflict.

Andrew Frederick Weatherby Proctor – his full name at birth – was born in the small port of Mossel Bay, Cape Colony, South Africa, on 4 September 1894. He was the son of Captain John James Proctor, who had served voluntarily in both the Basutoland Rebellion and, afterwards, in the Second Anglo-Boer War. However, by profession his father was a teacher, employed as headmaster of a school at George, Cape Colony, and, later, at Mafeking. The young Proctor was educated in South Africa: first at a school in Beaconsfield and then in his birthplace, Mossel Bay. Next, he boarded at College House, South African College School (later the University of Cape Town), where he eventually studied for an engineering diploma.

Shortly after the outbreak of the Great War in August 1914, Proctor broke off from his studies and voluntarily enlisted as a signaller into the Duke of Edinburgh's Own Rifles ('The Rifles') on 1 October 1914, having turned twenty less than a month earlier. He soon saw active service in the German South-West Africa campaign where, amid the desert and mountains, he had to confront not just the enemy but a searing heat and the constant presence of flies. Proctor, diminutive at just 5ft 2in. tall and at this time preferring to be called 'Frederick' rather than 'Andrew', played a full part in the campaign. He also kept a brief, daily diary that revealed his discontent with the bad living conditions, unpleasant climate, poor food, shortage of sleep, lack of frontline action and sheer boredom. On 24 March, Proctor wrote, tongue in cheek: 'Am afraid I will have to send my eldest son up to fight as I will be too old if they don't hurry up.' His entire diary entry, more than two months later, for 28 June 1915 read: 'Got up late (as usual). Received a week's rations today. Absolutely nothing doing. Shall die of melancholia.'

After witnessing the end of the campaign (which saw the enemy defeated in German South-West Africa), Proctor transferred to the South African Field Telegraph and Postal Corps. Three months later, in August 1915, he was demobbed and returned to Cape Town to resume his engineering studies, his wartime service career apparently over.

In late 1916, aged twenty-two, Proctor took some personal decisions relating to his name. He decided to drop 'Frederick' on the grounds that it sounded too Germanic and started calling himself 'Andrew'. He also decided to adopt a double-barrelled surname, taking on the name of 'Beauchamp' used by some of his distant Celtic ancestors. From then on, he was known as 'Andrew Weatherby Beauchamp Proctor' (not a hyphenated surname despite a hyphen later appearing in his gallantry medal citations).

It is not known how Beauchamp Proctor first developed an interest in flying but with the war in Europe ongoing, and as an engineer apparently keen 'to do his bit', he responded to one of the British government's recruiting campaigns and volunteered for the Royal Flying Corps (RFC). On 12 March 1917, he attested as an air mechanic, 3rd class, in the RFC, before sailing to England for pilot training.

On 26 March 1917, Beauchamp Proctor reported to No. 6 Officers' Cadet Battalion at Farnborough, Hampshire, before, on 13 April, being sent for a month's ground training at the Oxford School of Military Aeronautics. In May, he started his flying instruction with 5 (Reserve) Squadron, Castle Bromwich, Warwickshire, before further training at 24 (Reserve) Squadron at Netheravon, Wiltshire. On 10 June, he flew solo for five hours, but crashed on landing, destroying his aircraft's wheels. An advanced flying course at Central Flying School, Upavon, Wiltshire, in July 1917 led to him receiving his RFC 'wings' on 29 July. Thereafter, he was posted to Beaulieu, Hampshire, where he joined 84 Squadron, RFC, which had only been formed in January of that year.

His lack of height caused him some problems in aircraft even though he was able to overcome them. He was too short to be able to reach the rudder bar in a standard aircraft, while he was also too low in the cockpit for the cockpit view. However, he was able to fit the rudder bar with a pair of blocks so as to bring it within his reach and his cockpit seat was adjusted so as to provide him with a better view.

Commanded by the highly accomplished (and eventually highly decorated) Major Sholto Douglas, 84 Squadron was equipped with

SE5a Scouts and was preparing for its first tour of duty on the Western Front. On 24 September 1917, the squadron arrived in the war zone, initially flying routine patrols from its base in Flez, France. Soon, however, the fighter squadron actively sought out the enemy, achieving its first 'kill' on 22 November when Beauchamp Proctor and another pilot shot down a German kite balloon. Beauchamp Proctor suspected that he had achieved his first solo combat victory a week later when a German aircraft dived away, possibly out of control. However, with no eyewitness to the plane's demise, it was not possible to claim this as a 'kill'. On 5 December, he had a similar experience, but again without the necessary evidence needed for his first combat 'kill'. Christmas 1917 and the New Year of 1918 passed without the landmark solo victory that he was so keen to achieve.

His fortunes changed on 3 January 1918 when, with the trenches below him covered in snow, he spotted an enemy two-seater during an afternoon patrol. Beauchamp Proctor attacked the German aircraft and witnesses saw it spiral into the ground near St Quentin for his first confirmed 'kill'. In his own typed combat report for the day, Beauchamp Proctor wrote of this incident:

> In company with Lieut. Larson I engaged two E.A. [enemy aircraft] two-seaters near St Quentin. After various manoeuvres I managed to get onto the tail of one of the E.A. After emptying one drum of Lewis [gun] and about 100 rounds of Vickers [gun] into E.A at very close range, E.A. went into a steep nose dive. I dived after him. During the dive, I changed drums and again opened fire. The E.A. flattened out, stalled, and went into a steeper nose dive than ever. I still followed him, my pitot [tube – showing velocity] showing about 270 m.p.h. I saw my shots hitting the E.A. I got down to about 3000 feet about seven miles over, and was then being fired at very heavily from the ground. My cowling [engine cover] also blew off owing to the speed I was diving, so I turned West and returned under heavy

A.A. [anti aircraft] fire. When I last saw E.A. he was still in a vertical nose dive at about 2000 feet. I believe the E.A. was absolutely out of control as I fired in all about 400 rounds at him at a very close range, and saw my bullets hitting his planes [wings] and fuselage.

The very next day, Beauchamp Proctor hoped he had achieved his second confirmed 'kill' but, yet again, the necessary evidence that the enemy aircraft he attacked had hit the ground was lacking. Once again, it had to be classified as a 'probable' and more similar incidents took place early that year. By this time, Beauchamp Proctor's fighting spirit had impressed his superiors and, although he was not yet promoted in rank, he was appointed as a patrol leader. Undertaking his first flight in his new role on 15 February, he successfully forced down an enemy aircraft. Four days later, he took part in an action for which he was later awarded the Military Cross (MC), attacking a flight of enemy scouts. By March, he had eight confirmed victories but he almost perished himself when he was badly shaken in a serious landing accident. During the enemy spring offensive of 21 March, he was seen to great effect strafing approaching German aircraft.

On 1 April 1918, the date on which the Royal Air Force (RAF) was created, Beauchamp Proctor was promoted to lieutenant. A week later, 8 April, he was promoted to acting captain and flight commander. More daring combats and numerous 'kills' followed: in May, with the German night-bombing raids increasing on Allied towns and other targets, Beauchamp Proctor even embarked on a solo sortie in an attempt to intercept numerous enemy flyers, successfully attacking one bomber. On 28 May, he was awarded, 'in the field', a Bar to his (as yet unannounced) MC, after achieving six victories in a week – four aircraft and two kite balloons.

The scale of Beauchamp Proctor's achievements at this time are perhaps best recorded by providing the citations to the three gallantry awards that he was formally awarded between June and September 1918. The citation for his first MC, announced on 22 June, stated:

For conspicuous gallantry and devotion to duty. While on offensive patrol he observed an enemy two-seater plane attempting to cross our lines. He engaged it and opened fire, with the result that it fell over on its side and crashed to earth. On a later occasion, when on patrol, he observed three enemy scouts attacking one of our bombing machines. He attacked one of these, and after firing 100 rounds in it, it fell over on its back and was seen to descend in that position from 5,000 feet. He then attacked another group of hostile scouts, one of which he shot down completely out of control, and another crumpled up and crashed to earth. In addition to these, he has destroyed another hostile machine, and shot down three completely out of control. He has at all times displayed the utmost dash and initiative, and is a patrol leader of great merit and resource.

On 3 August, Beauchamp Proctor became one of the earliest recipients of the Distinguished Flying Cross: the DFC had only been instituted on 3 June that year to mark George V's fifty-third birthday. On 3 August, Beauchamp Proctor's citation paid tribute to his leadership skills and his sheer courage:

A brilliant and fearless leader of our offensive patrols. His formation has destroyed thirteen enemy machines and brought down thirteen more out of control in a period of a few months. On a recent morning his patrol of five aeroplanes attacked an enemy formation of thirty machines and was successful in destroying two of them. In the evening he again attacked an enemy formation with great dash, destroying one machine and forcing two others to collide, resulting in their destruction.

The Bar to Beauchamp Proctor's MC was announced in the *London Gazette* on 19 September when his citation stated: 'For conspicuous gallantry and devotion to duty while leading offensive patrols. He has lately destroyed three enemy machines, driven down one other completely out of control, and carried out valuable work in attacking enemy troops and transport on the ground from low altitudes. He has done splendid service.'

By the time that his third gallantry award was formally announced, Beauchamp Proctor was well into the most prolific phase of his flying career. For it was his actions in the air, after returning from leave, between 8 August and 8 October 1918 that eventually led to him receiving the ultimate reward for his courage – the VC – on top of the Distinguished Service Order (DSO) that was announced earlier the same month (November 1918).

Once again, the formal citations tell an impressive story. The one for his DSO, published on 2 November 1918, stated:

> A fighting pilot of great skill, and a splendid leader. He rendered brilliant service on 22 August, when his Flight was detailed to neutralise hostile balloons. Having shot down one balloon in flames, he attacked the occupants of five others in succession with machine-gun fire, compelling the occupants in each case to take to parachutes. He then drove down another balloon to within fifty feet of the ground, when it burst into flames. In all he has accounted for thirty-three enemy machines and seven balloons.

The citation for Beauchamp Proctor's VC, announced on 30 November, stated:

> Between August 8th, 1918, and October 8th, 1918, this officer proved himself victor in twenty-six decisive combats, destroying twelve enemy kite balloons, ten enemy aircraft, and driving down four other enemy aircraft completely out of control.
>
> Between October 1st, 1918, and October 5th, 1918, he destroyed two enemy scouts, burnt three enemy kite balloons, and drove down one enemy scout completely out of control.
>
> On October 1st, 1918, in a general engagement with about twenty-eight machines, he crashed one Fokker biplane near Fontaine

and a second near Ramicourt; on October 2nd he burnt a hostile balloon near Selvigny; on October 3rd he drove down, completely out of control, an enemy scout near Mont d'Origny, and burnt a hostile balloon; on October 5th, the third hostile balloon near Bohain.

On October 8th, 1918, while flying home at a low altitude, after destroying an enemy two-seater near Maretz, he was painfully wounded in the arm by machine-gun fire, but, continuing, he landed safely at his aerodrome, and after making his report was admitted to hospital.

In all he has proved himself conqueror over fifty-four foes, destroying twenty-two enemy machines, sixteen enemy kite balloons, and driving down sixteen enemy aircraft completely out of control.

Captain Beauchamp-Proctor's work in attacking enemy troops on the ground and in reconnaissance during the withdrawal following on the Battle of St. Quentin from March 21st, 1918, and during the victorious advance of our Armies commencing on August 8th, has been almost unsurpassed in its brilliancy, and as such has made an impression on those serving in his squadron and those around him that will not be easily forgotten.

Capt. Beauchamp-Proctor was awarded Military Cross on 22nd June, 1918; D.F. Cross on 2nd July, 1918; Bar to M.C. on 16th September, 1918; and Distinguished Service Order on 2nd November, 1918.

As stated in the above citation, Beauchamp Proctor's astonishing run of success throughout 1918 was brought to an end by the wound that he received on 8 October, just over a month before the Great War ended. It took a surprise attack by no fewer than eight German fighters to cause the damage and he was very fortunate to escape with his life. Weaving and twisting, Beauchamp Proctor somehow managed to use his one good arm to get away from his determined pursuers. After landing back at Assevillers Aerodrome, he received immediate medical attention for the injuries to his arm before being invalided back to England, where he was sent to Northumberland Hospital, near Newcastle-upon-Tyne, to recuperate. On 2 October 1918, a confidential report was drawn up recommending Beauchamp Proctor for a Bar to his DSO but this was never granted – probably because it was superseded by a recommendation for him to be awarded the VC.

Perhaps the most affectionate tribute to the young pilot came from Sholto Douglas, his CO, who said of Beauchamp Proctor in the aftermath of his war being ended by injury:

> He had been showing an extraordinary zest for attacking the enemy at any height and under any conditions, and in a manner that has become the talk of the Air Force. He had had only one spell of leave during the entire time we had been in France – by then over a year – and he had always been most persistent in his wishes to remain with the squadron. For all his size, that little man had the guts of a lion.

It was Douglas, too, who had personally written the recommendation that led to Beauchamp Proctor's VC.

His total of fifty-four victories represented almost one third of 84 Squadron's combat total for the war. Beauchamp Proctor's total was particularly remarkable given that, at the start of 1918, he had not so far claimed a single confirmed solo 'kill'. His final total of victories made him the joint sixth-highest Allied ace of the war and with just two German flyers, including the legendary Manfred von Richthofen – the 'Red Baron' with a war record of eighty victories – claiming a higher 'kill' count. Beauchamp Proctor was comfortably South Africa's leading ace of the 1914–18 conflict and its most decorated pilot. His success came from his abilities as a 'natural' pilot and his talents as a superb shot – added, of course, to his immense courage. Some believe that his tiny frame – he was some twenty-five pounds lighter than a typical pilot – also gave him an added advantage in the air.

After being discharged from hospital in March 1919, Beauchamp Proctor embarked on a lecture tour of the United States. Four months later, he returned to the UK where he underwent a seaplane training course at Lee-on-Solent, Hampshire. Afterwards, he went to RAF Cranwell, Lincolnshire, where, on 1 November 1919, he took up a permanent commission in the rank of flight lieutenant. He received his VC from George V at an investiture at Buckingham Palace on 27 November 1919, when The King also presented him with his DSO and DFC. Beauchamp Proctor was the first, but not the last, South African to be awarded Britain and the Commonwealth's most prestigious gallantry award. Shortly afterwards, he was arrested by two constables accused of wearing medals that they could simply not believe he was entitled to, but he eventually provided proof that he was no fraud.

At this point, Beauchamp Proctor was given permission to return to South Africa in order, finally, to complete his BSc in engineering. While in his homeland, the Mayor of Cape Town hosted a lunch at the City Hall in Beauchamp Proctor's honour on 5 February 1920. Additionally, George Crosland Robinson, the South African artist, painted his portrait. When he arrived back in Britain at the end of 1920, after his year's leave, he not only resumed his RAF career but also enrolled on further engineering studies at RAF Henlow, Bedfordshire. Officially, however, he was attached to No. 24 Squadron, a new communications unit.

In 1921, Beauchamp Proctor was chosen to take part in the second annual RAF Tournament at RAF Hendon, an air show conceived by Sir Hugh (later Viscount) Trenchard, a founder and, later, Marshal of the RAF. On 21 June, while rehearsing at RAF Upavon for the actual display the next day, Beauchamp Proctor commenced a loop in his Sopwith Snipe. At the top of the loop, his aircraft fell away and dived into an inverted spin, before crashing into the ground. Flight Lieutenant Andrew Beauchamp Proctor VC, DSO, MC & Bar, DFC – the hero who had survived so many highly dangerous dogfights – had been killed in a peaceful Wiltshire meadow in a flying accident. 'Proccy', as he was often affectionately called by his friends, was just twenty-six when he died.

The cause of his accident has never been fully explained although it has been speculated that the seat cushion, which he used to compensate for his lack of height, may have become caught in the controls. Initially, Beauchamp Proctor, who was unmarried but had a girlfriend, was buried in Upavon. Later, however, his body was returned to South Africa aboard the *Balmoral Castle* and, in his homeland, he was accorded what amounted to a state funeral, being re-interred at Mafeking on 8 August 1921. A lengthy report of his funeral in the *Cape Times* of 9 August was headlined 'A warrior borne home to rest'. In the report itself, he was described as 'one of South Africa's noblest sons'.

Today, Beauchamp Proctor is commemorated with headstones at both Upavon and Mafeking. Additionally, his name is on the RAF Memorial in St Clement Danes Church, central London, and a plaque inside the porch at St Mary's Church, Droylsden, near Manchester.

As stated earlier in this book, I bought Beauchamp Proctor's medal group privately in September 2016 after lengthy negotiations: his VC thereby became the 200th in my collection. I felt hugely privileged to become the custodian of this courageous man's splendid medal group, which was accompanied by a war diary, combat reports, newspaper cuttings and other documents (some of which have been used in this write-up). I also felt that it was entirely appropriate that such a magnificent VC should be the one to achieve this landmark decoration in my collection, fully thirty years after purchasing my first VC.

7

THE SECOND
WORLD WAR

The Allied Powers, led by the British Empire, the Commonwealth, the United States and the Soviet Union, defeated the Axis Powers of Germany, Italy and Japan. The war was fought in response to the expansionist aggression of Nazi Germany under Adolf Hitler, a racist dictator, and the imperial ambitions of Japan in Asia. It was, by far, the largest and deadliest war in history, culminating with the dropping of two atomic bombs on Japan.

Estimates of casualties vary greatly. But it is likely that around sixty-two million people, or 2 per cent of the world's population at the time, died in the war. Of these, perhaps twenty-five million were military and thirty-seven million civilian, with the Allies suffering some 80 per cent of the total casualties. The civilian deaths were the result of disease, starvation, massacres, aerial bombing and genocide (it is estimated that the Holocaust alone accounted for at least nine million people, most of them Jews).

Britain and France had tried to avoid another world war by following a policy of appeasement to placate Hitler: in 1938, Neville Chamberlain, the British Prime Minister, famously returned from Munich with an 'agreement' which partitioned Czechoslovakia, declaring that this guaranteed 'peace in our time'. On 1 September 1939, nine days after signing a secret pact with the Soviet Union, Germany invaded Poland. Two days later, Britain and France declared war on Germany.

During the first six months of 1940, the war spread rapidly. The Soviet Union attacked Finland and occupied Latvia, Lithuania and Estonia, then annexed Bessarabia and Northern Bukovina from Romania. Germany,

in turn, invaded Denmark, Norway, Luxembourg, Belgium, the Nether-
lands and France, and made preparations to invade Britain. In June, Italy
declared war on Britain, and later invaded British Somaliland but failed
in its attempt to overrun Greece.

In 1941, Germany first invaded Greece then betrayed its partner, the
Soviet Union: Operation Barbarossa, the largest invasion in history, began on
22 June. Meanwhile, the war spread to north Africa and the Middle East.
America showed its support for the Allies by signing a treaty – the Atlantic
Charter – with Britain in August 1941; and on 7 December the Japanese
launched a surprise air attack on the US Pacific Fleet in Pearl Harbor,
Hawaii. The following day the United States declared war on Japan.
On the same day, China officially did the same, while Germany declared
war on the United States on 11 December.

During 1942 and 1943, the war was fought in several theatres:
Europe, the Soviet Union, the Pacific, north Africa, China and south-east
Asia. In January 1944, a Soviet offensive relieved the siege of Leningrad
and soon the Allies started to gain ground elsewhere. On 6 June 1944 –
'D-Day' – the Allies, mainly forces from Britain, Canada and America,
invaded German-held Normandy; by 25 August, Paris had been liber-
ated. By April 1945, the Allies had advanced into Italy, and the Western
Axis Powers knew the war was lost. The Allies celebrated VE (Victory in
Europe) Day on 8 May, while the Soviets celebrated their Victory Day the
following morning.

US President Harry Truman then used a new 'super weapon' to bring
the war against Japan to a swift end. On 6 August 1945, a nuclear
bomb was dropped on Hiroshima, destroying the city. The United States
immediately called upon Japan to surrender but received no response, so,
three days later, a second bomb was dropped on Nagasaki. The Japanese
finally surrendered on 15 August (VJ Day), while Japanese troops in
China formally surrendered to the Chinese on 9 September. The war was
finally over.

The Second World War saw weapons and technology improve rapidly over
its six-year duration. This played a crucial role in determining the outcome

of the war. Many technologies were used for the first time, including radar, jet engines and electronic computers, as well as nuclear weapons. Aircraft, battleship and tank designs made enormous advances so that planes, boats and vehicles that were cutting edge at the beginning of the conflict had become obsolete by its end. The war also saw a shift of power from the British Empire and Western Europe to two new 'superpowers': the United States and the Soviet Union. And it led to the creation in 1945 of the United Nations, which was intended to prevent another world war and thereby succeed where the League of Nations had failed.

During the Second World War, 182 VCs were awarded, of which the Ashcroft VC Trust now has thirty, including ten purchased in the past decade and which make up this chapter.

The Army

Britain entered the war – and committed substantial land forces to the Allied effort – after Germany invaded Poland in 1939. A British Expeditionary Force (BEF) was sent to France, but was hastily evacuated as Germany swept through the Low Countries and into France in 1940. Only the Dunkirk evacuation saved the entire BEF from capture. The British Army was largely spared the horrors of trench warfare that had dominated the First World War and, as the global conflict progressed, the Army asserted itself as a formidable fighting force.

The British defeated the Italians and Germans at El Alamein in north Africa, in Italy and in the D-Day invasions of Normandy. In the Far East, the Army successfully fought the Japanese in Burma. As the war progressed, the Army developed its Commando units and the Special Air Service (SAS), which both repeatedly proved their worth.

SECOND LIEUTENANT (LATER CAPTAIN)
RICHARD WALLACE ANNAND
Army: The Durham Light Infantry
DATE OF BRAVERY: 15/16 MAY 1940
GAZETTED: 23 AUGUST 1940
Special feature of the VC: the magnificent 'wheelbarrow VC' who was awarded the Army's first VC of the Second World War.

Richard Wallace Annand was born in Westoe, South Shields, Co. Durham, on 5 November 1914. He was the son of Lieutenant-Commander Wallace Annand, who served with the Royal Naval Volunteer Reserve (RNVR) during the Great War, and his wife Elizabeth (*née* Chapman). Richard Annand was just seven months old when his father was killed at Gallipoli and an uncle became his guardian. Annand, who was known to his friends as 'Dickie', was educated at Pocklington School, East Yorkshire. After leaving school, he worked for the National Provincial Bank from 1933 to 1937, first working in its South Shields branch before also working in Rugby, Warwickshire, and London. His move to London saw him attend three nights of drill at HMS *President* stationed on the River Thames, for he intended to follow his father into naval service.

In 1933, Annand fulfilled his desire when he was commissioned as a midshipman into the Tyne and London Divisions, RNVR. He was promoted to substantive lieutenant in 1936 and in the same year attended a navigation course in Portsmouth, Hampshire, and a gunnery course on Whale Island, Portsmouth. In 1937, Annand applied for a regular commission in the Royal Navy as a seaman officer but he was refused on the grounds that, at twenty-two, he was too old. However, he was still young enough for an Army commission and, in January 1938, and by then twenty-three, Annand was gazetted as a second lieutenant into the Durham Light Infantry (DLI), thereby ending his career as a banker. After one month's Army training in Newcastle-upon-Tyne, he was attached to the regiment's

2nd Battalion based at Woking, Surrey. On 26 September 1939, Annand joined the British Expeditionary Force (BEF) in France and in October 1939 he moved to Bercy, Lille, on the Belgian Frontier during the so-called 'Phoney War'.

The German invasion of Belgium began on 10 May 1940, with the attack on Liège, after it was refused passage through the country. As the invasion of the Low Countries progressed, the River Dyle in Belgium formed an Allied defensive line east of Brussels. It was on one night in May that Annand, then aged twenty-five, distinguished himself in resisting a fierce German attack. The citation for his VC, published on 23 August 1940, detailed his action:

> For most conspicuous gallantry on the 15th–16th May 1940, when the platoon under his command was on the south side of the River Dyle, astride a blown bridge. During the night a strong attack was beaten off, but about 11 a.m. the enemy again launched a violent attack and pushed forward a bridging party into the sunken bottom of the river. Second Lieutenant Annand attacked this party, but when ammunition ran out he went forward himself over open ground, with total disregard for enemy mortar and machine-gun fire. Reaching the top of the bridge, he drove out the party below, inflicting over twenty casualties with hand grenades. Having been wounded he rejoined his platoon, had his wound dressed, and then carried on in command.
>
> During the evening another attack was launched and again Second Lieutenant Annand went forward with hand grenades and inflicted heavy casualties on the enemy.
>
> When the order to withdraw was received, he withdrew his platoon, but learning on the way back that his batman was wounded and had been left behind, he returned at once to the former position and brought him back in a wheelbarrow, before losing consciousness as the result of wounds.

During the initial battle, and after receiving his first wound, Annand had returned for more ammunition. In a letter from Sergeant Terry O'Neil, the platoon sergeant to Annand, published in the *Journal and North Mail*, County Durham's newspaper, he detailed Annan's bravery more fully:

> On the night of 15 May Mr Annand came to me at platoon head-quarters and asked for a box of grenades as he could hear Jerry trying to repair the bridge. Off he went and he must sure have given them a lovely time because it wasn't a great while before he was back for more. Just like giving an elephant strawberries.
>
> The previous night while the heavy stuff of both sides were send-ing over their mutual regards he realised that he had not received word from our right forward section which held a pillbox about 250 yards to our right front, so he went out to see how they were fixed. He had [been] gone about two hours and we had come to the conclusion that they had got him when something which I found hard to recog-nise came crawling in. It was just Jake [Annand] – that is the name by which we knew him. He looked as though he had been having an argument with a wild cat. His clothes were torn to shreds and he was cut and bruised all over. How he got there and back only he knows because he had the fire of our own troops to contend with as well as Jerry's. I don't suppose he knows the meaning of fear. He never asked a man to do anything he could do himself. He wouldn't talk much about it. He wasn't that kind. It was just another job of work for him.
>
> Another platoon of RWF [Royal Welch Fusiliers] came to reinforce us and had been there only half an hour when one of our own mor-tar bombs dropped right among them. Jake came dashing up, asked me what had happened and then off he went galloping up the hill-side to stop the mortar platoon. He didn't even stop to take his steel helmet and he was under fire all the way.

Sergeant-Major Martin McLane, of the 2nd Battalion, DLI, also praised Annand's bravery:

How that man never got hit with all the shooting going on, I don't ever know. It was a miracle really. I say this honestly, not because I know the man now and we're great friends. He ran across this bridge with his grenades, dodging here and there, ducking and skipping down, moving around, he got to the edge of this bridge and he just unloaded his grenades and came back. He caused devastation in that area. I don't know who was in there but you could hear them yelling, you know. Don't think a soldier dies peacefully, they yell when they're hit, the wounded; they scream for their mothers, a lot of them; and you could hear the screams coming from the place of men badly hit. The dead wouldn't have anything to say about it all – they were out of it.

In his book *VCs of the Second World War*, John Frayn Turner praises Annand's determination to continue fighting and carry out more brave deeds after receiving his first wound. He wrote:

Groping his way back to his former position, Annand discovered the [wounded] batman and managed to find a wheelbarrow as well. Without this, he could never have got the man back. He tumbled the wounded batman into the wheelbarrow and wheeled him towards the new rear line. Soon afterwards the exertion in his own wounded state took effect, and Annand lost consciousness through loss of blood.

Annand's VC was the Army's first VC action of the Second World War and one of just five awarded for the bitter battle for France.

The man Annand rescued, his batman Private Joseph Hunter, was later captured by the enemy and died from his wounds in a Dutch hospital. After being wounded in his VC action, Annand was evacuated back to the UK for hospital treatment to his injuries that included a significant loss of hearing. It was a memorable journey: for two days, he rattled his way through France on board a Belgian hospital train without food or water. When he arrived at the hospital in Calais, it had to be evacuated: Annand was put aboard the first of two hospital ships, only to learn later that the second had been bombed and sunk.

Long after the war ended, Annand gave a recorded interview to the Imperial War Museum, in which he described his injuries.

> They saw I was wounded with blood all over and I was ordered by the adjutant into a vehicle to be taken to hospital. I was in hospital in Brussels and then put on to a train, which took me to a hospital near Le Touquet. I remember writing home to my guardian uncle saying that we'd had a go at the Boche and that the Boche had had a go at me and I was in a hospital miles behind the lines – as I thought. But the Germans entered that place the next day and the hospital was evacuated and I was taken on a hospital ship to Southampton.
>
> I was in hospital for about a month after that and then rejoined the battalion, which by that time was reforming at Bridlington [Yorkshire] on the coast. I rejoined having no idea about the VC until August. It took some time, you see. I think that they had to get witnesses and so forth.

In 1940, in recognition of his VC, he was given the Honorary Freedom of the County Borough of South Shields. Having rejoined the re-formed 2nd Battalion of the DLI, based at Bridlington, he lost the remainder of his hearing during rifle training and served the remainder of the war in the UK. His jobs included training commandos in Scotland and working in the War Office. Annand's investiture by George VI took place at Buckingham Palace on 4 September 1940. Air raid warning sirens had been sounded shortly before the ceremony, so the investiture was held inside the Palace instead of the quadrangle, as originally intended. On 9 November 1940, Annand married Shirley Osborne at St George's Church, Hanover Square, London.

In 1948, Annand was invalided out of the Army as a captain having refused the opportunity to be transferred out of the DLI. Then, a chance encounter on a train resulted in him acquiring one of the earliest hearing aids. For the next three decades, Annand devoted himself to the welfare of the disabled, including those people who were deaf or hard of hearing. In 1947, he was a founder member of the British Association for the Hard of Hearing and, from 1948 to 1970, he was personnel officer for the Finchale Abbey Training Centre for the Disabled near Durham. His other roles included being president of the Durham County Branch of the Normandy Veterans, president of the Durham County Association for the Disabled, Deputy Lieutenant of Durham and president of the Durham and Cleveland branch of the Royal British Legion. Annand was renowned for his modesty, telling a newspaper in 1997 of his VC action: 'Every man who was with me deserved a medal. Countless deeds were done that went unrewarded. When I received my award, my feelings were of communal satisfaction, not an individual one.'

Once a brave man, always a brave man. On 26 February 1979, when aged sixty-four, Annand saved his wife's life by diving into the bitterly cold River Tyne in the dark after she had fallen off a ship's gangplank. The couple, who did not have children, celebrated their diamond wedding anniversary on 9 November 2000.

Annand died at the University Hospital of North Durham on Christmas Eve, 2004, having celebrated his ninetieth birthday less than two months earlier. His funeral was held at St Cuthbert's Church, Durham, on 5 January 2005 and he was then cremated. At the memorial service in Annand's honour at Durham Cathedral on 7 February 2005, more than 1,000 people came to pay their respects to Annand's wartime heroism and his later work in helping disabled people. There is a plaque in Annand's memory, which details his bravery, at the bridge over the River Dyle in Belgium. Likewise, there is a memorial stone in his honour in the grounds of the DLI Museum, Durham, and a portrait of him at the office of the DLI Old Comrades' Association.

HAVILDAR (LATER SUBADAR-MAJOR AND HONORARY CAPTAIN) GAJE GHALE

Indian Army: 5th Royal Gurkha Rifles
DATE OF BRAVERY: 27 MAY 1943
GAZETTED: 30 SEPTEMBER 1943
Special feature of the VC: an outstanding Gurkha award for bravery during the Burma campaign.

Gaje Ghale is believed to have been born on 1 August 1918 in Bar-pak village, the Gorkha district of Nepal (although at one point he also gave his date of birth as 1 July 1922). He was one of fourteen children – seven sons and seven daughters – born to Bikram Ghale and Mainli Ama, the second of his three wives. Bikram Ghale was a member of the somewhat exclusive Ghale clan, while his son, Gaje Ghale, worked as a shepherd boy before enlisting into the 2nd Battalion, 5th Royal Gurkha Rifles (Frontier Force) as a boy soldier on 1 August 1935. In fact, three of his brothers eventually joined the Gurkha Regiment.

From 1936 to 1939, Gaje Ghale served in Waziristan during yet another North-West Frontier campaign and from the outbreak of war until June 1942 he was a regimental instructor based in Abbottabad, now part of Pakistan. In 1942, he was sent to Burma with his regiment but he came out of the country when the first Burma campaign ended later that year. After re-equipping, the 5th Royal Gurkha Rifles were ready for battle once again in May 1943.

In late May 1943, the Japanese began to move into the Chin Hills of north-west Burma and overran No. 2 and No. 3 Stockades on the road west from Kalemyo to Fort White. On 26 and 27 May, the British attacked Basha East Hill, which overlooked No. 3 Stockade. After two unsuccessful attempts to capture Basha East Hill, a third attempt was made by troops that included the platoon commanded by Havildar Ghale. The citation for his VC, published on 30 September 1943, takes up the story:

In order to stop an advance into the Chin Hills of greatly superior Japanese forces it was essential to capture Basha East hill which was the key to the enemy position.

Two assaults had failed but a third assault was ordered to be carried out by two platoons of Havildar Gaje Ghale's company and two companies of another battalion. Havildar Gaje Ghale was in command of one platoon: he had never been under fire before and the platoon consisted of young soldiers.

The approach for this platoon to their objective was along a narrow knife-edge with precipitous sides and bare of jungle whereas the enemy positions were well concealed. In places, the approach was no more than five yards wide and was covered by a dozen machine guns besides being subjected to artillery and mortar fire from the reverse slope of the hill.

While preparing for the attack the platoon came under heavy mortar fire but Havildar Gaje Ghale rallied them and led them forward.

Approaching to close range of the well-entrenched enemy, the platoon came under withering fire and this N.C.O. was wounded in the arm, chest and leg by an enemy hand grenade.

Without pausing to attend to his serious wounds and with no heed to the intensive fire from all sides, Havildar Gaje Ghale closed his men and led them to close grips with the enemy when a bitter hand to hand struggle ensued.

Havildar Gaje Ghale dominated the fight by his outstanding example of dauntless courage and superb leadership. Hurling hand grenades, covered in blood from his own neglected wounds, he led assault after assault encouraging his platoon by shouting the Gurkha's battle-cry.

Spurred on by the irresistible will of their leader to win, the platoon stormed and carried the hill by a magnificent all out effort and inflicted very heavy casualties on the Japanese.

Havildar Gaje Ghale then held and consolidated this hard won position under heavy fire and it was not until the consolidation was

> well in hand that he went, refusing help, to the Regimental Aid
> Post, when ordered to do so by an officer.
>
> The courage, determination and leadership of this N.C.O. under
> the most trying conditions were beyond all praise.

Incidentally, the chilling battlecry from Ghale was 'Ayo Gurkhali'
('The Gurkhas are upon you'). In August 1943, Ghale was promoted to
jemadar and the following year he received his VC from Lord Wavell,
the Viceroy of India, at the Red Fort, Delhi. He was also decorated
by the King of Nepal with the extraordinarily rare Medal of the Order
of the Star of Nepal. He later served with his battalion in Japan in
1945 as part of the Commonwealth Occupation Force, and the following year represented his regiment at the Victory Parade in London.

In 1947, after India gained its independence, Ghale remained
with his regiment, which was redesignated as the 5th Gurkha Rifles
(Frontier Force). In 1948, he was promoted to subadar and later still
was promoted again to subadar-major of his battalion. From 1962
to 1963, Ghale served with the United Nations Force in the Congo.
He retired on 4 February 1966, apparently aged forty-six and with
the honorary rank of captain.

Ghale had two wives, Dhansuba Ghale, who died in 1950 and
with whom he had two sons, and Dhankuri Ghale, the younger sister of his first wife, with whom he also had two sons as well as five
daughters. After retiring to Almora, Uttar Pradesh, India, he was
elected as a member of the Almora Cantonment Board, a position
he held for nearly twenty years until his death.

Ghale, who had a round face and a relentlessly cheerful disposition, regularly attended the Victoria Cross and George Cross
Association reunions in the United Kingdom, and he was presented
to The Queen during her State Visit to Nepal in February 1986. On
19 August 1995, Ghale was present at the 'Last Big Parade', the
national event in London to commemorate the 50th anniversary of
the end of the Second World War.

Ghale died in New Delhi on 28 March 2000, apparently aged eighty-one. He was cremated in Almora the next day and his death prompted obituaries in both *The Times* and the *Daily Telegraph*. His name is listed on the Memorial Gates, Hyde Park Corner, London.

Ghale was a much-loved and hugely respected figure in both India and Britain. In June 2015, he was referred to affectionately in a House of Lords speech from Lord Bilimoria, speaking on the occasion of the Gurkha pageant at the Royal Hospital Chelsea. Lord Bilimoria, whose late father had commanded the 2/5th Royal Gurkha Rifles, told his fellow peers:

> Gaje Ghale VC and Agansing Rai VC [another Second World War Gurkha VC recipient and whose medals are also in my collection] were living legends, who I was fortunate to have grown up with and have been inspired by for the rest of my life. Agansing Rai VC was subadar-major when my father was commanding his battalion. Legend has it that when my father, as a young captain in a remote area in north-east India, received the telegram of my birth, Gaje Ghale was next to him and jumped for joy. The ground shook, because he was such a large man.
>
> What I learned about the Gurkhas really quickly is that they are the kindest, most caring and most gentle people. For example, when I took my South African possible future wife on her first visit to India, my father's retired driver, Bombahadur, who continued to serve with my father at retirement, took me aside and said, 'Baba, you should marry her!' My father's beloved Gurkha had given his approval, and of course then there was no question but that I was marrying Heather.
>
> However, these kind, gentle people in peacetime are the fiercest warriors mankind has known. Just reading the citations of the Gurkha VCs makes your jaw drop with feats that are, quite frankly, superhuman. Sir Ralph Turner, a former officer of the 3rd Gurkhas, had written:
>
> > 'Bravest of the brave, most generous of the generous, never had [a] country more faithful friends than you.'

MICHAEL ASHCROFT

COMPANY SERGEANT-MAJOR PETER HAROLD WRIGHT

Army: The Coldstream Guards
DATE OF BRAVERY: 25 SEPTEMBER 1943
GAZETTED: 7 SEPTEMBER 1944
Special feature of the VC: the first and only Salerno VC which was uniquely upgraded from a DCM at King George VI's specific insistence.

Peter Harold Wright was born in Mettingham, near Bungay, Suffolk, on 10 August 1916. His father was Gordon Wright, a farmer, and his mother was Helen (*née* Easter). He was from a large family of fourteen siblings and had eight brothers and five sisters. Wright was educated at Brooke Village School, Norfolk, and Woodton School, Norfolk. Initially, after leaving school, he worked on his father's farm but he was planning a career in the police force. However, he had a change of heart and enlisted into the Coldstream Guards in October 1936 and, later, joined the 3rd Battalion.

On 7 August 1937, Wright was promoted to acting lance-corporal and from November 1937 to October 1938 he served in Egypt. On 29 September 1938, Wright was confirmed in the rank of lance-corporal and from October 1938 to April 1939 he served in Palestine. However, after the outbreak of the Second World War in early September 1939, he returned to Egypt and was based in Alexandria. Wright was promoted to acting lance-sergeant on 1 September before being confirmed in the rank on 1 December. On 4 August 1941, Wright was appointed as acting sergeant, a rank confirmed on 21 January 1942. On 28 May 1942, Wright was wounded – above the eye – during fighting in Tobruk, Libya, and he was evacuated for hospital treatment. After nearly two months of recuperation, he rejoined his battalion on 16 July 1942. On 7 September 1942, he was promoted to acting colour-sergeant and was confirmed in this rank on 6 June 1943.

His VC action took place on 25 September 1943 when, after yet another promotion, Wright was in the rank of warrant officer class 2 – company sergeant-major – aged twenty-seven years old. The background to this remarkable **VC** was that Sicily had been invaded on the night of 9/10 July 1943 and formally fell to the Allies on 17 August. The following month marked the start of the long campaign to gain control of Italy, Hitler's southern Axis ally, and the first landings on the Italian mainland took place in Calabria on the night of 2/3 September. Italy's own armistice with the Allies was announced on 8 September, but at this point Germany still controlled most of the country and the situation everywhere was very confused and dangerous. On 9 September, America's 5th Army landed south of Salerno and, on 25 September, the 56th Division sought to advance north of Salerno as part of the break-out from the original 5th Army bridgehead.

As Wright's citation for his first gallantry medal makes clear, he showed outstanding courage:

In Italy on the 25th September, 1943, the 3rd Battalion, Coldstream Guards, attacked the Pagliarolli [*sic*] feature, a steep wooded hill near Salerno. Before it reached the crest the right hand company was held up by heavy spandau and mortar fire and all the officers had become casualties.

C. S. M. Wright, seeing that his company was held up, went forward to see what could be done. Finding that there were no officers left he immediately took charge and crawled forward by himself to see what the opposition was. He returned with the information that three spandau posts were holding them up. He collected a section and put it into a position where it could give covering fire. Single-handed he then attacked each post in turn with hand grenades and bayonet and silenced each one. He then led the company on to the crest but realised that the enemy fire made this position untenable. C. S. M. Wright therefore led them a short way down the hill and up on to the objective from a different direction.

Entirely regardless of enemy fire, which was very heavy, C. S. M.

Wright then re-organised what was left of the company and placed them into position to consolidate the objective.

Soon afterwards the enemy launched a counter-attack which was successfully beaten off. Later, with complete disregard of heavy enemy shell-fire on the area of company headquarters and the reverse slopes of the hill and of machine-gun fire from the commanding slopes on the left flank of the position, he brought up extra ammunition and distributed it to the company.

It is due to this Warrant Officer's superb disregard of the enemy's fire, his magnificent leadership and his outstanding heroism throughout the action that his battalion succeeded in capturing and maintaining its hold on this very important objective.

In fact, Wright originally received the Distinguished Conduct Medal (DCM) but when George VI learned exactly what he had done he considered that this decoration was insufficient reward for Wright's incredible courage. 'If ever a man deserved the VC, it is this man to whom I have awarded the DCM,' The King told General Harold Alexander when he visited Italy to bestow gallantry awards. George VI was adamant that the Army had erred and he asked Alexander to look into the precise circumstances of Wright's VC and to report back to him. The King felt that Wright had virtually captured a position single-handed and had repeatedly put his life at great risk. The general adhered to The King's request and, as a result, the DCM was fairly swiftly upgraded to the VC.

This required a short, additional paragraph being inserted in the *London Gazette* at the same time as Wright's VC was announced on 7 September 1944. It read: 'The King having been graciously pleased to approve the award of the Victoria Cross to C. S. M. Wright, the award of the Distinguished Conduct Medal for the same acts of gallantry, announced in the *London Gazette* of the 27th January, 1944 (No. 36349), is cancelled.' Although cancelled, the DCM was not recalled, meaning that Wright initially kept possession of both gallantry medals.

Wright, who was 6ft 1in. tall and extremely modest, greeted the news of his VC with utter surprise: 'VC? Can't be me – some other Sergeant-Major Wright maybe?' When told the reason, he still insisted: 'There's some mistake. I got the DCM for that.' When he wrote home just days after being told of his VC award, he signed off to his mother: 'I have not got much to write about, but here's hoping this finds you all O.K. Best of luck and love to all, Peter.'

At the time of his VC announcement, Wright was no longer on the frontline for, at the end of 1943 and having recovered from malaria, he had been sent back to the UK. After completing more than six years overseas, he was given a role training the battalion that was personally guarding Winston Churchill at the Prime Minister's country home at Chequers, Buckinghamshire.

Wright finally received his VC – as opposed to his earlier DCM – from George VI at an investiture at Buckingham Palace on 21 September 1944. Wright's Salerno VC was one of twenty awarded to the British and Commonwealth forces for bravery in the Italian Campaign. Eight of those twenty men are still buried on the battlefield on or close to where their courageous deeds took place.

On 30 March 1946, Wright was discharged to the Reserve and he went to work as a farmer at Blythburgh, Suffolk, and, later, at Helmingham in the same county. In June 1946, he married Mollie Hurren and the couple went on to have a son and two daughters.

In his home county, his roles included being president of the Witnesham branch of the Royal British Legion. In 1984, he was presented with the Royal British Legion's Gold Badge for his service to the charity. In the same year, he said of his VC action: 'It was the day the lads reckon I went quietly bloody mad!'

Five years later, Wright gave a lengthy interview to BBC Radio Cambridge about his life and his Army career. He described how, shortly after arriving in Italy in September 1943, his unit had orders to hold a canal at all costs.

One morning, when we were on this canal, the company commander and the second in command were sitting on the side of their slit trenches, with their servants, getting some breakfast. A shell came over and killed the second in command and took the company commander's right arm off. We got these casualties back to company headquarters. The RSM at the battalion headquarters asked me 'Had I seen a ghost?' – because I was dead white. I said: 'No. It's worse than that'.

In his radio interview, he described how, prior to his VC action, his battalion had been ordered to take Hill 270.

It had been attacked by another battalion but they failed to capture it. But our orders were to attack and capture that hill at all costs. We weighed the situation up from another hill.

The time of the attack was 12 o'clock on a two company front – with our company on the right and the other company on the left. We wound our way down through, under cover of trees and grape vines, into a valley and moved along to the bottom of the hill.

At 12 o'clock, we attacked and all hell let loose then. The Germans attacked with machine guns, mortars and everything. The actual hill in places got alight. I was behind with the stretcher-bearers. I decided to run forward then to see what was happening.

The first casualty I came across was the company commander. He was splattered [wounded] from head to foot from a mortar bomb. He then gave me orders to see the second in command of the company who was with one of the platoons. I found him: he was seriously wounded.

He then told me to find the next [most] senior officer to tell him what the situation was. I then rushed back again to where I thought he would be. I found him – he had been killed. That left the young officer who had joined us the night before. I then looked for him and I found him – he had been killed. I then went to see what was happening on the right flank of this hill and, as I was looking for this other platoon, I ran into these German machine-gun posts.

I ducked down and crawled back. I don't think they had seen me. I collected some grenades from some of the dead and wounded, and got a chap to give me covering fire. And I then got sort of up the hill a bit, they [the enemy] were on the slope.

I then wiped out the first one [machine-gun post] with grenades, then wiped out the second one with grenades and [with the help] of the boy who was giving me covering fire with his rifle. Then the third one – they ran away. I grabbed my rifle and bayonet and chased them but they got away.

I regrouped the company and made sure they were in position in case the Germans counter-attacked. I then sent a message back to the Commanding Officer that we had captured the hill and were consolidating our position: two officers killed, two seriously wounded, [so] would he send an officer to command the company? And he came himself.

We then tried to see how many we had lost but our main priority was then to get the wounded back. We got most of them back that night, and then it fell dark. The Germans counter-attacked just before dark but we drove them off. We then accounted for nearly all of the wounded: we had two we couldn't account for but we eventually found them. Then we went ahead and buried the sixteen NCOs and men that had been killed and the two officers.

Wright said that he had gone to Buckingham Palace to receive his VC from The King, accompanied by his mother and his fiancée (later his wife). When asked what George VI had said to him, Wright replied that The King had told him: 'I personally altered the award from the DCM to the Victoria Cross.' Wright said that he replied simply: 'Thank you, sir'.

Wright, who was affectionately known as 'Old Misty', died in Ipswich Hospital, Suffolk, on 5 April 1990, aged seventy-three.

He is buried at All Saints Churchyard, Ashbocking, Suffolk, a church that is mentioned in the Domesday Book of 1086. As well as having a headstone and an oak in Wright's honour in the churchyard, there is also a memorial to him at nearby Helmingham Parish Church. Additionally, his regiment commissioned a painting of his VC action by the artist Peter Archer and this can be seen at Wellington Barracks, central London.

Harry Bucknall, a fellow member of the Coldstream Guards and who knew Wright, said of him:

> I had the privilege to know Peter, who, after the war, returned to Suffolk to farm; he was a kind, gentle man, who I genuinely do not believe had a bad bone in his body... Peter would later chuckle to me, how no one ever asked for the other medal [the DCM] back.

JEMADAR ABDUL HAFIZ
Indian Army: 9th Jat Regiment
DATE OF BRAVERY: 6 APRIL 1944
GAZETTED: 27 JULY 1944
Special feature of the VC: a splendid Indian Army posthumous award for gallantry at Imphal.

Abdul Hafiz was born in Kalaampur village in the Rohtak district, Punjab, India (now Pakistan). He is believed to have been born on 1 July 1915 but it is possible, in fact, that he was born on 4 September 1919. Little is known of his early life, but he was the son of Hamidan and Nur Muhammad. On 4 September 1934, he enlisted into the Indian Army in the 3rd Battalion, 9th Jat Regiment. On 1 February 1941, nearly two years into the Second World War, he was promoted to jemadar.

The Japanese launched a major offensive against the British in Assam in March 1944 and, if it had been successful, it would have enabled them to push deep into India. After suffering heavy losses, the British were forced to withdraw to the plain around Imphal, the capital of Manipur. By 4 April 1944, the Japanese had reached Kohima, where the British also had a garrison. As the British were preparing a counter-attack, a Japanese unit captured Nungshigum Hill on 6 April 1944. This was a strategically important position some 14 miles north-east of Imphal so the 3/9th Jats launched a counter-attack and succeeded in removing the Japanese from the hill.

It was on this day that Hafiz showed such outstanding bravery that he was later awarded the VC. His citation, published on 27 July 1944, gave a full and vivid account of his bravery:

In Burma, in the early hours of the 6th April, 1944, in the hills 10 miles North of Imphal, the enemy had attacked a standing patrol of 4 men and occupied a prominent feature overlooking a Company position. At first light a patrol was sent out and contacted the enemy, reporting that they thought approximately 40 enemy were in position. It was not known if they had dug in during the hours of darkness.

The Company Commander ordered Jemadar Abdul Hafiz to attack the enemy, with two sections from his platoon, at 0930 hrs. An artillery concentration was put down on the feature and Jemadar Abdul Hafiz led the attack. The attack was up a completely bare slope with no cover, and was very steep near the crest. Prior to the attack, Jemadar Abdul Hafiz assembled his sections and told them that they were invincible, and all the enemy on the hill would be killed or put to flight. He so inspired his men that from the start the attack proceeded with great dash. When a few yards below the crest the enemy opened fire with machine-guns and threw grenades. Jemadar Abdul Hafiz sustained several casualties, but immediatetly [sic] ordered an assault, which he personally led, at the same time shouting the Mohammedan battle-cry. The assault went in without hesitation and with great dash up the last few yards of the hill, which was very steep. On reaching the crest Jemadar Abdul Hafiz was wounded in the leg, but seeing a machine-gun firing from a flank, which had already caused several casualties, he immediately went towards it and seizing the barrel pushed it upwards, whilst another man killed the gunner. Jemadar Abdul Hafiz then took a Bren gun from a wounded man and advanced against the enemy, firing as he advanced, and killing several of the enemy. So fierce was the attack, and all his men so inspired by the determination of Jemadar Abdul Hafiz to kill all enemy in sight at whatever cost, that the enemy, who were still in considerable numbers on the position, ran away down the opposite slope of the hill. Regardless of machine-gun fire which was now being fired at him from another feature a few hundred yards away, he pursued the enemy, firing at them as they retired. Jemadar Abdul Hafiz was badly wounded in the chest from this machine-gun fire and collapsed holding the Bren gun and attempting to fire at the retreating enemy, and shouting at the same time 'Re-organise on the position and I will give covering fire.' He died shortly afterwards.

The inspiring leadership and great bravery displayed by Jemadar Adbul Hafiz in spite of having been twice wounded, once mortally, so encouraged his men that the position was captured, casualties inflicted on the enemy to an extent several times the size of his own party, and enemy arms recovered on the position which included 3 Lewis Machine-guns, 2 grenade dischargers and 2 officers' swords. The complete disregard for his own safety and his determination to capture and hold the position at all costs was an example to all ranks, which it would be difficult to equal.

In fact, on 11 April, the Japanese seized Nungshigum Hill again only to be removed yet again on 13 April.

Hafiz had died, apparently aged twenty-eight (though possibly aged twenty-four) and so his VC was a posthumous award. Hafiz had been married to Jigri Begum and his decoration was presented to his widow by Lord Wavell, the Viceroy of India, at an investiture at the Red Fort, Delhi, on 24 October 1944. Hafiz is buried at the

Imphal Indian Army War Cemetery at Manipur State, India, and there is a commemorative headstone in his honour at Waken Hill, Imphal, India.

LIEUTENANT (LATER MAJOR SIR) TASKER WATKINS

Army: The Welch Regiment

DATE OF BRAVERY: 16 AUGUST 1944

GAZETTED: 2 NOVEMBER 1944

Special feature of the VC: one of the handful of immediate post D-Day VCs.

Tasker Watkins was born in Nelson, Glamorgan, on 18 November 1918. The son of a Welsh-speaking miner, Bertram Watkins, and his wife Jane (*née* Phillips), the young Watkins divided his early childhood between his own parents' home in Station Road, Nelson, and the nearby home of his grandparents in Shingrig Road. He was the middle of seven children and had been christened with his grandmother's maiden name. While still living in south Wales, he attended Llanfabon School and Pontypridd Grammar School. After his family moved to Essex, he attended Romford County School before working for Crookes Laboratory in the chemical industry. However, he was released from his job in order to take a degree in law and commerce at London University.

After the outbreak of the war, he served in the ranks of the Duke of Cornwall's Light Infantry from 16 October 1939 to 16 May 1941 until, on 17 May 1941, he was granted an emergency commission as a second lieutenant in the Welch Regiment and was promoted to substantive lieutenant on 3 April 1942. Various significant postings followed, including, while in the rank of temporary major, a role as a senior instructor at the War Office Battle School at Llanberis, north Wales. Here Watkins earned a reputation as a hard taskmaster and he later recalled in a television interview: 'We climbed [Mount]

Snowdon very often indeed, a sort of inducer of pain in those who were on the course. There had to be a fair amount of sadism in you to become an instructor. Making them go up Snowdon was part of that.'

Shortly after the D-Day landings of 6 June 1944, Watkins reverted to his role as a substantive lieutenant and returned to the frontline, serving with the 1/5th Welch Regiment in Normandy from the end of July that year. He was part of the reinforcements that were sent out as the Allies tried to push their way through France in the wake of the Normandy landings.

On the evening of 16 August 1944, Watkins's battalion attacked targets near the village of Bafour. His B Company came under a heavy and relentless machine-gun fire while advancing through cornfields that had been booby-trapped with mines. By the time the men reached two enemy machine-gun posts, Watkins was the only officer left standing. By then his men were isolated from the main British force and, to make matters worse, all radio communications were down between the two companies that had led the attack and Battalion HQ. The regimental records recorded a feeling of fear as the enemy appeared to be advancing from all sides: 'The atmosphere was one of tenseness and helplessness. It was impossible to restore the situation.'

As the enemy closed in on the company, Watkins decided that he and his men would fight their way out of trouble and somehow get back to the British lines – and that he would lead from the front. He charged the first machine-gun post with his Sten gun, shooting the enemy manning it. Next, he led the charge on an anti-tank gun that was targeting his men. When his Sten gun jammed, he threw the weapon in the face of a German anti-tank gunner before shooting him dead with his pistol.

As B Company continued to try to get back to the Allied lines, it crossed the cornfield where it had come under attack earlier. Once again, the Germans opened up on the British soldiers. Watkins directed operations yet again and, when the enemy appeared to falter under the company's rifle fire, he led a bayonet charge, killing several more enemy soldiers. At dusk, having by then manoeuvred around the enemy's flank, the company still found themselves separated from their battalion. At this point, Watkins, having assessed the situation, ordered his men to scatter. Before bringing his men to safety, he personally charged yet another enemy machine-gun post single-handed, killing or wounding all the enemy manning it. For a time, he hoped to keep the position until reinforcements arrived. However, still with no communications and with no signs of support, he eventually withdrew. At 1 a.m., he brought in the remaining twenty-seven members of his company, along with some German prisoners: thirty-three men from his company had become casualties, killed or wounded. Watkins himself was unharmed and unbowed. 'It didn't surprise me at all. It was typical of him,' said Captain Morgan, one of those present, many decades later.

Watkins, by then an acting major, was, however, severely wounded in a subsequent action. He received his injures as the Allied forces advanced on Hertogenbosch, southern Holland: while crossing a canal in October 1944, he was hit by shrapnel in the right leg and lower abdomen. While in hospital in Brussels, it looked as if he might need to have his leg amputated but, having been transferred to the Queen Elizabeth Hospital in Birmingham, it was decided that his limb could be saved.

It was while recuperating in hospital in Birmingham that Watkins learned he had been awarded the VC for his earlier bravery. His citation concluded: 'His superb gallantry and total disregard for his own safety during an extremely difficult period were responsible for saving the lives of his men, and had a decisive influence on the course of the battle.' Watkins never returned to the frontline but, after recovering from his injuries, was appointed Commanding Officer of the Royal Engineers Battle School at Penmaenmawr, north Wales. He received his VC from George VI at an investiture at Buckingham Palace on 8 March 1945.

He once said of his VC award:

I'm pretty grateful now ... life's very precious after all, it's all we've got really. It's easy to be philosophical out of battle but when you are heavily involved you don't have time to think of such things. You get on with what you are doing, what you are called upon to do.

However, most of the time, his only comment on the VC was: 'I am proud of that.'

During the war, in 1941, Watkins had married Eirwen Evans in Dagenham, Essex, and the couple went on to have a daughter and son. After leaving the Army in 1946, he left a considerable mark in two very different spheres of life: the judiciary and in rugby. After moving to Llandaff, near Cardiff, Watkins trained as a lawyer and was called to the Bar in 1948. In 1965, he became a Queen's Counsel and, in 1971 (the same year that he was knighted), he was appointed as a judge in the Family Division, followed later by The Queen's Bench Division and the Court of Appeal.

Watkins was appointed Deputy Chief Justice of England in 1988 and worked closely with Lord Lane, then the Lord Chief Justice, on judicial postings and the administration of the criminal justice system. He asked High Court judges to fill in time sheets to show how they spent their working days, in an attempt to boost the case for more judicial manpower.

In 1991, he sat alongside Lord Lane in the historic appeal case that established that husbands living with their wives could be convicted of raping them. According to Lord Lane, this was 'the removal of a common law fiction that has become anachronistic and offensive'.

Two years later Watkins himself delivered another well-received judgment, recommending that Derek Bentley be given a posthumous conditional pardon. An epileptic with a mental capacity 'just above the level of a feeble-minded person', Bentley had been hanged in 1953 after allegedly encouraging Christopher Craig to shoot PC Sidney Miles with the words 'Let him have it, Chris' during an attempted burglary.

Watkins retired from his legal career, aged seventy-five, having by then taken on a senior role in rugby: in 1968, he was elected as president of Glamorgan Wanderers (the team he had played for as fly half in his younger days) and then became chairman of the Welsh Rugby Union Charitable Trust, set up to help seriously injured players, in 1975. Finally, in 1993 he was elected as president of the Welsh Rugby Union, a post he held for eleven years until 2004. During his time as president, he sometimes addressed the Welsh players before a match, likening rugby to warfare since both required 'a cool mind, discipline and self-sacrifice'.

Upon standing down from the presidency of the WRU in 2004, Watkins was made honorary life vice-patron of the WRU, of which The Queen is patron. For a time from 1947, Watkins was also variously a member of the TA Association, Glamorgan and Wales, and he served as president of the Royal British Legion of Wales from 1947 to 1968. He was also president of the University of Wales College of Medicine from 1987 to 1998.

In common with most VC recipients, Watkins was proud of his award, but he always preferred to be remembered for his career achievements in the worlds of law and rugby rather than for his actions in war. However, shortly before Armistice Day 2001, he was asked to reflect on his VC award and replied:

> You must believe me when I say it was just another day in the life of a soldier. I did what needed doing to help colleagues and friends, just as others looked out for me during the fighting that summer … I didn't wake up the next day a better or braver person, just different. I'd seen more killing and death in 24 hours – indeed been part of that terrible process – than is right for anybody. From that point onwards I have tried to take a more caring view of my fellow human beings, and that, of course, always includes your opponent, whether it be in war, sport or just life generally.

In August 2007, Watkins fell heavily at his home in Llandaff. He was admitted to the University of Wales Hospital, where he died on 9 September, aged eighty-eight. Later that same day, the Welsh players wore black armbands for their opening match of the Rugby World Cup in Nantes, France. He was cremated after a funeral service at Llandaff Cathedral, where there is also a memorial to him in the Welsh Regiment Memorial Chapel. There is also a fine statue in his honour at the Millennium Stadium, Cardiff.

There were many affectionate tributes to Watkins after his death. Rhodri Morgan, then the First Minister of Wales, described him as 'one of the outstanding Welshmen of the twentieth century'. Dennis Gethin, the president of the Welsh Rugby Union, said he was 'arguably the greatest living Welshman ...: He was small in stature, but in every way a colossus and Wales is a poorer place without him. Sir Tasker was without doubt the greatest president the Union ever had and the rugby world certainly mourns his passing.'

There is a lengthy and splendid tribute to Wakins by W. Alister Williams in his book *Heart of a Dragon: The VCs of Wales and the Welsh Regiments 1914–82*. Williams writes: 'Tasker Watkins was one of those rare men who rose from very humble beginnings to succeed in whatever field of endeavour he turned his hand to.'

ACTING SUBADAR RAM SARUP SINGH

Indian Army: 1st Punjab Regiment
DATE OF BRAVERY: 25 OCTOBER 1944
GAZETTED: 8 FEBRUARY 1945
Special feature of the VC: a poignant posthumous Indian Army award for 'cool bravery' in the Burma campaign.

Ram Sarup Singh was born in the village of Kheri Talwana in Patiala state, India, on 13 April 1919. Little is known about his early life other than he was the son of Jorawar Singh.

On 12 April 1937, the day before his eighteenth birthday, Singh enlisted into the Indian Army and he was to serve in Arakan, Burma, with the 2nd/1st Punjab Regiment. In March 1944, the regiment was sent to Imphal, India, as part of 5th Division, which was deployed on operations in the Litan-Ukhrul Road area, and in the same month Singh was promoted to jemadar. The regiment was involved in engagements between April and September 1944, following which most Japanese troops had been driven out of India and the British were ready to march into Burma.

In October 1944, Singh was promoted to acting subadar and in the same month, south of Imphal, the British pushed forward along the Tiddim road, making for Kalewa on the Chindwin. The road south to Fort White was dominated by Kennedy Peak, while to the north was another Japanese stronghold at Sialum Vum that, in turn, guarded the ridge leading to Kennedy Peak. The position of Sialum Vum was attacked on 29 September but the enemy held out for almost a month against the assault.

On 25 October, Singh was in charge of a platoon of the 1st Punjab Regiment that was ordered to attack the flank of the enemy position. The Japanese had received plenty of warning of an attack and all the approaches to the heavily armed position were covered by machine-guns sited in bunkers.

It was for his bravery that day that Singh was awarded the VC, when the citation for his award, published on 8 February 1945, stated:

> In Burma on the 25th October, 1944, two platoons of the 1st Punjab Regiment were ordered to put in a diversionary attack on the flank of an enemy position. This feature was of exceptional natural strength and was defended by a large force of fresh Japanese troops who had turned the hill into a fortress. Every approach was covered by medium and light machine guns sited in bunkers. The platoon of Subadar Ram Sarup Singh at once charged the position with another section. This instantaneous action completely bewildered

the enemy, who fled from the bunkered positions suffering casualties in their retreat. The Subadar was wounded in the legs but took no notice of his wounds.

While he was consolidating his position, the enemy opened heavy fire with grenade dischargers, and at the same time put in a strong counter-attack in three waves of twenty each from a flank. It seemed that the platoon must be overwhelmed, but Subadar Ram Sarup Singh got another light machine gun into position and led a charge against the advancing enemy, bayonetting four himself, and checking them. Although badly wounded in the thigh, he got up and, ignoring his wound, again went for the enemy shouting encouragement to his men. He bayonetted another Japanese and shot a further one, but was mortally wounded by a burst of medium machine gun fire in the chest and neck.

It would be difficult to find a finer example of cool bravery, cheerfulness, leadership and determination. His action had a profound effect on the rest of the Company, and when volunteers were called for to bring in his body, under the heaviest fire, the entire Company volunteered.

Subadar Ram Sarup Singh's gallantry will inspire the Regiment for all time.

Partly as a result of Singh's bravery, the Japanese Army was driven back on 25 October. As the Allied forces pushed forwards, Fort White was reached on 8 November 1944 and Kalewa was occupied soon afterwards on 2 December.

Singh had died, aged twenty-five, and so his VC was a posthumous award. He had been married to Nath Kanwar and his decoration was presented to his widow by Lord Wavell, the Viceroy of India, at the Red Fort, Delhi, on 1 April 1945. Singh has no known grave but his name is commemorated on the Memorial Gates, Hyde Park Corner, London, and on the Rangoon Memorial, Burma (now Myanmar).

ACTING NAIK FAZAL DIN

Indian Army: 10th Baluch Regiment
DATE OF BRAVERY: 2 MARCH 1945
GAZETTED: 24 MAY 1945
Special feature of the VC: an outstanding Burma campaign award for arguably the finest hand-to-hand combat of the war.

Fazal Din was born in the village of Hussainpur, Hoshiarpur, India, on 1 July 1921. A Punjabi Muslim, he was the son of Nur Bakhsh, although little is known about his early life or his education. However, in either 1939 or 1940, Din enlisted into the 7th Battalion of the 10th Baluch Regiment and he later served in the Burma campaign.

On 1 March 1945, the British launched an attack on the town of Meiktila, east of the Irrawaddy River in Burma (now Myanmar). In a carefully co-ordinated attack, the 63rd Brigade advanced from the west, the 48th Brigade from the north and the 255th Indian Tank Brigade swung around to advance from the east in order to capture the enemy airfield. Heavy fighting continued throughout the next day as the British tried to force the last of the Japanese troops out of Meiktila.

On 2 March, Fazal Din, by then aged twenty-three and an acting naik (the equivalent of corporal) was involved in an outstanding act of bravery which cost him his life. His posthumous VC was announced on 24 May 1945 when his citation detailed exactly what he had done to earn his award:

> In Burma, on 2nd March, 1945, Naik Fazal Din was commanding a section during a Company attack on a Japanese bunkered position. During this attack, the section found itself in an area flanked by three bunkers on one side and a house and one bunker on the other side. This was the key of the enemy position and had held up a Company attack made earlier. Naik Fazal Din's section was accompanied by a tank but, at the time of entering the area, it had gone on ahead. On reaching the area, the section was held up by Light

Machine Gun fire and grenades from the bunkers. Unhesitatingly Naik Fazal Din personally attacked the nearest bunker with grenades and silenced it. He then led his section under heavy fire against the other bunkers. Suddenly six Japanese, led by two officers wielding swords, rushed from the house. The Bren gunner shot one officer and a Japanese other rank but by then had expended the magazine of the gun. He was almost simultaneously attacked by the second Japanese officer who killed him with his sword. Naik Fazal Din went to the Bren gunner's assistance immediately but, in doing so, was run through the chest by the officer, the sword point appearing through his back. On the Japanese officer withdrawing his sword, Naik Fazal Din, despite his terrible wound, tore the sword from the officer and killed him with it. He then attacked a Japanese other rank and also killed him. He then went to the assistance of a sepoy of his section who was struggling with another Japanese and killed the latter with the sword. Then, waving the sword, he continued to encourage his men. He staggered to Platoon Headquarters, about 25 yards away, to make a report and collapsed. He died soon after reaching the Regimental Aid Post.

Naik Fazal Din's action was seen by almost the whole Platoon who, undoubtedly inspired by his gallantry and taking advantage of the bewilderment created amongst the enemy by the loss of its leaders, continued the attack and annihilated the garrison which numbered 55.

Such supreme devotion to duty, even when fatally wounded, presence of mind and outstanding courage, have seldom been equalled and reflect the unquenchable spirit of a singularly brave and gallant N.C.O.

By the end of the day on 2 March, almost all the Japanese troops had been driven out of Meiktila and the loss of this strategically important town threatened the enemy's lines of communication with their troops north of Burma. Din's VC was presented by Lord Wavell, the Viceroy of India, on 19 December 1945, at the Red

Fort, Delhi, although it is not known who accepted it on behalf of Din's family.

Din, who had been married to Sardar Bibi, a young woman from his home village in India, has his name commemorated on the Rangoon Memorial in Myanmar, and also on the Memorial Gates at Hyde Park Corner, London.

CORPORAL (LATER COMPANY SERGEANT-MAJOR) EDWARD THOMAS CHAPMAN

Army: The Monmouthshire Regiment
DATE OF BRAVERY: 2 APRIL 1945
GAZETTED: 13 JULY 1945
Special feature of the VC: A superb VC for the final month of the war.

Edward Chapman was born in Pontlottyn, Glamorgan, on 13 January 1920. He was the second of four sons born to Evan Chapman, a miner, and his wife Rachel (*née* Saunders). Edward Chapman, who spoke Welsh, attended Fochriw School until the age of fourteen when he followed his father 'down the pit', working at Ogilvie Colliery, New Tredegar.

On 19 April 1940, Chapman, who was usually known as 'Ted', was posted to the Monmouthshire Regiment and assigned to the 2nd Battalion, based in Northern Ireland. Here, his regiment was part of 160th Brigade of the 53rd (Welsh) Division that had two principal tasks: to protect the province from invasion and to guard civilians against any terrorism from the IRA. In October 1941, the battalion was transferred to Leominster, Herefordshire. While on a visit to Belfast, Chapman had met and, eventually, become engaged to a local girl, Rhoda Watkins.

Their wedding was arranged in Belfast for early 1942 by which point Chapman was still based in Leominster. Because he was determined to get married in a civilian suit rather than in uniform, and with time short, Chapman went absent without leave for the final fitting. On his return to camp, he was arrested and his sentence was to be confined to barracks for a week. This meant he could not get to Belfast and, after he failed to turn up and his fiancée had heard nothing from him, she became convinced she had been jilted. Eventually, when she learned of Chapman's predicament, the wedding was postponed by a week. On 26 March 1942, at Richview Church, Belfast, the couple married with the groom in his military uniform: it was a double marriage celebration, as Rhoda Watkins's sister married her fiancé at the same time.

In the same month, Chapman and his regiment were moved to Rochester, Kent, to act as part of Britain's defensive frontline. On 25 June 1944, less than three weeks after the D-Day landings, the battalion arrived in Normandy and then advanced into the Low Countries, the Rhine Crossing and north-west Germany. By this point the 2nd Battalion, The Monmouthshire Regiment, had spent four years of relative inactivity and its members were anxious to see action. In August 1944, Chapman was wounded in the Falaise Pocket break-out, the decisive engagement in the Battle of Normandy, when a shell landed on his foot.

He made a quick recovery, however, and, after just five weeks in hospital, he was back on the frontline, this time posted to D Company in the regiment's 3rd Battalion. By 30 November, he was again in the thick of the action, when part of the battalion helped push the enemy back to the River Maas and then stormed a castle at Broekhuizen, near Horst. Despite suffering heavy casualties during heavy fighting, the 3rd Battalion took the village against a larger, dug-in enemy force.

There was no let-up for the battalion: after three weeks in Holland, it was moved to the Kleve area of western Germany, where it took part in the attack on the Schlieffen Line, the enemy's last major position before the River Rhine. Yet again, both the fighting and the casualties were heavy. However, the Allies pressed on deep into Germany with the enemy soldiers now fighting desperately to defend their homeland. By the third week of March, with the Allies by then across the Rhine, the 3rd Battalion was positioned in the Teutoburger Wald hills, preparing to advance and attack the Dortmund–Ems canal. Because of the difficult terrain, which included steep-sided woods, the area was unsuitable for tanks and other mechanised vehicles. This meant the advance would have to be an infantry assault and, at dawn on 2 April 1945, four companies from Chapman's battalion were ordered to enter the forest and try to clear the western edge of the ridge, north of Riesenbeck.

It was at this action, with the forest shrouded in mist, that Chapman showed such outstanding bravery that he was awarded the VC. The citation, published on 13 July 1945, gives a full account of what happened:

> On 2nd April, 1945, a Company of the Monmouthshire Regiment crossed the Dortmund-Ems canal and was ordered to assault the ridge of the Teutoberger [*sic*] Wald, which dominates the surrounding country. This ridge is steep, thickly wooded and is ideal defensive country. It was, moreover, defended by a battalion of German officer cadets and their instructors, all of them picked men and fanatical Nazis.
>
> Corporal Chapman was advancing with his section in single file along a narrow track, when the enemy suddenly opened fire with machine guns at short range, inflicting heavy casualties and causing some confusion. Corporal Chapman immediately ordered his section to take cover and, seizing the Bren gun, he advanced alone, firing the gun from his hip, and mowed down the enemy at point blank range, forcing them to retire in disorder.
>
> At this point, however, his Company was ordered to withdraw but Corporal Chapman and his section were still left in their advanced position, as the order could not be got forward to them.

The enemy then began to close up to Corporal Chapman and his isolated section and, under cover of intense machine gun fire, they made determined charges with the bayonet. Corporal Chapman again rose with his Bren gun to meet the assaults and on each occasion halted their advance.

He had now nearly run out of ammunition. Shouting to his section for more bandoliers [belts of ammunition], he dropped into a fold in the ground and covered those bringing up the ammunition by lying on his back and firing the Bren gun over his shoulder. A party of Germans made every effort to eliminate him with grenades, but with reloaded magazine he closed with them and once again drove the enemy back with considerable casualties.

During the withdrawal of his Company, the Company Commander had been severely wounded and left lying in the open a short distance from Corporal Chapman. Satisfied that his section was now secure, at any rate for the moment, he went out alone under withering fire and carried his Company Commander for 50 yards to comparative safety. On the way a sniper hit the officer again, wounding Corporal Chapman in the hip and, when he reached our lines, it was discovered that the officer had been killed.

In spite of his wound, Corporal Chapman refused to be evacuated and went back to his Company until the position was fully restored two hours later.

Throughout the action Corporal Chapman displayed outstanding gallantry and superb courage. Single-handed he repulsed the attacks of well-led, determined troops and gave his battalion time to reorganise on a vital piece of ground overlooking the only bridge across the canal. His magnificent bravery played a very large part in the capture of this vital ridge and in the successful development of subsequent operations.

Chapman's wound had been received when he was carrying the wounded officer, Captain Mountford, back to the Allied lines.

An enemy bullet first hit the officer's head and then went on into Chapman's thigh. As soon as Chapman put Mountford down, he realised he was dead. Chapman's wound, however, was not serious and he was soon able to return to his battalion. In fact, soon after his return, while based at Sonsfeld, Chapman got into a scrap with a friend and was hospitalised again, this time with a perforated eardrum. On 13 July 1945, a nurse gave him some clean pyjamas and told him to prepare for the arrival of a senior officer. Chapman was puzzled and feared he was going to face further disciplinary action over his brawl. In fact, the officer told Chapman that it was about to be announced that he had been awarded the VC.

Those who knew Chapman, by then twenty-five years old, were not surprised by his VC: although slightly built, he was a hugely determined, courageous individual. When his VC was announced, however, there was initially some confusion in his home village over whether this was the same Ted Chapman who had been born and brought up in south Wales. This was because the press had stated that Chapman was 'from Belfast'. The confusion was soon resolved: with his wife having returned to Belfast for the duration of the war, Chapman had given her home address for his next of kin. In fact, this was very much a Welsh VC, not a Northern Ireland one. Chapman received his VC from George VI at an investiture in Buckingham Palace on 31 July 1945, just eighteen days after the award was announced.

Chapman was demobilised to the Reserve in 1946 but within two years had rejoined The Monmouthshire Regiment as a territorial. On 1 June 1953, he was awarded the British Empire Medal (BEM) for his contribution to the Territorial Army (TA) when his citation stated:

> Sergeant Chapman won the coveted and supreme award for valour
> for his devotion to duty in the field of battle during the last war.
> Joining the Territorial Army when it was reformed in 1947, he has

taken a full and active part in all activities of the Company and Battalion. He is the type who is proud to be in the Territorial Army and in addition considers it his duty to serve his country. He was recently taken in for a fourth tour of duty despite the calls of his own business. Unlike many others who sit back and consider they have done their duty, this sergeant is only happy when he is taking part in the activities of the Regiment. I cannot over emphasise what it has meant to his Company and Battalion to have such a man volunteer time and again. His Company has grown in stature by having Sergeant Chapman on its strength.

The very next day after this announcement, Chapman was one of five men who represented his regiment at the coronation of Queen Elizabeth II. Although he was discharged from the TA in October that year, he re-enlisted again the following year, before finally stepping down from military service in 1957 in the rank of company sergeant-major.

After the war, Chapman returned to married life with his wife Rhoda and the couple had two sons and a daughter. After 1946, he worked for Rhymney Engineering before switching to work for the Great Western Railway in his home town: Pontlottyn station, Glamorgan. After these two jobs, Chapman then spent twenty-five years working as a nylon spinner for ICI Fibres of Pontypool. Chapman had two main hobbies: fly fishing and breeding Welsh Cobs, and, after retiring in 1982, he founded the Ynyswen stud farm of Welsh mountain ponies and was a life member of the Welsh Pony and Cob Society.

In a moving tribute to Chapman in his book *Heart of a Dragon: The VCs of Wales and the Welsh Regiment*, W. Alister Williams writes: 'In his private life, Chapman was something of a contradiction, always shying away from publicity, particularly with regard to his VC, while placing himself in the spotlight as an ordinary member of the public and in his working life.' For example, in April 1962,

Chapman took part, as a contestant, in the television panel game *What's My Line?* with Eamonn Andrews, where he was, albeit accurately, described by a panellist as a 'nylon spinner' (rather than a VC recipient).

On 3 February 2002, Chapman was taken ill at his home in New Inn, near Pontypool. Despite being reluctant to leave his home, he attended Nevill Hall Hospital in Abergavenny where he died later the same day, aged eighty-two. Chapman is buried at Panteg cemetery, New Inn, and a building at the TA Centre, Cwmbran, is named Chapman House in his honour.

The Royal Navy

The Royal Navy had emerged from the First World War with its reputation as the most formidable navy in the world still intact. During the inter-war years, a series of treaties aimed at preventing a naval arms race saw the Royal Navy lose much of its power and world dominance. By 1938, the supposed restrictions of the treaties were effectively null and void, and the Royal Navy re-armed. Many of the Royal Navy ships appeared dated, but there were exceptions, notably the aircraft carriers Ark Royal *and* Illustrious.

During the Second World War, the Royal Navy played a vital role in guarding shipping lanes, escorting convoys, and undertaking mine clearance and laying operations, and it enabled British forces to fight in remote parts of the world, including north Africa and the Far East. Naval supremacy was also important to the amphibious operations carried out, including the invasions of north Africa, Sicily, Italy and Normandy.

Capital ships, cruisers, corvettes and destroyers aside, the Royal Navy's Fleet Air Arm and Submarine Service also performed vital work across a broad range of theatres, while gallant work was undertaken by Motor Gun Boats (MGBs), Motor Torpedo Boats (MTBs) and Motor Launches (MLs) of Coastal Forces.

COMMANDER (LATER REAR-ADMIRAL SIR) ANTHONY CECIL CAPEL MIERS

Royal Navy

DATE OF BRAVERY: 4 MARCH 1942

GAZETTED: 7 JULY 1942

Special feature of the VC: one of the finest submariner VCs of the Second World War, awarded to one of only three submarine commanders to be awarded the VC for actions in the Mediterranean.

Anthony Cecil Capel Miers was born in Birchwood, Inverness, Scotland, on 11 November 1906. He was the younger son of Captain Douglas Miers, of The Queen's Own Cameron Highlanders, and his wife, Margaret (*née* Christie). Miers was proud of both his Scottish and military roots: through his grandmother, Mary Macdonald, he was a direct descendant of Donald Macdonald, the sixteenth Chief of Clanranald, while his grandfather, Lieutenant-Colonel Capel Miers, also served in The Queen's Own Cameron Highlanders and was killed in action during the opening year of the Great War at Bourg on the Aisne. Young Anthony Miers was educated at Stubbington House School, Fareham, Hampshire, before attending the Edinburgh Academy in Scotland and Wellington College, Berkshire.

In 1924, Miers joined the Royal Navy as a special entry cadet and from 1925 to 1927 he served as a midshipman in the battleship HMS *Valiant.* On 1 January 1928, he was promoted to sub-lieutenant and on 29 April the following year he joined the Submarine Service. Miers was a fine athlete, playing tennis, squash and rugby, being chosen for the latter sport to play for London Scottish, the Combined Services and Hampshire, and also selected for trials for the Navy and Scotland.

After various appointments and promotions, he then suffered a career setback as a first lieutenant in 1933, when he voluntarily reported an attempt to strike a rating after a football match. Miers, who could be volatile and short-tempered, was court-martialled and

dismissed from his ship, the fishery protection vessel *Dart*. Fortunately, he soon put that unhappy episode behind him and in 1936
was given his first submarine command, *L54*, and on 1 January 1938
was promoted to lieutenant-commander. From 1939 to 1940, the
opening year of the Second World War, he was on the staff of
the Commander-in-Chief Home Fleet, serving in HM ships *Nelson*,
Rodney and *Warspite*. However, on 12 November 1940, Miers
returned to the Submarine Service as Commanding Officer of one
of the new T-class boats, HM Submarine *Torbay*. For a time he was
based in Scotland but, from May 1941 to May 1942, *Torbay* operated out of Alexandria, Egypt. On 5 July 1941, while based in the
Mediterranean, *Torbay* sank the Italian submarine *Jantina* and two
tankers. Controversially, in the same month, Miers attacked four
German vessels carrying soldiers from a German garrison and, during
the operation, he ordered the machine-gunning of German soldiers
leaving their boat in a rubber raft.

On 31 December 1941, Miers was appointed to the rank of commander. For bravery in 1941 while commanding his submarine,
Miers was awarded the Distinguished Service Order (DSO) and, the
next year, he was awarded a Bar to his DSO: these two awards followed the sinking or damaging of more than 70,000 tons of Axis
shipping and rescuing more than 130 Allied soldiers from Crete.

Yet even during this courageous rescue of Allied soldiers, Miers's
temper had flared again during an encounter with fellow Scot Corporal George Bremner, one of two Army commandos from the Special
Boat Section (SBS). Bremner, who was awarded the Military Medal
(MM) for his bravery during the rescue, later recalled:

> Miers tried to insist that I paddled ashore in a force eight gale. I knew
> from past experience that I could not survive in such stormy weather
> and I refused to embark in my canoe. Miers threatened to shoot me
> for mutiny and he called through the voice pipe for his revolver.
> After he got his revolver he seemed to calm down and agreed to my

suggestion that we should go below and study the local charts for a more sheltered embarkation, which we found. Over a period of three nights we eventually rescued over 130 Allied troops off Crete, in which I played a major role.

Miers, who was nicknamed 'Gamp', could be utterly terrifying when in the midst of a rage. In his book *Gamp VC: The Wartime Story of Maverick Submarine Commander Anthony Miers*, Brian Izzard wrote: 'Men would dread his volcanic eruptions, which for those on the receiving end might culminate in a black eye, close arrest or the sack. For someone really unlucky, it was all three. But when the fire-eater cooled down he could be charm personified.'

Late February 1942 witnessed the start of a frantic period of action for Miers and his submarine crew. *Torbay* sailed from Alexandria on 20 February in order to patrol off the west coast of Greece. On the morning of 26 February, having surfaced to recharge batteries, *Torbay*'s crew sighted a tanker escorted by a destroyer. With Miers at the periscope, *Torbay* dived, surfaced astern of the enemy and fired one torpedo that was spotted. Once *Torbay* had been seen, she had to dive again and eleven depth charges were dropped in the hope of disabling her but they all missed. Miers had endured great difficulty shutting the upper hatch as the destroyer advanced towards his submarine and he later discovered that this was because the hatch was jammed by his own pillow.

On both 1 and 2 March, *Torbay* was once again depth-charged by destroyers and six near-misses saw the submarine lifted several feet upwards in the sea. When Miers later spoke of the stresses and strains of being depth-charged, he was full of praise for the calmness of his crew:

> I am bound to confess that on many occasions I have felt extremely frightened when the depth-charges have been going off around us. Yet even then the crew of *Torbay* has never failed to amaze me.

In fact they almost seem to enjoy themselves keeping a scoreboard of the number of enemy depth-charges dropped.

On 3 March 1942, an enemy convoy escorted by three destroyers was seen by *Torbay* as it entered Corfu harbour. 'All out of range,' Miers told Lieutenant Hugh Kidd. 'I am going to trail 'em. May take some time, but it should be worthwhile.' Overnight, having already surfaced once only to have to dive again to avoid a motor-ship, Miers followed the convoy through a narrow channel in heavily patrolled waters having commented to Kidd: 'They're going in. We'll follow later. Can't catch them otherwise, and we're not coming all this way for nothing – don't you agree, Kidd?' There were dangers aplenty – grounding, striking a mine or being spotted, engaged and sunk by enemy ships. Once *Torbay* was deep inside the harbour, Miers upped periscope and could see he was surrounded on three sides by enemy territory and several enemy vessels. Knowing it was too dangerous to attack at night and then escape afterwards, he decided to wait until the morning. However, first, *Torbay* was forced to surface in a full moon to recharge her batteries, before diving again having not been spotted. By dawn on 4 March, Miers discovered that the convoy had sailed again, leaving only two 5,000-ton transport ships and a destroyer at anchor. 'Right. Stand by to attack,' were Miers's orders to his first lieutenant.

The *Torbay* fired a torpedo at each of the three ships, missing the destroyer but hitting both transport ships, both of which subsequently sank. Miers took his submarine to the seabed, not knowing if the torpedoes had hit their targets, and waited there for an hour. That was the easier part: the submarine now had to make a hazardous withdrawal to the open sea in broad daylight, enduring constant depth-charging by the pursuing enemy. In all, some forty depth-charges were dropped but none found its target.

Miers had made for the nearest exit in a straight line and, at one point, was caught among small boats searching for the submarine.

He also avoided the enemy anti-submarine craft that were hovering along the long exit channel, as well as enemy aircraft continuously patrolling overhead. It was mid-morning when Miers finally reached open water, fully seventeen hours after he had led *Torbay* into the enemy's lair. During their ordeal, Miers had been reassuring his crew that they would be able to escape. 'Well, there's many a patrol to be done after this, so don't worry – we'll get her back to base,' he told one young crew member.

Miers's VC was announced on 7 July 1942, when his citation read:

> For valour in command of H.M. Submarine *Torbay* in a daring and successful raid on shipping in a defended enemy harbour, planned with full knowledge of the great hazards to be expected during seventeen hours in waters closely patrolled by the enemy. On arriving in the harbour he had to charge his batteries lying on the surface in full moonlight, under the guns of the enemy. As he could not see his target he waited several hours and attacked in full daylight in a glassy calm. When he had fired his torpedoes he was heavily counter-attacked and had to withdraw through a long channel with anti-submarine craft all round and continuous air patrols overhead.

After the announcement of his VC and other gallantry awards for *Torbay*'s officers and crew, it was suggested that the four officers would be invested at one ceremony and the ratings at another. Miers is said to have responded that if they could not all attend together, he would turn down his VC. This meant that, on 28 July 1942, the ship's company remained united, as they had been under the sea, for the investiture at Buckingham Palace by George VI. In all, twenty-eight officers and men from *Torbay* were decorated by The King: Miers received his VC, the engineer officer, Lieutenant Kidd, received the Distinguished Service Order (DSO), Lieutenants P. Chapman and D. S. Verschoyle-Campbell received Bars to their Distinguished

Service Crosses (DSCs) and twenty-four ratings either received the Distinguished Service Medal (DSM) or Bars to their DSMs.

Miers continued to serve with considerable distinction for the rest of the war. On 30 June 1942, just a week before his VC was announced, Miers was appointed as Submarine Staff Liaison Officer on the Staffs of Admiral Chester W. Nimitz, Commander-in-Chief Pacific, and Admiral Lockwood, Commander Submarines Pacific. As part of this role, he accompanied a 56-day war patrol with the US submarine *Cabrilla*. From 1944 to 1945, Miers was Commander Submarines, 8th Submarine Flotilla, which was based at Trincomalee, Ceylon (now Sri Lanka), and, later, Perth, Australia.

Miers's character and career are summed up well by John Winton in his book *The Victoria Cross at Sea*. The author says of the multi-decorated submarine commander:

> Of all the twentieth-century naval VCs, Anthony Miers perhaps most closely resembles those nineteenth-century officers who won the VC and went on to flag rank and knighthoods. His VC, like theirs, was the most dramatic incident of his career, but it was only one incident of many in a naval service which lasted, in his case, for thirty-five years. Miers' naval career had an almost Victorian symmetry: a hectic youth and an active middle age, followed by a later phase in which he became an 'elder statesman' and the 'senior submariner' of the Navy.

On 20 January 1945, Miers married Patricia Miller, who had served in the Women's Royal Australian Naval Service (WRANS), in Perth. The couple went on to have a son, who served in the Royal Navy, and a daughter. After the war ended, Miers was promoted – on 31 December 1946 – to captain, and during the same year he was given command of the shore-based HMS *Vernon II*. From 1948 to 1950, he commanded HMS *Blackcap*, the Royal Naval Air Station at Stretton, Cheshire, and during this time he gained his pilot's licence. After that, he commanded the depot-ship HMS *Forth* and the 1st Submarine Flotilla until 1952, and then was in charge of the Royal Naval College, Greenwich, London, until 1954. For the next year, he commanded the aircraft carrier, HMS *Theseus*. Miers was promoted to rear-admiral on 7 January 1956 and on 15 March of the same year he was appointed Flag Officer, Middle East. He retired on 4 August 1959, having been made a Companion of the Order of the Bath (CB) in 1958 and a Knight Commander of the Order of the British Empire (KBE) in 1959.

Miers led an interesting and active life after his retirement, at one point ending up as the manager of a button factory in Birmingham. Other posts included being president of the Royal Navy Lawn Tennis Association from 1954 to 1978, president of the Royal Navy Squash Rackets Association from 1960 to 1970, president of the Submarine Old Comrades' Association from 1967 to 1981 and chairman of the Royal Navy Scholarship Fund from 1968 to 1973.

During his final years, Miers and his wife lived in Roehampton, London. He died at his home on 30 June 1985, aged seventy-eight; his last word was 'Cheerio.' Sir Anthony Cecil Capel Miers VC, KBE, CB, DSO and Bar is buried in Tomnahurich cemetery, Inverness, where he has a Roman Catholic headstone.

Even after his death, Miers continued to be a controversial figure. Ludovic Kennedy, the writer and broadcaster, published his autobiography, *On My Way to the Club*, in 1989 and his book devoted several pages to 'a submarine atrocity' off Crete during the war. Kennedy suggested a 'much decorated officer' had been guilty of war crimes, in having seven enemy soldiers, who had survived in a dinghy/raft after their troop-carriers had been sunk, shot. Although Kennedy did not identify Miers or *Torbay* by name, newspapers picked up on the story knowing that they could not libel the dead. On 5 February 1989, the *Sunday Telegraph* ran a front-page story headlined: 'Was Royal Navy VC submariner a war criminal?' In the paper's article, both Miers and *Torbay* were identified. In this article, which was littered with inaccuracies, the journalist claimed there had been a near mutiny by *Torbay*'s crew when they were ordered to shoot the enemy soldiers. No mention was made that at the time of the shooting, the enemy soldiers were actually still in the water, armed and active: one had apparently tried to open fire with a rifle and another had thrown a hand grenade at the submarine. John Miers, Anthony's son, and John Winton, the author, were among the many to spring to Miers's defence. Winton wrote: 'In the luxury of peace we can criticise men like Miers. In wartime we desperately need them.'

In 1991, Kennedy went on to write another article for the *Telegraph Magazine*, headlined 'War Crimes', in which he *did* identify Miers by name. Kennedy was knighted in 1994 for services to journalism, but Miers's family remained angered by his accusations. John Miers said:

> To do something like that is unbelievable. It had nothing to do with the facts. Here were men who were the enemy, with guns, in uniform. The shore was two miles away, they could swim, let alone go in a boat. They could go and kill some of our soldiers. That's war. We're not sitting in armchairs. Kennedy was trying to make it into something it wasn't. I thought it was disgraceful.
>
> My mother was very upset. The thing that upsets all our family is that, as a result of this man putting something in print, my father is now an alleged war criminal. He's not an alleged war criminal. Just because someone decides he wants to accuse him doesn't mean he's an alleged war criminal. It's like saying he's probably innocent but he might not be. He <u>is</u> innocent.

The Royal Air Force (RAF)

After the end of the First World War, the RAF, which had only been founded in 1918, was significantly cut back. However, shortly before and during the Second World War, it again underwent a massive expansion. Military leaders on both sides could see that bomber aircraft were capable of not just inflicting substantial damage, but also demoralising the inhabitants of the nation that was being targeted.

Fighter aircraft also came into widespread use and dramatic aerial duels took place between rival 'aces' who, even if highly skilled at their job, had a short life expectancy. A defining period of the RAF's existence came during the Battle of Britain in 1940, when it held off the German Luftwaffe and helped to turn the tide of the war. The largest – and most controversial – effort of the RAF was the strategic bombing campaign against Germany by RAF Bomber Command in the latter stages of the war.

WING COMMANDER HUGH GORDON MALCOLM

Royal Air Force
DATE OF BRAVERY: NOVEMBER/DECEMBER 1942
GAZETTED: 27 APRIL 1943
Special feature of the VC: an outstanding posthumous award for self-sacrifice and gallantry in the air.

Hugh Malcolm was born in Broughty Ferry, Dundee, Scotland, on 2 May 1917. He was the son of Kenneth Malcolm, a Dundee jute merchant, and his wife Majorie (*née* Smith). The young Malcolm was educated at Craigflower Preparatory School, Dunfermline, and Trinity College, Glenalmond, Perthshire. As a young man, Malcolm was shy and quiet, but he was sporty and excelled at golf and hunting.

After completing his schooling, he entered RAF College Cranwell, Lincolnshire, as a cadet in January 1936, where he graduated as a commissioned pilot in December 1937. The following month Malcolm was posted to No. 26 Squadron (Lysanders), based at RAF Catterick, Yorkshire, where he took part in various training exercises. On 20 May 1939, he was piloting a Lysander 4784 in a practice flight for a forthcoming Empire Air Day display when he was involved in a major accident with his observer that wrote-off the aircraft. 'It just fell out'er me hands,' he noted in his log book, with masterly understatement. Malcolm suffered serious injuries, including a fractured skull, and was told he would never fly again. He spent four months in the Princess Mary Hospital at RAF Halton in Buckinghamshire and it was while recuperating there that Malcolm met a nurse, Helen Swan, who would become his wife: the couple married in Sussex in 1940. Malcolm's eventual recovery was so complete that he returned to his squadron in September 1939. As the Second World War intensified, Malcolm was promoted, first to flight lieutenant in September 1940 and then to squadron leader in December 1941.

Malcolm served as a flight commander in No. 18 Squadron (Blenheims) based at RAF Wattisham, Suffolk. With this squadron, he flew mainly night sorties, the first being on 6 May 1942. Many of these sorties were in support of main bomber force raids and his role was to attack German night-fighter airfields. Malcolm and his crew participated in Bomber Command's first '1,000-bomber raid' on Cologne on the night of 30/31 May 1942. It involved eighteen Blenheim IVs from No. 18 Squadron which flew intruder sorties against three Luftwaffe air bases, with Malcolm leading seven of these aircraft against Sint-Truiden airfield. On 1 June 1942, while involved in another major raid, this time on Essen, Malcolm and his crew again returned to attack St Trond.

Malcolm and his crew also participated in the next '1,000-bomber raid', this time to Bremen, on the night of 25/26 June. On 1 July, Malcolm and his crew were commended for their bravery in searching for and locating a dinghy – containing British aircrew – some 50 miles off the Dutch coast. This was carried out in daylight and in clear weather – which put them at great risk of an enemy attack – and Malcolm remained in the air for four hours to obtain seven 'fixes' on the dinghy so that the crew could be rescued.

In September 1942, Malcolm was promoted to wing commander and also to the command of the squadron. Two months later, he moved with his squadron to north Africa, where he was initially based at Blida airfield in Algeria. By then, his squadron, part of 326 Wing, was flying new Blenheim Vs, which were proving unreliable in these very different conditions. The aircraft's failings became apparent on their first operational sortie in north Africa on 17 November 1942. Malcolm and his squadron attacked Bizerta airfield in Tunisia at low-level in daylight and without a fighter escort. They bombed and strafed their target, but encountered both bad weather and the Luftwaffe on their return flight: No. 18 Squadron lost two bombers to the German fighter aircraft and two more in an air collision. Undeterred, the squadron returned to Bizerta eleven days later to bomb and strafe the airfield a second time, despite a massive barrage of fire from the German air defences.

By this point, the ground war in north Africa had become intense and, on 4 December, eleven Blenheim Vs from No. 326 Wing were flown to Souk-el-Arba in Tunisia to support the Army units in the battle area. Six Blenheims, led by Malcolm, took off at 9.15 a.m. to search for targets in the Chouigui area. When they located a Luftwaffe landing strip some 10 miles north of Chouigui, they bombed and strafed it before flying to Canrobert, to refuel, and then returned to Souk-el-Arba. However, less than an hour after landing, Malcolm received a message from the forward Army battle zone, requesting urgent air support in the area they had just come from. This meant flying in broad daylight over a battle area without fighter aircraft support: it was not possible to organise this in the time available. Malcolm was aware quite how hazardous the mission would be but, knowing the infantry desperately needed support, he did not hesitate. He was, however, ordered to abandon the attack if there was insufficient cloud cover to complete the task satisfactorily.

Eleven Blenheims from No. 326 Wing were chosen for the sortie but one burst its tail wheel attempting to take off and was taken out of service. The ten remaining aircraft kept a tight formation, knowing that this was their only defence against the Luftwaffe, but within twenty minutes, one of the planes had to make a crash-landing 15 miles east of Souk-el-Arba. The crew survived but the mission was now down to only nine aircraft. On arrival at the target area, the much-needed cloud cover was lacking, but Malcolm refused to abandon his mission. After circling their target, the Blenheims started to bomb but they were set upon by a huge number of Me 109 fighters, as many as sixty at any one time. One by one, in a five-minute 'battle' that was more like a massacre, the Blenheims were shot down until only Malcolm and his crew remained. Then, their Blenheim was hit, too, and the aircraft, with its crew of three, crashed and burst into flames some 15 miles from its target. Malcolm and his navigator, Pilot Officer James Robb, did not survive the crash.

The process by which Malcolm received his posthumous VC was anything but straightforward, as Stephen Snelling detailed in an article for the *Journal of the Victoria Cross Society* in October 2004. Group Captain (later Air Vice-Marshal Sir) Laurence Sinclair, who described Malcolm as 'one of the bravest officers I had known', had no hesitation in submitting a recommendation for the VC. Others, however, questioned his judgement and suggested a lesser award while he was officially still 'missing in action': the Distinguished Service Order (DSO). Once it emerged Malcolm had died, this award was ruled out (it was not and is not awarded posthumously), leaving him eligible for the VC or a mere Mention in Despatches, but fortunately the arguments of Sinclair and others eventually won the day.

Malcolm, who died aged twenty-five, was gazetted for a posthumous VC on 27 April 1943, both for his bravery during his final sortie and his earlier courage in north Africa. His lengthy citation ended with a summary of the final minutes of his life:

> Wing Commander Malcolm fought back, controlling his hard-pressed squadron and attempting to maintain formation. One by one his

aircraft were shot down until only his own aircraft remained. In the end he, too, was shot down in flames.

Wing Commander Malcolm's last exploit was the finest example of valour and unswerving devotion to duty which he constantly displayed.

After learning of her late husband's posthumous award, his widow, Helen, who lived in Worth, Sussex, said:

My husband's commanding officer wrote and told me of his last flight. I can only say how very proud I am of him. After his [1939] crash, he was told he would never fly again but he was determined to get back. He made an amazing recovery, and was able to return to his unit in September 1939, just after war was declared.

Malcolm's mother was equally proud of her son's bravery and VC. She said after the award was announced: 'My son was always keen on flying, and never thought of anything else. He was just an ordinary, straightforward boy, not studious, nor particularly fond of games, and there was nothing about him to suggest he might ever win a VC.'

Malcolm's widow received his VC from George VI at an investiture at Buckingham Palace on 11 June 1943. Malcolm is buried at the Beja War Cemetery in Tunisia and his name is on the RAF Memorial at St Clement Danes in central London.

Sub-Lieutenant K. G. Wallace, of the Royal Naval Volunteer Reserve, who had been loaned to the RAF for special observer duties, was one of three men to survive their crash landing after being shot down during the raid that claimed Malcolm's life. After returning home to Britain, Wallace, who was not in Malcolm's actual plane, provided a vivid description of the final attacks and his own remarkable survival. He said:

Our bombs were still going down when fifty to sixty Messerschmitt fighters came in at us. In the tightest possible formation we weaved as a single unit through the valley of the hills. We could see the fighters' cannon shells bursting all along the mountain-sides on a level with our faces. Finally, we were forced out of formation, and, with the starboard engine on fire, the fuselage on fire, and a large piece of wing missing, we went into the hillside at about 150 miles per hour.

Out of the blazing aircraft all three of us emerged more or less in one piece, and as we were in No Man's Land, we began to run like hell. Behind us were a party of men running down a hillside, and ahead was a second party of men – our own troops – coming to meet us. We were accelerated by cannon-shells from an enemy fighter who was trying to get us, but we made it. Then I passed out, and the party was over.

Wallace also provided an affectionate tribute to Malcolm, explaining that every member of the crew knew there was only the smallest chance of surviving the mission. 'But we would have gladly followed Malcolm anywhere. He was superb. Malcolm radiated a joy of living and fighting which was irresistible.'

In his book *For Valour: The Air VCs*, Chaz Bowyer writes: 'Hugh Malcolm's cool determination to complete this ill-fated sortie, against all the odds but in his constant endeavour to fulfil his duties, was the culmination of a flying career in which his qualities of courage and leadership had been manifest.'

Several months after Malcolm's death, Lady Tedder, the wife of the Middle East Air Commander-in-Chief, came to open the first in a series of rest and leisure recreation centres in north Africa. To people's surprise, she named it the 'Malcolm Club' despite the fact that she had barely known him. However, the name stuck and was soon applied to other similar clubs in the region.

ABOUT THE AUTHOR

Lord Ashcroft KCMG PC is an international businessman, philanthropist, author and pollster. He was deputy chairman of the Conservative Party and is founder and chairman of the board of trustees of Crimestoppers. He is a trustee of Imperial War Museums, chairman of the trustees of Ashcroft Technology Academy and Chancellor of Anglia Ruskin University.

Lord Ashcroft has had a lifelong interest in bravery, and his many substantial charitable donations include more than £5 million for a new gallery bearing his name at the Imperial War Museum, London, which is home to the author's VC and GC collections as well as those decorations in the care of the IWM. Lord Ashcroft also donated more than £1 million towards the RAF Bomber Command Memorial in Green Park, central London, which was officially unveiled by The Queen in 2012.

www.lordashcroft.com
www.lordashcroftmedals.com
www.victoriacrossheroes2.com
@LordAshcroft

SELECT BIBLIOGRAPHY

Abbott, P. E. and Tamplin, J. M. A., *British Gallantry Awards*, Nimrod Dix, London, 1981.

Arthur, Max, *Symbol of Courage: The Men Behind the Medal*, Sidgwick & Jackson, London, 2004.

Ashcroft, Michael, *Heroes of the Skies*, Headline Publishing Group, London, 2012.

Ashcroft, Michael, *Special Forces Heroes*, Headline Review, London, 2008.

Ashcroft, Michael, *Victoria Cross Heroes*, Headline Review, London, 2006.

Baird, Catherine, *'Little Doctor', V.C. (Harry Andrews)*, Salvationist Publishing and Supplies, London, 1964.

Batchelor, Peter and Matson, Christopher, *VCs of the First World War: The Western Front 1915*, The History Press, Stroud, 2011.

Best, Brian, *Journal of the Victoria Cross Society*, 8th edition, The Victoria Cross Society, Crowborough, March 2006.

Best, Brian, *Journal of the Victoria Cross Society*, 28th edition, The Victoria Cross Society, Crowborough, March 2016.

Best, Brian, *The Victoria Crosses That Saved the Empire: The Story of the VCs of the Indian Mutiny*, Frontline Books, Barnsley, 2016.

de la Billière, General Sir Peter, *Supreme Courage: Heroic Stories from 150 Years of the Victoria Cross*, Little Brown, London, 2004.

Birch, Gerry, *Journal of the Victoria Cross Society*, 27th edition, The Victoria Cross Society, Crowborough, October 2015.

Biggs, Maurice, *The Story of Gurkha VCs*, FireStep Books (in association with The Gurkha Museum), Brighton, 1993.

Bowyer, Chaz, *For Valour: The Air VCs*, William Kimber, London, 1978.

Carter, M. C., *South African Military History Society Journal*, South African National Museum of Military History in association with The South African Military History Society, Volume 2, No. 1, June 1971.

Churchill, Winston, *The Story of the Malakand Field Force: An Episode of Frontier War*, Dover Publications, New York, 2010.

Clayton, Ann, *Chavasse Double VC*, Pen & Sword Military, Barnsley, 2006.

Cooksley, Peter G., *VCs of the First World War: The Air VCs*, Sutton Publishing, Stroud, 1996.

Crook, M. J., *The Evolution of the Victoria Cross*, Midas Books in association with The Ogilby Trusts, Tunbridge Wells, 1975.

Davies, J. D., *Britannia's Dragon: A Naval History of Wales*, The History Press, Stroud, 2013.

Dinesen, Thomas, *Merry Hell! A Dane with the Canadians*, Jarrolds Publishers, London, [no date].

Doherty, Richard and Truesdale, David, *Irish Winners of the Victoria Cross*, Four Courts Press, Dublin, 2000.

Dutton, Roy, *Forgotten Heroes: The Charge of the Light Brigade*, Info-Dial, Oxton, 2007.

Elkin, Peter, *Tamworth's Forgotten Hero: Samuel Parkes VC*, Wonderworks Studios, Nantwich, 2004.

Frayn Turner, John, *VCs of the Air*, Airlife Publishing, Shrewsbury, 1993.

Frayn Turner, John, *VCs of the Second World War*, Pen & Sword Military, Barnsley, 2004.

Glanfield, John, *Bravest of the Brave*, Sutton Publishing, Stroud, 2005.

Gliddon, Gerald, *VCs of the First World War: 1914*, The History Press, Stroud, 2011.

Gliddon, Gerald, *VCs of the First World War: Arras and Messines*, The History Press, Stroud, 2012.

Gliddon, Gerald, *VCs of the First World War: Cambrai 1917*, The History Press, Stroud, 2014.

Gliddon, Gerald, *VCs of the First World War: Road to Victory 1918*, The History Press, Stroud, 2014.

Gliddon, Gerald, *VCs of the First World War: Somme 1916*, The History Press, Stroud, 2011.

Gliddon, Gerald, *VCs of the First World War: Spring Offensive 1918*, The History Press, Stroud, 2013.

Gliddon, Gerald, *VCs of the First World War: The Final Days 1918*, The History Press, Stroud, 2014.

Gliddon, Gerald, *VCs of the First World War: The Sideshows*, Sutton Publishing, Stroud, 2005.

Gummer, Selwyn, *The Chavasse Twins*, Hodder and Stoughton, London, 1963.

Hamilton, Robert, *Victoria Cross Heroes of World War One*, Atlantic Publishing, Croxley Green, 2015.

Harvey, David, *Monuments to Courage: Victoria Cross Headstones & Memorials*, The Naval & Military Press, Uckfield, 2008.

Heathcote, T. A., *The British Admirals of the Fleet 1734–1995: A Biographical Dictionary*, Leo Cooper, Barnsley, 2002.

Hunt, Derek, *Journal of the Victoria Cross Society*, 7th edition, The Victoria Cross Society, October 2005.

Izzard, Brian, *Gamp VC: The Wartime Story of Maverick Submarine Commander Anthony Miers*, Haynes Publishing, Yeovil, 2009.

Laffin, John, *British VCs of World War 2: A Study in Heroism*, Sutton Publishing, Stroud, 1997.

Loraine, Petre F., *The 1st King George's Own Gurkha Rifles, the Malaun Regiment 1815–1925,* Royal United Service Institution, London, 1925.

Napier, Gerald, *The Sapper VCs*, The Stationery Office, Norwich, 1998.

Oldfield, Paul, *Victoria Crosses on the Western Front August 1914–April 1915*, Pen & Sword, Barnsley, 2014.

Oldfield, Paul, *Victoria Crosses on the Western Front April 1915–June 1916*, Pen & Sword Military, Barnsley, 2015.

Parker, Lawrence V., *Journal of the Victoria Cross Society*, 25th edition, The Victoria Cross Society, Crowborough, October 2014.

Percival, John, *For Valour: The Victoria Cross, Courage in Action*, Thames Methuen, London, 1985.

Richards, Miriam M., *It Began with Andrews {The Saga of a Medical Mission}*, Salvationist Publishing and Supplies, London, 1971.

Ross, Graham, *Scotland's Forgotten Valour*, MacLean Press, Isle of Skye, 1995.

Rundell, Anthony J., *Kars: Victory into Defeat*, Impress, Nether Westcote, 2005.

Sandall, Robert, *The History of the Salvation Army: Volume III 1883–1953, Social Reform and Welfare Work*, Thomas Nelson and Sons, Edinburgh, 1955.

Sheppard, Ruth, *Extraordinary Heroes*, Osprey Publishing, Oxford, 2010.

Small, Hugh, *The Crimean War: Queen Victoria's War with the Russian Tsars*, Tempus Publishing, London, 2007.

Smith, Melvin Charles, *Awarded for Valour: A History of the Victoria Cross and the Evolution of British Heroism*, Palgrave Macmillan, Basingstoke, 2008.

Snelling, Stephen, *Journal of the Victoria Cross Society*, 4th edition, The Victoria Cross Society, March 2004.

Snelling, Stephen, *Journal of the Victoria Cross Society*, 5th edition, The Victoria Cross Society, October 2004.

Snelling, Stephen, *VCs of the First World War: Gallipoli*, The History Press, Stroud, 2010.

Snelling, Stephen, *VCs of the First World War: Passchendaele 1917*, The History Press, Stroud, 2012.

Snelling, Stephen, *VCs of the First World War: The Naval VCs*, Sutton Publishing, Stroud, 2002.

Snelling, Stephen, 'The Reluctant Hero', *Britain at War* magazine, Key Publishing, August 2015 monthly issue.

The Register of the Victoria Cross, This England Books, Cheltenham, (3rd edition) 1997.

The Victoria Cross and the George Cross: The Complete History (Volumes I, II and III), Methuen, London, 2013.

Uys, Ian S., *For Valour: The History of Southern Africa's Victoria Cross Heroes*, Ian S. Uys, Johannesburg, 1973.

Wallace, Lieutenant-General Sir Christopher and Cassidy, Major Ron, *Focus on Courage: The 59 Victoria Crosses of The Royal Green Jackets*, The Royal Green Jackets Museum Trust, Winchester, 2007.

Whitworth, Alan; *VCs of the North: Cumbria, Durham & Northumberland*, Pen & Sword Military, Barnsley, 2015.

Wilkins, Philip A., *The History of the Victoria Cross*, The Naval and Military Press, Uckfield, 2007.

Williams, W. Alister, *Heart of a Dragon: The VCs of Wales and the Welsh Regiments 1854–1902*, Bridge Books, Wrexham, 2006.

Williams, W. Alister, *Heart of a Dragon: The VCs of Wales and the Welsh Regiments 1914–82*, Bridge Books, Wrexham, 2006.

Winton, John, *The Victoria Cross at Sea*, Michael Joseph, London, 1978.

Woodyatt, Major-General Nigel G. (editor), *The Regimental History of the 3rd Queen Alexandra's Own Gurkha Rifles from April 1815 to December 1927*, P. Allen & Co., London, 1929.

Wrigley Wilson, Herbert, *After Pretoria: The Guerilla War*, General Books, Memphis, 2012.

PICTURE CREDITS

CREDITS TO PLATE SECTION 1

p. 1: top left © IWM (Q80484); top right © 19thCenturyPhotos.com;
bottom left, with permission from The Queen's Royal Hussars Regiment;
bottom right © Lord Ashcroft Collection

p. 2: top left © Getty Images; top right © Lord Ashcroft Collection;
bottom left © IWM; bottom right © Lord Ashcroft Collection

p. 3: top left © IWM (VC641); top right supplied by Dix Noonan Webb;
bottom left © IWM (Q80496); bottom right © IWM (VC570)

p. 4: top left © IWM (HU71322); top right © Lord Ashcroft Collection;
bottom © Lord Ashcroft Collection

p. 5: top left IWM (VC385); top right © IWM; bottom © Lord Ashcroft Collection

p. 6: top © Getty Images;
bottom left © IWM (Q114639); bottom right © IWM (VC694)

p. 7: top left © IWM (VC696); top right © IWM (Q68240); bottom © IWM (Q54252)

p. 8: top © IWM (Q67309); bottom © IWM (S041)

CREDITS TO PLATE SECTION 2

p. 1: top left © IWM (HU93411); top right © IWM (VC331);
bottom left © IWM; bottom right © IWM (Q85896)

p. 2: top left © IWM (VC259); top right © IWM;
bottom left © IWM (VC719); bottom right © IWM (Q79804)

p. 3: top © Lord Ashcroft Collection; bottom right, from the Lord Ashcroft Collection

p. 4: top © IWM (A5403);
bottom left © Lord Ashcroft Collection; bottom right © IWM (Q68027)

p. 5: top left © IWM (Q67242); top right © IWM (Q67596);
bottom © Dix Noonan Webb

p. 6: top left © Lord Ashcroft Collection; top right © IWM; bottom © Getty Images

p. 7: top left © IWM (IND3508); top right © Getty Images;
bottom left © Illustrated London News Ltd / Mary Evans;
bottom right © Lord Ashcroft Collection

p. 8: top © IWM (A10216); bottom Marcus Adams / Camera Press

INDEX